WRITERS INC

SCHOOL TO WORK

A Student Handbook

Written and Compiled by

Patrick Sebranek, Verne Meyer, Dave Kemper, and John Van Rys

WRITE SOURCE

GREAT SOURCE EDUCATION GROUP

a Houghton Mifflin Company
Wilmington, Massachusetts

Acknowledgements

School to Work is a reality because of the help and advice of a number of people, among them Laura Bachman, Diane Barnhart, Colleen Biehn, Carol Domblewski, Tom Gilding, Kathy Henning, Bev Jessen, Chris Johnson, Nancy Jones, Kim Rylaarsdam, Connie Stephens, Rita Sullivan, Ken Taylor, Randy VanderMey, Sandy Wagner, and Dawn Weis. Also, several of our students allowed us to use their papers as samples in the handbook. We thank them all.

Editorial: Lois Krenzke, Dave Kemper, Pat Sebranek

Book Design: Julie Sebranek

Production: Sherry Gordon

Illustration: Chris Krenzke

Printed in the United States of America

International Standard Book Number: 0-669-40874-3 (hardcover)

4 5 6 7 8 9 10 -RRDC- 01 00 99 98 97

International Standard Book Number: 0-669-40873-5 (softcover)

4 5 6 7 8 9 10 -RRDC- 01 00 99 98 97

Using the Handbook

Your *Writers INC: School to Work* handbook emphasizes writing in school and the workplace. But the handbook does not stop with writing. It also provides information on speaking, listening, thinking, using information, taking tests—you name it.

In addition, the **Almanac** at the back of the book provides many extras like full-color maps, helpful tables and lists, and a historical time line.

The **Table of Contents** near the front of the handbook gives you a list of the major sections and the chapters found under those sections. It also tells you the topic number on which each unit begins.

The **Index** at the back of *Writers INC: School to Work* is one of its most useful parts. It is arranged in alphabetical order and includes every specific topic discussed in the handbook. The numbers after each word in the index are topic numbers, not page numbers. Since there are often many topic numbers on one page, we've used topic numbers to help you find information more quickly.

Look through the **Body** of your handbook and notice the wide variety of material. Notice in particular the material that will be most useful to you—then use it.

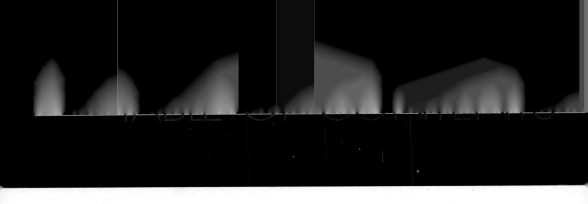

The Communication Process

The Writing Process

The Basic Elements of Writing

Forms of Writing

Writing in the Workplace

Research Writing

Searching for Information

Speaking and Listening

Issues in the Workplace

Reading, Thinking, Learning

Proofreader's Guide

Almanac

001

Why write?

- A few words written correctly or incorrectly in a sales proposal can mean the difference between future business and trouble.
  —J.F., Electrical Contractor

speak?

- Speaking helps a person understand a problem and how to solve it.
  —J.V., Hardware Store Manager

read?

- Reading develops your writing by example—one insight after another.
  —S.D., Paralegal Secretary

listen?

- Listening is the greatest learning tool on earth. You can obtain a mountain of information by listening to others.
  —L.V., President, Pizza Ranch Corp.

- Be a thinker! That idea you have may be just what the world is looking for.
  —J.L., Student, Machinist

think?

- Why be a thinker? Try the alternative sometime!
  —N.B., Student, Computer Science

002   **Why write?** You may as well ask, "Why breathe?" To succeed in school or in the workplace, you have to (1) be a writer-reader-speaker-listener-thinker and (2) breathe.

Like breathing, learning to write, read, speak, listen, and think is something that no one can do for you. You have to do it yourself. However, *Writers INC: School to Work* will help. Check the table of contents right now and think about the different kinds of information included in this handbook.

What's the best way to use *Writers INC: School to Work*? To find out, answer the multiple-choice question below.

Question:

_____ Select the best way to use *Writers INC: School to Work*.

(A) In English class to learn about the . . .
- **process of writing:** prewriting to proofreading
- **elements of writing:** style, sentences, paragraphs, essays
- **forms of writing:** personal, subject, academic, persuasive
- **rules for punctuation, grammar, mechanics, usage**
- **research paper:** finding information, writing, documenting sources
- **speaking process:** giving speeches and listening to others

(B) In Business Communication class to learn about . . .
- **business writing:** summaries, reports, proposals, messages, instructions, 10 kinds of letters
- **setting goals, planning a career, preparing a portfolio**
- **communicating on the job:** giving instruction, taking criticism, working in groups
- **getting a job:** résumé, application, interview, job acceptance

(C) In your other classes for help with . . .
- **writing essays, reports, research papers**
- **thinking clearly and logically**
- **finding, understanding, and using information**
- **reading, speaking, listening**
- **taking tests**
- **using maps, charts, graphs**

(D) All of the above.

Answer: While all the answers are correct, the best one is "D."

PROCESS

The Writing Process

The Writing Process in Action

003   Writing is a process. Remember that. If you try to figure out everything you want to say before you push your pen or click your keys, you may get that dreaded form of paralysis—writer's block.

To avoid that from happening to you, launch yourself into your writing by writing freely, clustering, brainstorming, whatever. One way or another, get your initial thoughts down on paper. Then work with those ideas one step at a time. Remember, writing flows best when you do it in stages, from prewriting to writing to revising and editing. That process is what this chapter is all about.

What's Ahead?

The pages that follow in this opening chapter review the basic steps in the writing process and provide an example of one writer's work in progress so you can see firsthand how the process works.

The Writing Process

004 Quick Guide

Prewriting

1. Find an interesting idea to write about; begin by doing a free writing, clustering, or other selecting activity. (See 011-013.)
2. Learn as much as you can about your subject. (See 015-016.)
3. Once you have a topic, find an interesting way (a focus) to write about it. (See 018-019.)
4. Think about an overall plan for organizing your writing. (See 020.)

Writing the First Draft

1. Write the first draft while your prewriting is still fresh in your mind; give special attention to your opening paragraph. (See 021-025.)
2. Refer to your plan or outline, but be flexible.
3. Keep writing until you come to a natural stopping point.

Revising

1. Review your first draft; add, cut, reword, or rearrange as necessary. (See 029-032.)
2. Review the opening and closing paragraphs. (See 033.)
3. Ask someone to react to your writing and revise as necessary. (See 036-040.)

Editing and Proofreading

1. Reread your final draft aloud to test it for sense and sound.
2. Check for errors in usage, punctuation, spelling, etc.
3. Look your writing over one last time and prepare a final copy.

Publishing

1. Prepare your copy for its final audience—your teacher, classmates, school paper, student magazine, etc.
2. Collect your best writing in a portfolio so you can refer to it now and in the future. (See 048-050.)

One Writer's Process

Lydia O'Neal is a high-school senior and editor of the school paper. She uses the writing process to develop her biweekly editorials because it helps her record her own ideas, gather information from other sources, organize, discard, add, and polish.

005 Prewriting: Searching and Selecting

Lydia starts the process by thinking about her readers—particularly fellow seniors about to graduate. She decides that her subject will be the challenges these seniors face, and her purpose will be to encourage them to trust in their education.

006 Shaping the Experience

Lydia uses a cluster (see 011) to help her think about her topic and develop a list of challenges. First she records her own ideas, and then she adds items that she gleans from *Time* and *Newsweek* magazines. Lydia then makes a short outline (see 119) that helps her organize her ideas and write the first draft.

Cluster

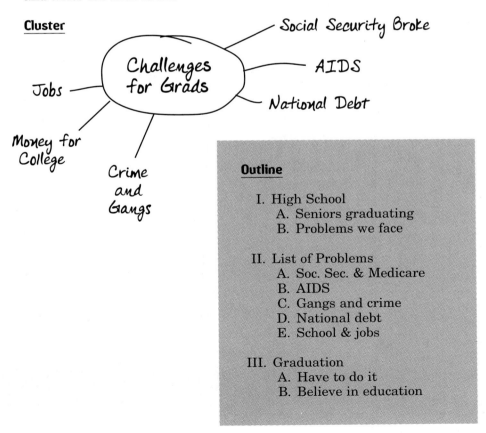

Social Security Broke

Challenges for Grads

AIDS

National Debt

Jobs

Money for College

Crime and Gangs

Outline

I. High School
   A. Seniors graduating
   B. Problems we face

II. List of Problems
   A. Soc. Sec. & Medicare
   B. AIDS
   C. Gangs and crime
   D. National debt
   E. School & jobs

III. Graduation
   A. Have to do it
   B. Believe in education

007 Writing the First Draft

Lydia glances at her outline a few times to recall specific ideas, but basically she writes nonstop—just trying to get all her ideas on the page. At this point she isn't concerned about errors in spelling or grammar.

The writer introduces her topic explaining why she chose it.

This is it! The last edition of the Elk River Voice before graduation. In just 31 days, the other 71 seniors and me will put on the long gowns and flat hats, walk across the stage at Elk River High, take our diplomas, smile, and step into the real world. But what kind of world is that? And can we make it? That's what I want to talk about in this editorial.

She lists her own ideas and those "in the news."

In 2002 the Medicair Program will go broke. In 2035 the Soc. Sec. fund will go broke. AIDS is growing with no cure in sight. The national debt is also growing-no cure either. And in a few months we'll be in job training, tech school, or college, trying to keep up with new technology. Gangs and crime are getting worse and speading into small towns. Hey, Class of '95, that's the world outside these high-school walls. What do you think?

The writer uses an illustration to suggest a solution to the problem.

Remember how Mr. Graham responded when we complained about problems and grades in geometry class? "What's an education for?" he'd ask. "To get A's- or to learn how to survive in the world out there? As I sit here writing my last piece for the Voice, I think that Mr. Graham was right. He made us work hard and think. But we got a good education that made us tougher.

She uses a question as a transition into the final paragraph.

Will life be hard outside E.R.H.S. and will we fail? Sure, sometimes. But teachers did there parts by giving us a strong education. Now we must do our part; graduate, step into the big, bad world, work hard, and try to make the world a better place.

008 Revising the First Draft

Lydia's first goal is to cut and reorganize information so every sentence clearly supports her main point about a strong education helping her and her classmates face real-life challenges. She corrects only obvious errors in grammar and punctuation.

The writer revises the introduction by cutting and adding.

She turns paragraph two into a list, using indentations and bullets to make the list easy to read.

She adds a second question for emphasis and specific adjectives to clarify the meaning.

The writer adds an important detail and uses a pronoun for smoother reading.

This is it! ~~The last edition of the Elk River Voice before graduation.~~ In just 31 days the other 71 seniors and me will put on the long gowns and flat hats, walk across the stage at Elk River High, take our diplomas, smile, and step into the real world. But what kind of world is that? And can we make it? That's what I want to talk about in ~~this editorial.~~ *my last editorial for the ER Voice—the challenges we'll soon face:*

- AIDs continues to spread with no cure in sight.
- The national debt is still growing—also, no cure.
- New technology is making jobs harder to git.
- Medicair and Social Security are going broke.
- The crime rate is growing like mad.

Hey, Class of '95, that's the world outside these high-school walls. What do you think? *Are you ready?*

Remember how Mr. Graham responded when we complained about *hard* problems and *low* grades in geometry class? "What's an education for?" he'd ask. "To get A's-or to learn how to survive in the world out there? As I sit here writing my last piece for the Voice, I think that Mr. Graham was right. He made us work hard and think. But we got a good education that made us tougher.

Will life be hard outside E.R.H.S. and will we fail? Sure, sometimes. But teachers *and parents* did there parts by giving us a strong education. Now we must do our part; graduate, step into the big, bad world, work hard, and try to make ~~the world~~ *it* a better place.

⓿⓿⑨ Editing and Proofreading

Lydia's final concern is finding and correcting all errors in spelling, punctuation, and grammar.

The writer adds a title.

The writer changes "me" to "I."

She adds periods after E.R. and underlines the name of the school paper.

She corrects spelling of "AIDS," "get," "Medicare," and changes a hyphen to a dash.

The writer correctly uses a dash, adds quotes after "there" and underlines "Voice."

She corrects "there" and changes the semicolon to a colon.

Stepping Up—and Out

This is it! In just 31 days the other 71 seniors and *I* ~~me~~ will put on the long gowns and flat hats, walk across the stage at Elk River High, take our diplomas, smile, and step into the real world. But what kind of world is that? And can we make it? That's what I want to talk about in my last editorial for the E.R. Voice—the challenges we'll soon face:

- *AIDS* ~~AIDs~~ continues to spread with no cure in sight.
- The national debt is still growing, also, no cure.
- New technology is making jobs harder to *get* ~~git~~.
- *Medicare* ~~Medicair~~ and Social Security are going broke.
- The crime rate is growing like mad.

Hey, Class of '95, that's the world outside these high-school walls. What do you think? Are you ready?

Remember how Mr. Graham responded when we complained about hard problems and low grades in geometry class? "What's an education for?" he'd ask. "To get A's, or to learn how to survive in the world out there?" As I sit here writing my last piece for the Voice, I think that Mr. Graham was right. He made us work hard and think. But we got a good education that made us tougher.

Will life be hard outside E.R.H.S. and will we fail? Sure, sometimes. But teachers and parents did *their* ~~there~~ parts by giving us a strong education. Now we must do our part: graduate, step into the big, bad world, work hard, and try to make it a better place.

A Guide to Prewriting

010   Prewriting is probably the most important step in the writing process. It involves selecting, shaping, focusing, and planning. You **select** a meaningful subject that reflects your personal needs or interests (and meets the requirements of your assignment). You **shape** your thoughts about this subject to understand it better. You **focus** your attention on a specific part of the subject that you would like to write about. And, finally, if it is needed, you **plan** a few basic writing moves before starting your first draft.

What's Ahead?

Whenever you have a question about your prewriting, turn to this section for help.

011 Guidelines for Selecting a Subject

The following activities will help you find a worthwhile subject for your writing. Read through the entire list before you choose an activity to begin your subject search.

1. **Journal Writing** Write on a regular basis in a journal. Explore your personal feelings, develop your thoughts, and record the happenings of each day. Underline ideas in your personal writing that you would like to explore in writing assignments.

2. **Free Writing** Write nonstop for 10 minutes to discover writing ideas. Begin writing with a particular focus in mind; otherwise, pick up on something that has recently attracted your attention. (See 014.)

3. **Clustering** Begin a cluster with a nucleus word (like *pollution*) related to your writing topic or assignment. Then record or cluster ideas around the nucleus word. Circle each idea as you write it, and draw a line connecting it to the closest related idea.

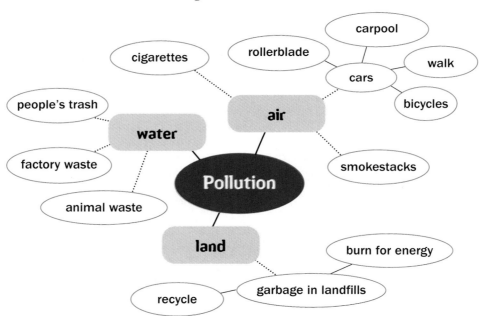

NOTE: After 3 or 4 minutes of clustering, scan your cluster for a word or an idea to explore in a free writing. A specific writing subject should begin to emerge during this writing.

4. **Listing** Freely listing ideas as they come to mind is another effective technique for finding a writing subject. Begin with an idea or a key word related to your assignment and simply start listing words. You can also brainstorm (list ideas) with members of a group.

5. Imaginary Dialogue Create an imaginary dialogue between you and someone else or between two strangers. The subject of this dialogue should be related to your writing assignment. Continue the conversation as long as you can, or until a writing idea begins to unfold.

6. Sentence Completion Complete an open-ended sentence in as many ways as you can. Try to word your sentence so that it leads to a subject you can use for a particular writing assignment:

We once . . .	How does . . .	I hope . . .
Too many people . . .	I never realized . . .	I wonder . . .
The good thing about . . .	On one hand . . .	If . . .

NOTE: Try alternating responses with a friend or classmate and work from each other's ideas.

7. Reflecting, Participating, and Listening Think about possible writing ideas as you read, as you ride (or drive) to school, and as you wait in the cafeteria line. Watch for unusual events, persons, objects, or conversations. Participate in activities related to your writing assignment. Interview someone who is knowledgeable or experienced about a writing idea. Also talk with family members and friends about possible subjects.

8. Using the "Essentials of Life Checklist" Below you will find a checklist of the major categories into which most essential things in our lives are divided. The checklist provides an endless variety of subject possibilities. Consider the first category, clothing. It could lead to the following writing ideas:

- the changing fashions in school clothing
- clothing as a statement ("we are what we wear")
- the clothing industry
- a favorite piece of clothing

Essentials of Life Checklist

clothing	communication	exercise	health/medicine
housing	purpose/goals	community	entertainment
food	measurement	arts/music	literature/books
exercise	machines	faith/religion	recreation/hobby
education	intelligence	trade/money	personality/identity
family	agriculture	heat/fuel	natural resources
friends	environment	rules/laws	tools/utensils
love	science	freedom/rights	plants/vegetation
senses	energy	land/property	work/occupation

> "The faster I write, the better my output. If I'm going slow, I'm in trouble. It means I'm pushing the words, instead of being pulled by them."
>
> —Raymond Chandler

014 Guidelines for Free Writing

Reminders . . .

- ◉ **Thoughts are constantly passing through your mind;** you never have nothing on your mind.
- ◉ **Free writing helps you get these thoughts down on paper.**
- ◉ **Free writing is also a way to develop these thoughts;** you do this by adding details and making meaning out of them.
- ◉ **Many things seem awkward or difficult when you first try them;** free writing will probably be no different. Just stick with it.

The Process . . .

- ◉ **Write nonstop and record whatever comes into your mind.** (Write for at least 10 minutes if possible.)
- ◉ **If you have a particular topic in mind, begin writing about it.** Otherwise pick up on anything that comes to mind and begin writing.
- ◉ **Don't stop to judge, edit, or correct your writing;** that will come later.
- ◉ **Keep writing even when you think you have exhausted all of your ideas.** Switch to another mode of thought (sensory, memory, reflective) if necessary, but keep writing.
- ◉ **When a particular topic seems to be working, stick with it;** record as many specific details as possible. If your ideas dry up, look for a new idea in your free writing or begin a new nonstop writing.

INSIDE

info

Carry your journal with you and write freely in it whenever you have an idea you don't want to forget, or even when you simply have nothing else to do. These free writings will help you become a better writer.

The Result . . .

- ◉ **Review your writings and underline the ideas you like.** These ideas will often serve as the basis for more formal writings.
- ◉ **Make sure your free-writing idea meets the requirements of your assignment;** also make sure it's one you feel good about sharing.
- ◉ **Determine exactly what you plan (or are required) to write about;** add specific details as necessary. (This may require a second free writing.)
- ◉ **Listen to and read the free writings of others;** learn from them.

015 Guidelines for Searching and Shaping a Subject

The following activities will help you develop your subjects for writing. If you already have a good "feel" for a particular writing subject, you might attempt only one of the activities. If you need to explore your idea in some detail, you might attempt two or more of the activities.

1. **Free Writing** At this point, you can approach free writing in two different ways. You can do a focused free writing to see how many ideas come to mind about your subject as you write, or you can approach your free writing as if it were an instant version of the finished product. An instant version will give you a good feel for your subject and will also tell you how much you know or need to find out about it.

2. **Clustering** Try clustering with your subject as the nucleus word. This clustering will naturally be more focused or structured than your earlier prewriting cluster since you now have a specific subject in mind. (See 011 for a model cluster.)

3. **5 W's of Writing** Answer the 5 W's—Who? What? Where? When? and Why?—to identify basic information about your subject. (You can add How? to the list for even better coverage.)

4. **Directed Free Writing** Do a variation of free writing by selecting one of the six thinking modes below and writing whatever comes to mind. (Repeat the process as often as you need to, selecting a different mode each time.)

   Describe it. What do you see, hear, feel, smell, taste . . . ?

   Compare it. What is it like? What is it different from?

   Associate it. What connections between this and something else come to mind?

   Analyze it. What parts does it have? How do they work (or not work) together?

   Apply it. What can you do with it? How can you use it?

   Argue for or against it. What do you like about it? Not like about it? What are its good points? Its bad points?

5. **Imaginary Dialogue** Create an imaginary dialogue between two people in which your specific subject is the topic of the conversation. The two speakers should build on each other's comments.

6. **Audience Appeal** Select a specific audience to address in an exploratory writing. Consider a group of preschoolers, a live television audience, readers of a popular teen magazine, the local school board . . .

016 7. **Structured Questions** Answering structured questions will help you understand what is important or unique about your writing idea.

    a.   What makes your subject different from others that are similar to it?

    b.   How is your subject changing?

    c.   How does your subject fit into his or her (its) world or environment?

    d.   What larger group is your subject a part of? What are the features of this larger group?

    e.   What features make your subject part of this larger group?

    f.   What features make your subject different from this group?

    g.   What other questions can you think of?

8. **Offbeat (Unstructured) Questions** Creating and answering offbeat questions will help you see your writing idea in different ways. The sample questions below will get you started. (Add your own questions.)

Writing About a Person
- What type of clothing is he or she like?
- What does his or her menu look like?

Writing About a Place
- What is the place's best sense (sight, smell, hearing, etc.)?
- Where does this place go for advice?

Writing About an Object
- What does this object look like upside down?
- What kind of shadow does it cast?

Writing About an Issue or Event
- What kind of car would you drive to this event?
- What machine does it most resemble?

Writing to Persuade
- What clubs or organizations would your argument or viewpoint join?
- Would your argument take the stairs or the elevator?

Writing to Explain a Process
- What restaurant is this process like?
- Where in a hardware store would this process feel most at home?

Writing a Narrative
- What fruit does this story resemble?
- What would your great-grandmother say about this story?

TAKE NOTE

You might try answering your structured and unstructured questions in the form of mini-free writings (5 minutes) to unlock creative ideas.

017 Taking Inventory of Your Thoughts

Let's say you still don't feel comfortable with your subject after thinking and writing about it. That is, you've done some searching and you've discovered some interesting things about your writing idea, but you still don't feel ready to write a first draft. Now may be a good time to see how well you match up with your subject.

After carefully considering the questions that follow, you should be able to decide whether to move ahead or look for another approach, or even another subject.

Assignment: What are the specific requirements of this assignment?

Do I have enough time to do a good job with this subject?

Self: How committed am I to my writing subject?

What can I learn or gain if I continue writing on this topic?

Subject: How much do I now know about this subject?

Is additional information available?

Have I tried any of the searching activities? (See 015-016.)

Purpose: Why am I writing?

Do I want to inform, entertain, explain, or persuade?

Audience: Who is my audience and what response do I want from them?

How much do they care or already know about this subject?

How can I get my audience interested in my ideas?

Form: In what form could I present my ideas: story, essay, poem, personal narrative, parody, interview? (See 134.)

Can I think of an interesting way to lead into my paper?

What is my subject?
Why am I writing?
Who is my audience?
What form should I use?

> "An effective piece of writing has focus. There is a controlling vision that orders what is being said."
>
> —Donald Murray

018 Focusing Your Efforts

Searching, selecting, shaping—these activities will produce a cloud of ideas and feelings in your mind. That cloud has to produce "lightning" before the information can jump from your mind to the page. That happens when you find a **focus** and are able to express it in a single statement.

019 Forming a Focus Statement

A focus statement usually expresses a specific feeling about a subject or highlights a specific feature of it. State your focus in a sentence that you feel effectively expresses what you want to explore in your essay. Write as many versions as it takes to come up with a sentence that establishes the right tone and direction for your writing. Use the following formula if you have trouble forming that statement:

> **Formula:** A specific subject *(Bungee jumping)*
> + a specific feeling or feature *(stretches safety to the limit)*
> = an effective focus or thesis statement.

NOTE: A focus statement is often called a *thesis statement*. It is similar to a topic sentence, the controlling idea in a paragraph. (See 108.)

020 Designing a Writing Plan

With a clear focus in mind, you may be ready to start your first draft. If, however, your subject is quite complex, you may need to design a writing plan before you start your first draft. Your plan can be anything from a brief list of ideas to a detailed sentence outline. (See 120.) Use the guidelines that follow to help you plan and organize your writing:

1. Study your focus statement. It may suggest a logical method of organization for your writing.

2. Review all of the facts and details you have produced so far to see if an overall pattern of organization begins to emerge.

3. Consider the methods of organization in the handbook. (See 111.)

4. Organize your ideas into some kind of list, cluster, or outline.

5. If nothing seems to work, consider gathering more information, or simply write your first draft to see what unfolds.

A Guide to Drafting

021   This is it. You're into your first draft, your first complete look at your writing idea. All of your searching and planning have led up to this point. Write as much of your first draft as possible in your first sitting while all of your prewriting is still fresh in your mind. Refer to your planning notes as you write, but be flexible. A more interesting approach may unfold during the drafting process. Concentrate on developing your ideas, not on producing neat copy. Remember that first drafts are often called *rough* drafts. Keep these additional points in mind during the drafting stage:

- ◉ Speak naturally and honestly so the real you comes through.
- ◉ Pay special attention to your opening paragraph. Try to grab your readers' attention and keep your writing focused on your main idea.
- ◉ Include as many specific details in your draft as possible.
- ◉ Continue writing until you make all of your main points or until you come to a logical stopping point.

What's Ahead?
Whenever you get stuck during the drafting process, turn to the appropriate strategy for help.

Writing Naturally
Writing an Opening or Lead Paragraph
Selecting a Method of Development
Bringing Your Writing to a Close

022 Writing Naturally

Write naturally—be yourself, they say. But, you say, I don't like the way I "naturally" write. It never sounds natural, for one thing. Sometimes it even sounds dumb or boring. Don't worry. Your writing will seem natural and pleasing if you keep one thought above all others: **The writer is never alone.** Your writing is one-half of a conversation with a reader you invent. Talk to your "silent partner."

1. Clustering and free writing can help you write in your true "voice."

2. Know your subject.
A good knowledge base makes the job of drafting much easier.

3. Be honest; don't try to fake it.
Readers are drawn to writers who are honest and trustworthy.

4. Be personally involved in your writing.
Share your personal thoughts and feelings; make connections between your subject and your own experience.

5. Be at ease; don't rush or nervously bounce around.
Think about what you've already said—repeat it in your mind or on paper—and let that help you decide what you should say next.

> "Voice is the imprint of ourselves in our writing. Take the voice away . . . and there's no writing, just words following words."
> —Donald Graves

023 A Natural Writing Style in Action

To develop a natural writing style, write about subjects that genuinely interest you, and tell good stories about these subjects, stories that share real feelings and specific details. The following excerpt from "The Bike" by Tony Rogers speaks naturally. As you will see, he genuinely cares about his subject and is able to bring it to life for his readers. (The writer capitalizes "The Bike" throughout the narrative.)

The Bike hung from its own spot in the ceiling next to the big front window, away from the other bikes. Dad and I would stare up at the glossy paint and shimmering spokes as the wheels spun lazily around. My eyes would travel along The Bike's exquisite lines and trace through the intricate pattern of bolts and springs that all joined together to form a brake or a shift lever. The price was written in black marker on a cardboard rectangle and knotted with twine to the handlebars. It was steep. The price was one that would typically accompany such a work of art, or a particularly rare vintage wine. Suddenly The Bike escaped like smoke through my fingers. Dad had seen the glint in my eye, but, "It's just too expensive," he said.

024 Writing an Opening or Lead Paragraph

Writing an opening or lead paragraph should help clarify your thinking about a subject, and it should set a number of things in motion: It should (1) point the way into your essay, (2) spark your readers' interest, (3) commit you to a certain voice, and (4) establish a form for your writing. It is one of the most important parts of each composition you write. Several possible starting points are listed below.

- ◉ **Begin with a funny story to set a humorous tone.**
- ◉ **Challenge your readers with a thought-provoking question.**
- ◉ **Open with an impressive or fitting quotation.**
- ◉ **Offer a little "sip" of the conclusion to get your readers' attention.**
- ◉ **List all your main points and treat your subject in a very serious, straightforward manner.**
- ◉ **Provide a dramatic or eye-opening statement.**

Remember: The angle or approach you use in your opening will affect the direction and style of your entire piece of writing. This is why your opening is so important.

025 Sample Opening Paragraph

In the following opening, student Donna Actie begins with four dramatic ideas to get the readers' attention. She then challenges readers with a thought-provoking question: "Why do so many of us have problems at school?" In her brief analysis of this question, the writer identifies the subject of her essay—the dangers of lead poisoning.

Get the Lead Out!

Low grades on exams. Failing classes. Lack of interest in school. Plans of dropping out. Why do so many of us have problems at school? There are many reasons: drugs, poverty, poor schools . . . But there's another reason you may not have heard about—lead poisoning. Recent studies indicate that young children exposed to even low levels of lead often face major difficulties later in life.

If you have been successful in writing an opening paragraph, you should have a pretty good idea of how the rest of your first draft will develop. Your opening paragraph should also establish the tone for the rest of your writing. In the sample above, the writer has clearly established a serious tone to reflect the seriousness of her subject.

INSIDE

A form usually unfolds naturally as you write, so don't worry if you can't see too far into your first draft. Remember that your destination is often unknown when you first start writing.

026 Selecting a Method of Development

Chris bought the first pair of shoes she tried on. The style, the color, and the fit were that good. Larry tried on five pairs of shoes before he found what he was looking for. Not unusual. Sometimes we know that the first thing we try on is right for us; other times we aren't so sure. The same holds true with the way you develop your ideas in a piece of writing. At times, the first method that comes to mind will be the best approach. At other times, you will have to do some comparison shopping before you feel comfortable with a method for developing your writing.

Several methods are listed here. Any one of them can help you shape your writing. You may choose to . . .

narrate: tell a story or re-create an experience. (See 104 and 138-145.)

describe: tell in detail how something or someone appeared. (See 105 and 147-157.)

define: clarify or explain the meaning of a term, idea, or concept. (See 164-166 and 546-547.)

explain: prove a point by providing specific examples or reasons.

analyze: break down a thing or a process into its parts and subparts.

classify: divide a large and complex set of things into smaller groups and identify each group.

compare: measure one thing against something more or less like it, or explain something new or complex by using an analogy to something quite familiar. (See 162-163.)

argue: use logic and evidence to prove that something is true or that something should be done. (See 178-180 and 558-574.)

027 Bringing Your Writing to a Close

Sometimes your writing will come to an effective stopping point after the last main point is made. Whenever that is the case, don't try to tack on a closing paragraph. Leave well enough alone.

Closing paragraphs are important when you feel it is necessary to tie up any loose ends or clarify certain points in the body of your writing. You may also want to leave readers with a final thought that helps them see the importance of your message. Experiment with a number of possible endings before you settle on one. (For ideas, check the endings of the models in "Forms of Writing.")

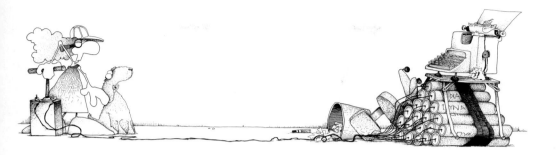

A Guide to Revising

028   The first step in the revising process is to review your first draft to see how you feel about it . . . and to see how much work you have ahead of you. Use these questions as a basic guide when you review a first draft:

- Is the content interesting and worth sharing?
- Is the style natural and effective in getting my message across?
- Are there any major gaps or soft spots in my writing?
- How can I improve what I have done so far?

Once you have a good feel for your first draft, you're ready to turn it into a more complete and effective piece of writing. In very basic terms, that is what revising is all about—making changes in your writing until it says exactly what you want it to say. How many changes you make depends on the quality of your first draft and your commitment to your writing. Revising, like most work, requires an honest, personal commitment.

What's Ahead?

Whenever you have a specific question about revising a piece of writing, turn to one of the strategies in this section for help.

> "I work on a word processor for the first drafts, but for revisions, I always print out a copy . . . and do my corrections by hand."
>
> —Betsy Byars

029 Using Basic Revising Strategies

Making the Right Moves

No writer gets it right the first time. Few writers get it right the second time. In fact, professional writers often have to write several revisions before they are satisfied with their work. Don't be surprised if you have to do the same. The guidelines that follow should help:

- ◉ **First look at the big picture.** Take it all in. Decide if there is a focus or main idea either stated or suggested in your writing. If you can't find the focus, write one. Or, if your original thinking on your subject has changed, write a new focus statement.

- ◉ **Then look at specific chunks of information** in your writing and reorder them if you feel they could be arranged more effectively.

- ◉ **Also cut information** that doesn't support your focus; **add information** if you feel additional points need to be made. Make sure that your writing answers the basic questions your readers may have; **rewrite parts** that aren't as clear as you would like them to be.

- ◉ **Finally,** look very closely at your writing style and **refine it** so your ideas are interesting, colorful, and clear.

INSIDE info

Each of your paragraphs should develop an important point related to your subject. In addition, each paragraph should serve as an effective link to the information that comes before it and after it. (See 113.)

030 Revising on the Run

Writer Peter Elbow recommends "cut-and-paste revising" when you have very little time to make changes in your writing. For example, let's say you are working on an in-class writing assignment and have only 15 minutes to revise your writing. Use the five steps that follow:

1. Don't add any new information to your writing.
2. Remove unnecessary facts and details.
3. Find the best possible information and go with it.
4. Put the pieces in the best possible order.
5. Do what little rewriting is necessary.

031 The R-R-R-R-Revising Strategy

The 5-R's strategy covers everything from reading the first draft to refining or polishing the revised copy. (If you're looking for an in-depth revising strategy, you've just found it.)

Read: Sometimes it's hard to keep an open mind when you read your first draft. You need to put some distance between you and your writing.

- Whenever possible, put your writing aside for a day or two.
- Read it out loud.
- Ask others (family, friends, classmates) to read it out loud to you.
- Listen to your writing: How does it sound? What does it say?

React: Here are six questions that will help you react to your own writing on the second or third read-through:

- What parts of my writing work for me?
- Do all of these parts work together? Are they logical?
- Do all the parts point to one idea? What is the main idea?
- Do the parts say what I want them to say?
- Have I arranged the parts in the best possible order?
- Where do I need to go from here?

Rework: Reworking your writing means making changes until all of the parts work equally well. There is usually plenty of reworking to do in the early stages of writing.

Reflect: One of the best ways of keeping track of your revising progress is to write comments in the margins of your paper. Margins are the perfect place for you to explore your feelings concerning what you have written. Here are some guidelines:

- Explore your thoughts freely and naturally.
- Note what you plan to cut, move, explain further, and so on.
- Reflect upon the changes you make. (How do they work?)
- If you are unsure of what to do, write down a question to answer later.

Refine: Refining is putting some style into your written copy— shining up your thoughts and words. Here's what you can do:

- Read your paper out loud to make sure that you haven't missed anything.
- Listen for both the clarity and quality of your words and sentences.
- Make the final changes so your writing reads smoothly and clearly.

Making Your Writing More Interesting

032 Escaping the "Badlands"

The later stage of revising is one of the most important in the whole composing process. Why? Because here you can escape the "badlands" of writing—those stretches of uninspired words and ideas that can make writing boring. Use these questions as a guide to check for problem areas.

1. **Is my topic worn-out?** "My Weekend at the State Tournament," for example, can be revived into "March Madness!"

2. **Is my purpose stale?** If you have been writing merely to please a teacher or to get a good grade, start again. But this time try writing to learn something or to trigger a response in your readers.

3. **Is my voice predictable or fake?** If it sounds phoney ("A good time was had by all"), start again. This time, be honest. Be real.

4. **Does my first draft sound boring?** Maybe it's boring because it pays an equal amount of attention to everything. Shorten some parts by summarizing them; lengthen others by explaining. If you're sharing a story, skim through the less significant parts by "telling" what happened; then focus on the more important parts by "showing" what happened. Summarize and explain. Tell and show.

5. **Does my essay follow a formula too closely?** The five-paragraph essay (introduction, three main points, conclusion) provides you with an important organizing frame to build on. However, if this frame is followed too closely, it may actually get in the way. So read your draft again, and the first time your inner voice starts saying "formula, formula," cross out some words and start blazing a more interesting trail.

INSIDE **info**

Think of revising as a special opportunity rather than a chore. Try a number of different things to make your writing come to life, including any one of the prewriting activities listed in the handbook. (See 015-016.)

033 Reviewing the Opening and Closing Paragraphs

After making changes in the body of your writing, you may need to change the opening paragraph as well. Make sure that it draws your reader into the main part of your paper and accurately introduces the focus of your writing. (See 024-025.)

Also review (or write) the closing paragraph for your essay. The closing should tie up any loose ends left in the body of your paper and remind readers of the importance of your subject. Remember, however, that it may not be necessary to add a closing paragraph if your writing comes to a natural stopping point after the last main point is made.

034 Using the Right Level of Language
Jaquar or Jalopy?

As you revise, be sure your word choice sticks to an appropriate level of language or diction. Your choice of words should reflect and reinforce the purpose of a particular writing assignment.

You might, for example, write a composition in which the **informal English** (also known as colloquial English) used in casual conversation is the best choice. Informal English is characterized by contractions, sentence fragments, popular expressions (*you know, like, forget it*), cliches (*like a chicken with its head cut off*), and frequent references to oneself (*I couldn't quite figure out . . .*).

> We weren't afraid to admit we were scared silly when the cops stopped us that time. Who wouldn't be?

Or you might write an essay or a research paper in which the word choice meets the standards of **semiformal English**. When writing is published, it usually is edited to meet such standards. In semiformal English, slang and conversational phrases are replaced by more carefully chosen words.

> Semiformal English, such as you are reading in this sentence, is worded correctly and cautiously so that it can withstand repeated readings without seeming tiresome, sloppy, or cute.

Or you might write a report or set of instructions in which the word choice is more **technical**. Technical language is also the level of language used most often in the workplace. It requires the writer to be clear and accurate at all times, defining terms and giving examples whenever necessary.

> Acid rain, the term for precipitation that contains a high concentration of harmful chemicals, is gradually changing our environment. The greatest change is caused by sulfur dioxide, a gas produced from the burning of coal.

> "Advice to young writers? Always the same advice: learn to trust your own judgment, learn inner independence, learn to trust that time will sort the good from the bad."
>
> —Doris Lessing

035 **Checking the Style of Your Writing**

Don't worry too much about style as long as you still face major questions about the content, focus, and organization of your writing. All of the reviewing, reworking, and refining that you do will naturally bear the stamp of your personal style. But at some point, you will want to look closely at your writing to make sure that all of your ideas speak clearly and effectively. The following list of reminders should help.

1. Write clearly.

Clarity is the foundation of good writing. Until your ideas are clearly expressed, nothing else really matters.

2. Strive for simplicity.

Essayist E. B. White advises young writers to "approach style by way of simplicity, plainness, orderliness, and sincerity." That's good advice from one of America's most stylish writers.

3. Know when your writing doesn't work.

Watch for sentences that all sound the same and sentences that hang limp like wet wash. Rely on your writer's sixth sense to help you sort the good from the bad in your writing.

4. Know when to cut.

And as writer Kurt Vonnegut says, "Have the guts to do it." Cut any words and phrases that don't strengthen your sentences and any sentences that don't strengthen your paragraphs.

5. Write with details.

Writing without details (examples, figures of speech, anecdotes, etc.) is like baking bread without yeast. One of the most important ingredients is missing. But be careful. Your writing will sound forced if you overdo the details.

6. Write with specific nouns and verbs.

Writing with specific nouns (*Bruce Springsteen*) and verbs (*swaggers*) gives your writing energy. Writing with vague nouns (*man*) and weak verbs (*is, are, was, were,* etc.) forces you to use a lot of modifiers.

7. Write active, forward-moving sentences.

Make it clear in your sentences that your subject is doing something (Anita asked . . . , He rebelled . . . , Marine biologists discovered . . .).

036 Group Advising and Revising

All writers can benefit from an interested audience, especially one that offers constructive and honest advice during a writing project. And who could make a better audience than your fellow writers? Some of you might already work in writing groups, so you know the value of writers sharing their work. Others of you might want to start a writing group so you, too, can experience the benefits.

How exactly can a writing group help you? For starters, your fellow writers can tell you what does and doesn't work for them in your writing. This feedback is especially helpful early in the revising process so you can find out if your writing idea is one others would really be interested in reading about.

Some experts go so far as to say that talking about writing is *the* most important step in the process of writing. By sharing ideas and concerns, a community spirit will develop, a spirit that will help make writing a meaningful learning experience rather than just another assignment. This enthusiasm is bound to have a positive effect on the final product.

> "At first, I thought, 'Why bother?' What did we know about writing? I resented the group discussions about my writing and offered very few suggestions for the others. It took me a while to realize that in my small group we were talking about what we each really needed right now, for this paper. That was something even the teacher couldn't tell me."
>
> —Paul, a student

037 Maintaining Good Relations

To maintain good relations among group members, focus your comments on specific things in their writing. For example, an observation such as "I noticed many 'There is' statements in your opening" will mean much more to a writer than a general, personal comment such as "You need to put some life into your opening." A specific observation will help the writer see a problem without hurting her or his confidence.

Give praise when praise is due, but base it on something you observe or feel in the writing: "Your series of questions and answers is an effective way to organize this essay" or "There is an energy in this writing that I really like."

INSIDE info

At first, your observations may seem limited. You may be able to comment only on the nice sound the writing has or a point you don't understand. Fine. Just keep trying—and listening. Your ability to make a variety of observations will improve with practice.

038 Writing Group Guidelines

The guidelines that follow will help you conduct effective group revising sessions.

The Author/Writer

- **Come prepared with a substantial piece of writing.** Prepare a copy for each group member if this is part of normal group procedure.

- **Introduce your writing.** However, don't say too much; let your writing do the talking.

- **Read your copy out loud.** Speak confidently and clearly.

- **As the group reacts to your writing, listen carefully and take brief notes.** Don't be defensive about your writing, since this will stop some members from commenting honestly about your work. Answer all of their questions.

- **If you have some special concerns or problems, share these with your fellow writers.**

The Group Members

- **Listen carefully as the writer reads.** Take notes, but make them brief so that you don't miss part of the reading. You may find it more helpful to listen to the entire work, and then do a mini-free writing immediately after the reading. (There are other reaction methods to choose from, as well. See 039-042 for four strategies.)

- **Keep your comments positive and constructive.**

- **Focus your comments as much as you can on specific things you observe in the writing.**

- **Ask questions of the author:** "Why? How? What do you mean when you say . . . ?" And answer questions the author might have for you.

- **Listen to other comments and add to them.** In this way, you help each other become better writers.

NOTE: Reviewing the guidelines from the writing process, writing style, and the special forms of writing sections in your handbook will also help you prepare for group sessions.

Group Revising Strategies

039 Critiquing a Paper

Use the checklist that follows to help you evaluate compositions during group revising sessions.

Purpose: Does the writer have a clear purpose in mind? That is, is it clear that the writer is trying to entertain, to inform, to persuade, etc.?

Audience: Does the writing address a specific audience? And will the readers understand and appreciate this subject?

Form: Is the subject presented in an effective or appropriate form?

Content: Does the writer consider the subject from a number of angles? For example, does he or she try to compare, classify, define, and/or analyze the writing idea?

Writing Devices: Does the writing include specific examples, figures of speech, anecdotes, quotations, etc.? Which ones are most effective?

Voice: Does the writing sound sincere and honest? That is, do you "hear" the writer when you read his or her paper?

Personal Thoughts and Comments: Does the writer include any personal thoughts or comments in the writing? Are they needed or appropriate?

Purpose Again: Does the writing succeed in making a person smile, nod, or react in some way? What is especially good about the writing?

040 Reacting to Writing

Peter Elbow, in *Writing Without Teachers,* offers four types of reactions group members might have to a piece of writing: *pointing, summarizing, telling,* and *showing.*

1. **Pointing** refers to a reaction in which a group member "points out" words, phrases, or ideas in the writing that make a positive or negative impression.

2. **Summarizing** refers to a reader's general reaction to the writing. It may be a list of main ideas, or a word that gets at the heart of the writing.

3. **Telling** refers to readers expressing what happens as they read a piece: first this happens, then this happens, later this happens.

4. **Showing** refers to readers expressing their feelings metaphorically. A reader might, for example, refer to something in the writing as if it were a voice quality, a shape, a type of clothing, etc. ("Why do I feel like I've been lectured to in this essay?" or "Your writing has a neat, tailored quality to it.")

041 Good Writing: A Matter of Choice

What makes for good writing? Six basic points appear on the lists of most experienced writers. Use these points as a guide during group revising sessions. Good writing is . . .

- **original** (the subject or the way the subject is covered is fresh),
- **organized** (the ideas are presented in a sensible order),
- **detailed** (the details are specific and colorful),
- **clear** (the sentences clearly and smoothly move the writing forward),
- **correct** (the final product is clean and correct), and
- **effective** (the writing is interesting and informative).

042 Feeling Your OAQS

Here's a simple and effective four-step scheme you can use to comment on early drafts in group revising sessions:

> **O**bserve
> **A**ppreciate
> **Q**uestion
> **S**uggest

- **Observe** means to notice what another person's essay is designed to do, and to say something about that design, or purpose. For example, you might say, "Even though you are writing about your boyfriend, it appears that you are trying to get a message across to your parents."

- **Appreciate** means to praise something in the writing that impresses or pleases you. You can find something to appreciate in any piece of writing. For example, you might say, "You have a wonderful main idea" or "With your description, I can actually see his broken tooth."

- **Question** means to ask whatever you want to know after you've read the essay. You might ask for background information, or a definition, or an interpretation, or an explanation. For example, you might say, "Why didn't you tell us what happened when you got to the emergency room?"

- **Suggest** means to give thoughtful advice about possible changes. Offer this advice honestly and courteously. Be specific, and be positive. For example, you might say, "With a little more physical detail—especially sound and smell—your third paragraph could be the highlight of the whole essay. What do you think?"

A Guide to Editing and Proofreading

043   There comes a point in any writing project (like a fast-approaching due date) when you must prepare it for publication. At this point you must edit and proofread your revised writing so that it speaks clearly and accurately. Your first concern when editing is to replace any words, phrases, and sentences that sound awkward or confusing. Then you should check your writing for spelling, usage, mechanics, and grammar errors.

    Make sure to ask a classmate or teacher to help you edit your writing. Also make sure to have all of the necessary editing tools on hand (handbook, dictionary, thesaurus, computer spell checker, etc.) when you work. Follow any guidelines provided by your teacher when preparing your final draft. Then proofread your finished product for errors before submitting it.

What's Ahead?

The checklists and strategies in this section will help you edit and proofread your work.

Editing Checklist

Cut, Clarify, Condense

Testing Your Sentences

Proofreading Checklist

044 Editing Checklist

Have you ever used a shopping or study list? Isn't it helpful to have your thoughts organized? The following checklist should help you each time you edit your writing. You might think of it as a "chopping" list, but it's really more: chopping, connecting, rearranging, polishing . . .

1. Read your final draft aloud to test it for sense and sound. Better yet, have someone read it aloud to you. Listen carefully as he or she reads. Your writing should read smoothly and naturally. If it doesn't, you have more editing to do.

2. Does each sentence express a complete thought? Does each paragraph have an overall point or purpose?

3. Have you used different sentence types and lengths? Are any sentences too long and rambling? Do you use too many short, choppy sentences?

4. Have you used a variety of sentence beginnings? Watch out for too many sentences that begin with the same pronoun or article (*I, My, The, There,* etc.).

5. Check each simple sentence for effective use of modifiers, especially prepositional phrases, participial phrases, and appositives. Have you punctuated these modifiers correctly?

6. Check your compound sentences. Do they contain two equal ideas, and is the relationship between the two ideas expressed by the proper conjunction (*and* versus *but* versus *or* . . .)?

7. What about your complex sentences? Have you used the most appropriate subordinating conjunction (*although, before, because, since, when, while,* etc.) or relative pronoun (*that, who, which,* etc.) to connect the two clauses in these sentences?

8. Make sure your writing is concise and to the point. Have you omitted slang, wordiness, and flowery language? Strive for simplicity and clarity in your writing.

9. Is your writing fresh and original? Have you avoided overused words and phrases? If not, substitute nouns, verbs, and adjectives that are specific, vivid, and colorful.

10. Replace any words or phrases that may be awkward, confusing, or misleading.

045 Cut, Clarify, Condense

Would you like an easy and effective strategy for fixing problems with wording? Try the 3 C's of editing.

Editing Code:

● **CUT** [brackets]

If you find a section in your writing that seems unnecessary or wordy, put brackets around it. If you later decide that this section is definitely unneeded, cut it.

● **CLARIFY** 〰〰〰

If you see something confusing or unclear in your writing, put a wavy line under it. Then, when you go back to this section, reword it or add to it.

● **CONDENSE** (parentheses)

If you come across part of your writing that is wordy or over-explained, put a set of parentheses around it. Then rewrite this section so that it reads more simply and clearly.

046 Testing Your Sentences

Another effective editing strategy is to test your sentences for variety, verb choice, and length. Here's how you can do just that:

◉ In one column on a piece of paper, list the opening words in each of your sentences. (Then decide if you need to vary some of your sentence beginnings.)

◉ In another column, list the verbs in each sentence. (Then decide if you need to replace any overused verbs—*is, are, see, look,* etc.—with more vivid ones.)

◉ In a third column, identify the number of words in each sentence. (Then decide if you need to change the length of some of your sentences.)

TAKE NOTE

Remember that your goal is to write sentences that sound natural. The best test for that is to simply read your sentences out loud and listen.

047 Proofreading Checklist

The following guidelines will help you check your writing for spelling, usage, mechanics, and grammar errors before you share it.

1. Have you spelled all your words correctly? Here are some tips:
- Read your writing backward and aloud—one word at a time—so you focus on each word.
- Circle each word you are unsure of.
- For help, consult the list of commonly misspelled words in your handbook. (See 686-690.) For additional help, check a dictionary.

2. Does each sentence end with a punctuation mark?

3. Are coordinating conjunctions (*and, but, or, so,* etc.) in compound sentences preceded by a comma? Have you used commas to set off items listed in a series, after introductory clauses, and so on?

4. Is all dialogue or written conversation properly punctuated?

5. Do all complete sentences in general copy or in dialogue begin with a capital letter? Have you capitalized all proper names?

6. Have you misused any of the commonly mixed pairs of words: *there / their / they're, accept / except,* etc.? (Refer to the "Using the Right Word" section in your handbook, 692-701.)

7. Have you used any words, phrases, or sentences that may confuse the reader?

8. Do your subjects and verbs agree in number?

9. Do your pronouns agree with their antecedents?

10. Have you used any sentence fragments, run-ons, or rambling sentences?

11. Have you chosen an appropriate title if one is needed?

12. Is your paper labeled correctly with your name and the class's name?

13. Does the form meet the requirements of the assignment?

Preparing a Writing Portfolio

048   A portfolio is a collection of your best writing that you submit for assessment. It is different from the traditional writing folder (also known as a working folder) that contains writing in various stages of completion. Portfolios contain only your finished work. Compiling a portfolio allows you to participate in the assessment process. You decide what writing to include; you reflect upon your writing progress; you make sure that all the right pieces are in all the right places. You are pretty much in control.

     A portfolio can be used even after you've shared it with your classmates and instructor. Very often employers are interested in seeing the kind of work you did in school, since this is a good indication of the kind of work you will do on the job.

What's Ahead?

This section of your handbook provides guidelines for putting together a writing portfolio and for preparing the writing pieces you plan to include.

     What You Should Include

     How You Should Work

049 What You Should Include

Most writing portfolios contain the following basic components: (Check with your teacher for the specific requirements.)

- A **table of contents** listing the information included in your portfolio
- An **opening essay** or **letter** detailing the story behind your portfolio (how you compiled it, how you feel about it, what it means to you)
- A **specified number of finished pieces** representing your best writing in the class (Your teacher may require you to include all of your planning, drafting, and revising work for one or more of these pieces.)
- A **best "other" piece** related to your work in another content area
- A **cover sheet** attached to each piece of writing discussing the reason for its selection, the amount of work that went into it, and so on
- **Evaluation sheets** or **checklists** charting, among other things, the basic skills you have mastered as well as the skills you still need to work on (Your teacher will supply these sheets.)

050 How You Should Work

1. Keep track of all of your writing (including planning notes and drafts) throughout the term. This way, when it comes to compiling your portfolio, you will have the necessary pieces to work with.

2. Make sure that you understand all of the specific requirements for your portfolio.

3. Work with an expandable or pocket-type folder. You will avoid dog-eared or ripped pages if you keep the components in a "safe environment."

4. Maintain a regular working schedule. It will be impossible to produce an effective portfolio if you approach it as a last-minute project.

5. Develop a feeling of pride in your portfolio. Allow it to reflect as positive an image of yourself as possible. Look your best!

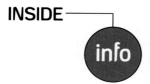

INSIDE — info

The guidelines provided on this page deal with a portfolio that showcases your abilities as a writer. You would normally submit this type of portfolio prior to the end of a semester or final grading period.

Writing with a Computer

051 When asked whether a computer helps them with their writing, most students answer *yes*. If you ask these students to explain their answer, they tell you that they stay at a piece of writing longer with a computer, that they experiment more, that they like the way they can move information around, and that they have a better attitude toward writing in general.

Teachers agree that computers help students with their writing, especially when it comes to writing research papers and reports. Teachers will also say, however, that computers are better suited for certain parts of the writing process than they are for others. This section discusses the upside and the downside of computer-assisted writing. We hope it helps.

What's Ahead?

In this section of your handbook, you'll find many helpful tips on how to use a computer when you write.

Prewriting
Writing the First Draft
Revising
Editing and Proofreading
Booting Up!
Outputting Your Copy

052 Prewriting

Upside:

Prewriting can be a breeze on a computer. For example, think about free writing. You can fill the screen any way you want and keep going as long as you want, without so much as having to flip over a sheet of paper.

If you type fairly well, you can get ideas down much faster by keyboarding than by writing.

If you prewrite messily in longhand, using the computer can free you from worry about handwriting you (or your teacher) can't read later.

Some people are more inventive in front of a screen. It may be that you have a different style of learning or creating. Using a computer may well free your thinking and help you get words on paper.

Downside:

Some writers do less prewriting and planning when they are using a computer, partly because they aren't able to use some forms of prewriting, like clustering.

The monitor is too tempting for some writers; they constantly stop to read what they have written. *Solution:* Turn the resolution of the monitor down to stop yourself from deleting or editing.

Best Advice: Try it out! Find out whether prewriting on paper or prewriting on a screen is better for you. If you think it's simpler or easier to approach prewriting with paper and pen, you're not alone: many writers find this to be the case. At the same time, don't overlook the possibility that using a computer may help you get ideas down more quickly and effectively.

TAKE NOTE

Save your work at frequent intervals throughout a writing project. Before you turn off your computer, print out a hard copy and make a backup copy of your work on a disk. No one wants to lose an entire paper by default!

> "For me it [the word processor] was obviously the perfect new toy. I began playing on page 1—editing, cutting, and revising—and have been on a rewriting high ever since."
>
> —William Zinsser

053 Writing the First Draft

Upside:

 Using a computer helps a writer stay with a piece of writing longer and develop it more thoroughly.

 Computers allow you to concentrate on ideas rather than on the finished copy.

 Using a computer allows you to get your thoughts on paper much faster than writing them out in longhand. Computers can improve your flow of words and help cure writer's block.

 Drafting on a computer can make it easier for you to share ideas. You can simply print out a hard copy for your teacher or classmates to react to. As a result of this sharing, you also become more aware of a real audience.

Downside:

 Deleting sections of copy on a computer is very tempting for some writers. Most experts agree that it is important to save all of your ideas in early drafts. *Solution:* Don't push that delete key no matter what—at least not in your early drafts!

Best Advice: Do your drafting on your computer. If you can't resist the temptation to make a lot of changes during first drafts, turn down the brightness on your monitor and type "blind" for a while. Print out and share copies of what you've written.

INSIDE

Knowing when to stop drafting is as important as getting started. When you have worked on your draft for a good chunk of time, stop and give it a rest. Coming back with fresh eyes and a clear mind will increase your objectivity as well as your creativity.

054 Revising

Upside:

A big plus for computer writing is the time and toil it saves you when writing or typing revision after revision, especially on longer essays and research papers.

A computer makes revising easier because you can move, delete, and add large chunks of information by using a few simple commands. As a result, you no longer have to be afraid to try new things during revision.

Group revision is also made easier with quick, clean printouts for everyone to read and react to.

Downside:

Some people are not as good at carefully evaluating on a screen as they are on paper. *Solution:* Print out the document, make the changes on paper, and then input them.

Best Advice: Use your computer for revising, but also read through a printed copy of your work so that you can reflect on what you've written. (If you print out a copy before you revise, you can easily undo any hasty revising later.)

055 Editing and Proofreading

Upside:

Because making changes is so easy, you can easily produce a clean final copy.

Programs are available to help you prepare your writing for publication. The spell checkers and search-and-replace capabilities in some word-processing programs are especially helpful.

Some programs make it simple to create the bibliography or works cited section for a research paper.

Downside:

You may not see errors such as missing words, misplaced commas, or misspelled words as easily on a screen as on paper. Or you may come to rely too much on your spell and grammar checkers. *Solution:* Do a final, thorough reading yourself.

Best Advice: Do your editing and proofreading on a computer. Clearly, the computer works best in this final stage of preparing a paper.

056 Booting Up!

If you are just getting into computers, you should find the following observations helpful:

- **Don't put your pens and paper into storage just because you are using a computer.** You will still do plenty of old-fashioned longhand during most of your writing projects. Many writers like to do their initial writing on paper and their revising and editing on computers. After a little experimenting, you can decide what works best for you.

- **To hunt and peck with a computer is slow and tedious, so you must know how to type.** There are keyboarding programs available to use on your computer if you can't take a basic typing or word-processing course in school.

- **Word-processing programs make a computer a hi-tech writing machine.** Programs are the software (disks, cartridges, cassettes, etc.) that instruct a computer to perform certain tasks. All word-processing programs allow you to enter, delete, add, and move data. Others will actually help you with your spelling, grammar, and research-paper work.

- **All word-processing programs come with step-by-step instructions.** Follow them carefully. When you do get stuck and you can't find your own answers, ask for help. It may seem difficult at first, but you'll soon be an expert!

- **Keep a written (or typed) copy of your writing handy.** That way, if your writing suddenly vanishes from your computer screen, you'll have a copy to fall back on. Remember: *Save!*

- **Give it a rest!** Staring at a monitor for a long period of time can cause eyestrain. Make sure that you adjust the contrast and brightness on your monitor so that it feels comfortable to your eyes. Also make sure that the lighting in the room does not cause a glare on your screen. When your eyes begin to ache, save your text, and take a rest.

057 Outputting Your Copy

Using a computer allows you to add some nice touches to your final copy. Here are just a few of the things you can use to make your work look more professional.

- Different typestyles for variety
- Boldface or italics for emphasis
- Indents and centering for page balance
- Tables and charts for clarity
- Uniform margins for neatness
- Graphics for illustration

ELEMENTS

Basic Elements of Writing

Writing with Style

Writing Sentences

Writing Paragraphs

Writing Basic Essays

Writer's Resource

Writing with Style

058 What's your style when you greet people? Are you a "Hey-dude-what's-up?" kind of person? Or are you more formal? "Hello, Mr. Jordan, It's good to see you." And what about your style when it comes to clothes or music or cars?

In speech and in writing, the words you choose and the way you put them together make up your style. In speech, the best style is the one that fits you, your purpose, and your listener. In writing, the best style also is one that fits you, your purpose, and your reader. If, for example, you're writing for the school newspaper, your readers will appreciate a style that falls within the guidelines for good journalism. In the work-place your readers will appreciate a style that falls (1) within the broad guidelines of business writing and (2) within the specific guidelines set by your company or organization.

What's Ahead?

This section includes information and models to help you improve your personal writing style.

> Traits of an Effective Style
> Common Ailments of Style
> Showing Versus Telling
> Using Strong, Colorful Words
> Using Repetition

059 Traits of an Effective Style

Just as your vocabulary will improve as you continue to read, your style will improve as you continue to write. Developing an effective style doesn't happen all at once like passing a driving test. It happens a little bit each time you write—or read. It is a slow, creative process. But you can help things along if you take a little time to study the traits of an effective style and apply them to your own writing:

Concreteness ● For a writing style to be effective, it must be specific or concrete—not general or vague. In most academic and business writing, writers use specific words to help the reader think and understand. For example, in order to help a builder clearly understand what to do, an engineer writing instructions uses specific construction terms like *12-inch I-beam* rather than creative, colorful words like *thick-shouldered steel girder.*

Focus ● Stylistic writing has a clear focus. Keep the focus of your writing clear by (1) thinking about your general purpose, like informing or persuading, and (2) concentrating on the specific feelings and ideas that you must convey in order to achieve that purpose.

Vitality ● Stylistic writing is lively and every word is worth reading. Give vitality to all your writing by speaking honestly and presenting interesting information. Give vitality to your business writing by talking directly to your reader—not to your computer screen or memo pad.

Originality ● Stylistic writing is fresh: there are no worn-out phrases or tired ideas. The writer takes risks with word choice and sentence structure to get and keep the readers' attention. In general you have more freedom to experiment in personal and creative writing than in academic and business writing, but even a one-sentence statement on a company fax form is an opportunity to choose interesting words and phrases.

Grace ● Like a shortstop who backhands a line drive, spins, and throws to first base all in one smooth motion, stylistic writing moves gracefully from start to finish. It ties pieces of information together into a smooth flow of ideas. You achieve graceful writing—in the classroom and in the workplace—by writing as naturally as possible without interruptions.

Commitment ● Stylistic writing takes commitment. Whether you're writing a poem, a research paper, or the minutes of a business meeting, you achieve style by (1) believing that your writing is worth doing and (2) refining the writing until it moves with style.

Common Ailments of Style

060 Primer Style

The Ailment: If your writing has many short sentences one right after the other, it may sound like a grade-school textbook, or "primer."

> Abigail Bruins works at Child Life Preschool. She teaches four-year-olds. Abigail plans her lessons carefully. She communicates well with her students.

The Cure: The main cure is to cut unnecessary words and combine some ideas into longer, smoother sentences. Here's the same passage revised:

> Abigail Bruins is an effective teacher at Child Life Preschool who prepares her lessons carefully and communicates well with her four-year-old students.

061 Passive Voice

The Ailment: When a verb is in the passive voice, the subject of the sentence receives the action of the verb. Because the passive voice uses more words and is less lively than the active voice, overuse of the passive voice may make your writing seem slow and impersonal.

> The meeting was called to order by President Nathan Vanderlaan, and the minutes were read by Secretary Jesse Nieboer.

The Cure: Unless you need the passive voice, change it to active.

> President Nathan Vanderlaan called the meeting to order, and Secretary Jesse Nieboer read the minutes.

062 Insecurity

The Ailment: Qualifiers *(to be honest, to tell the truth, I really think)* and intensifiers *(really, truly, actually)* are useful when it's necessary to clarify or strengthen a statement. However, you should use these words and phrases only when necessary because they suggest that you lack confidence in your ideas.

> I totally and completely agree with Mary Beth that the pay scale is probably unfair, but that's only my opinion.

The Cure: Think through your idea carefully, write it clearly, and let the idea stand on its own strength.

> I agree with Mary Beth that the pay scale is unfair.

TAKE NOTE

For other ailments of style, see "Wordiness" (095), "Flowery language" (091), "Jargon" (093), and "Cliche" (096).

063 Showing Versus Telling

Writer Don Murray suggests that you put people in your writing and let their actions communicate ideas for you. Let them show your readers something in a lively and interesting way rather than you telling them matter-of-factly. **Showing** is a tool that you can use in all your writing—from short stories to business proposals.

Example No. 1

The paragraph below is from an essay in which student writer Martina Lowry defines the word "tact" by showing how her mother treats Martina's brother.

Sensitivity is a major component of tact. If a person isn't sensitive to another's feelings, there is no way he can be tactful. Children are especially vulnerable and must be treated sensitively. Sometimes a child's proudest accomplishments actually cause parents more work. Yesterday my 5-year-old brother proudly announced that he had cleaned the screen of our television set. Unfortunately, he used Pledge furniture polish, which produced a smeared, oily film on the television screen. My mother smiled and thanked him for his efforts—and then showed him how to clean the screen properly. Her sensitivity enabled my brother to keep his self-respect. . . .

Example No. 2

Notice that while the paragraph above illustrates an idea by telling about people, the one below, taken from a business report, tells about a machine. By describing how the model #736 performed in a product-evaluation test, the writer illustrates the quality of an entire line of lawn mowers.

The new generation of Grass Eater lawn mowers have larger engines, greater cutting capacity, and better pickup than last year's models. In fact, we chose the #736 Grass Eater as the best-performing self-propelled, rotary lawn mower that we tested. In the test area with shorter grass, the six-horsepower, two-cycle engine turned the twenty-one-inch blade with ease at walking speeds of slow, medium, and fast. In the area of taller grass, the #736 also moved easily at both the slow and medium speeds. With the shift in the fast position, the engine pulled noticeably but never coughed or cut out. In both areas and at all three speeds, the #736 earned its name Grass Eater by cutting clean, even swaths, picking up 80 percent of the clippings, and leaving a manicured turf that even landscapers would love.

Discussion: The first example above illustrates how *showing* helps the reader understand a concept that is difficult to define (*tell*). The second example illustrates how showing helps the reader evaluate a product. Both help the reader picture the ideas being discussed.

064 Using Strong, Colorful Words

Without the right colors you can't paint an accurate picture of your subject. This is true both in art and in writing. Whether you're describing, instructing, or informing, you need the right words to communicate exactly what you're feeling and thinking.

065 Choose specific nouns: General nouns (like *person, disease,* and *form*) communicate vague and sometimes misleading information. More specific nouns (*child, melanoma,* and *W-2 form*) give the reader clearer, more precise information. Read the table below and notice that as you move down each column, the nouns get more specific.

General to Specific Nouns

person	*place*	*thing*	*idea*
woman	building	vehicle	pain
actress	shop	van	headache
Meryl Streep	Galen's Garage	minivan	migraine

066 Use vivid verbs: Like nouns, verbs also can be general or specific. For example, *run* is less precise than *dash, gallop,* or *lope*. Notice that the verbs below are more specific as you read down each column.

General to Specific Verbs

went	worked	talked	stood
walked	studied	requested	slumped
stumbled	crammed	pleaded	slouched

067 Select specific adjectives and adverbs: Use precise, colorful adjectives to describe the nouns in your writing. Strong adjectives can help make the nouns you choose even more interesting and clear to the reader. For example, when describing your uncle's new car as a "*sleek red* convertible," you are using adjectives to give the reader a clearer picture of the car.

NOTE: Use adjectives selectively. If your writing contains too many adjectives, they will simply get in the way and lose their effectiveness.

Too many adjectives: A tall, shocking column of thick, yellow smoke marked the exact spot where the tanks exploded.

Revised: A column of thick, yellow smoke marked the spot where the tanks exploded.

068 Using Repetition

Another important stylistic technique is to repeat similar grammatical structures (words, phrases, or ideas) for the purpose of rhythm, emphasis, and clarity. When used effectively, **repetition** can do more to improve your style of writing than just about any other technique.

INSIDE info

When using repetition, remember to keep the words or ideas parallel, or stated in the same way. For example, here is a series of infinitives: *to research, to evaluate,* and *to invest.*

For Rhythm and Balance: Notice in each sentence below that repeated words or phrases are balanced and flow smoothly from one to the next.

> Feel cool, look cool, and be cool in this new suit from Sasser!

> To get an M.D. in family practice, you'll need four years of college, four years of medical school, and three years of a hospital internship.

> Who was the great NBA center who starred at U.C.L.A., adopted an Islamic name, and studied ballet?

For Emphasis and Effect: Notice in the examples below how repetition in sentence structure adds intensity.

> Mutual respect, race-to-race, is built on honest dialogue, face-to-face.

> Just as a gardener who plants little in the ground can expect little from the harvest, a society that invests little in its schools can expect little from its graduates.

> Please take time to follow all safety precautions. At Slenk Automation we value no project and no contract as highly as we value the health of our employees.

For Unity and Organization: Repetition is a useful tool in all types of writing. The following are examples of how repetition is used to organize and clarify business writing:

- Stating steps in a process (See "Writing Instructions," 218-219.)
- Numbering items within a list (See "Minutes of a Meeting," 224.)
- Introducing elements in a daily schedule (See "Model Short Report," 228.)
- Stating conclusions in a report (See "Short Report," 229.)
- Repeating patterns of a graphic layout (See "The Informative Letter," 195, and "The Résumé," 206.)
- Writing paragraphs with parallel structure (See "Model Letter of Complaint," 198.)

Writing Sentences

069   Let's start with some good news: You don't have to be a grammar expert to write effective sentences. Yes, you have to know the basic rules, but rules are secondary to the real thing. You learn the most about sentences by experiencing them—by seeing them in print (in the books and magazines you read) and by writing regularly (in a variety of forms).

And now for some more good news: This chapter provides a quick, easy-to-use set of guidelines for writing clear, effective sentences. It's the place to turn whenever you have a question about sentence sense.

What's Ahead?

This section of your handbook includes answers to nearly all your sentence questions.

⬤070 Combining Sentences

Most sentences contain several basic ideas that work together to form a complete thought. For example, if you were to write a sentence about the construction of the Great Wall of China, you would actually be working with several different ideas. Each of these ideas could be written as a separate sentence:

- The longest construction project in history was the Great Wall of China.
- The project took 1,700 years to complete.
- The Great Wall of China is 1,400 miles long.
- It is between 18 and 30 feet high.
- It is up to 32 feet thick.

⬤071 The Process in Action

Of course, you wouldn't express each idea separately like this. Instead, you would combine these ideas (some or all of them) into longer, more mature sentences, using one of the following approaches:

1. Use a **series** to combine three or more similar ideas.

> The Great Wall of China is **1,400 miles long,** between **18 and 30 feet high,** and up to **32 feet thick.**

2. Use a **relative pronoun** (*who, whose, that, which*) to introduce the subordinate (less important) ideas.

> The Great Wall of China, **which is 1,400 miles long and between 18 and 30 feet high,** took 1,700 years to complete.

3. Use an **introductory phrase or clause.** (You can also use a **colon** to introduce a list of details.)

> **Having taken 1,700 years to complete,** the Great Wall of China was the longest construction project in history: 1,400 miles long, between 18 and 30 feet high, and up to 32 feet thick.

4. Use a **semicolon** (and a conjunctive adverb if appropriate).

> The Great Wall took 1,700 years to complete; it is 1,400 miles long and up to 30 feet high and 32 feet thick.

5. Repeat a **key word** or phrase to emphasize an idea.

> The Great Wall of China was the longest and largest construction **project** in history, a **project** that took 1,700 years to complete.

6. Use a **correlative conjunction** (*either, or; not only, but also*) to compare or contrast two ideas in a sentence.

> The Great Wall of China is **not only** 1,400 miles long, **but also** up to 30 feet high and 32 feet thick.

7. Use an **appositive** (a phrase that renames) to emphasize an idea.

> The Great Wall of China—**the largest construction project in history**—is 1,400 miles long, 32 feet thick, and up to 30 feet high.

072 Modeling Sentences

What you will find if you study the sentences of your favorite authors may surprise you. You may find sentences that seem to flow on forever, sentences that are so direct that they hit you right between the eyes, sentences that sort of sneak up on you, and "sentences" that aren't complete thoughts. (Writers do occasionally break the rules.)

INSIDE
info

Generally speaking, most popular authors write in a relaxed, somewhat informal style. This style is characterized by sentences with a lot of personality, rhythm, and varied structures.

073 The Modeling Process

You will want to try imitating certain sentences in your own writing because you like the way they sound or the way they make a point. This process is sometimes called **modeling**. Like sentence combining, sentence modeling can help you improve your writing style. Here's how you can get started:

- **Reserve** a special section in your notebook or journal to list effective sentences you come across in your reading.
- **List** sentences (or short passages) that flow smoothly, that use effective descriptive words, or that contain original figures of speech.
- **Study** each sentence so you know how it is put together. Read it out loud. Look for phrases and clauses set off by commas. Also focus on word endings (*-ing, -ed,* etc.) and on the location of articles (*a, an, the*) and prepositions (*to, by, of,* etc.).
- **Write** your own version of a sentence by imitating it part by part. Try to use the same word endings, articles, and prepositions, but work in your own nouns, verbs, and modifiers. (Your imitation does not have to be exact.) Practice writing several different versions.
- **Continue** imitating different sentences to help you fine-tune your sentence style. The more you practice, the better your style will get.

074 The Process in Action

Study the following interesting sentence:

> He has a thin face with sharp features and a couple of eyes burning with truth oil.
>
> —Tom Wolfe

Now look carefully at the modeled version and compare it part by part to the original sentence. Can you see how the imitation was carried out?

> He has an athletic body with a sinewy contour and a couple of arms bulging with weight-room dedication.

075 Expanding Sentences

Strangely enough, when you compose sentences, finer often means fatter. In other words, to make a more finely focused point, you need to add modifiers, which "fatten" the sentence. Take a simple "base clause" like this one: Toni shrieked.

We could fatten or expand that sentence by adding a variety of modifiers to show exactly how and when and why Toni shrieked. Here are some types of modifiers we could choose:

Single words:	Suddenly
Phrases	
Prepositional:	with her hands on her face
Infinitive:	to cover her embarrassment
Participial:	gasping sharply
Absolute:	her mouth gaping
Clauses	
Subordinate:	when the game show host called out her name
Relative:	who was waving a $10,000 bill

076 Moving Modifiers

We could make all kinds of expanded sentences using modifiers like these, just by moving them around into exactly the combinations we wanted. We could put modifiers before the base clause, after it, even in the middle of it if we wanted. Study these samples:

When the game show host, who was waving a $10,000 bill, called out her name, Toni, gasping sharply, suddenly shrieked, with her hands on her face, her mouth gaping.

Toni shrieked, covering her face in embarrassment when the game show host, waving a $10,000 bill, called out her name.

With a shriek, her mouth gaping, an embarrassed Toni covered her face as the game show host waved a $10,000 bill and suddenly called out her name.

077 Cumulative Sentences

The type of sentence we have just created is called a cumulative sentence. Remember these facts about cumulative sentences:

● They usually have a relatively simple base clause.
● The idea in the base clause is made more exact with modifiers.
● Modifiers can come before the base clause, in the middle of it, or after it.
● You may use many modifiers or just a few, as it suits you.
● Modifiers can modify words in the base clause, or they can modify other modifiers.

> "To err is human, but when the eraser wears out ahead of the pencil, you're overdoing it."
>
> —J. Jenkins

078 Writing Complete Sentences

With a few exceptions in special situations, you should use complete sentences when you write. By definition, a complete sentence expresses a complete thought. However, a sentence may actually contain several ideas, not just one. The trick is getting those ideas to work together to form a clear, interesting sentence that expresses your exact meaning.

Among the most common errors that writers make when attempting to write complete and effective sentences are **fragments, comma splices, rambling sentences,** and **run-ons.**

079 A **fragment** is a group of words used as a sentence. It is not a sentence, though, because it lacks a subject, a verb, or some other essential part. That missing part causes it to be an incomplete thought.

Fragment: Lettuce all over the table. (This phrase lacks a verb.)

Sentence: Lettuce flew all over the table.

Fragment: When the waiter served the salad. (This clause does not convey a complete thought. We need to know what happened "when the waiter served the salad.")

Sentence: When the waiter served the salad, lettuce flew all over the table.

Fragment: Kate asked, "Is that what you call a tossed salad?" Laughing and scooping up a pile of lettuce. (This is a sentence followed by a fragment. This error can be corrected by combining the fragment with the sentence.)

Sentence: Laughing and scooping up a pile of lettuce, Kate asked, "Is that what you call a tossed salad?"

TAKE NOTE

When you write dialogue, fragments are not mistakes and are often preferable to complete sentences because that's how people talk:

"Hey, Rico. My house?"
"Yeah, right. On Tuesday afternoon."
"Whatever."

080 A **comma splice** is a mistake made when two independent clauses are connected ("spliced") with only a comma. The comma is not enough: a period, semicolon, or conjunction is needed.

Splice: We want employees to understand the system, we need a good manual.

Corrected: We want employees to understand the system, but we need a good manual. (Coordinating conjunction *but* has been added.)

Corrected: We want employees to understand the system; we need a good manual. (Comma has been changed to a semicolon.)

081 A **rambling sentence** is one that seems to go on and on. It is often the result of the overuse of the word *and*.

Rambling: Until around 1850, shoes were made "straight" and fit either the left or the right foot and this did not change until machines were invented that made it easy to customize shoes for each foot.

Corrected: Until around 1850, shoes were made "straight" and fit either the left or the right foot. Then machines were invented that made it easy to customize shoes for each foot.

082 A **run-on sentence** is two sentences joined without adequate punctuation or a connecting word.

Run-on: I thought the ride would never end my eyes were crossed, and my fingers were numb.

I thought the ride would never end. My eyes were crossed, and my fingers were numb.

> "If any man wishes to write a clear style, let him first be clear in his thoughts."
>
> — Johann Wolfgang von Goethe

083 Writing Clear Sentences

Writing is thinking. Before you can write clearly, you must think clearly. Nothing is more frustrating for the reader than writing that has to be reread just to understand its basic meaning.

Look carefully at the common errors that follow. Do you recognize any of them as errors you sometimes make in your own writing? If so, use this section as a checklist when you revise. Conquering these errors will help to make your writing clear and readable.

084 An **incomplete comparison** is the result of leaving out a word or words that are necessary to show exactly what is being compared to what.

Incomplete: I get along better with Rosa than Gina. (Do you mean that you get along better with Rosa than you get along with Gina? . . . or that you get along better with Rosa than Gina does?)

Clear: I get along better with Rosa than Gina does.

085 **Ambiguous wording** is wording that is unclear because it has two or more possible meanings. It often occurs when sentences are combined.

Ambiguous: Mike decided to take his new convertible to the drive-in movie, which turned out to be a real horror story. (What turned out to be a real horror story—Mike's taking his new convertible to the drive-in, or the movie?)

Clear: Mike decided to take his new convertible to the drive-in movie, a decision that turned out to be a real horror story.

086 An **indefinite reference** is a problem caused by careless use of pronouns. As a result, the reader is not sure what the pronouns are referring to.

Indefinite: In *The Light Touch*, **he** describes how to use humor for business success. (Who is *he*?)

Clear: In *The Light Touch*, the author, Malcolm Kushner, describes how to use humor for business success.

Indefinite: As he pulled his car up to the service window, **it** made a strange rattling sound. (Which rattled, the car or the window?)

Clear: His car made a strange rattling sound as he pulled up to the service window.

087 <u>**Misplaced modifiers**</u> are modifiers that have been placed incorrectly; they can lead to confusion.

Misplaced: We have an assortment of combs for physically active people with unbreakable teeth. (People with unbreakable teeth?)

Corrected: For physically active people, we have an assortment of combs with unbreakable teeth.

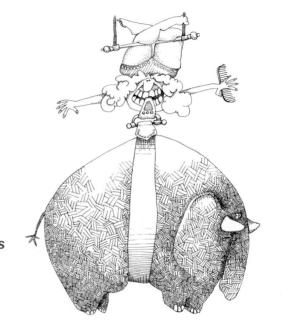

We have an assortment of combs for physically active people with unbreakable teeth.

088 <u>**Dangling modifiers**</u> are modifiers that appear to modify the wrong word or a word that isn't in the sentence.

Dangling: Trying desperately to finish the work, Paul's boss called him. (The phrase *Trying desperately to finish the work* appears to modify *Paul's boss.*)

Corrected: Trying desperately to finish the work, Paul heard his boss call him. (Here the phrase modifies *Paul.*)

Dangling: After standing in line for five hours, the manager announced that all the tickets had been sold. (In this sentence, it appears as if the manager had been *standing in line for five hours.*)

Corrected: After standing in line for five hours, Ian heard the manager announce that all the tickets had been sold. (Now the phrase clearly modifies the person who had been standing in line: *Ian.*)

> "Read over your compositions and, when you meet a passage which you think is particularly fine, strike it out."
>
> — Samuel Johnson

089 Writing Natural Sentences

Samuel Johnson, a noted writer of the eighteenth century, was undoubtedly talking about one of the greatest temptations facing writers—to use lots of words (big words, clever words, fancy words). For some reason, we get into our heads the idea that simple writing is not effective writing. Nothing could be further from the truth.

The very best writing is ordinary and natural, not fancy or artificial. That's why it is so important to master the art of free writing. It is your best chance at a personal style. A personal voice will produce natural, honest passages you will not have to strike out. Learn from the following samples, which are wordy and artificial.

090 **Deadwood** is wording that fills up lots of space but does not add anything important or new to the overall meaning.

Wordy: At this point in time, I feel the study needs additional work before the subcommittee can recommend it be resubmitted for consideration.

Concise: The study needs more work.

091 **Flowery language** is writing that uses more or bigger words than needed. It is writing that often contains too many adjectives or adverbs.

Flowery: The cool, fresh breeze, which came like a storm in the night, lifted me to the exhilarating heights from which I had been previously suppressed by the incandescent cloud in the learning center.

Concise: The cool breeze was a refreshing change from the muggy classroom air.

092 A **trite expression** is one that is overused and stale; as a result, it sounds neither sincere nor natural.

Trite: It gives me a great deal of pleasure to present to you this plaque as a token of our appreciation. Let me read it.

Natural: The words on this plaque speak for all of us.

093 **Jargon** is language used in a certain profession or by a particular group of people. It usually does not sound natural in everyday writing.

Jargon: I'm having conceptual difficulty with these employee mandates.

Natural: I don't understand these work orders.

094 A **euphemism** is a word or phrase that is substituted for another because it is considered a less offensive way of saying something. (Avoid overusing euphemisms.)

Euphemism: I am so *exasperated* that I could *expectorate*.

Natural: I am so mad I could spit.

095 <u>**Wordiness**</u> is unnecessary repetition of a word (or a synonym for that word).

Redundant: He had a way of keeping my attention by the way he raised and lowered his voice on every single word he spoke.

Concise: He kept my attention by raising and lowering his voice when he spoke.

Double
Subject: Some people they don't use their voices as well as they could. (Drop *they*, since *people* is the only subject needed.)

Concise: Some people don't use their voices as well as they could.

Tautology: *widow woman, descend down, audible to the ear, return back, unite together, final outcome* (Each phrase says the same thing twice.)

096 A **cliche** is an overused word or phrase that springs quickly to mind but just as quickly bores the user and the audience. A cliche gives the reader nothing new or original to think about—no new insight into the subject.

Cliche: Our plan is as dead as a doornail.

Natural: Our plan won't work.

cliches
to
avoid

acid test	food for thought
after all is said and done	in a nutshell
a tough road ahead	in one ear and out the other
back to square one	in the nick of time
beat around the bush	last but not least
believe it or not	lesser of two evils
best foot forward	more than meets the eye
bread-and-butter issue	needs no introduction
came through with flying colors	no time like the present
cart before the horse	put your foot in your mouth
chalk up a victory	reinvent the wheel
don't rock the boat	run it up the flagpole
drop in the bucket	see eye-to-eye
easier said than done	shot in the arm
face the music	sink or swim
fish out of water	state of the art

> "You can be a little ungrammatical if you come from the right part of the country."
>
> —Robert Frost

Writing Acceptable Sentences

097   What Robert Frost says is very true. Much of the color and charm of literature comes from the everyday habits and customs—especially the speech—of its characters. Keep that in mind when you write fiction of any kind. However, when you write essays, reports, and most other assignments, remember that it's more important to use language that is correct and appropriate.

098 **Substandard (nonstandard) language** is language that is often acceptable in everyday conversation, but seldom in formal writing (except fiction).

Colloquial:
Avoid the use of colloquial language such as *go with*, *wait up*.

Can I go with? (Substandard)
Can I go with you? (Standard)

Double
preposition:
Avoid the use of certain double prepositions: *off of*, *off to*.

Reggie went off to the movies. (Substandard)
Reggie went to the movies. (Standard)

Substitution:
Avoid substituting *and* for *to* in formal writing.

Try and get here on time. (Substandard)
Try to get here on time. (Standard)

Avoid substituting *of* for *have* when combining with *could*, *would*, *should*, or *might*.

I should of studied for that test. (Substandard)
I should have studied for that test. (Standard)

Slang:
Avoid the use of slang or any "in" words.

Hey, dude, what's happenin'? (Substandard)

099 **Double negative** is a sentence that contains two negative words. Because two negatives make a positive, this type of sentence can take on a meaning opposite of what is intended. Usually, it just sounds bad.

Awkward:
I haven't got no money. (This sentence actually says—after taking out the two negatives that are now a positive—I have got money.)

Corrected:
I haven't got any money. / I have no money.

NOTE: Do not use *hardly, barely,* or *scarcely* with a negative; the result is a double negative.

100 <u>Shift in construction</u> is a change in the structure or style midway through a sentence. (Also see "Agreement of Subject and Verb," 761-771.)

Shift in number: When *a person* goes shopping for a used car, *he or she* (not *they*) must be careful not to get a lemon.

Shift in tense: The trunk should be checked to see that it *contains* a jack and a spare tire that *are* (not *should be*) in good shape.

Shift in person: *One* must be careful to watch for heavy, white exhaust or *one* (not *you*) can end up with real engine problems.

Shift in voice: As you continue to look for the right car (active voice), many freshly painted ones are sure to be seen (passive voice).

Corrected: As you continue to look for the right car, you are sure to see many freshly painted ones. (Both verbs are in the active voice.)

101 <u>Inconsistent (unparallel) construction</u> occurs when the writer fails to use a consistent grammatical structure for each of the parallel items in a series.

Inconsistent: To improve your memory, picture in your mind what you hear or read, repeat the main points to yourself, and taking notes is important, too. (The sentence has two verbs that are parallel—*picture* and *repeat*—and then switches to an *-ing* word, *taking*.)

Consistent: To improve your memory, picture in your mind what you hear or read, repeat the main points to yourself, and take notes. (Now all three things being discussed are consistent, or parallel.)

THE BOTTOM LINE

Use sentence combining, modeling, and expanding to build your sentences; use the four guidelines below to build them correctly:

- ◉ **Be Complete** Avoid fragments, comma splices, run-ons, and rambling sentences.

- ◉ **Be Clear** Avoid incomplete comparisons, ambiguous wording, indefinite references, and misplaced and dangling modifiers.

- ◉ **Be Natural** Avoid deadwood, flowery language, euphemisms, wordiness, trite expressions, jargon, and cliches.

- ◉ **Be Grammatically Correct** Avoid substandard language, double negatives, shifts in construction, and inconsistent construction.

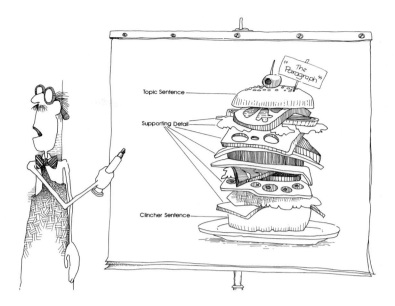

Writing Paragraphs

The sentences you're reading right now are arranged in a paragraph. What's a paragraph? It's a group of sentences beginning with a five-space indentation. But it's more than that. It's a sequence of thoughts that make sense together, something like a sandwich. That is, you'll find a layer of details or illustrations (the lettuce, meat, tomatoes) sandwiched between a topic sentence and a concluding or clinching sentence (the bread). If you'll look at this paragraph, you'll see that's exactly how it's made.

Think of a paragraph as one especially long sentence. Or, if you like, think of it as an especially short essay. Both are true! That's why, if you can master the art of the paragraph, you can master the art of writing.

What's Ahead?

This section of your handbook will help you sort through all the details related to writing good paragraphs.

Types of Paragraphs

The Topic Sentence

Paragraph Unity

Types of Details

Methods of Arranging Details

Adding Variety

Writing a Paragraph

103 Quick Guide

A good paragraph hangs together and gives readers what they need and want. Readers need to know what the topic is. And they need information about that topic. But they appreciate it when the information is interestingly detailed. And they love it when the information is given a colorful, original voice. Here are some tips to help you give your readers what they want:

1. If you haven't already been assigned a topic, select one that interests you (and your reader) and can be covered in one paragraph.

2. For your paragraph, write a topic sentence that clearly states your topic and a specific impression. (See 108.)

3. List the details you plan to cover in your paragraph. Be sure to consider both personal details and details from other sources. (See 110.)

4. Write the sentences in your paragraph in a natural order. Let your own personality and creativity be your guide, along with (of course) your topic sentence.

5. If you are having difficulty putting your thoughts into a logical order, refer to the "Methods of Arranging Details," 111, for help.

6. Use a variety of sentence beginnings, lengths, and types. (See "Adding Variety," 112.) Don't, however, worry about variety until after you have all your ideas down in writing.

7. Also make sure that your sentences read smoothly and connect well with one another. (See "Combining Sentences," 070, and "Transitions and Linking Words," 114.)

8. Once the first draft of your paragraph is complete, check it over to be sure your topic reads clearly from start to finish and that all your sentences belong in the paragraph. (See "Paragraph Unity," 109.)

9. If necessary, add a final sentence (*a concluding sentence*) to bring your paragraph to a logical stopping point.

10. Proofread your paragraph carefully for usage, punctuation, spelling, and so on.

Types of Paragraphs

There are four basic types of paragraphs: *narrative, descriptive, expository,* and *persuasive.*

104 A **narrative paragraph** tells a story with a beginning, a middle, and an end. Narrative writing is common in short stories and novels; however, writers in the workplace use it as well. The following example is a news release written by a person in the Fedora Police Department.

> As a result of a citizen's prompt reporting, John Jones of Fedora, Nevada, was convicted of operating a motor vehicle while under the influence of alcohol. On February 22 an anonymous caller informed the Fedora Police Department that a brown Ford pickup had nearly struck a person in the McDonald's parking lot. When Officer Bill Hamilton stopped the pickup, he saw beer cans on the floorboards. Jones took an intoxilyzer test at the sheriff's office, and the test indicated a breath alcohol concentration of .290, almost three times over the legal limit. Jones pled guilty to operating a motor vehicle while under the influence of alcohol. Because of earlier drunk-driving convictions, Jones lost his driver's license for six years. Thanks to a citizen's phone call, a drunk driver was taken off the streets.

105 A **descriptive paragraph** is one in which the sentences work together to present a single, clear picture (description) of a person, a place, a thing, or an idea. Description is commonly used in novels, short stories, and essays. The example below is a realtor's newspaper advertisement.

> The three-bedroom, ranch-style home pictured above is attractive, well built, and modestly priced. Located at 605 11th Avenue, this home has light-gray vinyl siding, black shutters, vinyl-clad Pella windows, and a double-door garage—all of which look crisp against the row of 30-foot pines that line the south and west edges of the 100' x 110' lot. The walls are built with 2" x 4" studs, insulation baffles between the studs, plus Tyvec and one-inch styrofoam insulation outside the studs. The seven rooms on the first floor are all trimmed in dark oak: 24' x 12' living room, 9' x 9' dining area, 10' x 11' kitchen, 6' x 11' full bath, 11' x 13' master bedroom, and two 10' x 10' bedrooms. Except for the light oak floor in the living room, the floors of all other first-floor rooms are covered with a clean, two-year-old carpet. The full basement includes two rooms: a 10' x 9' paneled bathroom with a tile floor, shower, and double sink; and a 12' x 10' utility room with a laundry area, water softener, and a three-year-old gas furnace and air-conditioning unit. The rest of the downstairs area is unfinished with a cement floor. Priced at $85,000 and located within two blocks of Children's Park, this 30-year-old ranch is a very good buy.

106 An **expository paragraph** is one that presents facts, gives directions, defines terms, and so on. Most of the writing that you do in school or the workplace is *expository* in the sense that your main purpose is to present or explain facts or ideas. (However, within an expository piece like an essay or a business proposal, you will often write either a series of sentences or an entire paragraph that is *narrative, descriptive,* or *persuasive.*) The following paragraph is from a company pamphlet.

> Discrimination based on race, nationality, religion, sex, or marital status is not allowed at Ulferts' Manufacturing Company. Discrimination is any language or behavior (including hiring decisions, promotions, or job assignments) that either demeans an employee or gives an employee special treatment based on his or her race, nationality, religion, sex, or marital status. If you believe that someone at Ulferts' has discriminated against you in this way, report the incident to your supervisor or to the personnel manager. The supervisor or personnel manager will begin the disciplinary process described later in this chapter.

107 A **persuasive paragraph** is one that presents information to support or prove a point. The writer expresses an opinion and tries to convince the reader that the opinion is correct. The example below is a personnel manager's recommendation to hire an applicant.

> During her interview I found Carmen Chen to be an interesting, articulate person who should be a fine Events Coordinator for Colonial Inn. Dressed neatly in a navy blue suit, she arrived on time and introduced herself politely. When I asked why she felt qualified for our position, Carmen gave a well-organized response. First she asked if I had had an opportunity to review her résumé. When I said that I had looked through it briefly, Carmen offered details of two experiences mentioned in the résumé: her two-year program in hotel management at Kandiyohi and her one year as hostess at the Summer House Resort. Throughout the interview Carmen listened carefully to my questions and answered them thoroughly. While she is young and the job of Events Coordinator carries a lot of responsibility, Carmen has demonstrated excellent communication skills and good organizational skills. In addition, her grade transcripts and recommendations (included with the enclosed résumé) all show that she would work hard for Colonial Inn.

INSIDE

info

You will find a number of other paragraph models throughout your handbook. Each one can serve as an additional model of how to properly construct a well-written, effective paragraph.

108 The Topic Sentence

Most paragraphs contain a sentence that states (or strongly suggests) the focus or topic of the paragraph. This sentence is sometimes called the **topic sentence** and is often found at or near the beginning of the paragraph, although it can appear in the middle or at the end.

In a tightly organized paragraph, every sentence is closely related to the topic sentence, bringing a sense of unity and clarity to your writing. As you work your way through your overall topic or idea, you move from one paragraph (or unit of thought) to the next. Eventually you tie all the paragraphs together into an essay, a report, an analysis, or any other type of composition that calls for highly organized writing.

A well-written **topic sentence** tells your reader what your subject is and what you plan to say about it. Here's a simple formula to follow:

> *Music helps people relax.*
>
> **Formula:** A limited topic *(Music)*
> + a specific impression *(helps people relax)*
> = a topic sentence.

109 Paragraph Unity

In a unified paragraph every sentence (1) closely relates to the topic sentence and (2) fits in well with the other sentences. Notice in the paragraph below that all the sentences except the one in boldface fit well together. While this sentence deals with the topic of the paragraph, it breaks the rhythm of the other sentences and repeats what the reader already knows. Take out the boldfaced sentence, and the paragraph is clearer and smoother.

Before the blue Buick slammed into his green Chevy and left his left side numb, the high-school sophomore thought about life in terms of jump shots, fast breaks, and left-handed layups. But when the passenger door banged open and no seat belt held him down, the boy bounced out of the car into a paralytic's world that had completely different challenges. How do you wash both hands when only one hand can hold the soap? How do you cut your right-hand fingernails when your left-hand fingers can't squeeze the clipper? How do you look cool while walking with friends when the clop-clop noise of your left-footed limp sounds louder than a bleacher full of fans? **He found that really embarrassing.** Eventually the boy found joy in his new world, but first he had to learn to accept new challenges and to find fulfillment in different victories.

110 Types of Details

Personal Details

If writing consisted only of general statements, it would all look pretty much alike. The genius, as they say, is in the details. Details are those extra bits of information that show exactly what something is, how it feels, how it looks, how it's made, what it reminds you of, and so forth. Your mind is a storehouse of details like those, so, before you ransack other sources for information, turn to your own senses, your own memories, and your own reflections.

Sensory details are those that come to you through the senses *(smell, touch, taste, hearing,* and *sight)*. Sensory details are especially important when you are attempting to describe something you are observing (or have observed) firsthand.

> I could feel heat radiating from the kerosene stove and smell its oily fumes even before I squeaked open the door to his third-floor apartment.

Memory details are those that you recall from past experiences. Often, memory details will come to you in the form of mental images, which you can use to build strong, colorful descriptions.

> I can remember as a kid how I walked the noisy, wooden stairway to his attic room and how he was always waiting at the half-opened door to take the newspaper from my shaking hand.

Reflective details are those that come to mind as you wonder about or reflect on something (*I wish, hope, dream, wonder,* etc.). Reflective details bring a strong personality to your writing and allow you to write about the way things might have been or may yet be.

> I wonder if he ever knew how frightened I was then and how I imagined there to be all varieties of evil on the other side of that half-opened door—beyond the kerosene stove.

Details from Other Sources

After you have gathered all your personal details about the topic, you may want to add details—*facts, figures, examples*—from other sources. You can find these "secondhand" details in a number of ways:

- **First**, you can simply ask another person—a parent, a teacher, a neighbor—anyone who has interesting information or experiences to share.
- **Second**, you can ask an expert, someone who knows a great deal about the topic.
- **Third**, you can gather details from magazines, newspapers, books, videotapes, and so on, in your media center or library.
- **Finally**, you can use a computer to tap into a wide range of informational services.

⟨111⟩ Methods of Arranging Details

If your writing is flowing smoothly, it will most likely have an inner logic or natural direction that will hold it together for the reader. However, if necessary, you can purposely arrange the details in your paragraph in any of several basic ways:

- ◉ **Chronological** *(time)* **order** is effective for writing about personal experiences, summarizing steps, and explaining events. Details are arranged in the order in which they happen.

- ◉ **Order of location** is useful for many types of descriptions. It helps provide unity by arranging details left to right, right to left, top to bottom, edge to center, the distant to the near, and so on.

- ◉ **Illustration** *(deduction:* general to specific) is a method of arrangement in which you first state a general idea (topic sentence) and follow with specific reasons, examples, facts, and details to support the general idea.

- ◉ **Climax** *(induction:* specific to general) is a method of arrangement in which you present details followed by a general statement or conclusion drawn from the specific information provided. (If you use a topic sentence, place it at the end.)

- ◉ **Cause and effect** arrangement helps you make connections between a result and the events that preceded it. The general statement (a result or cause) can be supported by specific effects, or the general statement (an effect) can be supported by specific causes.

- ◉ **Comparison** is a method of arrangement in which you measure one subject against another subject that is often more familiar. State the main point of the comparison early and present the likenesses (details) in a clear, organized fashion. (See 548-551.) **Contrast** uses details to measure the differences between two subjects.

- ◉ **Definition** or **classification** can be used when explaining a term or concept (a machine, theory, game, etc.). Begin by placing the subject in the appropriate class, and then provide details that show how your term or concept is different from others in the same class. Do not include more than a few features, or distinctions, in one paragraph. (See 547 and 553.)

TAKE NOTE

The transitions listed in your handbook (114) can help you tie your points together smoothly, whether you use one of the methods above or follow your own natural method.

112 Adding Variety

You can bring interest, emphasis, and balance to your paragraphs by using a variety of words and sentences. Here are some suggestions:

Word Variety

- Use your own vocabulary as much as possible. Your best words will be those that sound as if you are simply talking to your reader.
- Use synonyms to avoid the monotony of using the same words or phrases over and over again.

Sentence Variety

- Vary your sentence beginnings. Rather than beginning each sentence with the subject, use modifiers, phrases, and clauses instead.
- Vary the length of your sentences to suit the topic and tone of your paragraph. Short, concise sentences, for example, are appropriate for explaining complex ideas. Longer sentences help to show the relationship between ideas and usually read more smoothly.
- Vary the arrangement of the material within each sentence by using different kinds and types of sentences. (See 757-760.)

Notice the change in tone and maturity of the paragraph below after some of the repeated words (in boldface) have been eliminated or replaced (by the words in parentheses). Also notice the variety of sentence beginnings, lengths, and types.

> January in northern Wisconsin can be **bitter cold**. The temperature is often 20 to 30 degrees below zero. If the wind also blows, the result can be a windchill of 70 to 80 degrees below. **That's cold!** (eliminate altogether) It is so **cold** (frigid) at times that you can't go outside for fear of having some real problems with **the cold hurting your hands or face** (frostbite). On these **really cold** (face-numbing) days, people are warned against traveling except for an emergency. If the **cold** (arctic-like weather) continues for more than a couple of days, almost all traffic stops. You simply cannot trust your car. It can suddenly stall in the middle of nowhere, leaving you stranded in the **extreme cold** (frozen air). About the only way to beat the **incredible cold** of a northern Wisconsin winter is to huddle around the fireplace and dream of the warm, sunny days of summer.

INSIDE

info

Look for variety in the words and sentences of other paragraphs throughout the handbook. Remember, though, that your wording should not get in the way of what you're trying to say. If your paragraph is clear and effective, don't change it just to add variety.

Reviewing Paragraphs in Essays

113 Quick Guide

Look at each paragraph in your essays and reports in two ways: (1) as an individual unit and, (2) as one part of the whole piece. (Use the paragraph symbol [⁋] to indicate where each paragraph begins as you review your writing. This symbol will remind you to indent each new paragraph in your final copy.)

1. Each paragraph should say enough to stand on its own. One way to check the effectiveness of a paragraph is to imagine a title for it, as if it were the only thing you had written. Another way is to form a simple question that the paragraph answers clearly. (If one of your paragraphs doesn't pass either of these tests, consider revising it or leaving it out.)

2. Consider arranging your opening paragraph like an upside-down pyramid. That is, start with general statements that get the readers' attention, and then state the specific subject, or thesis, in the last sentence or two.

NOTE: If you feel your opening paragraph is effectively structured in another way, leave it alone.

3. The concluding paragraph often begins with a general review of the important ideas discussed in the essay and ends with a statement that reminds the reader of the overall importance of the paper.

4. All of the paragraphs in the body of your paper should help develop your thesis (main idea) in some way. A paragraph might explain, define, compare, or classify information to support your thesis statement. Another paragraph might relate a personal experience or recent incident that adds to or clarifies your main idea.

5. Transitions should be used to connect one paragraph to the next. They unify the paragraphs, and they make your writing easier to follow and understand. (See 114.)

6. The bottom line? If you want readers to really listen to your writing, you must make it worth reading. Readers want to learn something and be entertained in the process. They want writing that is original and clearly moves from one point to the next. Finally, readers want to hear the real voice of the writer—the real you.

Transitions and Linking Words

Words that can be used to **show location**:

above	away from	beyond	into	over
across	behind	by	near	throughout
against	below	down	off	to the right
along	beneath	in back of	onto	under
among	beside	in front of	on top of	
around	between	inside	outside	

Words that can be used to **show time**:

about	first	meanwhile	soon	then
after	second	today	later	next
at	third	tomorrow	afterward	as soon as
before	till	next week	immediately	when
during	until	yesterday	finally	

Words that can be used to **compare things** (show similarities):

in the same way	likewise	as
similarly	like	also

Words that can be used to **contrast things** (show differences):

but	otherwise	although	on the other hand
however	yet	still	even though

Words that can be used to **emphasize a point**:

for this reason	again	truly
to emphasize	to repeat	in fact

Words that can be used to **conclude** or **summarize**:

as a result	finally	to sum up	in conclusion
therefore	last	all in all	in summary

Words that can be used to **add information**:

again	another	for instance	finally
also	and	moreover	as well
additionally	besides	next	along with
in addition	for example	likewise	equally important

Words that can be used to **clarify**:

in other words	for instance	that is	put another way

Writing Basic Essays

Weight lifting builds biceps, and essay writing builds communication skills. So it's no wonder that coaches—from gymnastics to track—make their athletes "pump iron" now and then. And it's no wonder that teachers—from high school to tech school—make their students write "essays."

This chapter will help you write all kinds of essays—from explanations to proposals, from evaluations to essay tests. It will help you understand the structure of an essay, how to organize your ideas, and how to support them. Finally, the chapter will illustrate a process that will build an essay even a football coach would love.

What's Ahead?

This chapter discusses the basics of the essay: structure, organization, and support. It also includes writing guidelines, models, and helpful tips.

The Importance of Structure

The basic essay has a tight structure; that is, it contains an opening paragraph, several body paragraphs, and a closing paragraph.

116 Beginning

Your **opening paragraph** should accomplish several things: It should gain your readers' interest in your subject, identify your focus or thesis, and set up the rest of the essay. The trick is to do all of these things smoothly and naturally. (See 018-019 for more about your focus, or *thesis statement.*)

There are several ways to draw your readers' attention to your subject. Five effective techniques are listed here.

- Open with a series of questions about the topic.
- Provide an interesting story or anecdote about the subject.
- Present a startling or unusual fact or figure.
- Quote a well-known person or literary work.
- Define an important subject-related term.

117 Middle

The **developmental paragraphs** are at the heart of the essay. They must clearly and logically support your thesis. If, for instance, you are going to present information about paper recycling, each developmental paragraph in your essay should discuss an important element related to that subject.

It's important that these paragraphs are arranged in the best possible way—chronologically, by order of importance, or by an order of your own making. (See 111.) It's also important that your paragraphs flow smoothly from one to the next. To achieve this flow, make sure that the first sentence in each new paragraph serves as an effective link to the preceding paragraph. Transitions like *in addition, on the other hand,* and *as a result* are often used for this purpose. (See 114.)

INSIDE Start a new paragraph whenever there is a shift or change in the essay. This change is called a paragraph shift and can take place for any of these reasons: (Also see 113.)

1. A change in emphasis or ideas
2. A change in time or speaker
3. A change in place or setting

118 Ending

The **closing** or summary paragraph should tie all of the important points together and draw a final conclusion for the readers. It should leave readers with a clear understanding of the essay topic.

The Importance of Organization

119 The Topic Outline

A **topic outline** is a listing of the topics to be covered in a piece of writing; it contains no specific details. Topics are stated in words and phrases rather than in complete sentences. It is always a good idea to begin your outlining task by placing your thesis statement, or controlling idea, at the top of your paper. This statement will serve as a reminder of the specific topic you are outlining. Outline each main point, but do not attempt to outline your opening or closing paragraph unless specifically told to do so.

Introduction
  I. Paper recycling big business
     A. Industry involved
     B. Recyclable paper plentiful
     C. Countries buy wastepaper
 II. Simple process
     A. Collect and sort paper
     B. Form a pulp
     C. Dry pulp to make paper
     D. New paper used in many ways
III. Some papers not recyclable
     A. Glossy, envelopes, glued papers
     B. Must be sorted out
     C. New process coming for glossy paper
Conclusion

120 The Sentence Outline

The **sentence outline** not only contains the major points to be covered but lists supporting details as well. It is used for longer, more formal writing assignments; each point should, therefore, be written as a complete sentence.

Introduction
  I. Paper recycling is a booming business today.
     A. Industry believes recycling paper makes good sense.
     B. A large supply of recyclable paper is thrown away by Americans.
     C. Taiwan actually buys paper waste from the U.S.
 II. Paper recycling is a simple process.
     A. Paper is collected and sorted.
     B. Paper is mixed with water and chemicals to form pulp.
     C. Pulp is dried and new paper is formed.
     D. The new paper is used for a wide range of products.
III. Some types of paper cannot be recycled presently.
     A. Equipment cannot handle glossy paper, envelopes, glued papers, etc.
     B. These types must be sorted out.
     C. A new technology is being perfected that will make glossy papers recyclable.
Conclusion

121 The Importance of Support

If you were a ruler and your subjects were slaves, you could say what you wanted and your slaves would have to agree. But you're a writer, not a slave driver, and your readers are free to think for themselves. They'll believe what you say only if you show evidence why they should—facts, quotations from authorities, examples, illustrations, explanations, definitions, arguments, etc. Pieces of evidence like these are called **support**.

Using Facts

In the model persuasive essay in this chapter, the writer asks if metal detectors are the answer to student safety. He makes this statement: "The answer to this question for Somerset High School is, I believe, 'no.' " Here are two supporting facts he presents to get the readers to accept his opinion:

1. The only weapons found so far at SHS have been knives.
2. We've had very few weapon-related expulsions compared to other area campuses.

Using Quotations

A quotation from an expert can go a long way toward lending support. For example, in an essay about sports and children, a writer made this claim: "Competitive sports can be harmful for preschoolers." Later, he shared this supporting quotation to help convince the readers:

Dr. M. Jones recently reported, "The high stress of athletic training and conditioning in youngsters can damage their bone structure."

Using Examples

Examples will strengthen your writing by making it more concrete. In the model expository essay in this chapter, the writer states, "Paper recycling has truly become part of the daily lives of many Americans." Here are two of the examples the writer uses to prove his statement is true:

1. Recyclable paper is collected at home (curbside) and at the office.
2. Americans recycled 20 million tons of paper last year.

TAKE NOTE

An essay stands or falls on the strengths of its support. If the support is missing, your readers will not value your writing.

122 Guidelines for Writing an Expository Essay

Informing Your Readers

You write an expository essay to present information. Your goal is to share facts, explain them as necessary, and guide your readers to a clear understanding of your subject. Gather facts by referring to at least two different sources—books, periodicals, etc. Your final essay should read smoothly from the opening paragraph to the closing thought. Refer to the guidelines and model that follow for help.

Searching and Selecting

1. **Searching** • Think of a subject you would like to know more about. Consider subjects related to your course work, as well as interests outside of school. Page through textbooks or newspapers, or brainstorm for ideas with classmates. Make a list of possible subjects.

2. **Selecting** • Look over your list and focus your attention on interesting subjects that you know you can find plenty of facts about—in a textbook, reference book, or magazine. Now choose your favorite.

Generating the Text

3. **Collecting** • Find at least two good sources of information and begin reading. List important facts as you come across them. (Don't worry about their order at this point.) To be certain you understand the information you're collecting, use your own words as much as possible.

4. **Planning** • Review your facts, looking for a main idea or impression that could serve as the focus, or thesis, of your essay. Once you identify a possible focus, write it out in a sentence. Next, put a check mark by the facts and details that support this idea. Then plan and organize your writing accordingly. You may find it helpful at this point to prepare an outline. (See 119-120.)

Writing and Revising

5. **Writing** • Develop your first draft according to your plan. Devote extra time to your opening paragraph, which should catch your readers' attention and identify the focus of your writing.

6. **Revising** • Carefully review your first draft, making sure that the main idea you had intended to share has, in fact, been clearly put forth. Also make sure that you have effectively supported this idea and that your writing flows smoothly. (See topic 129 for more ideas.)

Evaluating

Is the essay well organized?

Do the facts effectively support the focus?

Will readers appreciate the treatment of this subject?

123 The Expository Essay

The purpose of an **expository essay** is to present important information about a specific subject. In the following example, student writer Todd Michaels shares timely information about paper recycling. You will notice that his essay follows the traditional five-paragraph pattern (opening paragraph, three developmental paragraphs, and closing paragraph).

Paper Recycling

From large paper chutes at the office to home curbside collection, paper recycling has become an everyday thing. Americans have changed their throwaway attitude for a recycling consciousness, and they are recycling in record numbers. Last year 20 million tons of paper were recycled—a substantial increase from the previous year. Paper recycling has truly become part of the daily lives of many Americans.

The focus, or thesis statement, is clearly presented.

Paper recycling has indeed become a big deal, and a big business. Today, industry recycles paper not just because it is a good thing to do, but because it makes good business sense. Since Americans throw away more paper than anything else, there is much to be gained by recycling paper. For example, Fort Howard Corporation of Green Bay, Wisconsin, produces bathroom tissue made entirely of recycled paper. The company recycles enough paper each year to cover 100 acres 18 feet deep (Grove 104). Foreign countries are even buying our paper waste. If you see a MADE IN TAIWAN tag on a manufactured paper product, in another life it was probably a newspaper in America. Taiwan buys all of its paper from the United States.

Specific facts are used to support main points.

The process of paper recycling is a simple one. First, paper is collected and sorted. Recyclable paper includes typing paper, newspaper, cardboard boxes, scrap paper, index cards, and computer printouts. This recyclable paper is dumped into a vat of water and chemicals. A large spinning blade mixes the paper to a pulp. This pulp is dried on screens, and the new paper is formed on cylinders. Items made from this new recycled paper include newspapers, cereal and shoe boxes, toilet tissue, paper towels, building insulation, egg cartons, and even livestock bedding.

The writer clearly explains the recycling process.

124

Each developmental paragraph addresses a specific aspect of recycling.

Not all types of paper can be recycled, however. Recycling equipment at this time cannot handle envelopes, carbon paper, glossy paper, photographs, or paper with scotch tape, glue, or staples attached. These types of paper must be sorted out. Advancements are being made, though, to accommodate these items. Recycling equipment currently is being perfected that will remove ink from glossy magazine and catalog paper, enabling the paper to be recycled.

The closing line reminds readers of the importance of the subject.

Although landfills are still filling up with over two-thirds of our recyclable waste, paper recycling has become a success story. While only 18 percent of metal cans and 2 percent of plastics are recycled, 40 percent of recyclable paper is, in fact, recycled. Five thousand community programs exist nationwide for the recycling of paper products, and big business has discovered the advantages of a product-material that can be reused up to eight times. Recycling fever hasn't been as high in the United States since World War II, when people in a wartime situation felt it was their duty to recycle. Perhaps people today have realized that the world is in a different kind of emergency situation, and that, again, it is their duty to recycle. @

166

The closing lines not only summarize the essay, but also emphasize the importance of tact in society.

Sensitivity, truthfulness, and careful thought are all necessary components of tact. No one component will do; they must all be utilized in situations where people's feelings are at stake. Tact is a wonderful skill to have, and tactful people are usually admired and respected. Without tact our society would nurture insensitivity and disregard for others. ☻

167 <u>Writing a Problem/Solution Essay</u>

"A problem well stated is a problem half solved."

At some point, you may be asked to write an essay in which you analyze a problem and present one or more solutions. Begin by choosing a problem related to the work in one of your classes or related to the world around you and analyze it completely before suggesting possible solutions. Use the guidelines below and the example that follows to help you develop your writing.

Searching and Selecting

1. **Reviewing** • If your assignment is related to a specific subject, review your text and class notes for possible topics. Also consider brainstorming for ideas with a small group of classmates.

2. **Searching** • Otherwise, think about the things students complain most about: crowded classrooms, jobs, grades, discrimination, safety. What about a problem in the neighborhood, at your school, or in your personal life? What about environmental issues, politics, or other areas that affect your world? What is being done to address these problems? Do you have suggestions or solutions?

Generating the Text

3. **Forming** • After you've selected a problem, write it out in the form of a clear statement. Then analyze it thoroughly, exploring the problem's parts, history, and causes. Weigh possible solutions. Try listing reasons why solutions might work, or why they might not.

4. **Assessing** • Make sure you are dealing with a manageable problem and that you have enough background material to write intelligently about it. (You may need to gather more facts and statistics to establish the problem or propose solutions.)

Writing and Revising

5. **Writing** • Once you have assessed the problem, write your first draft. Discuss the problem and possible solutions as clearly and completely as you can.

6. **Revising** • Carefully review your first draft for clarity and logic. Also have a classmate review your work. Revise accordingly.

Evaluating

Does the essay present a real solution to a real problem? Is the writing interesting? The opening engaging? The conclusion logical?

Will readers understand and appreciate the essay?

168 Problem/Solution Essay

Nicolette Francis and Jennifer Morales team up to research the problem of secondhand smoke. The writers draw on a number of sources to establish the seriousness of the problem and then conclude with the commonsense solution and a touch of humor. (This essay originally appeared in *New Youth Connections: The Magazine Written By and For New York Youth,* Sept./Oct. 1991. It is reprinted with permission.)

"Secondhand smoke" is defined.

The writers quote a prominent authority to support their point.

The writers use another quotation to add details about the problem.

Other People's Smoke: In Your Face

Monica Pearson, 19, of the HS of Fashion Industries, doesn't like it when people smoke around her. "The smoke bothers me, it makes my eyes burn and messes up my lungs just being around me," she explained.

According to the U.S. Environmental Protection Agency (EPA), secondhand smoke is one of the most widespread and harmful indoor pollutants around. That's the smoke people blow in your face or the smoke coming off the end of their cigar.

Sometimes you can't even see it. It comes through the ventilation system or lingers in the air after the smoker's already gone home. But the fact is that secondhand smoke kills.

"A substantial number of the lung-cancer deaths that occur among non-smokers can be attributed to involuntary smoking," according to the ex-Surgeon General C. Everett Koop. Coupled with heart disease and other related illnesses, many experts put the total number as high as 50,000 a year. That's as many Americans as were killed in the entire Vietnam War, and makes it the third most common preventable cause of death after smoking itself and alcoholism.

Kids Are Hardest Hit

One group particularly hard hit are children. "Young, growing tissues are much more susceptible to carcinogens [cancer causing agents] than adult tissues are," Dr. William G. Cahan of the Sloan Kettering Memorial Cancer Center has said. "Bringing up a child in a smoking household is tantamount to bringing him or her up in a house lined with asbestos and radon."

In addition to cancer, the EPA reports that children of smokers are hospitalized much more often for bronchitis and pneumonia and their lungs develop at a slower rate than other kids'. Chronic ear infections and asthma are

169

also more common in children whose parents smoke. In general, secondary smoke substantially increases respiratory problems in children.

Another way smoking affects other people's lives is that it starts fires. According to the new book, *Kids Say Don't Smoke,* 1,500 Americans a year are killed in fires started by cigarettes—people smoking in bed, things like that. The book says companies could make cigarettes that go out when you stop puffing, but they worry that would be bad for business.

In New York City, it's now against the law to smoke indoors in public. Joe Cherner, chairman of Smokefree Education Services, an organization fighting for a smoke-free environment, says these laws came about because "it's not fair to give [cancer and] heart disease to people who don't smoke. What smokers do to themselves is their own business. What they do to those around them is everybody's business."

People are still allowed to smoke in the privacy of their own homes, in cars, and in designated smoking areas, but even that's becoming less socially acceptable. Andrea Johnson, 16, of HS of Fashion Industries lets people know she doesn't appreciate it when they smoke around her: "I tell them either they can put it out or leave." Monica says she asks politely, "Please don't smoke in my house."

Just Like Spitting

The *Kids Say Don't Smoke* book says that in the old days spitting used to be common practice in restaurants:

> There were spittoons beside each table. You'd be eating, and someone at the next table would be spitting. If you did this in a restaurant today, you'd probably be thrown out. (And spitting doesn't cause cancer.) Just as it's hard to imagine how our grandparents permitted spitting in restaurants, it's going to be hard for our grandchildren to understand how we allowed smoking.

In New York City, smoking is banned in elevators, offices, schools, hospitals, subways, and buses, among other places. If someone is smoking around you, Cherner says, "Number one, move. Number two, ask that person not to smoke. [And] number three, throw a bucket of water on them, 'cause they might be on fire." ❷

Editor's Note: Some of the quotations from experts in this article are from secondary sources.

Each paragraph explains another reason why the smoke is a problem.

The analogy to spitting implies that smoking is not only unhealthy—it's also disgusting.

Persuasive Writing

Getting other people (or things) to do what you want them to is sometimes easier said than done. It may require that you offer them something in return, a "carrot" or some small reward, for instance. Or you might simply build a strong, logical case for your side, one that convinces others to change their mind and do what you ask.

Whether you are selling a product or training a pet, one ground rule in **persuasive writing** is that your best offense is a good defense. You need to know what the other side thinks, whether that other side is an individual consumer or an entire government agency.

What's Ahead?

This section addresses persuasive writing, from publicizing and promoting products to taking and defending positions on issues.

Writing an Ad Script

Writing a Brochure or Flier

Writing a Position Paper

Writing an Essay of Argumentation

171 ## Guidelines for Writing an Ad Script
"And now, a brief message . . ."

We've all seen TV ads—way too many of them. Some work well, others not so well. Have you ever thought, "I could write a better commercial than that"? Well, by following the guidelines below, you can do just that. You can write your own television commercial script, remembering that the purpose of your script is to sell a product using the same techniques used by advertisers. Begin by studying ads on TV to see what kinds of images and ideas are developed. Then refer to the guidelines below and the model that follows to help you develop your writing.

Searching and Selecting

1. **Searching** • Put together a list of products you would like to sell: shoes, bungee cords, blue jeans, whatever.

2. **Selecting** • After each, list three possible names for your product and a description of who might buy it. Then select one product to sell.

Generating the Text

3. **Collecting** • Determine (1) what your product can do, (2) how it can do it better than related products, and (3) what kind of story (plot, characters, conflict) would best sell this product to your audience.

4. **Focusing** • Remember that you need to decide on one primary appeal, or hidden message, for your commercial, one that is right for the product and audience.

Writing and Revising

5. **Writing** • When you write the first draft of your ad, keep in mind you are writing for TV. Try to visualize what your ad will look like on the screen. Focus on telling a simple story, one with characters who have a fairly simple problem they are able to solve in 30 to 60 seconds. (Try to include camera and/or stage directions for your ad.)

6. **Refining** • Read your draft aloud and try "walking through" the actions with a group of classmates to see how the script sounds. Is it realistic and catchy enough to hold your viewers' interest? Hint: Studies show that if you can capture your viewers' attention for the first five seconds, they will usually watch the entire commercial.

Evaluating

Does the ad script tell a clear, clever story with a plot, characters, and visual effects?

Is the story strong enough to convince a specific audience to buy the product?

172 Ad Script

This 30-second TV ad script was created for a boat company running a spring tent sale. The video part (what you see on the screen) is described in italics. The audio part (called the voice-over—VO) is indicated in bold type. (This ad script is used with permission of Morse Advertising, Traverse City, Michigan.)

Spicer's Boat City Tent Sale

Opening Video and Graphics:
The Big Boat Store is outside and under the big top . . . It's SPICER's big Spring Tent Sale.

Graphic: Tent Sale Bargains
With great Tent Sale bargains on everything at Spicer's . . .

Shot of Model with Graphic:
1992 2050 Capri, V6-MercCruiser Stern Drive (for co-op), full canvas, stereo, power steering, power trim and more
Like this big 20-foot Bayliner, a great big boat for the whole family—with V-6 MercCruiser Power and tons of extras, including trailer

Change Graphic:
$12,988 + freight and prep
Plus your choice of two free accessory packages!

List Accessory Packages:
O'Brien Ski Package-O'Brien OR Tube Package, -OR-USCG Safety Package, -OR-Eagle LCD Fish Finder
for under thirteen grand.

Quick Shots of Inventory (show pontoons):
Save on boats, motors, accessories, and hoists. Choose from cuddys and runabouts to pontoons and fishin' boats!

Exterior with Tent in Background; Add Graphic:
It's a great time to be outside and under the big top . . . at the Big Boat Store, Spicer's Boat City, your Mercury and Force Outboard Dealer!

:903 Close Sing
Spice up your life! @

Note that a lot of territory is covered in this sales pitch: The purpose of the ad is identified, examples of new inventory are previewed, prices and package options are given, and a reason to buy is provided.

Ad ends with a closing song.

173 **Writing a Brochure or Flier**

A Real Deal

Brochures and fliers are common ways of conveying a sales pitch. Both are short, powerful advertising pieces that are easy and inexpensive to make. The guidelines below will help you understand better how to put together your own brochure or flier. The model on the following page will show you a flier made by a student writer on a home computer.

Searching and Selecting

1. **Selecting** • Think of a product or service you would like to promote or sell to others. Refer to the "Essentials of Life Checklist" (013) if you can't think of a topic.

2. **Searching** • Once you've selected a topic, use the "Structured Questions" (016) to help you understand what is important or unique about your topic.

Generating the Text

3. **Collecting** • Determine (1) what your product or service can do, (2) how it can do it better than related products, and (3) what kind of brochure or flier would best sell your product or service.

4. **Focusing** • To determine the focus of your piece, ask yourself (1) what audience is the product suited for, (2) is the piece intended to close a sale or create interest, and (3) what do you most want to make clear to your readers?

Writing and Revising

5. **Writing** • When you write the first draft, keep in mind that your space is strictly limited. Try to visualize what your completed piece will look like. Focus on your central idea, and remember that you will want to use a minimum number of words to get your idea across.

6. **Refining** • Design your piece with large headlines and attention-getting visuals and graphics. Your major headline should summarize the primary benefit of the product or service offered. Then add facts, figures, and testimonials to encourage a positive response. Finally, include reader-response instructions, offering the necessary names, addresses, and phone numbers.

Evaluating

Can readers get the main message at a glance?

Are the who, what, when, and how questions answered clearly?

Has clutter been eliminated?

Flier

Lin Armstrong produced this flier on her home computer and distributed copies by taking them door-to-door and placing several on community and store bulletin boards. Notice how she uses both words and graphics to catch her readers' attention and sell her services.

The main point is stated as a bold question and answer and is given first.

The writer uses bullets to highlight her services.

She lists special qualities of her services.

Clients' statements support the writer's claims.

Reader receives instructions.

Need Help with Your Pet?

Call **Lin Armstrong**, every pet's favorite care provider!

Services
- Bathe and brush
- Walk your pet
- Feed and change water
- Take for veterinary appointments

Perks
- Will go to any location within city limits
- Available mornings, evenings, and weekends
- Reasonable prices and documented, monthly bills

What Clients Say . . .

"I trust Lin to take my poodle to all her health-care appointments. She's careful, sensitive, and always on time!"
—Ann Vega

"Lin gave my Siamese cat all the love and attention he deserved while I was gone."
—Gigi Hernandez

"My sheltie gets regular exercise, thanks to Lin. She keeps Trooper in tip-top shape!"
—Joe Wexler

Call 723-6589 TODAY!

175 **Guidelines for Writing a Position Paper**

Heavy on My Mind

Two intelligent people can disagree on a serious issue and both of them could make a good case. Writing a position paper lets you put your best case forward. From the opening claim to your analysis of arguments and supporting evidence, your aim must be to spell out your train of thought clearly. As you develop your paper, refer to the guidelines below and the model on the next page.

Searching and Selecting

1. **Selecting** • Think of current issues in the news (decisions, trends, laws, or controversies) that will be of interest to you and your readers. Also study magazines, journal entries, class notes, etc., for ideas.

2. **Reviewing** • Consider reviewing a current issue of the *Readers' Guide to Periodical Literature* or other such guides for possible subjects. Think about possible ideas in your other classes, in the cafeteria, or at home.

Generating the Text

3. **Noting** • Determine what you already know about your subject and how you feel about it. You might express these feelings (take a position) in a free writing or an exploratory draft. Also state what you hope to find out during your investigation of the issue.

4. **Investigating** • Collect as many facts and details as you can to help you develop your writing. While reading may be your most important source of information, also consider conducting interviews, writing letters, gaining firsthand experiences, and so on.

5. **Assessing** • Now that you have thoroughly researched your subject, reassess and restate your position. Then decide where to start writing and how to organize your main points. (Also see 558-574.)

Writing and Revising

6. **Writing** • Write your first draft as thoughtfully and carefully as you can, making sure each part clarifies and strengthens your position.

7. **Revising** • Carefully review your writing; have at least two of your classmates read and react to your work as well. Revise and refine your writing accordingly.

Evaluating

Does the paper present an in-depth discussion of a timely issue?

Has a position been effectively presented and supported?

Will readers appreciate the treatment of the subject?

176 Position Paper

A well-developed position paper gives reasons for the writer's point of view and may also mention contrasting positions. In this feature for their school newspaper, students Tanya Ypma and Kim Rylaarsdam present two sides of the tanning-bed controversy, followed by their own conclusions.

Tanning Beds in Health Clubs: Marriage or Mismatch?

What does a healthy body look like? Are you thinking fit and trim . . . and tan? In magazines and on TV a healthy person is often a bronzed person who has spent a lot of time in the sun. Because many people connect healthy with tan, it's not surprising that many health and fitness centers have tanning beds. The Sioux Fitness Center even offers a package deal for fitness classes and tanning. But do tanning beds even belong in health clubs?

The topic of the paper is introduced as a question.

Obviously many health club owners think so. Having tanning beds is an additional service for their clients and an additional source of income for themselves. Besides, say these owners, tanning beds have something in common with their physical fitness equipment—both help people look good. We agree—trim and tan bodies are attractive.

Arguments are presented clearly.

Some health club owners even claim that a tanning-bed tan is healthy. For example, Connie Grevengoed, owner of Sioux Fitness Center, says that using a tanning bed creates a base tan that can protect you from sunburn. Many of her clients use the beds before going on beach vacations. Some tanning-bed operators also say that using the bed is safer than sunbathing because the tanning booth is a controlled environment: sessions are usually limited to 20 minutes.

In fact, these owners would probably be annoyed that we're even asking the question: Do tanning beds belong in health clubs? After all, they could argue that the beds are legal and regulated by the state. (In Iowa, for example, children aged 16 and under need parental permission to use the beds.) So if the beds are legal, why shouldn't club owners be free to rent them, and adults be free to use them?

The writers introduce their position with a question.

It's hard to argue with owners' freedom to rent the beds. But one could ask owners what the purpose of their health club is. Do tanning beds really help their clients achieve good looks and good health?

177

If the purpose is for clients to look good, tanning is a short-term answer with long-term consequences. People who have spent a lot of time exposed to ultraviolet rays, especially between the ages of birth and 18, will eventually experience premature aging-wrinkles! The effects of overexposure may not be obvious right away but will appear in the future.

It's also doubtful whether a tanning-bed tan is "healthy" in terms of providing a protective base tan for future exposure to the sun. The ultraviolet rays used in tanning booths turn the skin brown but don't create a thick, tough layer that protects lower layers of skin. So users may feel secure and protected from sunburn when they're really still at risk.

Details indicate the extent of the problem.

Skin specialists and cancer researchers say that any kind of tanning is a health risk. Incidents of skin cancer have greatly increased in the last couple of decades. The American Cancer Society estimates that 700,000 Americans will develop skin cancer each year, plus 32,000 will be diagnosed with melanoma, the deadliest form of skin cancer. Researchers blame the increase in skin cancer on the diminishing ozone layer and overexposure to ultraviolet rays.

Details indicate the seriousness of the problem.

Even though the ultraviolet rays used in tanning beds are different from the sun's, they're still dangerous. A recent study in Sweden showed that heavy use of tanning lamps increases a person's risk of melanoma, especially for people under 30. The study showed that anyone who had ever used sunlamps or sun beds faced a 30 percent greater risk of melanoma than those who had never used such devices. People under 20 who "fake-baked" more than 10 times a year were eight times more likely to develop melanoma than nonusers.

Finally, while cancer is serious, it's not the only health problem associated with the use of sunlamps. For example, tanners using salons in Iowa need to sign a paper warning them of potential eye injury (such as increased chance of developing cataracts), activation of some viral conditions such as cold sores, and allergic reactions.

The writers draw their own conclusion.

So do tanning beds belong in health clubs? Sure, owners are free to rent the beds—no law prevents them. But the flip side of freedom is responsibility. If health club owners feel responsible for their clients' health, they'll use their money and space for exercise equipment, not tanning beds. @

178 Guidelines for Writing an Essay of Argumentation

Proving a Point

Writing an essay of argumentation is more than just expressing an opinion. It's selecting and presenting a topic that you have some real feelings about. To prepare your argument, you need to write out the following: (1) a main point (proposition) that you will argue for, (2) an argument(s) supporting your proposition, and (3) an argument(s) opposing your proposition. You must then look for information (evidence) that builds your arguments, and present the information in a way that will convince your readers that your proposition is right. Use the guidelines below and the example that follows. (Also see 558-574.)

Searching and Selecting

1. **Searching** • Review your texts or class notes for possible topics. Also think of related issues or problems you hear debated locally or nationally. (Focus on subjects that are serious, timely, and, most important, debatable.)

2. **Selecting** • Test a possible topic by (a) identifying a reasonable point or proposition to argue for, (b) listing one argument supporting this proposition, and (c) listing one argument opposing it.

Generating the Text

3. **Collecting** • Look in books, magazines, or newspapers for information. Take notes, especially on strong arguments supported by the opinions of authorities and by factual evidence. Label arguments "pro" (for your proposition) or "con" (against).

4. **Assessing** • Check the best pro and con arguments. If you need to change your main point in order to defend it more effectively, do that now. Then decide on the best arrangement of your ideas. (Consider saving your best pro argument for last.)

Writing and Revising

5. **Writing** • Develop your argument using your planning as a guide. If you become stuck, ask a classmate to be your "ear": read your proposition and talk through your argument.

6. **Revising** • Refine your argument before presenting it to your readers. Have a classmate review your writing as well.

Evaluating

?··

Is the proposition reasonable and clearly stated?

Are supporting arguments logical, clear, and convincing? Are opposing arguments dealt with?

Given the supporting arguments, is the conclusion valid?

179 Essay of Argumentation

Brian Lojeck tackles an age-old issue—dress codes. His carefully organized argument first appeared in the *Aviation High School Log Newsletter* in May 1992. It is reprinted with permission.

We Walk Alike, We Talk Alike, We Look Alike

You wake up in the morning. You smash your alarm clock to silence it (the dreaded Klaxon) and guzzle down a cold soda to fulfill your nutritional needs. Then you get dressed.

No matter what you wear, you are guaranteed one thing. You're original. The chances of meeting someone who is wearing the exact same outfit is slim at best. You feel good, right?

Now imagine this: You look into your closet and all of your clothes are blue. Blue shirts, blue pants, blue shoes, blue underwear. Everyone in school is also wearing blue-on-blue-on-blue-on-blue-on-blue. Nice, huh?

That's exactly what a bunch of people who call themselves "The Uniform Committee" want to do to us. They sent out a paper a long time ago to some of us asking if we agreed with the reinstatement of a mandatory uniform in Aviation High School.

The first reason they gave for supporting the mandatory uniform is to lower clothing costs.

Cool.

Lowering clothing costs is good.

Fine.

How? A school uniform is only good in school (unless it's a Nautica jacket and Levis). That means that you would still need your regular clothes for outside of school and you would have to buy the uniform in addition. I don't think you want to wear the same clothes every day so you will need to buy more than one uniform. These uniforms, of course, would only be available from the school itself. Do I hear a "brilliantly disguised plan to make money"? Nah, not a chance!

WILL SOMEONE TELL ME HOW THIS IS GOING TO SAVE MONEY!

The second reason is to promote school pride.

Cool.

School pride is good.

Fine.

The writer describes life with the present policy—no uniforms.

The writer imagines life with the new policy—uniforms required.

An argument supporting the new policy is presented and attacked.

How? How is dressing like Smurfs going to make us proud?

"Hi, I go to Aviation and my life is ruled by a nameless, faceless Uniform Committee and gosh, I'm proud of it!"

I'm proud of everything I do. Just because I don't wear an "I-Write-Editorials" shirt doesn't mean I'm not proud. I know some great basketball players. None of them wear "I-Can-Get-the-Ball-Through-the-Hoop" shirts. That doesn't make them any worse players or any less proud of it. If the school wants us to be proud, then it is going to have to earn our pride. How can we be proud if we are always hearing about how this was canceled or this can't be done or we have to wait to do this? Pride is like money; you have to earn it.

WILL SOMEONE TELL ME HOW DRESSING LIKE EVERYONE ELSE IS GOING TO MAKE ME PROUD?

The third reason is to keep the school safe.

Cool.

Safety is good, too.

Fine.

(Everybody now, repeat after me.) HOW? Why not LOCK THE DOORS! I know they can be locked because I've been locked in the building a couple of times already by these bolted-on clamps that looked like they would keep the devil himself out. How about making the guards guard instead of talking to the students? How about looking to the future instead of repeating the mistakes of the past?

The uniform was not, Not, NOT the reason for this school's past success. The reason was the people in the uniforms. Time and money should be spent cultivating the people rather than clothing us. Only when the money that goes into these outrageous ideas is spent on more luxurious items (like books and tools) will the school regain its past glories. Only when the faculty seeks to help students and stops trying to control us will we attain our past glories.

I close with this. Judge us by what we do . . . not by how we look. @

The writer supports his position by making fun of an opposing argument.

Parallel structure highlights the three arguments.

The essay concludes with a challenge to opponents.

WORKPLACE

Writing in the Workplace

Workplace Writing

Writing the Business Letter

Writing to Get a Job

Writing on the Job

Workplace Writing

181   All organizations—IBM, the Willmar Farmer's Co-op, the Buffalo Bills—need people who can not only speak well, but also write effectively. Whether you end up an engineer or a nurse, a lab technician or a social worker, good writing helps you *get* a job and *do* your job.

    Why the big deal about writing? It's very simple. In a world that depends so much on information and technology, organizations need people who can present information and ideas clearly. When you're on the job, you're no longer writing for a teacher, but for a living.

182 The Advantages of a Written Message

- Gives you time to think about and edit what you want to say.
- Communicates a specific message that stays on the topic.
- Provides both parties with an official record of the message.
- Generally is taken more seriously than the spoken word.
- Can be sent to many people conveniently.

What's Ahead?

This section explores the writing you will do on the job.

Writing the Business Letter
Writing to Get a Job
Writing on the Job

183 Workplace Writing Tasks

Anyone who feared that telephones and computers would make writing obsolete ought to revisit today's workplace. Look at the table below to see how many types of writing you could be asked to do at work.

TYPE	EXAMPLES
Letters	
Good news	inquiry • thank-you • congratulations • greeting • recommendation • order • extending credit • job offer • job acceptance • follow-up
Bad news	serious complaint • job claim or credit rejection • invitation or job refusal
Persuasive	collection • sales • special request • application
Reports, Memos	
Periodic	sales • production • inventory • inspection • budget • department • visit report • employee evaluation
Project	construction • progress • technical • experiment • lab • field-trip report
Proposals	troubleshooting • research • sales proposal • recommendation
Special	résumé • site inspection • meeting minutes • incident or accident report • research report • survey report • instructions • agenda • reminder
Media Relations	
For mass media	news release • fact sheet • feature article • speech • advertising copy
For the general public	pamphlet • brochure • annual report • policy and procedure statements
For readers inside the company	bulletin • newsletter • periodical • crisis plan • position paper

Workplace Writing

184 Quick Guide

All workplace writing—whether your first application form or a complex product manual—shares these characteristics:

⦿ **Starting Point:** Workplace writing begins with a need—either one you see or one assigned to you on the job. (*I'm writing to apply . . . , As you requested, . . .*)

⦿ **Purpose:** Workplace writing is practical—sharing ideas and information to solve a problem, to complete work, or to ask for action. This flow of information helps to build positive relationships with coworkers, customers, and others.

⦿ **Audience:** The specific readers vary for each piece. The key is understanding your reader's needs, knowledge, and position, and then tailoring the message accordingly.

⦿ **Form:** The shape of workplace writing also varies, though most pieces follow a standard format that has these two main qualities: (1) a basic three-part structure announcing the purpose, providing details, and spelling out an action, and (2) presentation strategies—lists, numbers, headings, boldface, underlining, visuals.

⦿ **Voice:** The tone of workplace writing is conversational but to the point—neither too chummy nor too formal. Think of your writing as part of a direct and sincere conversation with your reader. Speak clearly, concisely, and courteously.

⦿ **Point of View:** Personal pronouns are allowed, but keep the focus on the subject. Use "I" and "you" in person-to-person communication and "he," "she," and "they" in most general messages.

⦿ **The Big Picture:** Workplace writing is the process of sharing ideas and information so that readers know why you are writing and what they must understand or do. This writing has real-world impact. When writing, consider the effect of each piece on your reader, your organization, and yourself.

185

Expressions to Avoid in Workplace Writing

Formal and Awkward Phrasing: Replace with simpler, more modern language.

problem	solution
at the present writing	right now
you are hereby advised	I'm writing to let you know
ceased functioning	quit working
are in receipt of	have received
on a daily basis	daily

Slang: Replace with more broadly acceptable words.

problem	solution
chill out	relax
awesome	remarkable
burned out	exhausted
grease monkey	auto technician, mechanic

Cliches: Because they're worn-out, don't use them. Replace them with clear, simple statements. (See 096 for more cliches.)

problem	solution
last but not least	last, finally
water under the bridge	past, history
rock the boat	cause problems

Insensitive Language: Eliminate words insensitive to gender, race, religion, or class. Use neutral or positive terms. (Also see "Treating the Sexes Fairly," 775-784.)

problem	solution
foreigner	Canadian, Brazilian, etc.
lower class	working class
policeman	police officer

THE BOTTOM LINE

All writing done in the workplace must be clearly stated using honest, effective language. Language that is awkward, wordy, worn-out, or insensitive to a person's gender, race, or religion simply won't do.

Writing the Business Letter

Letters are workplace workhorses that help you apply for a job, file complaints, order supplies, or request information. Well-written letters result in true *communication*, an exchange between people; but poorly written letters can cause confusion and damage business relationships.

How do you write *effective* letters? Simple. Pay attention to the tips and models in this chapter; then use them as a guide the next time you need to communicate in writing.

What's Ahead?

This chapter of your handbook covers the business letter from start to finish. Included are tips on prewriting, organizing, style, form, revising, and proofreading a letter:

187 Form of the Business Letter

A letter must be professional and look professional—neatly typed or printed on good-quality paper. (See the guidelines below.)

semi-block

full block

Letter-Writing Guidelines

- Use a consistent style: semi-block or full block.
- Use a print size and typestyle that make reading easy.
- Use margins left and right from 1 to 1.5 inches.
- Center the letter vertically (top to bottom) on the page, leaving margins of 1 to 1.5 inches, or more.
- Present your information completely yet concisely.

188 Parts of the Business Letter

The **heading** gives the writer's complete address, either in the letterhead (company stationery) or typed out, plus the date.

The **inside address** gives the reader's name and address.

- ☐ If you're not sure which person to address or how to spell someone's name, you could call the company for the information.
- ☐ If the person's title is a single word, place it after the name and a comma. A longer title goes on a separate line.

The **salutation** begins with *Dear* and ends with a colon, not a comma.

- ☐ Use Mr. or Ms. plus the person's last name, unless you are well acquainted. Do not guess at Miss or Mrs.
- ☐ If you can't get the person's name, replace the salutation with *Dear* or *Attention* plus the title of an appropriate reader, such as *Customer Service Department, Sales Manager,* or *Personnel Manager.* (**Examples:** Dear Sales Manager: or Attention: Personnel Manager).

The **body** should consist of single-spaced paragraphs with double spacing between paragraphs. (Do not indent the paragraphs.)

☐ If the body goes to a second page, put the reader's name at the top left, the number 2 in the center, and the date at the right margin.

For the **complimentary closing**, use *Sincerely, Yours sincerely,* or *Yours truly* followed by a comma; use *Best wishes* if you know the person well.

The **signature** includes both the writer's handwritten and typed name.

☐ When someone types the letter for the writer, that person's initials appear (in lowercase) beside the writer's initials (in capitals).

☐ If a document (brochure, form, copy, etc.) is enclosed with the letter, the word *Enclosure* or *Encl.* appears below the initials.

☐ If a copy of the letter is sent elsewhere, type the letters *cc:* plus the person's or department's name beneath the enclosure line.

189

Heading

Savannah Chamber of Commerce
105 E. Bay Rd.
Savannah, GA 31404-1832
October 19, 1995

Four to Seven Spaces

Inside Address

Ms. Charlotte Williams, Manager
Belles Lettres Books
The Delta Mall
Savannah, GA 31404-0012

Double Space

Salutation

Dear Ms. Williams:

Double Space

Welcome to the Savannah business community. As the Chamber's executive director, I'd like to thank you for opening your store in Delta Mall.

Body

Belles Lettres is a welcome addition to the town's economy, especially with the store's emphasis on Southern authors. I wish you success. For this reason, I encourage you to join the Chamber of Commerce. Membership gives you a voice in your community's development and access to promotional materials. I've enclosed a brochure about our organization.

If you decide to join, I could set up a ribbon-cutting ceremony, which would provide some useful news coverage. Please call me at 944-0645 to discuss your membership.

Complimentary Closing

Double Space

Yours sincerely,

Signature

Ardith Lein　　**Four Spaces**

Ardith Lein

Double Space

Initials
Enclosure
Copies

AL:nk
Encl. membership brochure
cc: Peter Sanchez

⟨190⟩ The Letter-Writing Process

Prewriting Tips

- **Think first about your reader.** How well do you know her or him? How will she or he feel about your message? Is this person already well-informed on this subject? How will she or he use the message?
- **Think about your purpose.** Write out your reason for writing—what you want the reader to know or do—and keep it in front of you. This reason is your primary purpose, but don't forget your secondary goal—creating goodwill for any future communications.
- **Collect the information you will need.** It may be in your head, on your desk, in a database, or a phone call away. Jot down the details you need to include, and think about the best way to present them.

Effective Letter Organization

A letter that works is more than your first thoughts typed out. Your message must be organized for your reader's convenience. As a general rule, organize the body of your letter into three parts:

Situation: The opening introduces the message by stating the subject and purpose. It answers the question "Why are you writing this letter?"

Explanation: The middle of the letter presents the information and ideas at the heart of the message—the details. It answers the question "What's it all about?"

Action: The conclusion focuses on outcomes—what you want the reader to do, when, and how. It answers the question "What's next?"

Effective Letter Style

Letters should not be written to dazzle readers with flashy phrases. Because a letter is communication between people, the style should be conversational, courteous, and straightforward.

Be conversational. Your letter should sound like one person speaking to another. Be plain and simple in the words you choose, but avoid slang.

Be courteous. You accomplish nothing by talking down to or blowing off steam at your reader.

Avoid awkward or wordy phrases and insensitive language. The table at topic number 185 gives examples of each.

191 Proofreading the Business Letter

Whether you or someone else types your letters, you are the one responsible for the careful editing that makes each letter sound professional. Check out all these points:

Organization

☐ 1. The letter states its purpose clearly, right away.
☐ 2. The explanation gives the reader complete and accurate details.
☐ 3. The letter states exactly what you want the reader to do.

Wording and Tone

☐ 4. The letter avoids expressions that are wordy, cliched, vague, or sexist.
☐ 5. The letter begins, continues, and ends with a courteous tone.

Form and Appearance

☐ 6. The letter carefully follows either semi-block or full block format.
☐ 7. The letter is neatly typed or printed with no smudges or obvious corrections.
☐ 8. The margins are correct and even, the spacing is correct, and the message is centered on the page.
☐ 9. The letter is signed in ink, and the signature is readable.

Punctuation

☐ 10. A comma separates the city and state, but not the state and ZIP.
☐ 11. A colon is used after the salutation (except after an *Attention* line) and a comma after the complimentary closing.

Capitalization

☐ 12. The names of streets, cities, months, and people are capitalized.
☐ 13. The title of the reader, the name of the department, and the name of the company are capitalized in the inside address.
☐ 14. The word *Dear* and all nouns in the salutation are capitalized, but only the first word of the closing is capitalized.

Spelling

☐ 15. The reader's name is spelled correctly in both the inside address and the salutation.
☐ 16. The numbered street names from First to Tenth are spelled out, but figures are used for higher numbers.
☐ 17. The names of cities, streets, and months are spelled out. Any abbreviations used are correct. (Envelope rules vary. See 192.)

192 Folding the Letter

An 8½- by 11-inch letter should be mailed in a standard-sized 9½- by 4⅛-inch envelope.

1. Fold the bottom edge so that the paper is divided into thirds.

2. Fold the top third of the letter down and crease the edges firmly.

3. Insert the letter (with the open end at the top) into the envelope.

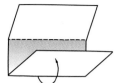

193 Addressing the Business Envelope

Address the letter correctly so it can be delivered promptly. Use the same addresses on the envelope that you used for the inside address and heading on the letter. The return address goes in the upper left corner, the destination address in the center.

> REP OLYMPIA SNOWE
> 2464 RAYBURN BLDG
> WASHINGTON DC 20515-0001
>
>
>
>
> MR LOUIS FREEN
> DIRECTOR
> FEDERAL BUREAU OF INVESTIGATION
> 10TH ST & PENNSYLVANIA AVE NW
> WASHINGTON DC 20535-0001

Sample addresses:

ATTN MANAGER TRAINING
MCDONALDS CORP
1 MCDONALDS PLZ
OAKBROOK IL 60521-1900

DR LESLIE MATHESON
GRACE MATERNITY HOSPITAL
5980 UNIVERSITY AVE
MADISON WI 53406

Official USPS Envelope Guidelines

1. Capitalize everything in the address and leave out ALL punctuation.

2. Use the list of common abbreviations found in the National ZIP Code Directory. (See 680.) Use numerals rather than words for numbered streets (9TH AVE NE, 3RD ST SW).

3. If you know the ZIP + 4 code, use it. You can get ZIP + 4 information by phoning the postal service.

194 The Letter of Inquiry (or Request)

An inquiring mind is curious. Out of curiosity or need, a person writes a letter of inquiry to check things out—to seek information about a job, person, product, service, policy, or procedure. Writing a letter of inquiry, or request, involves detective work. You need to follow clues to get the facts. Ask yourself these questions:

- Exactly what do I want or need? Why? By when?
- Where can I get it? From whom?
- Am I being realistic, or expecting too much?

456 Seventh Ave. N.E.
Cedar City, UT 84720-1697
September 17, 1994

Utah Jazz
301 W. South Temple
Salt Lake City, UT 84101-1836

The appropriate reader is addressed.

Attention: Public Relations Department

I'm writing for information about attending a Utah Jazz home game between December 7 and 24.

The request is stated in first sentences.

As the captain of the Cedar City Crusaders basketball team, I've been asked to set up a team trip. We would like to attend a weekend game and a practice, if possible. Could you send me the following:

1. ticket prices for a group of 12-15,

Specific details are listed.

2. a schedule of home games and practices between December 7 and 24, and

3. directions on how and when to book tickets.

Final statement looks forward to action.

I would appreciate the information by October 1. I look forward to your reply.

Sincerely,

Jenny Smithers

Jenny "Sky" Smithers

195 The Informative Letter

"This is to inform you . . . " Too many letters begin with this dry-as-dust statement as an introduction to some dry-as-dust information. But good informative letters convey information clearly and interestingly. They deliver their message with energy and purpose. You will need to write informative letters for many reasons:

- To send (by fax or mail) specific instructions or directions
- To keep your customers informed about the latest developments or opportunities in the company
- To provide a written record of a meeting or an agreement

It's All in the Packaging

To make your letter clear and interesting, package the information well. Here are some guidelines:

Be complete. A letter that's missing details makes extra work necessary—phone calls, faxes, follow-up letters. The costs? Time, money, and the embarrassment of a communication breakdown.

Be accurate. Little mistakes in the information can cause breakdowns as well. Imagine what would happen if an engineer misquoted stress specifications for building materials or if a pharmacist mislabeled a medication. Always double-check your facts before sending them.

Put the information in context. Think of yourself as an information carrier—a person delivering important information to another person. Anticipate your reader's questions about the information (Why are you giving it to me? What does it mean?) and make those answers part of your letter.

Organize and present the information effectively. Your reader needs to get to the information quickly and easily. Don't bury it. Organize the details logically—and present them clearly—using white space, lists, boldfacing, and underlining. It's your job to present information in a way that makes it easy to find and understand.

196 Model Informative Letter

The Travel Center

Member
ASTA
American Society
of Travel Agents

28 Second Street NE • Sioux City, Iowa 51250

Telephone 712-722-3727
Nationwide 800-553-6643
FAX 712-722-3827

March 15, 1995

Mr. Mark Melbourne
1590 E. Birch
Mitchell, SD 57301-1440

Dear Mr. Melbourne:

The letter's purpose is clearly stated.

Thank you for your inquiry about student tour packages to Europe. To give you the flexibility you described, I recommend that you buy your plane tickets separately from the tour. Airline fares allow you to stay 30-60 days, whereas the Image Tours package restricts you to a 20-day stay and return from Amsterdam only.

All the details are reader-friendly; key details are listed and framed in white space.

The following fares are in effect from Sioux Falls on Northwest and KLM airlines, routing Sioux Falls-Minneapolis-Amsterdam-Stockholm:

> **To Stockholm, round-trip** $809.45 including tax

> **To Amsterdam, with return** $834.45 including tax
> **from Stockholm**

Your friend could fly with you as far as Amsterdam and then go on to Stockholm while you meet the tour group. These fares are offered as part of a pre-book sale requiring ticket purchase by March 31, 1995.

The details are complete and accurate: dates, places, amounts, and restrictions.

The rest of your trip would involve the following costs:
1. Heart of Europe tour (minus the air): $1,392.00 per person sharing a double room.
2. Rail fare from Amsterdam to Gîteberg: $297.00 one way per person or $191.00 second class per person. The one-way trip takes about 17 hours.

A friendly close anticipates action.

We look forward to helping you book a great trip to Europe!

Yours sincerely,

Anne Maatman

Anne Maatman
Manager

197 The Letter of Complaint

What do you do when . . .

- your new CD arrives cracked in half?
- you receive a permanent stain on your new shirt from a freshly painted door in the mall?
- a new computer program malfunctions at work?

When such things happen, you need to make a complaint. Sometimes you can simply deal with the problem in person or over the phone. But often you put yourself in a better position when you write a letter: your message will not be interrupted, and you will have a written record of your complaint.

Letting off steam?

The purpose of the letter of complaint is **not** to blow off steam. Instead, you need to explain the problem and ask for a solution. In fact, the less whiny your letter sounds, the more likely you are to get a positive response from your reader. Most organizations are happy to get customer feedback because they want to provide quality products and services.

In a sense, you are like a prosecutor who has to prove that a crime has been committed: you need to produce evidence that a problem exists and that your reader has a responsibility to address the problem. Include facts about the following:

The Transaction Note where, when, and how you purchased the product or received the service. Include photocopies of any evidence such as a receipt, canceled check, or warranty.

The Product or Service Include the model or serial number.

The Problem Be specific about what is wrong and any inconvenience the problem is causing you.

Attempted Solutions If you have already tried to solve the problem, explain what you did and who you talked to.

The Solution Explain what action you want the reader to take—a refund, a replacement, or an apology.

Note: In most cases you will want to state the problem clearly in the first paragraph, following with explanation and details. However, if you are uncertain about the reader's response and feel that you need to be very persuasive, you may want to build up to the problem by providing complete background information first.

Be **Complete, Clear,** ◄─── and **Courteous.**

198 Model Letter of Complaint

2112 Jefferson Park Ave. #10
Charlottesville, VA 22903-5790
April 11, 1995

The Shoe Company
123 West Adams
Beaverton, OR 97005-9870

Dear Customer Service Department:

**Product
information**

On February 22, I bought size 10 Jump Max running shoes for $64.95 at the Runner's Roost in Walker, Virginia. The store was having a going-out-of-business sale, but the salesperson told me that even though the store would be closed, the shoes would keep your guarantee of satisfaction.

**Problem/
action taken**

I wore the shoes for six weeks with no problem. But on April 7 I noticed a loss of cushioning in my left shoe. I discovered that the exposed air-sole in the heel was punctured and was no longer holding air.

**Cause of
problem**

I don't believe that I misused the shoes because my runs were mostly on pavement and grass, and I used them almost exclusively for running. The popped air-sole must have resulted from a defect in the manufacturing process.

**Solution
desired**

I am enclosing my Jump Max running shoes along with a copy of the canceled check. Please send me a new pair of shoes in the same model and size.

I look forward to your response. I've enjoyed using your products over the years, and I expect to use them in the future.

Sincerely,

Mark Hammons

Mark Hammons

Encl. shoes and canceled check

199 The Bad-News Letter

People in the workplace do not enjoy sharing bad news. Who would want the job of refusing a request or turning down a job applicant? Even though delivering bad news is always tough, you can do it kindly. Cushion the main point by surrounding it with neutral or positive information. Here's what you should include:

Buffer: a neutral and supportive statement that establishes the writer-reader relationship

Reason: an explanation that supports the upcoming decision

Bad News: a gentle but clear decision (Try to state it positively and avoid using the word "you." If possible, provide an alternative.)

Friendly Close: a sincere, supportive statement

W. P. BACCAM Insurance Agency
200 Parkview Drive • Lakewood, NY 14750-1440 • (716)763-8102

January 14, 1995

Ms. Gloria Patton
96 Huron Street
Lakewood, NY 14750-1440

Dear Ms. Patton:

Neutral opening states purpose.

As your personal agent, I wanted to update you on the status of your automobile insurance.

Writer explains situation and states bad news objectively.

In order to keep their premiums low, some insurance companies will not cover high-risk drivers. In the past two years you have had an at-fault accident and four moving violations. Therefore, your current auto insurance company, Greentree Fire & Auto, has chosen not to renew your policy effective February 15, 1995. I do have six nonstandard auto insurance companies that are willing to provide you coverage in spite of your record.

Alternative provided.

Final statement suggests action reader may take to solve the problem.

Please call (ext. 7053) so that together we can determine how best to meet your auto insurance needs.

Sincerely,

Seth Baccam

Seth Baccam

200 The Thank-You Letter

"Thank you"—two simple but powerful words, both in life and in the workplace. Thank-you letters and other goodwill messages (welcome, congratulations) build strong workplace relationships. They make the workplace work well because work is more than business: it's people.

But why write to say thanks? Why not just say it? Well, for one thing, a written thank-you shows extra effort; it says, "I appreciate you." If you want to say thank you well, follow these guidelines:

Be selective. Select the right form—personal note, greeting card, or formal letter. Choose a situation where someone has truly impressed you. (A letter for every little act soon weakens the impact.) And never mix your thanks with some other purpose, like a sales pitch.

Be sincere. Sincere thanks is genuine, heartfelt. If you don't feel it, don't say it. Most readers can spot counterfeit thanks easily.

Be prompt. Don't wait until you have no other work on your desk. Respond immediately.

Be personal. After all, your reader does not want a form letter. Remember that you are thanking a real person.

Be specific. Instead of sending a vague thank-you that covers the moon and stars, be exact. Why are you thankful, and for what?

People who deserve a thank-you letter, memo, or note:

1. someone who interviewed you for a job (See 210.)
2. a host for a trip or tour
3. an employee, employer, or teacher at the end of the job or year
4. a person who wrote a recommendation letter for you
5. an organization or an individual who solved your problem or resolved your complaint promptly and effectively
6. someone whose extra efforts benefited you or your organization
7. a worker whose service on a committee, project, or charity brought about success
8. a worker whose suggestion or proposal improved quality, efficiency, safety, or some other workplace condition
9. a supervisor or coworker who effectively resolved a conflict or workplace difficulty for you
10. someone who helped you work through a problem

201 Sample Thank-You Letter

456 Seventh Ave. N.E.
Cedar City, UT 84720-1697
January 5, 1995

Thank-you is sent promptly, less than a week after the event.

Mr. Gene Ebert
Public Relations Department
Utah Jazz
301 W. South Temple
Salt Lake City, UT 84101-1836

Dear Mr. Ebert:

Person in the department is addressed directly.

I'm writing on behalf of the Cedar City Crusaders basket-ball team to thank you for the great time we had at the Jazz home game against the Knicks on December 31.

When I first wrote to you in September, I appreciated your help in suggesting possible games and in getting the whole team a 25 percent discount on tickets. But we never expected to meet three of the players, get our pictures taken with them, or play a game of 21 with Karl Malone! None of us will forget this team trip, believe me.

Writer specifically lists what she and teammates are grateful for.

While we still have nine games left to play, you have already made our season a success. Thank you. We will wear our Jazz shirts with pride while the Jazz make their run for the NBA Championship!

Letter ends with a sincere compliment.

Sincerely,

Jenny "Sky" Smithers

Jenny "Sky" Smithers

Writing to Get a Job

Applying for a job can be spooky. You can almost never guess the outcome (not to mention your income!). But if you can't control the result, you can at least manage to write the sort of letter of application that will get you to an interview. That's going to be a more and more important skill as years go by. Some authorities say that a worker entering the workforce in the next several years will change jobs an average of six times in his or her lifetime. As competition increases, those who write strong letters will have a distinct advantage.

What's Ahead?

This chapter concentrates on those skills needed to apply for and get a job. Here are the topics covered:

The Application Form

The Request Letter

The Résumé

Application and Follow-Up Letters

Interviewing for the Job

Accepting a Job Offer

203 The Application Form

Someone once said, "The closest to perfection a person ever comes is when he (or she) fills out a job application form." Oddly enough, it's probably true. When you fill out an application form, you want to present the very best picture possible. You want to make a positive impression by what you say and how you say it. Here are some tips that will help you fill out any form—from job application to health insurance.

Filling Out Forms

204 Quick Guide

1. Read the entire form, including instructions, before putting pen to paper.

2. Make a photocopy of the blank form to use as a rough-draft copy, or draft your answers on a separate piece of paper.

3. Don't write in spaces marked "For Office Use Only."

4. Type or print neatly with blue or black ink.

5. Make sure your hands are clean and that no food or drink is nearby to accidentally spill on the form.

6. Don't skip any blanks. If the item doesn't apply to you, write N/A (not applicable).

7. Answer honestly but give only the information requested.

8. If you make a mistake, don't scratch it out or write over it. Use correction fluid instead.

9. Double-check all numbers for accuracy.

10. Proofread for spelling, punctuation, and typos.

11. Ask someone else to also proofread your form.

12. Deliver or mail the form to the appropriate person.

205 The Request Letter

An important part of the job-hunting process is asking authority figures, like teachers or employers, to write recommendations or to serve as references. The best way to ask is by writing a letter of request. Here is a suggested outline:

- **Situation:** remind the reader of your relationship to him or her; then ask the person to write a recommendation or to serve as a reference for you.

- **Explanation:** describe the work you did for the reader.

- **Action:** ask the reader to respond to your request by a certain date.

2400 Sheridan Rd.
West Columbia, SC 29167-1440
August 28, 1995

Dr. Barbara Sadat
152 Benton Circle Dr.
West Columbia, SC 29167-5823

Dear Dr. Sadat:

Situation
I am applying for a part-time job at the Cribs and Crayons Child Care Center here in West Columbia. Since I have taken care of your son, Tyler, I am writing to ask if I may use your name as a reference.

Explanation
I feel I would be well qualified for the job. Taking care of Tyler taught me to be responsible and interact well with children.

Action
Please let me know by September 4 if you are willing to be a reference; my phone number is 739-6401. I have appreciated the opportunity to work for you, and I look forward to hearing from you.

Sincerely,

Mila Celis

Mila Celis

206 **The Résumé**

Your résumé is a vivid word picture of you. Its purpose is to interest the employer so he or she will call you for an interview. A résumé is not a brag sheet. Instead of *telling* about yourself, you *show* what skills and knowledge you have and the responsibilities you have had. The content and form of résumés may vary slightly, but generally all résumés contain the following information:

- **personal data** about you (address, phone, time available)
- your job **objective** (the job you want to have and the kind of organization you want to work for)
- your **work experience**
- details about your **education**
- **other experience** (organizations, volunteer work, etc.)
- your **achievements** or abilities

Résumé Writing Tips

1. Design each résumé to fit a particular job.

2. Be specific—use numbers, dates, names.
(. . . graduated in top 25 percent, . . . maintained a *B* average, . . . missed only one day of school, . . . supervised seven other workers)

3. Present information about your experience or education first, depending upon which is the most important to the job for which you are applying.

4. List your work experience. Include positions you've held, names of employers, specific duties, and dates you held each position.

5. Include information about achievements or special abilities. Also list volunteer work, club duties, other responsibilities that suggest you would be a responsible, dependable worker.

6. Use everyday language and short, concise phrases.

7. Use the techniques of boldface, underlining, white space, and indentations to make your résumé readable.

8. Get someone else's reaction before typing the final copy.

9. Proofread carefully for spelling, punctuation, and other errors.

10. Address and mail your résumé (and your cover letter) to the appropriate person.

207 **Sample Résumé**

MILA CELIS
2400 Sheridan Rd.
West Columbia, SC 29167-1440
(803) 739-6401

JOB OBJECTIVE:	Part-time caretaker in a child-care facility
EXPERIENCE:	
1994-1995	MOPS (Mothers of Preschoolers), West Columbia Cared for 4-6 two-year-olds for 2 hours every Tuesday evening
Summer 1994	Craft Assistant Arts & Recreation Council, West Columbia Assisted four-year-olds in the summer Arts and Crafts program (clay, tie-and-dye, paint) Supervised children on the playground
1993-Present	Baby-sitter Dr. Barbara Sadat Care for a toddler, sometimes overnight: prepare and serve meals, give baths, read books, and give prescribed medicine
EDUCATION:	Super-Sitter Certificate, Lexington Medical Center, June 1993
	Learned first aid, CPR, handling emergencies, child development and nutrition, appropriate behavior management, activities for children at different age levels
	Completed 11th grade, Irmo High School Grade Point Average: 3.0/4.0 Course work includes Child Psychology, Human Anatomy, Foods
AWARDS AND ACHIEVEMENTS:	
1995	Excellent Attendance Award, Irmo High School Student Council Member Peer Counselor
1994	Superior Rating, Humorous Acting, District Speech Contest
REFERENCES:	Available upon request

208 The Letter of Application

A letter of application (or cover letter) introduces you to an employer and often highlights information on an accompanying résumé. Your goal is to convince the employer to invite you for an interview. Before writing the actual letter, answer these questions:

● What job are you applying for?
● How did you find out about the job?
● What are the employer's needs? (List)
● How can you fill these needs?

Then write a brief business letter. Remember to keep your tone enthusiastic and positive. Your letter will create that all-important first impression and usually determine whether or not you are considered and interviewed for the job. So concentrate on your qualifications for the job, including any special talents you can offer.

TAKE NOTE

Once your letter gets you an appointment, check out 210 for tips on how to handle the interview.

Telling Your Story

◉ In the **salutation**, address a specific person. If you don't know the person's name, write "Attention: Personnel Manager" or "Dear Personnel Manager."

◉ In the **introduction**, state the job you are applying for and where you found out about it. Give your chief qualification (your #1 selling point).

◉ In the **body**, explain how your skills can meet the organization's needs.

• Provide a brief statement explaining your qualifications for the position.

• If possible, use words directly from the job ad to describe what you can do.

• Verbally highlight the parts of the enclosed résumé that relate to the job opening.

• Emphasize what you can do for an employer, rather than what he or she can do for you.

◉ In the **conclusion**, request an interview. Be sure to list the times you can be reached and the correct phone numbers. End by thanking the reader for his or her time and consideration.

209 Sample Application Letter

2400 Sheridan Rd.
West Columbia, SC 29167-1440
September 5, 1995

Ms. Joyce Denisenko
Cribs and Crayons Child Care Center
1010 Brown St.
West Columbia, SC 29167-7644

Salutation

Dear Ms. Denisenko:

Introduction

In response to your newspaper advertisement, I am writing to apply for the position of caretaker on the toddler floor. The enclosed résumé will show you the experience I have already had working with children.

Body

Any place caring for children needs responsible and dependable employees. I not only enjoy children, but I realize what an important job child care is. Toddlers need a loving, safe environment where they can learn and grow. Parents need to feel confident that caretakers will provide close supervision, creative activities, and nutritional food for their children. I am a person you and the parents could count on to provide consistently excellent care.

Conclusion

I would be happy to come in for an interview at any time. You can contact me at 739-6401 after 3:30 p.m. or by leaving a message on my family's answering machine. Thank you for considering my application.

Sincerely,

Mila Celis
Mila Celis

⑳ Interviewing for the Job

Your letter of application and résumé are pictures of you. If the employer likes the pictures and wants a closer look at the real thing, he or she will ask you to come for an interview. Here are some tips to help you get ready:

What to Do Before the Interview

Think about yourself.

What are your goals? Strengths? Weaknesses?

Think about the employer.

Why is the organization interested in you?
What are the business's goals, size, services, and reputation?

Think about the interview.

What questions can you expect: Your strengths?
   Weaknesses? Reason for seeking the job?
What materials may the employer want to see: Work
   samples? Portfolio? Additional copy of your résumé?

Think about the job.

What does the job involve? What are the hours? Wages?
   Opportunities for advancement?

How to Respond During the Interview

Be attentive.

Introduce yourself to the office staff and say why you're there.
Complete forms neatly and quietly.
Shake hands and look the interviewer in the eye.
Listen carefully.

Be clear.

Answer questions clearly and briefly.
Restate questions in your own words if you are unsure what
   the interviewer means.
State your strengths and how you use them.

Ask about the job.

What is the job description? Salary? Benefits? Opportunities
   for advancement? Work schedule? Starting date?

What to Do After the Interview

Tell when and where you can be reached.
Thank each person involved in the interview.
Write a follow-up letter.

211 Writing the Follow-Up Letter

Your application and résumé have gotten you an interview, and that interview went well. Now what? Pace the floor and chew your nails? No! Put your hands to work. A day or two after the interview you should send a follow-up letter. A good follow-up message contains the following:

- A thank-you comment
- A statement confirming your interest in the job and your value as an employee, with specific reference to the interview
- A statement about your willingness to answer further questions
- Your phone number and times you're available

806 E. Seventh St.
Del Rio, TX 78003-3667
February 16, 1995

Ms. Ruby Villanueva
Director of Personnel
Del Rio Community Clinic and Hospital
400 Valley Rd.
Del Rio, TX 78003-7829

Dear Ms. Villanueva:

Thank-you comment

Thank you for the interview yesterday. I enjoyed meeting you and the nurses at Del Rio.

Confirm your interest in the job

I would enjoy contributing to the important work that you and other staff members do in this community. After touring your impressive obstetrics unit, I'm convinced that my internship at the neonatal unit of El Paso General would make me an asset to your team.

Follow-up information

I appreciate your considering me for the position of registered nurse. If you have any further questions, I am available at 823-9667 from 8:00 to 10:00 weekday mornings, or you may leave a message any time after that.

Yours sincerely,

Jack Delaney

Jack Delaney

212 Accepting a Job Offer

Once you've been offered a job, your task is pretty simple, right? You just say yes or no. But how you communicate your decision is important for starting a job well. When you do receive an employment offer on paper, make your written response *professional, polite,* and *prompt,* whatever your decision. A good acceptance letter, direct and brief, contains the following:

- The actual acceptance, precisely stated
- Clarification of details: salary or wage, starting date, business to take care of before starting date
- A closing statement indicating that you look forward to starting

806 E. Seventh St.
Del Rio, TX 78003-3667
February 23, 1995

Ms. Ruby Villanueva
Director of Personnel
Del Rio Community Clinic and Hospital
400 Valley Rd.
Del Rio, TX 78003-7829

Dear Ms. Villanueva:

Acceptance

I am pleased to accept the position of registered nurse in the obstetrics unit of Del Rio, at the salary of $23,500.

Clarification

As we discussed on the phone, a starting date of March 15 works well for me. Before then, I will complete the forms you sent and return them. I also will forward my R.N. certification next week when Lone Star Technical College processes it.

Closing statement

I'm looking forward to caring for Del Rio's mothers and babies soon.

Yours sincerely,

Jack Delaney

Jack Delaney

Writing on the Job

213 In the business world, every stage of a project calls for writing: from proposals and instructions, to memos, telephone messages, E-mail, committee minutes, and progress reports, to final reports, executive summaries, evaluations, newsletters, and media reports.

As your responsibilities on the job grow, the demand for your writing will probably grow, too. You won't have to be a Nobel-prize-winning novelist to write well. You must simply be clear, thorough, focused, and sensitive to your reader.

What's Ahead?

This section of your handbook covers the writing forms you will use on the job.

Writing Memos and Messages

Writing Instructions

Writing Summaries and Minutes

Writing Proposals and Short Reports

Writing for the Media

Writing on the Job

214 Quick Guide

What Your Coworkers Expect

1. Listen to your coworkers carefully and reply to them promptly; be aware of any deadlines or special situations.

2. Use the form and style the company uses, but also be creative.

3. Show respect for the people you work with and write to by being sensitive to their culture, gender, religion, etc.

4. Be a team writer. A lot of writing in the workplace happens in groups, so learn how to collaborate.

5. Use your time wisely. Don't spend several hours on a simple memo when you need to dedicate quality time to another task.

What Your Readers Need

1. Be sure you know which person you should write to and address him or her by name or by position.

2. Organize your writing carefully, making your message easy to follow. Include times, dates, places, the 5 W's (*who, what, when, where, why*), and whatever else is necessary to give a full and accurate picture.

3. Be honest with your reader and work hard to help him or her understand your ideas and information.

4. Be clear about how you want your reader to respond to what you've written.

5. Become familiar with new ways of communicating information: E-mail, fax, voice mail, electronic bulletin boards, desktop publishing.

215 Writing Memos

Memos are written to ask and answer questions, give short reports, and remind people about appointments and meetings. They also serve as a written record of any action you take.

● Send memos only when necessary and only to those who need them.

● Get to the point: (1) state the subject,
　　　　　　　　　　 (2) give necessary details,
　　　　　　　　　　 (3) ask for the response you want.

● Distribute them in the best way—interoffice mail, bulletin board, fax, E-mail, etc.

INTER-TECH, INC.
MEMO

Date:　　October 22, 1995

To:　　　Inter-Tech Staff

From:　　Jane Brand, Personnel Director

Subject:　New Technology

Use standard memo heading.

This month's staff improvement meeting will be held next Thursday, October 29, at 8:00 p.m. It will feature Dr. G. F. Gillis, a professor at City Technical College. He will speak on the latest technology and how we can expect it to affect us and our work.

State your point clearly and concisely.

Dr. Gillis is planning a winter-term training program that will feature all facets of office technology and communication. Those attending the meeting will receive additional information on the program.

Please sign up with me before the end of the day on Tuesday if you plan to attend the meeting.

State the response you want.

> "If you're not smiling while you're talking on the phone, the customer can tell it."
>
> —Lawrence Vander Esch, Corporate President

216 Telephone Etiquette

Do telephone manners matter? Absolutely. Your voice over the wires is often the first or only impression a person receives of you and your organization. Below are ways to use the telephone effectively.

Telephone Talking Tips

- **Speak slowly and clearly** into the mouthpiece. Don't chew gum, eat, or drink.
- **Let your voice communicate** that you're capable and interested in the caller.
- **Be friendly,** but don't waste time. Get to the point of the call.
- **Be a good listener.** Put aside other work and pay attention.
- **Turn off background noise** such as a radio or TV.
- **Stay calm,** even if the person on the other end is not.
- **End the conversation with a courteous comment** such as "Thank you" or "Good-bye." Then replace the receiver quietly.

When placing a call . . .

- Identify yourself. "Hello, this is Anita Johnson from Hillview Computer Services."
- If you have several things to discuss, make a list beforehand so you don't forget anything. Have necessary information near you.
- If the person you are calling sounds busy, ask if you can call back at a more convenient time.
- If you want your call returned, give your name, number, and a good time to reach you.
- Use available technology such as answering machines, E-mail, and faxes to leave messages.

When answering a call . . .

- Try to answer the phone by the second or third ring.
- Identify yourself and the organization. "City offices. This is John."
- If the call needs to be transferred, politely ask who is calling. (Ask before putting people on hold, and don't leave them there for long.)
- Keep note-taking materials near your phone. If you need to take a message, be complete and accurate.

217 Writing Telephone Messages

Telephone messages in the workplace must be taken carefully and delivered promptly. Taking messages well requires two things: (1) being polite and professional on the phone and (2) getting down all the facts correctly. Double-check numbers and spellings with the caller, and use the 5 W's as a checklist. (Remember, each message you write well will help establish your reputation as an efficient, dependable worker.)

- **Who** is the message for? Who is the message from?
- **What** is the message?
- **When** is the meeting or appointment mentioned in the message? When was the message written?
- **Where** is the receiver of the message to go, or call back?
- **Why** is the message important—what's the purpose?

After you have taken the message, deliver it promptly. You may fill out a standard message form by hand or use electronic mail (E-mail), depending on the situation.

Standard Message Form

E-Mail Message

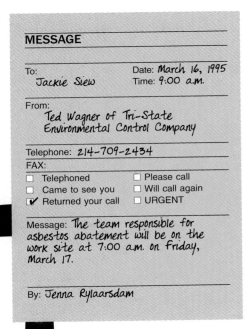

MESSAGE

To: Jackie Siew   Date: March 16, 1995
                                 Time: 9:00 a.m.

From: Ted Wagner of Tri-State Environmental Control Company

Telephone: 214-709-2434

FAX:

☐ Telephoned   ☐ Please call
☐ Came to see you   ☐ Will call again
☑ Returned your call ☐ URGENT

Message: The team responsible for asbestos abatement will be on the work site at 7:00 a.m. on friday, March 17.

By: Jenna Rylaarsdam

```
Date:    16 Mar 1995   09:00:39
From:    jrylaarsdam@western
To:   jsiew@western
Subject:   message from wagner
Priority:   normal

t wagner of tri-state environmental
control returned your call at 9 a.m.

1. team responsible for the asbestos
abatement will be on the work site at
7 a.m. on friday, march 17. phone:
214-709-2434.
```

> "When writing instructions, don't assume anything. If the reader knew what to do, he or she wouldn't need instructions."
>
> —Dennis Walstra, Plumbing Contractor

218 Writing Instructions

"Put whatchamacallit A into whosit B, turn 62.5 degrees, and crank it with a grummle wrench." Ugh! Help!

Do instructions frustrate you? You're not alone. Poorly written instructions can be a real problem, especially when your work depends upon them. Good instructions explain how to complete a process using a clear, step-by-step procedure. Nothing is left to chance.

Step-by-Step-by-Step

Know your goal.
What result do you want? A package delivered, a machine assembled, food prepared? Spell it out and keep the goal in front of you.

Know your reader.
What does the reader already know and need to know about the process? Does he or she understand technical terms? Develop your instructions with the reader in mind.

Know the process.
How well do you as the writer know the process? Make sure you know it backward and forward.

Organize the steps.
Part 1: an introduction that gives an overview of the whole process and states the end goal

Part 2: a list of required parts, equipment, or tools

Part 3: a step-by-step walk-through of the process

Write the steps.
Use clear, exact verbs that tell the reader what to do; also use precise terms for parts, tools, and measurements.

Clarify the steps.
Because a reader will work back and forth between the task and the instructions, your writing must be easy to get into and out of. Number the steps and use graphics to help the reader.

Test the steps.
Allow a couple of days to pass after you write the instructions. Then try to follow the directions. Ask a friend to do the same. Finally, revise your instructions as necessary to make sure they are clear.

TAKE NOTE

At times, you may need to give and take instructions in person, rather than in written form. For guidelines, turn to 395 in your handbook.

219

Sample Instructions
Closing Out the Cash Register

The steps below will help you (1) close out the cash register and (2) account for the day's receipts. You need four things:

- a daily account form
- an adding machine
- a deposit bag
- a pen

1. MAKE SURE THE STORE DOOR IS LOCKED. Then take the cash tray out of the register drawer and place it on the counter.

2. Turn the cash register key to the X setting and press the X key. The machine will print the X reading: the total amount of receipts (cash, credit card slips, and checks) taken in for the day.

3. Turn the key to the Z setting and press the Z key. The machine will print the Z reading: itemized, department-by-department subtotals (camera sales, film sales, film processing, etc.).

4. Count out $100 and place it in the envelope marked FLOAT. (The FLOAT is the $100 of cash placed in each cash register when the store opens.) The remaining cash, checks, and credit card slips make up the day's receipts. DO NOT PLACE THE FLOAT BACK IN THE DRAWER.

5. Using the adding machine, total the day's receipts and check them against the X reading. If the totals differ, count the receipts a second and third time if necessary. If the totals still do not agree, make a note of the difference and attach it to the receipts.

6. Fill out the daily account form by entering these totals: the X and Z readings and the day's receipts (credit card slips, checks, and cash). Place the day's receipts in the deposit bag.

7. Place the following in the safe: (1) the deposit bag, (2) the daily account form, (3) the X and Z readings, and (4) the envelope marked FLOAT. DOUBLE-CHECK THE SAFE DOOR TO MAKE SURE IT'S LOCKED.

220 Writing Summaries

When someone hands you a pot, you grab it by the handle. When somebody hands you a report (and time is short), you read the summary. In fact, the summary may be all you read. That's why clear summaries are vital to the smooth, efficient operation of a business.

Here are two of the many times a summary might be written.

- A production manager for an electric motor manufacturer provides a summary of her department's annual meeting to corporate heads.
- A researcher for a pesticide company writes a review of the articles she has found about organic methods of controlling corn borers.

221 Summarizing a Document

Why would someone need a summary of an article or a document?

Busy people can use summaries to get key ideas or an overview of a report, an article, or anything written.

How do I write a summary?

- First, skim the selection to get the overall meaning.
- Read the selection carefully, paying attention to key words.
- List the main ideas on your own paper.
- Write a summary of the major ideas, using your own words. Keep the following points in mind as you write:
  - Your opening (topic) sentence should be a clear statement of the main idea of the original selection.
  - Stick to the essential information throughout.
  - Try to state each important idea in one clear sentence.
  - Arrange your ideas in the most logical order.
  - Use a concluding sentence that ties all your points together.

222 Summarizing a Meeting

Are summaries used for other purposes?

Oftentimes, what goes on at a meeting is put into a summary. These special summaries are called minutes. (See 417-419 for more information on how a business meeting works.)

How do you write minutes well?

- Be neutral when you summarize discussion. Leave out personal feelings, emotions, and comments about personalities.
- Record motions, voting results, names, and duties as accurately as possible.

223 Summary of a Document

The summary below is a good example of what you need to do when you condense a news article or business report. Notice that the opening sentence introduces the topic and states the main point of the article. The writer goes on to list essential information and concludes with a sentence that brings the summary into final focus. (First appeared in *Working Woman* in March, 1995. Written by Elizabeth Weiss. Reprinted with the permission of *Working Woman* Magazine. Copyright © 1995 by *Working Woman*, Inc.)

SUITING UP FOR SUCCESS

Even the best-looking résumé won't win you a job if you don't look the part. Now a number of innovative nonprofits have started to help poor women dress—and interview—for success.

The first was Chicago's Bottomless Closet, which has served some 1,500 clients since opening in 1991; more than 600 have secured jobs and held them for a year or more. After that came Suited for Change in Washington, D.C., and the Career Closet in San Jose, Calif.

In a similar effort, hundreds of women have received free shampoos, cuts, and perms each week since Sister Bonita Steinlage opened the first of two salons for Cincinnati's indigent in 1990. She is now hoping to expand to four other states.

In New York, a group of women is raising $25,000 to open Suited for Success, where racks will be filled by donations of still-current career clothes. Graduates of approved job-training programs will be offered two outfits gratis—from shoes to earrings —and, once jobs are landed, two more outfits. "This is a way for a woman who can't possibly go out and buy a work wardrobe to put her best foot forward," says designer Andrea Jovine, who has donated 100 outfits.

The programs address more than dress. Volunteers at all four organizations, trained by professional image consultants and career counselors, also offer tips on workplace etiquette, interviewing, and job-search strategy, along with advice on hair, makeup, and nutrition. "We don't want to just hang clothes on a body," says Irene Tanner, a co-founder of the New York group. "We want to develop a sense of self-esteem."

– Elizabeth Weiss

Model Summary

Nonprofit organizations in several U.S. cities are offering free help to women searching for jobs. Recognizing that everyone needs to look right to land a job, the stores provide outfits or hair styling at no cost to those who can't afford to pay. Much of the merchandise is donated, and the store personnel volunteer their time. The programs also give advice on searching for jobs, interviewing, and behavior on the job. Together, the clothing, grooming, and counseling are designed to give all women an equal chance at getting and keeping a job.

224 Summary (Minutes) of a Meeting

Horace Mann High School: Student Council Meeting
Wednesday, September 27, 1995: Room 201

Identifying
information is
given first.

Present: Sherry West (pres.), Robert Ortez (v.p.), Kate Westlake (treas.), Brian McCarthy (sec.); Alex Wong, Adrienne Clark, Jim Watts, and Craig Harada (class reps), Ms. Martinez (faculty rep)

95.113   Sherry called the meeting to order and reviewed the agenda.

OLD BUSINESS

95.114   Brian read the minutes of the September 20 meeting. They were accepted without change.

Articles are
identified by
year (95) and
item number
(114).

95.115   The motion tabled in article 95.109 was opened again for discussion. The motion to use November's activity periods for intramural volleyball passed. Jim and Adrienne will set it up.

NEW BUSINESS

The key points
of a report
(and who
reported) are
noted.

95.116   Lisa Tremaine joined the meeting. As a SADD rep, she asked the council to consider these ways of observing Alcohol Awareness Week (Oct. 23-27):
          (1) place a wrecked car in front of the school,
          (2) tape white outlines of bodies in the halls,
          (3) read alcohol-related statistics during morning announcements,
          (4) hold an assembly with County Attorney Marsha Wag as speaker.

An idea is
moved,
seconded, and
voted on.

After discussion, Adrienne moved and Craig seconded that the council support activities 1, 3, and 4, but not 2 because it might upset some students, faculty, and janitors. Ms. Martinez will relay these plans to the administration.

NEXT MEETING

Future
business is
described.

95.117   Besides the homecoming preparations, we will deal with plans for AWOL Day (when juniors get to shadow a person in the workplace).

95.118   The meeting was adjourned.

Submitted by Brian McCarthy

Next Meeting: Rm. 201, 7:45 a.m., Oct. 4

225 Writing Proposals

People write proposals in the workplace to fix a problem, meet a need, or make an improvement. A proposal can be as simple as a piece of paper slipped into a suggestion box, or as complicated as a bid to build nuclear submarines. But having a good idea is not enough to make change happen. Your proposal should spell out any suggestion carefully if you want it to be positively received and to actually change the way things work.

Understand the problem.

Begin by carefully defining and researching your idea for change. Exactly what is the problem or need you see? Why is it important? What has been done or tried in the past? How will your idea solve the problem or meet the need?

Consider the reader's position.

Someone reading a proposal thinks, "How does this affect me and my organization? Is this the best idea? What's the bottom line? Do I have confidence in this writer?" A writer needs to jump into the reader's shoes and think about the questions he or she might have.

Prove that your idea is workable.

Above all, you must demonstrate with specific details that your idea is a good one. What will your plan accomplish? How much time do you need? How much will it cost? Who will be affected by the planned changes?

Organize your plan to persuade.

Most proposal writers offer their plans in this form:

1. Statement of the problem or need—what it is, why it's important, and how it has been dealt with in the past.

2. A plan to solve the problem or meet the need—what the plan is, why it makes sense, what the results will be, and how the results will be checked or measured.

3. A detailed program for putting the plan into action— what it will take in terms of people, technology, services, time, and money.

226 Model Proposal

Treebeard Lawn Service
Seattle, Washington

To: Robert Castillo

From: Donna Kao

Date: July 10, 1995

Subject: Employee T-Shirts

Suggestion stated

I have an idea for advertising Treebeard's name in Seattle. I propose that all employees wear company T-shirts to stick out like green thumbs.

Statement of problem and plan to solve it

Right now, we all wear clothes that feel good for hot-weather work. But while we work hard, we look bad. In fact, we're downright raggedy. Green T-shirts with the company name and logo on them would make us hard to miss. In fact, we'd be walking ads, feeling good and looking good.

Ideas for putting plan into action

I've called three stores that do shirts, but Sam's Slickprint has the best prices. Sam himself gave me these figures:

Logo design and preparation (one-time cost)	$25.00
Single shirt	$10.00

For orders of 10 or more shirts, he'd give us a 20 percent discount. The total cost for 32 employees would be $281. This cost, by the way, is $811 less than the cost of running our 2-column by 5-inch ads in the Seattle Times--and our green T-shirts will be walking around town all summer long, making people think "Treebeard."

Let me know what you think of this idea as soon as you can. Sam said his prices are good until the end of the month.

"The incident report is the link between the crime and the court case—maybe a year later."

—Dan Altena, Deputy Sheriff

227 Writing Short Reports

Short reports (also called memo reports) are important workplace tools. By *recording, organizing, analyzing,* and *interpreting* information, these reports help people answer day-to-day questions:

- How's it going?
- What's finished?
- What's left to be done?
- What's the problem?
- What's the solution?

Preparing the Report

- ◉ Know what information your reader needs and why. Decide whether to simply present information or to also analyze and discuss it—to provide conclusions only or to add recommendations.
- ◉ Present your information objectively (without emotion), accurately, and precisely.
- ◉ Organize the information using headings, white space, underlining, boldface, and visuals such as graphs and tables.
- ◉ Use the report forms and formats that your employer expects, but follow memo guidelines if forms do not exist.
- ◉ Write in a factual but conversational style, using personal pronouns such as *I* and *you*.

Organizing the Report

The Direct Approach

When you think the reader will like your conclusions and recommendations, talk about these first. Then add the facts and details that support your ideas.

Introduction: your statement explaining the purpose of the report

Conclusions/Recommendations: your conclusion about the information and/or a plan for action

Discussion of Findings: detailed, full information that shows where your conclusions and recommendations come from

The Indirect Approach

When the reader needs to be convinced of your conclusions and recommendations, give the hard facts first. This may help to make your report more persuasive.

228 Model Short Report

Date: February 28, 1995

To: Ms. Doriani

From: Eric Rowe

Subject: AWOL Visit with Recreational Director

The introduction states the purpose and previews the content.

On Tuesday, February 21, I shadowed Sandi Walker as part of the AWOL program. Sandi is the recreational director for Hobart, Ohio. This report covers (1) Sandi's schedule, (2) the work she does, and (3) my conclusions about her job.

The Day's Schedule

The findings section is clearly subdivided, using effective presentation techniques.

Sandi's schedule varies, but on this day she worked from 8:00 a.m. to 4:30 p.m. Here's what we packed into those hours:

8:00 - 9:00	met with her supervisor, Ruth Davidson, and replied to phone messages
9:00 - 10:00	led a stretching class for seniors
10:15 - 12:00	did paperwork
12:00 - 12:30	ate lunch (a healthy one, of course)
12:30 - 2:00	cleaned the pool and led a water aerobics class
2:15 - 3:00	inspected public tennis courts
3:00 - 4:30	worked on program planning

The report is factual and objective.

A Recreational Director's Work

Sandi showed me that a rec director is always on the go doing many different tasks:

The style is conversational.

Teaching Classes: Sandi led two fitness classes with about twenty people in each. She aimed each workout at the right level for the class, taught them how to do the exercises right, and gave them a nonstop pep talk.

Doing Paperwork: Sandi did a lot of administrative work.

1. She answered phone messages and mail. For example, she got a letter from the Hobart Bike Club asking her to help them plan a bike trail. She read the letter, thought about the idea, and phoned the club's president to set up a meeting.

2. She does paperwork to make sure programs run smoothly. For example, she . . .
   * ordered Red Cross certificates and pool supplies,
   * set up schedules for lifeguards and soccer refs,
   * sorted softball applications and set up teams,
   * made up a work order to repair a tennis court.

Details and examples support each point.

Creating and Planning Programs: What I enjoyed most was helping Sandi work on future programs. She explained how she researches them and writes proposals for her supervisor and the city council. For example, with the help of the Hobart police, she's putting together a rollerblading and bike safety class for kids.

Conclusions About Recreational Directors

Watching Sandi for just one day taught me a lot:

1. A rec director plans and runs many programs that help people enjoy their spare time.

Conclusions clearly follow from findings.

2. A rec director helps people get fit, learn new things, and meet others in their community.

3. A good rec director (like Sandi) needs to . . .
   * be a people person—understand people's needs and get them involved,
   * be fit and understand fitness,
   * be a good communicator—talk, listen, and write well,
   * be a good manager—organize things, people, and time,
   * be creative—come up with new ideas.

Closing comment states the usefulness of the report.

Spending a day with Sandi was positive. What I learned about her work will definitely help me write my report on careers in recreation. I've already written her a thank-you letter telling her this.

230 Writing for the Media

Organizations use the media to communicate with the general public. Regular communication is like regular exercise: it prevents little problems from developing into big ones. Rumors can be dealt with, and the truth can be shared, for example.

Media generally refers to television, radio, and print sources like newspapers and magazines. Because they carry information to masses of people, they're also called the mass media. The media can reach millions (World Cup Soccer fans), or they can focus on a special group (lovers of tuba music).

Here are some of the many types of writing people in business do for mass distribution through the media:

- news releases and newsletters
- pamphlets and brochures
- periodicals (magazines)
- feature articles
- annual reports
- fact sheets and surveys

Understanding the Process

When you write for the media, you become a public-relations writer. It's your job to create an honest dialogue between an organization and the public it serves. Keep these points in mind as you write:

- Open communication makes organizations personal, human.
- Honest writing helps people respond positively to an organization, even if the news is negative.
- Public-relations writing builds relationships with employees, clients, management, and other important groups.

Writing Effectively

1. Do your homework. Get the facts by learning about your organization's history, statistics, people, publications, and positions.

2. Give the straight facts. Even though you write to support your organization, you don't want to hide or distort information.

3. Write in a simple, forceful style, using short to medium length sentences with easily understood words. Make your writing personal yet professional.

INSIDE

Pay careful attention to form. Some types of writing, especially news releases, follow a specific form that the media has come to expect.

231 The News Release

Burlington High School
225 Robert Street
Burlington, WI 53105

Use the
correct form.

FOR IMMEDIATE RELEASE   For more information contact
March 8, 1995   Waynetta Mosser, 414-555-3679

Give the facts:
who, what,
where, and
when.

According to Waynetta Mosser, Burlington High School business
department, 15 students attended Mini-Business World, a two-
day business simulation competition held at the University of
Wisconsin-Whitewater, March 6-7. Professor Richard James,
UW-Whitewater, initiated the team competition 10 years ago.
Other participating area high schools, each sending 15
students, included Waterford, East Troy, and Whitewater.

Be sure that
names, titles,
and all other
facts are
accurate.

Students were divided into 10 six-member teams that
included at least one student from each of the four schools.
In addition to the 10 student teams, there were two teacher
teams—one in each of two divisions. Burlington community
leaders who served as team advisors were Mr. Bruce Spink,
First Banking Center; Mr. Scott Hoffman, Director of the
Community Education Department; and Mr. Dennis Eisenberg,
Executive Director of Southern Lakes United Educators.
Advisors worked with students as they developed their
products, made budgetary decisions, and reacted to market
changes simulated by the master computer.

Corri Henningfeld, a Burlington junior whose team won
(highest net profit) in their division, said each team came up
with a luxury product. Her team's Panther stereo helped them
win a separate television commercial competition as well.

A grant fully funded Burlington's participation in the
simulation.

RESEARCH

Research Writing

Writing the Research Paper

Writing Responsibly

Citing Sources

Student Models

Writing the Research Paper

One of your proudest achievements as a student would be to write a good research paper, since the research paper demands that you "put it together": thinking, speaking, reading, and writing. More than that, the research paper challenges you to take charge of your own education. You're the leader. It's your topic, your curiosity, and your energy that makes it happen. It's a big project, too, with many stages. So if you can write a good research paper, you can be trusted to manage many other complex and time-consuming tasks without losing your wits. If I were your employer, I'd be glad to know that.

What's Ahead?

This section of your handbook provides you with everything you need to write a research paper, from prewriting through the final proof-reading. (This chapter follows the MLA style sheet, the most popular research-paper form in use today.)

Research Update
Prewriting
Writing the First Draft
Revising
Preparing the Final Paper

233 Research Update

Traditionally, students headed straight for their libraries to find information (books, magazines, etc.) for their research papers. Today, students are urged to gather information firsthand by using interviews, observations, questionnaires, and so on. You, as a student, are personally involved in gathering facts, finding examples, and forming ideas. This process makes the whole research experience more meaningful and satisfying.

234 I-Search vs. Re-Search

One method of research that focuses almost entirely on firsthand research of information is the I-Search paper. An I-Search paper begins with an individual's own natural curiosity about something. One person may wonder if he or she has what it takes to become an emergency-room nurse. Another may wonder about the risks and rewards of becoming a police officer.

Once a personal need is identified, I-Searchers set out to find information and answers they need through visits and interviews. I-Searchers use books and magazines only when they are recommended by someone during an interview or a visit. (People first, books second.) An I-Search paper is the story of an individual's own searching adventure, a story that naturally includes original thought and genuine feelings.

235 A Personalized Approach

Here's what we recommend for your next research paper:

Get involved.	Start by selecting a subject that really interests you, and then carry out your research personally, using both primary and secondary sources.
Keep a journal.	Consider writing in a journal during your research. Thinking and writing about your work will help you make sense of and evaluate new information.
Personalize it.	Present the results of your searching in a way that sounds as if it comes from you. The more your research paper comes from your own thinking, the more you (and your readers) will like it.
Follow the steps.	Finally, we recommend that you follow the 20 steps suggested on the following pages.

Steps in the Process

> "My idea of research is to look at the thing from all sides; the person who has seen the animal, how the animal behaves, and so on."
>
> —Marianne Moore

236 Prewriting

Finding a Research Topic

1 Select an interesting subject.

Meaningful research projects start with a personal need to know or learn about something. Which used car has the best repair record? What are the best career opportunities for young people today? What are the real costs and benefits of a college education? Select a general subject that interests you and seems practical for the time and resources available. Also, get your teacher's approval for your subject.

2 Gather some general information.

Once you've selected a general subject, talk with people who may know something about your subject. Teachers in your school may be able to provide basic information about your subject, or they may direct you to local experts. Then do some exploratory reading in reference books, magazines, and newspapers. Look for videos, CD's, and on-line information.

NOTE: Ask an aide to help you find the basic sources of information in the media center or local library. Some computer databases may be available to you, as well as the usual resources. (See 359-383.)

3 Limit your subject.

As you read about your subject, ask questions such as *What do I really want to know about this subject? What makes it worth investigating? What interests me the most about it?* These types of questions will help you limit your subject. Put this limited subject into a **focus** or **thesis statement**—a sentence that states what you plan to research. Or state your focus in the form of a research question. The student model (307-310) uses the following thesis statement: "Car designers have to think up new safety features to deal with the greater dangers of increasingly higher speeds."

NOTE: Don't be surprised if your thesis changes as you do your research. You will probably consider a number of focuses before you settle upon the one you will finally use for your paper.

237 Searching for Information

4 Prepare a preliminary bibliography.

Continue to look for information related to your thesis statement. Often, you can find new sources by checking the bibliographies in books and materials you've already reviewed. Then make a list of these sources and put this information into a computer or on 3- by 5-inch cards. Arrange the cards in alphabetical order by the authors' last names. If you don't know the name of an author, alphabetize by the first word in the title (not including *A, An,* or *The*). Either number each entry in your computer list, or number each card in the upper right-hand corner.

Sample Bibliography Card

Flowers, Jack. "What's New in
NASCAR." Popular Mechanics
June 1994: 44–45.
②

Sample Note Card

Modified Steering Wheel   ②

- first appeared at 1994 Daytona 500
- much thicker, softer padding than
  before
- better impact protection
  "easier on the driver's wrists and
  finger muscles in long races"
                (p. 44)

5 Take notes.

As you begin reading the material listed in your bibliography, take notes and write down quotations related to your specific subject.

- Keep notes on cards of the same size and style (4- by 6-inch cards are recommended).
- Write down important details and quotations, along with the page numbers where this information can be found. Also place the number of the related bibliography card in the upper right-hand corner.
- Place quotation marks around word-for-word quotations.
- Use the ellipsis (. . .) when you leave words out of a quotation. Use brackets around words you add to a quotation. (See 246.)
- Look up unfamiliar words. If you find that a particular word is important, copy its definition onto a note card.
- Give each card a descriptive heading (a word or phrase to highlight the main idea of that note card: *Homeless—personal close-up*).

238 Note Taking: A Closer Look

Summarize ● To summarize, reduce what you have read to a few important points using your own words.

Paraphrase ● To paraphrase, restate what you have read using your own words. Use this method when you are trying to retrace the thinking of one of your sources. Put quotation marks around only key words or phrases you borrow directly from the sources. (See 245-246.)

Quote Directly ● To quote someone directly, record the statement or idea word for word and put quotation marks before and after.

6 Collect information from primary sources.

If possible, collect firsthand information by conducting interviews, passing out questionnaires, or making observations. (See 339-344.)

Designing a Writing Plan

7 Write your working outline.

Organize your note cards into their most logical order and use them to construct a working outline. Your descriptive headings may be used as main points and subpoints in your outline. (See 311.)

8 Continue developing your research.

Search for any additional information that may be needed to develop your focus, or thesis. Reconsider the thesis statement you wrote in step 3 to see if your thoughts about it have changed.

9 Revise your outline.

Revise your working outline as necessary when you find new information.

use your note cards to construct a working outline.

> "The guiding question in research is 'So what?' Answer that question in every sentence and you will become a great scholar; answer it once a page in a ten-page paper and you'll write a good one."
>
> —Donald N. McCloskey

239 Writing the First Draft

10 Write the introduction.

The introduction should do two things. The first part should say something interesting, surprising, or personal about your subject to gain your readers' attention. (See the list below for ideas.) The second part should identify the specific focus, or thesis, of your research.

- Start out with a revealing story or quotation.
- Give important background information.
- Offer a series of interesting or surprising facts.
- Provide important definitions.
- State your reason for choosing this subject.

11 Write the body.

The next step is to write the main part of your research paper, the part that supports or proves your thesis. There are two ways to proceed. You may write freely and openly, or you may work systematically, carefully following your notes and working outline.

Writing Freely and Openly

One way to go about writing the body of your research paper is to put your outline and note cards aside and write as much as you can on your own. Refer to your note cards only when you need a quotation, specific facts, or figures.

After you have completed this first writing, review your outline and note cards to see if you have missed or misplaced any important points. Then continue writing, filling in or reorganizing ideas as you go along.

Writing Systematically

You may also write the body of your paper more systematically—carefully following your working outline and note cards right from the start. Begin by laying out the first section of note cards (those covering the first main point in your working outline). Then write a general statement that covers the first main point. Using the note cards you have in front of you, add supporting facts and details. Repeat this process until you have dealt with all the main points in your outline.

240 Writing Tips

- Use your own words as much as possible. Use direct quotations only when the wording in the quotation is exactly as you want it.

- Present your ideas honestly and clearly. When you have something meaningful to say, you are more likely to write an interesting paper.

- Avoid fragments, abbreviations, or slang ("you know," "no way," "forget it") in your writing. Work to achieve a semiformal style.

- Drop statements that you cannot support with facts and details.

12 Write the conclusion.

The final section, or **conclusion**, of your paper should leave the readers with a clear understanding of the importance of your research. Review the important points you have made and draw a final conclusion. In a more personal approach, you may discuss how your research has strengthened or changed your thinking about your subject.

> "[Good] writing is concise. A sentence should contain no unnecessary words, a paragraph no unnecessary sentences, for the same reason that a drawing should have no unnecessary lines and a machine no unnecessary parts."
>
> —William Strunk

241 Revising

13 Revise your first draft at least two times.

Revise once to make sure you have covered all of the main points and effectively supported them. Revise a second time to make sure all of your sentences are clear and smooth. (See "A Guide to Revising," 028-035, for help.)

14 Document your sources.

Put the Works Cited section (bibliography) together, listing all of the sources you have cited in your paper. (See 257-300 for appropriate style guidelines.) Give credit in your paper for ideas and direct quotations that you have used from different sources. (See 247-256.) Also make sure you have copied the ideas and quotations accurately.

"Only the hand that erases can write the true thing."

—Meister Eckhart

242 Preparing the Final Paper

15 Edit your final revision.

Check and correct punctuation, capitalization, usage, and grammar. (See the "Proofreader's Guide," 575-788, for help.)

16 Prepare your final copy.

If you use a computer, print your final copy on a good quality printer. Leave a margin of one inch on all sides, except for page numbers. Double-space your entire paper, including long quotations and the Works Cited section. (See 306-318 for examples.)

17 Arrange and number your pages.

Begin numbering with the first page of your paper and continue through the Works Cited section. Type your last name before each page number. Place the page numbers in the upper right-hand corner, one-half inch from the top and even with the right-hand margin.

18 Add identifying information.

Type your name, the teacher's name, the course title, and the date in the upper left corner of the first page of the paper. (Begin one inch from the top and double-space throughout.) Center the title (double-space before and after); then type the first line of the paper. (See 307.)

INSIDE

info

If your instructor requires a title page, center the title one-third of the way down from the top of the page; then center your name, the name of the instructor, and any additional information two-thirds of the way down. (See 311.)

19 Type your final outline.

If you need to submit a final outline, make sure it follows the final version of your paper. (See 311.) Double-space your outline and number its pages with small Roman numerals.

20 Check your paper from start to finish.

When you hand in your paper, it should be error free.

Writing Responsibly

A research paper—like any other type of meaningful writing—should be a personal process of discovering new information. Once you've collected the information, you need to go about the business of making it part of your own thinking. You should look carefully at the points on which your sources agree and disagree, and decide which ones offer the best arguments and why. You can then determine how these findings stand up to your own thinking. Research will become your own when you

- ◉ believe in the subject,
- ◉ give yourself enough time to learn about it,
- ◉ involve yourself in active, thorough research, and
- ◉ make your own voice the primary voice in your writing.

What's Ahead?

This chapter will help you understand what you can and cannot do when you use other people's words and ideas in your research paper:

Writing Paraphrases

Using Quoted Material

244 Writing Paraphrases

When you write a report or research paper, you need to support your ideas with information from other sources and give credit to those sources. (Not giving credit is a serious error called **plagiarism**.) There are two ways to give proper credit: either quote directly or paraphrase what other people have written. When you **paraphrase**, you use your own words to restate the author's ideas; when you quote, you include the exact words of the author and put quotation marks around them.

Below you'll find some helpful guidelines, followed by two model paraphrases that could have been used in a research paper. One model is a basic paraphrase; the other is a paraphrase containing a direct quotation.

Quick Guide

1. Skim the selection first to get the overall meaning. (Concentrate on just the main ideas, not the details.)

2. Read the selection carefully, paying particular attention to key words and phrases. (Check the meaning of unfamiliar words.)

3. Try listing the main ideas on a piece of paper—without looking at the selection.

4. Review the selection another time so that you have the overall meaning clearly in mind as you begin to write.

5. Write your paraphrase, using your own words to restate the author's ideas. Keep the following points in mind:

- Stick to the essential information.
- State each important idea as clearly and concisely (briefly) as possible.
- Put quotation marks around key words or phrases taken directly from the source. (See 245.)
- Arrange the ideas into a smooth, logical order. (Your version of the author's views should be as easy to read as the original—maybe easier.)

6. Check your final summary by asking these questions:

- Have I kept the author's ideas and point of view clear in my paraphrase? Have I quoted where necessary?
- Have I cut enough of the original? Too much?
- Could another person get the author's main idea by simply reading my paraphrase?

245 Original Source

The human brain, once surrounded by myth and misconception, is no longer such a mystery. It is now understood to be the supervisory center of the nervous system that controls all voluntary (eating and thinking) and most involuntary behavior (blinking and breathing).

The brain functions by receiving information from nerve cells that are located throughout the body. Recent research has provided a clear picture of exactly what happens when information first reaches the brain. It has been discovered that the cells that receive the information in the cortex of the brain are arranged in a regular pattern in columns. The columns are, in turn, arranged into a series of "hypercolumns." Each cell within each column has a specific responsibility to perceive and analyze certain kinds of incoming information. Within the columns, the analysis of this information follows a formal sequence.

Eventually, the information is relayed to the higher centers of the brain where a complete picture is assembled. The brain then evaluates the information and either sends a return message or stores the information for later use. The return message travels through the body in the form of electrical and chemical signals via the billions of nerve cells (neurons). When the message reaches its destination, the muscles or glands respond with the appropriate reaction.

Basic Paraphrase

The human brain controls all voluntary and most involuntary behavior. The process begins when the brain receives information from nerve cells located throughout the body. This information is received by brain cells arranged in a series of columns with each cell having a specific responsibility to analyze certain kinds of incoming information. After the information has been analyzed, it is sent to the higher centers of the brain where a complete picture is put together. The brain then evaluates the information and either stores it for later use or sends a return message to the muscles and glands, which react appropriately ("The Brain" 26).

Paraphrase with Quotation

The human brain controls all voluntary and most involuntary behavior. The process begins when the brain receives information from nerve cells located throughout the body. "The cells that receive the information in the cortex of the brain are arranged in a regular pattern in columns. . . . Each cell within each column has a specific responsibility to . . . analyze certain kinds of incoming information" ("The Brain" 26). After the information has been analyzed, it is sent to the higher centers of the brain where a complete picture is put together. The brain then evaluates the information and either stores it for later use or sends a return message to the muscles and glands, which react appropriately.

Using Quoted Material

246 Quick Guide

A quotation can be a single word or an entire paragraph. You should choose quotations carefully, keep them as brief as possible, and use them only when they are interesting or necessary. When you quote directly, be sure that the wording, capitalization, and punctuation are the same as that in the original work. Any changes you make should be clearly marked for your readers.

Short Quotations

If a quotation is four typed lines or fewer, work it into the body of your paper and put quotation marks around it.

Long Quotations

Quotations of more than four typed lines should be set off from the rest of the writing by indenting each line 10 spaces and double-spacing the material. When quoting two or more paragraphs, indent the first line of each paragraph an extra three spaces. Do not use quotation marks.

Leave two spaces after a longer quotation before you cite a parenthetical reference. Generally, a colon is used to introduce quotations set off from the text. (See 630 for more information.)

Partial Quotations

If you want to leave out part of the quotation, use an ellipsis to signify the omission. An ellipsis (. . .) is three periods with a space before and after each one. (See 578.)

NOTE: Anything you take out of a quotation should not change the author's original meaning.

Adding to Quotations

Use brackets [like this] to signify any material you add within a quotation to help clarify its meaning.

Quoting Poetry

When quoting up to three lines of poetry, use quotation marks and work the lines into your writing. Use a diagonal (/) to show where each line of verse ends. For verse quotations of four lines or more, indent each line 10 spaces and double-space. Do not use quotation marks.

To show that you have left out a line or more of verse, make a line of spaced periods the approximate length of a complete line of the poem.

Citing Sources

247 Parenthetical References

The *MLA Handbook for Writers of Research Papers* suggests giving credit for your sources of information in the body of your research paper. To give credit, simply insert the appropriate information (usually the author and page number) in parentheses after the words or ideas taken from another source. Place them where a pause would naturally occur to avoid disrupting the flow of your writing (usually at the end of a sentence).

> The bubonic plague appeared in two forms, one affecting the bloodstream and spread by contact, the other infecting the lungs and spread by breathing (Tuchman 92).

Keep two points in mind when citing sources. First, indicate as precisely as you can where you found this information. (Use page numbers, volume numbers, acts, chapters, etc.) Second, make sure all of your sources are listed in the Works Cited section of your paper.

What's Ahead?

This chapter will help you understand how and when to "cite sources" (give credit) in your research paper:

Parenthetical References

Works Cited

Other Forms of Documentation

248 **One Author: Citing a Complete Work**

You do not need a parenthetical reference if you identify the author in your text. (See the first entry below.) However, you must give the author's last name in a parenthetical reference if it is not mentioned in the text. (See the second entry below.) A parenthetical reference could begin with an editor, a translator, a speaker, or an artist instead of the author if that is how the work is listed in the Works Cited section.

With Author in Text (This is the preferred way of citing a complete work.)

In No Need for Hunger, Robert Spitzer recommends that the U.S. government develop a new foreign policy to help Third World countries overcome poverty and hunger.

Without Author in Text

No Need for Hunger recommends that the U.S. government develop a new foreign policy to help Third World countries overcome poverty and hunger (Spitzer).

249 **One Author: Citing Part of a Work**

List the necessary page numbers in parentheses if you borrow words or ideas from a particular work. Leave a space between the author's last name and the page reference. No punctuation is needed.

With Author in Text

Bullough writes that genetic engineering was dubbed "eugenics" by a cousin of Darwin's, Sir Francis Galton, in 1885 (5).

Without Author in Text

Genetic engineering was dubbed "eugenics" by a cousin of Darwin's, Sir Francis Galton, in 1885 (Bullough 5).

250 **Two or Three Authors**

Give the last names of every author in the same order that they appear in the Works Cited section. (The correct order of the authors' names can be found on the title page of the book.)

Students learned more than a full year's Spanish in ten days using the complete supermemory method (Ostrander and Schroeder 51).

251 **More Than Three Authors**

Give the first author's last name as it appears in the Works Cited section followed by *et al.* or *and others* with no punctuation in between.

According to Culligan and others, communication on the job is more than talking; it is "inseparable from your total behavior" (111).

252 Corporate Author

If a book or other work was written by a committee or task force, it is said to have a *corporate* author. If the corporate name is long, include it in the text (rather than in parentheses) to avoid disrupting the flow of your writing. Use a shortened form of the name in the text and in references after the full name has been used at least once. For example, *Task Force* may be used for *Task Force on Education for Economic Growth* after the full name has been used at least once.

> The thesis of the Task Force's report is that economic success depends on our ability to improve large-scale education and training as quickly as possible (14).

253 An Anonymous Book (Work)

When there is no author listed, give the title or a shortened version of the title as it appears in the Works Cited section. (No page numbers are needed for single-page articles or nonprint sources.)

> The Information Please Almanac states that drinking water can make up 20 percent of a person's total exposure to lead (572).

254 Literary Works: Verse Plays and Poems

Cite verse (plays and poems) by divisions (act, scene, canto, book, part, and lines) using Arabic numerals unless your teacher prefers Roman numerals. Use periods to separate the various parts. If you are citing lines only, use the word *line* or *lines* in your first reference and numbers only in additional references.

> In the first act of the play named after him, Hamlet comments, "How weary, stale, flat and unprofitable, / Seem to me all the uses of this world" (1.2.133-134).

NOTE: A diagonal is used to show where each new line of verse begins.

Verse quotations of more than three lines should be indented one inch (10 spaces) and double-spaced. Each line of the poem or play begins a new line of the quotation; do not run the lines together.

> James A. Autry talks about "business" in his poem "Threads":
>
>> Listen.
>> In every office
>> you hear the threads
>> of love and joy and fear and guilt,
>> the cries for celebration and reassurance
>> and somehow you know that connecting those threads
>> is what you are supposed to do
>> and business takes care of itself. (23-30)

255 Literary Works: Prose

To cite prose (novels, short stories), list more than the page number if the work is available in several editions. Give the page reference first, and then add a chapter, section, or book number in abbreviated form after a semicolon.

> In The House of Seven Spirits, Isabel Allende describes Marcos, "dressed in mechanic's overalls, with huge racer's goggles and an explorer's helmet" (13; ch. 1).

When you are quoting prose that takes more than four typed lines, indent each line of the quotation one inch (10 spaces) and double-space it. In this case, you put the parenthetical citation (the pages and chapter numbers) *outside* the end punctuation mark of the quotation itself. Skip two spaces before you begin the citation.

> Allende describes the flying machine that Marcos has assembled:
>> The contraption lay with its stomach on terra firma, heavy and sluggish and looking more like a wounded duck than like one of those newfangled airplanes they were starting to produce in the United States. There was nothing in its appearance to suggest that it could move, much less take flight across the snowy peaks. (12; ch. 1)

256 Indirect Source

If you cite an indirect source—someone's remarks published in a second source—use the abbreviation *qtd. in* (quoted in) before the indirect source in your reference.

> Paton improved the conditions in Diepkloof [a prison] by "removing all the more obvious aids to detention. The dormitories are open at night: the great barred gate is gone" (qtd. in Callan xviii).

THE BOTTOM LINE

When you give credit to your sources within the research paper, follow these guidelines:

◉ Insert the appropriate information (usually author and page number) in parentheses after the words or ideas borrowed from another source.

◉ Place your parentheses where a pause would naturally occur (usually at the end of a sentence).

◉ Make sure all the sources you cite in your paper are also listed on your Works Cited page.

257 Works Cited

The Works Cited section includes all of the sources you have cited (referred to) in your text. It does not include any sources you may have read or studied but did not refer to in your paper (that's a bibliography). Begin your list of works cited on a new page (the next page after the text), and number each page, continuing from the last page of the text. The guidelines that follow describe the form of the Works Cited section.

The Works Cited Section

258 Quick Guide

1. Type the page number in the upper right-hand corner, one-half inch from the top of the page.

2. Center the title *Works Cited* one inch from the top; then double-space before the first entry.

3. Begin each entry flush with the left margin. If the entry runs more than one line, indent additional lines one-half inch (five spaces).

4. Double-space each entry and between entries.

5. List each entry alphabetically by the author's last name. If there is no author, use the first word of the title (disregard *A, An, The*).

6. A basic entry for a book would be as follows:

Guillermo, Kathy Snow. Monkey Business. Washington, DC:

National Press Books, 1993.

NOTE: For both books and periodicals, leave two spaces after the author and after the title. Leave a single space between other items of the publication information.

7. A basic entry for a periodical (a magazine) would be as follows:

Murr, Andrew. "The High Cost of Defense." Newsweek 21 Mar.

1994: 70.

8. Check the following pages for specific information on other kinds of entries.

Model Works Cited Entries: Books

The entries that follow illustrate the information needed to cite books, sections of a book, pamphlets, and government publications.

259 ## One Author

> Angell, David. The Internet Business Companion: Growing Your Business in the Electronic Age. Reading, MA: Addison-Wesley, 1995.

260 ## Two or Three Authors

> Bystydzienski, Jill M., and Estelle P. Resnik. Women in Cross-Cultural Transitions. Bloomington, IN: Phi Delta Kappa Educational Foundation, 1994.

261 ## More Than Three Authors

> Marine, April, et al. Internet: Getting Started. Englewood Cliffs, NJ: PTR Prentice Hall, 1994.

262 ## A Single Work from an Anthology

> Green, Mark. "The Pro-PAC Backlash: When Money Talks, Is it Democracy?" Points of View. Ed. Robert E. Diclerico and Allan S. Hammock. 3rd ed. New York: Random House, 1986. 154.

NOTE: If you cite a complete anthology, begin the entry with the editors.

> Diclerico, Robert E., and Allan S. Hammock, eds. Points of View. 3rd ed. New York: Random House, 1986.

263 Two or More Books by the Same Author

List the books alphabetically according to title. After the first entry, substitute three hyphens for the author's name.

> Laurence, Peter J. The Peter Pyramid. New York: William
>
> Morrow, 1986.
>
> - - -. Why Things Go Wrong. New York: William Morrow, 1985.

264 A Corporate Group Author

> United States. Dept. of Labor. Bureau of Statistics. Occupational
>
> Outlook Handbook. Washington: GPO, 1994.

265 An Anonymous Book

> The World Almanac Book of the Strange. New York: New Ameri-
>
> can Library, 1977.

NOTE: The Bible is considered an anonymous book. Documentation should read exactly as it is printed on the title page.

> The Jerusalem Bible. Garden City, NY: Doubleday, 1966.

266 A Multivolume Work

> Ziegler, Alan. The Writing Workshop. Vol. 2. New York: Teachers
>
> and Writers, 1984.

NOTE: If you cite two or more volumes in a multivolume work, give the total number of volumes after the title.

> Barnouw, Eric, ed. International Encyclopedia of Communications.
>
> 9 vols. New York: Oxford University Press, 1989.

267 An Introduction, a Preface, a Foreword, or an Afterword

> Peter, Tom. Foreword. The Service Edge. By Ron Zemke. New
>
> York: New American Library, 1989. vi-x.

NOTE: Give only the author's last name after *By* if he or she is the author of the piece cited and the complete work.

> Burnett, Rebecca E. Preface. Technical Communication. By Bur-
>
> nett. Belmont, CA: Wadsworth, 1990. xvi-xx.

268 Cross-References

To avoid unnecessary repetition when citing two or more entries from a larger collection, you may cite the collection once with complete publication information (see Hall below). The individual entries (see Abbey and Baldwin below) can then be cross-referenced by listing the author, title of the piece, editor of the collection, and page numbers.

> Abbey, Edward. "The Most Beautiful Place on Earth." Hall 225-41.
>
> Baldwin, James. "Notes of a Native Son." Hall 164-83.
>
> Hall, Donald, ed. The Contemporary Essay. New York: Bedford-
>
> St. Martin's, 1984.

269 An Edition

An edition refers to the particular publication you are citing, as in the 3rd edition. But the term "edition" also refers to the work of one person that is prepared by another person, an editor.

> Shakespeare, William. The Merchant of Venice. Ed. Sylvan
>
> Barnet. New York: Signet-NAL, 1963.

270 A Translation

> Turgenev, Ivan Sergeevich. Fathers and Sons. Trans. Michael R.
>
> Katz. New York: W. W. Norton, 1994.

271 An Article in a Reference Book

It is not necessary to give full publication information for familiar reference works (encyclopedias and dictionaries). For these titles, list only the edition (if available) and the publication year. If an article is initialed, check the index of authors (in the opening section of each volume) for the author's full name.

> "Multi-tasking." Jargon: An Informal Dictionary of Computer Terms.
>
> 1993 ed.
>
> "Technical Education." Encyclopedia Americana. 1992 ed.
>
> Lum, P. Andrea. "Computerized Tomography." World Book. 1994 ed.

272 Pamphlet with No Author or Publication Information Stated

If known, list the country of publication [in brackets]. Use N.p. (no place) if the country is unknown, n.p. (no publisher) if the publisher is unknown, and n.d. if the date is unknown.

> Pedestrian Safety. [United States]: n.p., n.d.

273 **Signed Pamphlet**

Treat a pamphlet as you would a book.

Grayson, George W. The North American Free Trade Agreement.

New York: Foreign Policy Association, Inc., 1993.

274 **Government Publications**

State the name of the government (country, state, etc.) followed by the name of the agency.

United States. Federal Trade Commission. Shopping by Mail or

Phone. Washington: GPO, 1994.

275 **A Book in a Series**

Give the series name and number (if any) before the publication information.

Bishop, Jack. Ralph Ellison. Black Americans of Achievement.

New York: Chelsea House, 1988.

276 **A Publisher's Imprint**

The name of a publisher's imprint appears above the publisher's name on the title page. Give the imprint followed by a hyphen and the name of the publisher (Signet-NAL).

Solzhenitsyn, Alexander. One Day in the Life of Ivan Denisovich.

Trans. Ralph Parker. New York: Signet-NAL, 1963.

277 **A Book with a Title Within a Title**

If the title contains a title normally in quotation marks, keep the quotation marks and underline the entire title.

Harte, Bret. "The Outcasts of Poker Flat" and Other Stories.

New York: Signet-NAL, 1961.

NOTE: If the title contains a title normally underlined, do not underline it in your entry, as in this example: A Tale of Two Cities as History.

278 **A Reference Book on CD-ROM**

If you use an encyclopedia or other reference book recorded on CD-ROM, use the form below.

Software Tool Works Multimedia Encyclopedia. CD-ROM. Novato,

CA: Software Tool Works, 1991.

Model Works Cited Entries: Periodicals

The entries that follow illustrate the information and arrangement needed to cite periodicals.

279 **Signed Article in a Magazine**

> Tully, Shawn. "The Universal Teenager." Fortune 4 Apr. 1994: 14-16.

280 **Unsigned Article in a Magazine**

> "Crafts Fair Showcases Women." Entrepreneur May 1995: 23.

281 **An Article in a Scholarly Journal**

> Chu, Wujin. "Costs and Benefits of Hard-Sell." Journal of
>
> Marketing Research 32.2 (1995): 97-102.

NOTE: Journals are usually issued no more than four times a year. Number 32 refers to the volume. The issue number is not needed if the page numbers in a volume continue from one issue to the next. If the page numbers start over with each issue, then put a period between the volume number and issue number: 32.2.

282 **Signed Newspaper Article**

> Bleakley, Fred R. "Companies' Profits Grew 48% Despite Economy."
>
> Wall Street Journal 1 May 1995, midwest ed.: 1.

NOTE: Cite the edition of a major daily newspaper (if given) after the date (1 May 1995, midwest ed.: 1). To cite an article in a lettered section of the newspaper, list the section after the page number. (For example, 4A would refer to page 4 in section A of the newspaper.) If the sections are numbered, however, use a comma after the year; then indicate sec. 1, 2, 3, etc., followed by a colon and the page number.

283 Unsigned Newspaper Article

"African Roots of American Music Traced at Westchester College

Program." Amsterdam News [New York] 29 Jan. 1994, sec. 1: 21.

NOTE: If the unsigned article is an editorial, put *Editorial* after the title. Also, if the city of publication is included in the newspaper's name, you do not have to add it in brackets.

284 A Letter to the Editor

Epsy, Mike. Letter. "Abolishing the Farmer's Home Administration."

Washington Post 5 Mar. 1994, 5A.

285 A Review

Olsen, Jack. "Brains and Industry." Rev. of Land of Opportunity,

by Sarah Marr New York Times 23 Apr. 1995, sec. 3: 28.

NOTE: If you cite the review of a work by an editor or a translator, use *ed.* or *trans.* instead of *by*.

286 Published Interview

O'Leary, Hazel. "Hazel O'Leary." By Linda Turbyville. Omni Apr.

1995: 75+.

NOTE: Type the word *Interview* after the interviewee's name if the interview is untitled.

287 A Title or Quotation Within an Article's Title

Merrill, Susan F. "'Sunday Morning' Thoughts." English Journal

76.6 (1987): 63.

NOTE: Use single quotation marks around the shorter title if it is a title normally punctuated with quotation marks.

288 An Article Reprinted in a Loose-Leaf Collection

O'Connell, Loraine. "Busy Teens Feel the Beep." Orlando Sentinel

7 Jan. 1993: E1+. Youth. Ed. Eleanor Goldstein. Vol. 4.

Boca Raton, FL: SIRS, 1993. Art. 41.

NOTE: The entry begins with original publication information and ends with the name of the loose-leaf volume (Youth), editor, volume number, publication information including name of the *information service* (Social Issues Resources Series), and the article number.

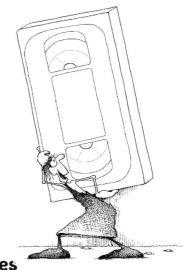

Model Works Cited Entries: Other Print and Nonprint Sources

289 A Publication on Diskette

Barker, Anthony. The New Earth Science. Diskette. Cincinnati:

Freeman's Press, 1991.

290 Television and Radio Programs

If your reference is primarily to the work of an individual, cite that person before the title. Otherwise, you may give other pertinent information (writer, director, producer, narrator, etc.) after the main title of the program (underlined).

"The Ultimate Road Trip: Traveling in Cyberspace." 48 Hours.

CBS. WBBM, Chicago. 13 Apr. 1995.

291 Recordings

Shocked, Michelle. Arkansas Traveler. LP. Polygram Records,

Inc., 1992.

NOTE: The person cited first in a recording (composer, conductor, performer, etc.) depends on the emphasis you want. If citing the booklet, liner notes, etc., accompanying a recording, give the author's name, title of material, and description (*Liner notes*) before the regular bibliographic information.

Also, if the recording is on CD, you need not indicate so. Other forms should be noted, however: *LP* for long-playing record, *Audiocassette,* etc.

292 Audiocassette

Allen, Jeffrey G. How to Turn an Interview into a Job. Audiocassette.

Simon and Schuster, 1985. 52 min.

93 **Films**

If it is important, cite the size and length of the film (for example: 16 mm, 32 min.) after the date.

> Trading Places. Dir. John Landis. Perf. Dan Akroyd, Eddie Murphy,
>
> Ralph Bellamy, and Jamie Lee Curtis. Paramount, 1983.

94 **Filmstrips, Slide Programs, and Videocassettes**

Cite the medium (filmstrip, slide program, etc.) after the title.

> How to Leave Your Job and Buy a Business of Your Own. Video-
>
> cassette. Self-Reliance Press, Inc., 1990. 55 min.

95 **Published Letters**

> Bottomley, Edwin. "To Father." 6 Dec. 1843. An English Settler in
>
> Pioneer Wisconsin: The Letters of Edwin Bottomley. Ed. Milo
>
> M. Quaife. Madison: State Historical Society, 1918. 60-62.

NOTE: "To Father" and 6 Dec. 1843 refer to the cited letter.

96 **Letter Received by the Author (Yourself)**

> Thomas, Bob. Letter to the author. 10 Jan. 1989.

97 **Personal Interview**

> Brooks, Sarah. Personal interview. 15 Oct. 1993.

98 **Maps and Charts**

> Wisconsin Territory. Map. Madison: Wisconsin Trails, 1988.

99 **Cartoons**

> Trudeau, Garry. "Doonesbury." Cartoon. Chicago Tribune 23 Dec.
>
> 1988, sec. 5: 6.

00 **Lectures, Speeches, and Addresses**

> Angelou, Maya. Address. Opening General Sess. NCTE Conven-
>
> tion. Adam's Mark Hotel, St. Louis. 18 Nov. 1988.

NOTE: If known, give the speech's title in quotation marks instead of the label *Address, Lecture,* or *Speech.*

301

Abbreviations for Research Papers

anon.	anonymous
bk., bks.	book(s)
©	copyright
chap., ch., chs.	chapter(s)
comp.	compiler, compiled, compiled by
ed., eds.	editor(s), edition(s), edited by
e.g.	for example; *exempli gratia*
et al.	and others; *et alii*
et seq.	and the following; *et sequens*
ex.	example
f., ff.	and the following page(s)
fig., figs.	figure(s)
GPO	Government Printing Office, Washington, DC
ibid.	in the same place as quoted above; *ibidem*
i.e.	that is; *id est*
ill., illus.	illustration, illustrated by
introd.	introduction, introduced by
l., ll.	line(s)
loc. cit.	in the place cited; *loco citato*
MS, MSS	manuscript(s)
narr., narrs.	narrated by, narrator(s)
n.d.	no date given
no., nos.	number(s)
n. pag.	no pagination
n.p.	no place of publication and/or no publisher given
op. cit.	in the work cited; *opere citato*
p., pp.	page(s)
pub. (or publ.), pubs.	published by, publication(s)
rev.	revised by, revision, review, reviewed by
rpt.	reprinted (by), reprint
sc.	scene
sec., secs.	section(s)
sic	thus (used within brackets to indicate an error is that way in the original)
tr., trans.	translator, translation
v., vv. (or vs., vss.)	verse(s)
viz.	namely; *videlicet*
vol., vols.	volume(s): capitalize when used with Roman numerals

302 Other Forms of Documentation

Use the guide below and the model notes on the following page **only if** you have been instructed to use footnotes or endnotes in your research paper instead of parenthetical references. Endnotes appear at the end of the text of your paper on a separate page; footnotes appear at the bottom of the pages in the text. The first endnote or footnote to a work contains the publication information found in the Works Cited section plus a page reference. Second and later references to a particular work contain less information. (See 304-305.)

Information to Include

Endnotes and footnotes contain all the information a reader would need to locate the source:

- ◉ . . . . **author's name** in normal order
- ◉ . . . . the **title** of the work
- ◉ . . . . **publication facts** (publisher, place, and date)
- ◉ . . . . specific **page reference** of the source

Using Footnotes and Endnotes
303 Quick Guide

1. Number your notes consecutively throughout a paper.

2. Place numbers at the end of a sentence or a clause so you don't interrupt the flow of ideas.

3. Raise all note numbers slightly above the typed line; leave one space after the number.

4. Indent the first line of each endnote or footnote one-half inch (five spaces).

5. For endnotes, center the title *Notes* one inch from the top of the endnote page. Double-space, indent one-half inch (five spaces), and type the note number slightly above the line. Leave one space and enter the reference. Additional lines in each note should be flush with the left-hand margin. Double-space throughout.

6. For footnotes, double-space twice between the last line of the text on a page and the first footnote. Single-space each entry and double-space between them. If a note continues to the next page, type a line one double space below the text on that page. Double-space again and continue the footnote.

Model Footnotes and Endnotes

304 ## First References

The model notes below illustrate the information needed the first time you refer to a source:

Book by One Author

[1] Arnold Shaw, Black Popular Music in America: From the Spirituals, Minstrels, and Ragtime to Soul, Disco, and Hip-Hop (New York: Schirmer Books, 1986) 34.

Article in a Magazine

[2] Shawn Tully, "The Universal Teenager," Fortune 4 Apr. 1994: 14-16.

Newspaper Article

[3] Alessandra Stanley, "Russians Find Their Heroes in Mexican TV Soap Operas," New York Times 20 Mar. 1994, national ed.: 1.

Personal Interview

[4] Sarah Brooks, personal interview, 15 Oct. 1993.

Periodically Published Database on CD–ROM

[5] Patricia Ackley, "Jobs of the Twenty-First Century," New Rochelle Informer 15 Apr. 1994: A4, New Rochelle Informer Ondisc, CD-ROM, Info-Line, Oct. 1994.

Material from On–Line Computer Service

[6] Douglas Stempel, "Loving Our Heritage," Annapolis Reporter 3 July 1992: 12, History Index, on-line, Comptell, 13 Nov. 1995.

305 ## Second and Later References

If you have fully documented a work in an endnote or a footnote, your succeeding references need only include the author's last name (or the title if no author) and the pages cited.

Book by One Author

[7] Shaw 45.

[8] Shaw 13-17.

NOTE: Simply repeat the necessary information—the author or title and page numbers—even when you are referring to the same work two or more times in a sequence.

Student Models

Before you put your final research paper together, you may want to check your work against other students' papers and see how it measures up. On the following pages, you will find two student papers. The first is a short report that uses only secondary sources (two magazine articles); the second is a longer, more formal report that uses a primary source (interview) along with newspaper and magazine articles.

Higher Speeds Without Sacrificed Safety

The writer of this short report introduces his topic by focusing on the popularity and risks of NASCAR racing. He builds to his thesis in the second paragraph: "Car designers have to think up new safety features to deal with the greater dangers of increasingly higher speeds." The rest of the paper lists and explains three safety innovations, using facts and details from two articles listed on the Works Cited page.

Corporate-Owned Hog Confinements in Iowa

The writer begins her introduction with the traditional notion of pig farming and builds to her thesis in the second paragraph: "The corporate-owned hog confinement promises to drastically change the hog industry in Iowa." She completes her introduction by listing three subtopics to be explored. In the rest of the paper, while examining the subtopics, the writer discusses the effects of hog-farming changes. She includes facts, figures, and expert opinion, ending her research paper with a number of unanswered questions.

Van Ravenswaay 1

Dan Van Ravenswaay
Ms. Kramer
English Class
1 March 1995

Higher Speeds Without Sacrificed Safety

On the NASCAR racing circuit, race-car drivers compete for the Winston Cup by running 31 races at superspeedways all over the country. These races have become very popular. Fans idolize their favorite drivers the way a basketball or football fan looks up to Michael Jordan or Troy Aikman.

Nobody wants to see a NASCAR driver injured or killed, but high-speed crashes happen. What if you had a car that could go 200 miles per hour and you slammed into a wall with it? Common sense and Newton's laws of physics would tell you that both you and your car would be history. Race-car drivers take this kind of risk every time they slip behind the wheel. Car designers and builders have a tough job preventing these tragedies. Motor builders keep giving drivers more horsepower so cars can go faster. Car designers have to think up new safety features to deal with the greater dangers of increasingly higher speeds. Three recent technological changes are helping: specially padded steering wheels, air deflectors, and new suspensions.

The first change is a modified NASCAR steering wheel. A new padded wheel appeared at the Daytona 500 in 1994 (Flowers 44). This wheel has a ring of foam that is much thicker than the old steering wheel's padding. The cushion does a better job of absorbing the impact of the driver's body before he or

---

The writer mentions sports heroes to get the reader's attention.

The writer states his thesis clearly and then lists how he will address it.

Van Ravenswaay 2

she feels the metal tubing underneath. Not only does
this wheel give better impact protection to the driver
in a crash, but it's also softer to the touch and
"easier on the driver's wrists and finger muscles in
long races" (Flowers 44). This padding might seem
like a minor change, but this simple safety feature
makes the sport safer for the drivers.

A second safety feature, air deflectors, helps
keep cars on the ground in an accident or spinout.
Once a car turns sideways on the track, too often it
lifts off the ground. When a car is in the air, it
becomes much more dangerous. It can easily roll
over and cause a major accident involving other cars.
After the 1993 season, NASCAR decided to take
action on this problem. It designed the air deflectors,
which were first used in February 1994 at Daytona
Speedway. What are these air deflectors? They are
20-inch by 8-inch sheets of metal mounted on the
rear portion of the roof (Flowers 44-45). When a
spinout happens, the backward flow of air over the
car causes the deflectors to flip up and create down
force that keeps the car on the track. These useful
flaps keep the car from "thinking" it's a plane.

Sometimes an accident can't be avoided, so the
third safety innovation helps make a crash less
serious. This high-tech change is a modified
suspension system. A car's suspension absorbs
shocks and helps the driver control the car. The
older system is based on a solid-frame construction,
but the newer ones are built to give way when an
impact happens. "The weak links," says chassis-
builder Butch Stevens of BSR Racing in Charlotte,

The writer explains a concept unfamiliar to the reader.

An idea from a previous paragraph is connected to an idea in this one.

309

Van Ravenswaay 3

North Carolina, "are the front and rear suspensions. They're made to bend, in specific ways, on impact" (qtd. in Lovell 35). A weak link sounds like a bad thing, but Stevens means it in a positive way. On impact, the front or rear suspension will absorb a lot of energy from the crash through the bending. This creates what's called "an energy-management crush zone" (Lovell 35). The give-way suspension makes the crash less direct for the driver than the old solid-frame suspension. The result is less serious injuries for the driver.

These three safety innovations help NASCAR drivers walk away from accidents to drive another day. Suspension modifications, air deflectors, and steering-wheel padding all show NASCAR designers working hard to make racing as safe as possible for drivers. As speeds at NASCAR tracks increase, chassis makers will be faced with more lifesaving challenges. The drivers depend on them. The fans depend on them. The future popularity of the sport depends on them. Until crash dummies can drive, safety technology is the best insurance for NASCAR racing.

Sources of quotations and borrowed information are given in parentheses.

The writer ends with the repetition of a key concluding point.

Van Ravenswaay 4

Works Cited

Flowers, Jack. "What's New in NASCAR." <u>Popular</u>
    <u>Mechanics</u> June 1994: 44-45.

Lovell, Bill. "Low Tech, High Speed." <u>Popular</u>
    <u>Mechanics</u> March 1993: 34-45, 111.

The sources
are listed
alphabetically.

The second
line is indented
five spaces.

311 Title Page and Outline

If your instructor asks you to include a title page and/or an outline with your paper, you can use the samples below as your guide. (Also see 242.)

TITLE PAGE

Corporate-Owned

Hog Confinements in Iowa

Lisa Tebben

Mr. Schelhaas

English 101

8 November 1994

**RESEARCH
PAPER OUTLINE**

Corporate-Owned Hog Confinements in Iowa

Introduction--The corporate-owned hog confinement is a new way of raising pork that promises to drastically change Iowa's hog industry.

I. Why is the issue important--Iowa's dependence on the hog industry

II. Defining and explaining the hog confinement

    A. Large-scale operations

    B. High-tech, computerized production process

    C. The growth in number and size of hog confinements

    D. Iowa as a prime confinement location

III. The effects of corporate hog confinements

    A. Increased hog production and market share for Iowa

    B. Waste management problem

    C. Overproduction and the family farm

    D. Monopoly and the family farm

Conclusion--Questions remain about what is best for the hog industry in Iowa. The choices will affect people's lives.

Lisa Tebben
Mr. Schelhaas
English 101
8 November 1994

Corporate-Owned Hog Confinements in Iowa

When many people think of the life of a pig, they picture Wilbur and his slop pail in E. B. White's children's story, Charlotte's Web. They think of mud and manure on the traditional family farm, of sows raising their piglets in the pigpen. The fact is that this traditional hog operation is changing. In Iowa especially, the nation's hog heartland, farmers and the farm industry are dealing with the trend toward large, corporate-owned hog confinements. As an article earlier this year in the Des Moines Register noted, "Hogs—and who will own them—have become a central question to this state's agricultural economy" (Wagner 1).

Experts are debating the pluses and minuses of the corporate hog confinement versus the family farm, but one thing is certain: the corporate-owned hog confinement promises to drastically change the hog industry in Iowa. We can see how important this change is if we look at (1) the place of hog farming in Iowa's economy, (2) the way hog confinements work, and (3) the effects of confinements.

Hog farming is crucial to Iowa's economy. In fact, Iowa leads the nation in pork production, claiming a 25 percent share. Its 34,000 hog-farm operators each year market 25 million pigs, generating 30 percent of the state's agricultural receipts ("Alliance" 1, 3). In addition, the pork industry in

The writer uses a familiar topic to introduce her paper's topic.

The writer supports her topic sentence with statistics.

Tebben 2

Iowa creates over 12 billion dollars in total state revenue and provides more than 93,000 jobs ("Pork" 15).

In Iowa, hog farmers really do bring home the bacon. My dad, Davis Tebben, co-owns Sioux Automation, a manufacturing company that makes equipment for raising livestock. I asked him what hog farming means to local economies—rural communities and towns. He said that farm income is turned over or circulated an average of seven times within the area it is generated. This money goes to farmers, feedmills, truck drivers, veterinarians, equipment dealers, local businesses, and many others. Clearly, losing a lot of the primary income from hog sales would weaken this cycle in Iowa communities. Other farm income can't easily pick up the slack, either. Producing and marketing corn, soybeans, and other products simply does not involve nearly as many people as producing and marketing hogs. If Iowa lost its share of the hog market, community revenue would decrease while unemployment and taxes would probably increase—affecting all citizens in the long run. A healthy hog industry helps keep Iowa's economy healthy.

How will Iowa's hog industry stay strong? Iowans are currently debating this question. Corporate hog confinements are at the center of the debate, because they change the system of hog production. Confinements are huge facilities that raise thousands of hogs. The hogs are born and grown in buildings that "use the same climate controls found in skyscrapers" (Kilman A1). Because

An interview is used as a source of information.

The writer suggests possible effects without stretching the facts.

Tebben 3

the risk of disease is high in these large facilities with their huge pig populations, all visitors must shower and change into company clothing, including underwear, before entering the buildings (Kilman A1).

In these high-tech facilities, hog production itself is carefully watched and controlled. The corporate hog confinement is a computerized barn. Already computers check humidity in the buildings and water consumption by pigs; soon software will check oxygen levels as well. Climate control is so precise that the temperature is lowered by half a degree each day as the pigs grow, since larger pigs like cooler conditions (Kilman A1). Each pig is tracked by a computer so that all important aspects of its life are documented precisely. Sows are carefully monitored to ensure that each gives birth to the most piglets possible. In fact, each sow is expected to produce 23 pigs a year for three years before being shipped to the slaughter-house. The piglets produced by these high-yield sows are soon weaned and moved to a nursery for three weeks. At 45 pounds, the pigs move to a finishing barn where high-potency diets prepare them for a market weight of 245 pounds.

This entire life span, from birth to butcher, takes five and a half months, much less time than hogs raised on family farms (Kilman A1). Confinements raise hogs more quickly, efficiently, and cheaply than the family farm can. And because these hogs are closely monitored and carefully bred, they are nearly carbon copies of each other. As a result, pork processing plants receiving these hogs can also be highly mechanized (Kilman A1). The corporate hog confinement is high-tech farming.

Specific details help the reader understand confinements.

A reference is given even when the information is put in the writer's own words.

315

Tebben 4

These corporate farms are growing in number and size. Murphy Family Farms, currently the largest pork producer in the country, owns 180,000 sows, but plans to have 210,000 sows by the end of 1994 (Freese 20-21). In other words, this farm could produce 4.8 million market hogs in one year. Premium Standard Farms has shown how quickly these confinements can grow. In only five years, this company has gone from zero sows to 96,800 (Freese 20). Sonny Faison, president of Carroll's Foods, the second largest producer, has big plans for expanding his company. "Ten years ago," he says, "we had 6,000 sows. . . . Now we know we can get to 200,000 in two years and 400,000 in five years. We are putting more sows in in one month than we used to in a year" (qtd. in Freese 24). These growth plans seem to be the rule in hog confinements, not the exception.

For many confinements, Iowa is an especially attractive place to be. Because corn and soybeans are grown locally, feeding hogs in Iowa is less expensive than in any other state. The support services of feedmills, vets, and trucking companies—services needed by the large firms—are all in place.

Supporters of hog confinements point to these factors and to the economic benefits of corporate farms. Hog confinements could increase hog production dramatically—and the state's share of the national market. A full discussion of the issue, however, needs to take into account other possible effects of growing hog confinements.

First of all, hog confinements produce more than

The writer explains why the person she quotes is an authority.

Each paragraph focuses on one effect of hog confinements.

Tebben 5

just ham and bacon. They produce waste—and a lot
of it. A confinement of 80,000 hogs can produce
about half a billion gallons of manure annually,
enough to fill the Pentagon (Kilman A1). Clearly,
this much waste is a problem for confinement owners.
Waste disposal is an important environmental issue.
Animal waste must be kept from polluting rivers,
streams, and groundwater supplies. The confinements
could use the age-old technique of spreading waste as
organic fertilizer, but most large hog operations don't
have the acres needed to take care of that much
manure. The odor alone can lead to angry residents,
lawsuits, and decreased property values.

A second effect of growing hog confinements
may be overproduction. Right now, 30 corporate
farms have 25% of Iowa's pork market. Analyst
Gene Johnston suggests in an editorial that if these
corporate farms "all grow to the size of the biggest
one, these 30 firms could raise more pigs than we
consume and export" (17). On the one hand,
increased production is a benefit. For example, Gene
Leman, head of IBP (a meat processing company),
says that he needs more hogs to fill his operation
schedule (Wagner 1). On the other hand, increased
corporate production might have a harmful effect on
traditional family farms, which use hog production as
a cushion of reliable income in case of crop failure.
Overproduction pushes prices down, and the small
operator can't compete. Many of the smaller producers will go out of business because they don't have
enough capital to survive the low prices created by
oversupply.

A second
major effect
is clearly
identified.

Only the page
number is
cited when the
author's name
appears in
the text.

Tebben 6

A third possible effect, then, of growing hog confinements is monopoly—the confinements "hogging" the market. They could certainly push small farms out of the hog business. Murphy Family Farms could by itself replace 2,000 independent family farmers. In addition, many large producers want to control the process of pork production from beginning to end, from owning their own feedmills to designing and operating their own packing plants. In North Carolina, where hog production has grown quickly to place it second behind Iowa, we hear of "small farmers who are turned away from hog-buying stations because packing plants are controlled by the big operators" (Wagner 1). Such important changes to the pork industry will clearly mean important changes for individual pork producers, industries tied to pork production, rural communities, and the state.

What should Iowa do to keep the hog industry healthy? That's a tough question. Should the state welcome the growth of hog confinements? Or should it make such confinements illegal? If it does this, these confinements might simply go to a state without anti-corporate laws, a move that would weaken Iowa's market share (Wagner 1). Smaller area farmers could group together to provide buyers with a larger volume of hogs and to share advice on technology, feeds, and genetics (Looker 21). Such a move might help cut costs. Whatever the answers, Iowa's hog industry is changing. The choices made will affect more than good old Wilbur the pig. They will mean major adjustments for people—for farmers, rural communities, and the whole state.

The conclusion asks questions that still need to be answered.

Tebben 7

Works Cited

"Works Cited" is centered one inch from the top.

"Alliance to Promote Iowa's Pork Industry." <u>Iowa Farm Bureau</u> 3 Sept. 1994: 1, 3.

Freese, Betsy. "Pork Powerhouses." <u>Successful Farming</u> Oct. 1994: 20-24.

Johnston, Gene. "Business." Editorial. <u>Successful Farming</u> Oct. 1994: 17.

Kilman, Scott. "Power Pork." <u>Wall Street Journal</u> 28 March 1994: A1.

The Works Cited page is double-spaced throughout.

Looker, Dan. "Strength in Numbers." <u>Successful Farming</u> Nov. 1994: 20-22.

"Pork Plays Important Role in Economy." <u>Herds & Plowshares</u> Oct. 1994: 15.

Tebben, Davis R. Personal interview. 1 Nov. 1994.

Wagner, Jay P., et al. "A Furor over Hogs." <u>Des Moines Register</u> 22 May 1994: 1.

INFORMATION

INFO

Searching for Information

Defining Information

FYI—*For Your Information.* It's a phrase we hear often. As students, workers, and consumers we depend upon information each day for everything from finishing the simplest task to making life-changing choices. But what is information, anyway? When you hear the word, what do you imagine?

- ◉ Stuff hidden away on shelves in the library?
- ◉ Rows of computer terminals with workers rapidly keyboarding data?
- ◉ CNN (Cable News Network) or television infomercials?

It seems that anything and everything is information. Here's the key point. Whatever you do in life—fix cars, work for Uncle Sam, design clothes, or run your own business—you'll need to get good at sorting through lots of information, finding what you need, and chucking the rest.

What's Ahead?

To succeed in this information age, you've got to learn how to sort through truckloads of information. This section will help you uncover the many ways you can look for and get information. Here are the topics covered:

Data vs. Information

Primary vs. Secondary Sources

Evaluating Sources

320 Data vs. Information

When people talk about "information," what they often mean is "data." But information isn't simply data—facts, figures, words, pictures, or images. Look at the data below. Do you understand any of it?

1 **2**  **3**

4 DEFAULT – I will be in default on this note and any agreement securing this note if any one or more of the following occurs:
(a) I fail to make a payment on this note in full within 10 days after it is due; or
(b) I fail to observe any other covenant of this transaction, the breach of which materially impairs the condition, value, or protection of your rights in the property securing this note, or materially impairs my prospect to pay the amounts due under this note.

Data becomes information when it means something to us, when it is something we understand or can use in our daily life. Need some help with the data above? Check the fine print at the bottom of the page.

321 Primary vs. Secondary Sources

Information sources can be divided into two categories—*primary* and *secondary*.

A **primary source** is an original source. When you write in your diary, you are the originator of the information. That makes it a primary source. When you read someone else's diary, you are reading a primary source. Of course, primary sources are often much more than a personal record. The Constitution of the United States, for example, is a primary source because it, too, is an original document.

Secondary sources are not original sources. They get their data or information from original sources, and then they basically do what they want with it. Most magazines, newspapers, and encyclopedias are very careful with how they use original material, but the old warning "Let the buyer beware" is always true when it comes to secondary sources. Some writers of secondary sources twist information so that it appears to support their argument.

Be Careful! ┄┄┄➤ Don't trust all information as absolute truth. Like a good reporter, you need to check your sources.

1. "slippery when wet" road sign 2. the "fate" motif from the first movement of Beethoven's Symphony no. 5 in C Minor 3. a blueprint 4. excerpt from a loan agreement

322 Information Packages

Information comes in all shapes and sizes. In later chapters, we'll talk about how to find and use information; but for now, look at the chart below to get an overview of the packages in which information comes wrapped.

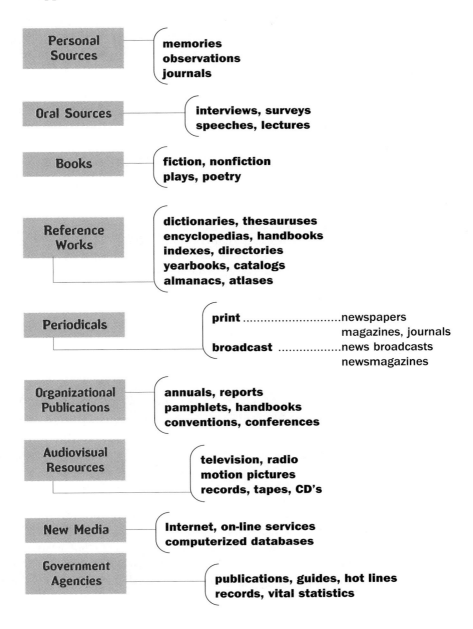

Personal Sources	**memories** **observations** **journals**
Oral Sources	**interviews, surveys** **speeches, lectures**
Books	**fiction, nonfiction** **plays, poetry**
Reference Works	**dictionaries, thesauruses** **encyclopedias, handbooks** **indexes, directories** **yearbooks, catalogs** **almanacs, atlases**
Periodicals	**print** ....newspapers magazines, journals **broadcast** ....news broadcasts newsmagazines
Organizational Publications	**annuals, reports** **pamphlets, handbooks** **conventions, conferences**
Audiovisual Resources	**television, radio** **motion pictures** **records, tapes, CD's**
New Media	**Internet, on-line services** **computerized databases**
Government Agencies	**publications, guides, hot lines** **records, vital statistics**

323 Evaluating Sources

In a bag of split peas you'll sometimes find a little stone that has slipped through the sieve. Same size, same shape as the peas, but different quality—you'll notice when you crunch down on it. Information is like that. One bit of information looks pretty much like another. But information, too, needs to be evaluated for quality. Some should be tossed out. Some should be chewed and swallowed with care.

How do you know which information to trust? Here are some key questions to ask about it:

Quality Control

1. **Is the source primary or secondary?** (See cautions at 321.)

2. **Is the information complete?** Try to see the whole picture. If you're given data from an experimental group, you should be given results from a control group for comparison. If your source shows you highlights, ask to see the "lowlights," too.

3. **Is the information accurate?** Mistakes can result from bad research design, misinterpreting results, poor reporting, computer goofs, problems in fax transmission, or even slipups by a keypunch operator. (Unfortunately, mistakes don't come with little red flags that say "Oops." You've got to detect them the old-fashioned way: by thinking about them.)

4. **Is the source an expert?** An expert is someone who has mastered a whole subject area, someone that everyone regards as an authority. Be careful. When experts go outside their fields of expertise, they may not have much more authority than the fire extinguisher.

5. **Is the information current?** A book on computers written five years ago may be ancient history by now. But a book on Abraham Lincoln could be 40 years old and still the best source on the market.

6. **Is your source biased?** A "bias" means literally a tilt toward one side. Biased sources—such as political "spin doctors," TV infomercials, or corporate spokespersons—have something to gain by slanting facts and emotions their way. Some of what they say may have value, but you must decide how much their language distorts the truth. (For help, see "Thinking Logically," 558-574.)

NOTE: Slanted language or distorted statistics may reveal many sorts of biases. Here are a few to watch out for: bias toward (or against) a region of the country, a political party, males or females, a certain race or ethnic group, a certain religion.

Working with Information

Finding good information is just a beginning. If you want to be "information literate," you have to weigh every piece of information, test it, and work with it until you balance the scales to your satisfaction. You need to understand the information and where it comes from. You need to know how to apply it, analyze it, evaluate it. Remember, a person with lots of information but no real understanding is just a walking atlas. You want to be more than that.

What's Ahead?

This section of your handbook looks at working with information by exploring these questions:

What is information literacy?

How do we work with information?

How do we send information?

325 What is information literacy?

To be literate you need to be able to read and write. But information literacy goes beyond simple reading and writing—it's being able to gather, evaluate, and communicate information clearly. It's being able to sort through all kinds of information and make sense of it.

James Pond, spy, meets Stephanie Jerkyl, student . . .

[Jerkyl is wearing a T-shirt that says, "Books Are for Worms."]

Pond: Psst! Hey, kid! Listen up. Wanna job?

Jerkyl: Nope, already got one. . . . Hmmm, what's the pay?

Pond: Well, you can't measure everything in money, you know.

Jerkyl: Hey, everybody needs cash. . . . Well, what's the job? Spit it out, already.

Pond: R.A.

Jerkyl: R.A.? Regular army? Resident alien? What?

Pond: Research assistant. I'm a spy, kid, an informant. I snoop out info and spoon it up to clients. Information is my business. Careful and clever research is my life.

Jerkyl: Research! That's a four-letter word!

Pond: It's eight, kid. Count 'em.

Jerkyl: That's twice as bad.

Pond: OK—so I used the "R" word. You should know, though, that research is more than digging up names and dates in the library to shovel into a report. It's also more than labs, microscopes, and atom smashers. Research is making sense of things. Research is my life!

Jerkyl: Nice slogan. It might win you a couple of votes . . . from librarians. What's research got to do with my life?

Pond: You do research every time you use information to make a choice: pick your courses, buy tennis shoes, make career choices. To figure it out and then do it, you've got to start with questions and be smart—information literate.

Jerkyl: Info what?

Pond: Information literate.

Jerkyl: Sounds like a disease.

Pond: It's the skills you need to dig up information and work it over to answer a question, fix a problem, make a decision, or follow a dream. Information literacy is the legwork and brain work you'll need to finish any project—from making a pizza to developing renewable energy technology.

Jerkyl: Okay, I give up. Where do I sign? Hey, do I get one of those shoe phones?

326 How do we work with information?

When we work with information, we work with our entire being—our hands, our hearts, our heads. The physical side involves locating, storing, and retrieving data. The mental side involves using any number of the following thinking skills: *recalling, understanding, applying, analyzing, synthesizing,* and *evaluating.*

327 Recalling Information

Your memory stores experiences and information; the act of recalling helps you locate and make sense of that stored information.

Upside: Your memory helps define and shape your life and makes it possible to repeat small and large tasks.

Downside: Memory is often unreliable; details may fade with time.

Shoptalk: Let's say that you are gathering information to purchase a car. You recall all you can about various cars—that Auntie Em's AMC Pacer was a lemon; that minivans are popular, but expensive.

328 Understanding Information

Understanding is the act of connecting raw data to your personal ideas and turning it into information. Answering the question "What does this mean?" is the key to understanding information.

Upside: Understanding information demands more complex brain work and may lead to changing your mind.

Downside: If your previous knowledge and ideas are limited, your ability to understand new data is also limited.

Shoptalk: Understanding cars is essential if you expect to make a good decision about which one to buy. What is the fuel efficiency of a Dodge Neon? What difference does it make if an engine has four cylinders or six? What is dual exhaust, and are two tailpipes better than one?

329 Applying Information

Applying information is putting information to use, bringing it into contact with an actual situation. Applying information is like painting: once a painter understands what a customer wants, she or he can mix the paint and start applying it to the walls.

Upside: Information is put to work to make and do things.

Downside: If the information is faulty, what you make or do may be flawed.

Shoptalk: You have read a consumer magazine article about front-wheel drive. You apply the information when you test-drive three front-wheel drive models (Metro, Civic, and Neon) to see how they handle and brake.

330 Analyzing Information

When you analyze information, you examine it closely, think and talk about it, and figure out what it means. A mechanic determining why your car won't start, a doctor diagnosing a medical condition, and a teenager comparing two brands of jeans are all analyzing information.

Upside: By thinking logically (comparison/contrast, cause/effect, categorizing, etc.), you can arrive at a reasonable conclusion.

Downside: By focusing too much on the details, you may lose sight of the whole picture.

Shoptalk: You create a table or chart on the three cars, comparing price, mileage, and other important similarities and differences.

331 Synthesizing Information

When you synthesize information, you reshape it into another form. Air pressure, temperature, and jet stream readings become a weather map, or many pages of data become a company's five-year plan.

Upside: Synthesizing connects ideas creatively, translating information from one form to another.

Downside: Some synthesizing, such as negative advertising, can be used to manipulate or mislead people.

Shoptalk: Car names are actually examples of synthesis. Instead of calling their cars Model #1 or Design Experiment #498, automakers consider the features of their cars and then try to capture their essence in imaginative names—Metro, Civic, Neon.

332 Evaluating Information

When you weigh or judge information, you are evaluating it in order to make informed decisions. A jury member thinks about the evidence presented and decides whether or not a witness is telling the truth. A supervisor reviews a clerk's sales record and treatment of customers for a performance review.

Upside: Evaluating helps us determine the worth or value of information. It provides a foundation for decisions and planning.

Downside: Evaluating is only as good as the information and thinking that go into it. If our synthesizing, analyzing, organizing, etc., are faulty, our evaluating will be faulty as well.

Shoptalk: You have compared and contrasted the Metro, Civic, and Neon. When you judge the pros and cons of each and make a decision, you are evaluating information.

333 Working with Information

When you are asked to . . .   **You should be ready to . . .**

Recall Information

recall	define
list	label
name	identify
record	memorize

- list details
- identify or define terms
- collect information
- remember information

Understand Information

understand	show
review	restate
cite	explain
summarize	describe

- give examples
- restate the important details
- explain how something works
- tell why something happened

Apply Information

utilize	select
choose	model
illustrate	organize
locate	demonstrate

- select the most important details
- put information in order
- make something work
- show how something works

Analyze Information

classify	compare
divide	contrast
edit	characterize
tell why	map
examine	break down

- look at each part and put it into the correct group
- make connections between things by using cause and effect, comparison and contrast, etc.

Synthesize Information

combine	develop
speculate	invent
design	blend
compose	propose
create	formulate
predict	imagine

- figure out a better way of doing something
- redesign or blend the old and the new
- make an educated guess
- come up with a theory

Evaluate Information

judge	rate
recommend	measure
argue	persuade
evaluate	assess
criticize	convince

- weigh its strengths and weaknesses (pluses and minuses)
- determine its clearness, accuracy, value, etc.
- judge its value/worth

334 Organizing Information

Okay, so you've chosen the Neon because it's a spunky compact car that best meets your needs. What's the best way to assemble that information for your friendly neighborhood banker so that she or he will see the beauty of your logic and give you a nice, fat loan?

1. Understand your audience, why he or she needs the information, and what information you need to pass on.

2. Organize the information so it's easy to understand.

3. Choose the best methods of presenting and displaying your information (lists, tables, graphs, explanations, displays).

335 Communicating Information

Once you've worked with your information and shaped it into the best possible form, it's time to choose a way to share it.

- **In Person:** If you want to explain your information, or if you want to hash over problems together, or if you want to keep up a personal working relationship, nothing beats face-to-face communication.

- **By Telephone:** Call forwarding, voice mail, and conference calls have taken the kinks out of telephoning. Use the phone for quick, informal contact, but don't rely on a phone call alone if your message is especially important.

- **In Writing:** If it's important, get it in writing. Writing is cheap. It's permanent. And, writing shows respect for the reader.

336 Using Technology to Send Written Messages

By Fax Machine: A fax machine combines writing and the telephone. Basically, a fax machine sends a copy of your original page(s) through the phone line. At the other end, another fax machine prints out copy.

Upside: fast, convenient, cheaper than overnight delivery

Downside: requires relatively expensive equipment at both ends; expensive for long documents.

By Electronic Mail (or E-Mail): In this method your computer sends a message to another computer (or even hundreds of computers) electronically; it can be used within a company or between computers that are thousands of miles apart.

Upside: fast, convenient, saves paper, allows two or more parties to have a "live" written conversation

Downside: requires computers and modems at both ends; may not always be private

Primary Sources

337   A primary source gives you firsthand information—information you gather yourself, straight from the "horse's mouth." You may collect this firsthand information through observation, a conversation or an interview, a survey, or attendance at some presentation or display. Getting it, of course, is only half the fun. Understanding and using it is your goal.

What's Ahead?

This chapter covers the most popular primary sources and suggests ways to gather information firsthand.

Making Observations

Using Surveys and Forms

Conducting Interviews

Observing Presentations and Displays

338 Selecting Primary Sources

Finding answers to your questions involves finding facts and ideas in a variety of reliable places. Finding firsthand—or primary—sources will get you closer to the grass roots and closer to the truth. Consider these examples:

- Instead of simply reading about the Great Depression for a school report, you interview a neighbor or family member who lived through it, or you go to the library and find a collection of letters written by people during that time.

- On the job as an insurance claims adjustor, you go directly to a home to assess fire damage. Later, you go to the city assessor's office to find records of the home's original value.

Examples of

Primary Sources

Where to Find

personal experiences	journals, memory
interviews	magazines
surveys	city assessor's office
court records	courthouse
diaries and journals	secondhand bookstores
letters	your grandmother's trunk
original documents	historical museum
speeches	CD-ROM in library
reports from an on-the-scene reporter	newspapers
autobiographies	library
E-mail correspondence	Internet
films	film library

INSIDE

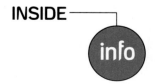
info

Although most primary sources are reliable, not all are. For example, have you ever heard two people describe an accident or incident they each witnessed (making them primary sources) in such totally different ways that it made you think the people came from different planets?

339 Making Observations

Observing people, situations, things, and places is a common method of gathering information at school, at home, in the workplace, even on the practice field. Observation is our everyday lab work.

> When do people observe?
> - A student observes the flood stages on a local river and then writes a report on what she observed.
> - A nurse monitors vital signs while a patient undergoes a kidney transplant.
> - A soil conservationist checks a farm field for erosion patterns after a severe rainstorm.

How do we observe effectively? Just by keeping our eyes open? That's a good start, but here is some more advice.

Before Observation

1. **Know what you want to accomplish.**
   Do you need to understand a place? Solve a problem? Answer a question?
2. **Do your homework before you go.**
   If you are observing production robotics, learn something about it so you know what to look for.
3. **Get permission to observe.**
   If the location or event isn't open to the public, get an okay before-hand. Explain why you want to observe.
4. **Bring what you need.**
   Yes, you need your eyes, but pen and paper, field journal, camera, camcorder, or tape recorder will help you record what you see and hear. Then you can review and evaluate what you observed.

During Observation

Follow your plan, but let the situation also shape your observing. Take notes on specific details and impressions—the sounds a machine makes, its motions, and the way people interact with it, for example. Get different viewpoints or perspectives by observing the scene from more than one position.

After Observation

1. **Look over your notes**.
   Think carefully about the information you've gathered.
2. **Arrive at conclusions about what you've observed.**
   List them, along with supporting details.

340 Using Surveys

Surveys and questionnaires are something like interviews, except in an easy-to-fill-out form. They can help you gather information quickly and easily—from simple facts to personal opinions and preferences. Surveys are also flexible. They can be done in person, over the phone, through the mail, or with computers. Here are some guidelines:

> When do people use surveys and questionnaires?
> - A student doing a report on the work lives of immigrants surveys local businesses about immigrant employees.
> - Volunteers distribute questionnaires for a politician seeking office.
> - A housing specialist surveys community residents in order to plan residential developments over the next 10 years.

Find a focus.

A good survey has a limited purpose and targets a specific audience.
1. It asks specific people questions they can answer.
2. It gathers information that cannot be easily obtained elsewhere.

Organize it with the respondent in mind.

A good survey is easy for readers to complete.
1. The title suggests the purpose.
2. The introduction states the purpose and explains how to complete and return the form.
3. Numbers, white space, headings, boldface, and underlining guide the reader.
4. The questions are clear, precise, and complete.

Test your survey.

Ask a friend or coworker to read the survey and help you revise it. Test it out on a small group before actually using it.

341 Conducting Interviews

The idea of an interview is simple: You talk with someone who has expert knowledge or has had important experiences with your topic. Such questioning can be as informal as a phone call to a neighbor or as formal as a videotaped interview on location with a local celebrity.

> When do people conduct interviews?
> - A student interviews a former professional ballplayer about his experiences.
> - A police officer interviews witnesses to an automobile accident.
> - A nursing home nutritionist talks with a new resident in order to set up a monthly meal plan.

342 Preparing for an Interview

1. **Know the person and the subject that you will discuss.** Come to the interview informed so that you can build on what you know.

2. **When you arrange the interview, be thoughtful.** Set it up at the interviewee's convenience. Explain your purpose, the process, and the topics to be covered.

3. **Write out some questions ahead of time.** This will give the interview some structure and help you cover the necessary topics.

   ◉ Avoid slanted or loaded questions that suggest you want a specific answer.
   Slanted: "Don't you agree that small businesses treat their employees better than large corporations do?"
   Better: "How do small businesses and large corporations treat their employees differently?"

   ◉ Understand open and closed questions. Closed questions ask for simple, factual answers; open questions ask for an explanation.

   Closed: How many personal computers did you sell last year?
   Open: How would you describe the current market for personal computers?

   ◉ Ask your questions in a logical order so that the interview moves smoothly from one subject to the next.

4. **Write the questions on the left side of the page.** Leave room for quotations, information, and impressions on the right side.

5. **Be prepared.** Take pens and paper. If you plan on taping the interview, get permission ahead of time. Bring along a tape recorder with blank tapes and extra batteries.

343 Doing the Interview

1. **Begin by reminding the person why you've come.** Provide whatever background information is necessary to help him or her feel comfortable and focus on the specific topic.

2. **If the person gives permission, tape the interview.** Use a tape recorder with a counter. When the expert makes an important point, jot down the number. Later you can find these points quickly and save yourself precious time.

3. **Write down key information.** Even if you are using a recorder, write down the important facts, quotations, and impressions.

4. **Use body language**—from nods to smiles—to show you're listening.

5. **Be flexible.** If the person looks puzzled by a question, rephrase it or ask another. If the discussion gets off track, gently redirect it to the main topic.

344 Following the Interview

1. **As soon as possible, review all your notes** and fill in responses you remember but couldn't record at the time.

2. **Thank the person** in a note or with a phone call. At the same time, check to make sure the information and quotations are accurate.

3. **Let the person see the outcome**—the report you plan to hand in, the proposal that you wrote, or the policy change you made.

345 Learning from Presentations

Speeches and lectures, plays and concerts, art exhibits and museum displays, television and radio shows—all of these can provide valuable information when you actively observe and think about them.

When do people gather information from presentations?
- Students listen to a journalist explain how to conduct a good interview.
- Child-care providers watch a video describing signs of physical abuse.
- Shop owners examine new CD-ROM products at a sales convention.

To get the most information from a speech, performance, or display, follow these guidelines:

1. **Read about the topic or presenter before attending.**

2. **Take notes on key ideas and details.**

3. **Ask questions.**

4. **Collect brochures, handouts, and other useful information.**

Secondary Sources

If a primary source is the word-by-word transcript of a trial, a secondary source might be a news commentary based on the transcript. Or it might be a magazine article based on interviews with jurors or even a movie loosely based on the trial. Get the picture? A secondary source is at least once removed from the original. Secondary sources offer information not included in the primary source by extending, analyzing, evaluating, or interpreting the original source.

Where should you look for secondary sources? The library is a good place to start. There you'll find secondary sources in the form of micro-films, CD-ROM's, atlases, editorials, articles, and more. (And don't forget the book in your hand at this moment! It's a secondary source that's just about to show you how to use other secondary sources.)

What's Ahead?

This chapter explains each type of secondary information and how to use it.

Reference Works

Periodicals: Magazines, Newspapers, Journals

CD-ROM's

347 Reference Works

When you think of reference works, do you see a sagging shelf of heavy encyclopedias? A dog-eared pocket dictionary? That's a start, but picture these reference works in these places:

<u>Home</u>   cookbooks, phone directories, medical dictionaries, gardening encyclopedias, and product guides

<u>School</u>   atlases, encyclopedias, dictionaries, and handbooks—in the classroom and the library

<u>Work</u>   directories, shipping manuals, vendor catalogs, procedure statements, handbooks, and specialized dictionaries

Using Reference Works

⊚ **Discover the work's structure.** In order to find the information you want, look at the structure of the reference. Check how items are organized, and look for instructions at the beginning.

⊚ **Understand what the work covers.** Each reference work contains a limited amount of information. Check those limits by looking for these at the beginning:

- date the reference work was published
- time frame the work covers (**Example:** July 1994-June 1995)
- specific materials the work covers (**Example:** *Dictionary of American Negro Biography* contains summaries of lives of prominent African-Americans but only up to 1970. No living persons.)

⊚ **Use precise words in your searches.** For example, in an encyclopedia the word *immigrants* will lead you to different information from the word *aliens*. Also check whether you have spelled these words correctly.

Different Types of Reference Works

To help you understand reference tools better, we have divided them into the following groups:

- Encyclopedias
- Dictionaries and Thesauruses
- Books and Pamphlets
- Organizational Publications
- Yearbooks, Almanacs, Atlases, . . .
- Periodicals
- CD-ROM's

348 Encyclopedias

Like a dictionary, an encyclopedia is made up of alphabetically arranged entries. An encyclopedia's articles give you an overview of a topic and suggest further research topics.

Kinds of Encyclopedias

General encyclopedias contain entries covering as many fields of knowledge as possible.

> *Encyclopedia Britannica, Encyclopedia Americana, Collier's Encyclopedia, Grollier's Multimedia Encyclopedia* (on **CD-ROM**)

Specialized encyclopedias focus on a single area of knowledge.

> *The Encyclopedia of Careers and Vocational Guidance*
> *The Encyclopedia of Computer Science*
> *Encyclopedia of Food Technology*
> *McGraw-Hill Encyclopedia of Science and Technology*
> *The Encyclopedia of Environmental Studies*
> *Encyclopedia of Animal Care*

Using Encyclopedias Effectively

- Begin by checking to see how old the encyclopedia is. This will tell you whether or not the information is current and reliable.
- Look for your main topic first. After reading this main entry, check out cross-referenced words. Finally, go to the index for further leads.
- Read articles carefully and take note of the topic subdivisions. These can help you in further research.

349 Dictionaries

Kinds of Dictionaries

Dictionaries list words alphabetically and define them. But not all dictionaries are the same. Below are four kinds:

General dictionaries are major volumes such as the *Webster's New Twentieth Century Dictionary* and the *Oxford English Dictionary*. They define a broad variety of words.

Specialized dictionaries define only those words common to one field or used by one group of people: *Dictionary of Engineering and Technology, Dictionary of Occupational Titles, Stedman's Medical Dictionary.*

Biographical dictionaries include information about people: *Current Biography, Who's Who in America.*

Bilingual dictionaries translate words from one language to another. For example, a Spanish-English dictionary translates English words into Spanish and Spanish words into English.

350 Using the Dictionary

And you thought dictionaries just dished out definitions. Look again. There can be more than 10 kinds of information packed into one little entry. Each type is described below, and most are illustrated on the next page.

Spelling

Wondering how to spell a word or whether or not to capitalize it? Check it out. Use the word's sounded-out spelling to locate it.

Plurals, Verb Forms, and Compounds

Is *octopi* the plural of *octopus*? Is *thunk* or *thought* the past participle of *think*? A dictionary will help you answer these questions.

Syllabication

Where should you hyphenate a long word at the end of a typed line? The dictionary will tell you that, too.

Pronunciation

Saying a word properly helps you understand, remember, and communicate its meaning. (The dictionary gives you a pronunciation key at the bottom of pages or in the introduction.)

Parts of Speech

A dictionary shows how a word is used (part of speech)—whether *implode* is a verb or a noun, for example.

Etymology

Some dictionaries offer the word's history (where it came from) in brackets. This little bit of history can help you understand and remember the word's meaning.

Restrictive Labels

Field or usage labels limit a definition. A field label restricts a meaning to a subject area (*aeron.* for aeronautics). A usage label shows how a word is used (*slang*).

Synonyms and Antonyms

Some dictionaries list words with similar or opposite meanings after the definition.

Illustrations

In some dictionaries, especially technical dictionaries, a picture helps to clarify the word's meaning.

Meaning

Most words have several meanings. How do you sort them out? First read all the meanings, and then decide which one best fits the context in which the word is used.

351 Sample Dictionary Page

GUIDE WORDS

SYLLABICATION AND
PARTS OF SPEECH

MEANING

SPELLING OF VERB FORMS

SPELLING AND
CAPITAL LETTERS

ILLUSTRATION

PRONUNCIATION

ETYMOLOGY (History)

ACCENT MARK

SYNONYMS

USAGE

PRONUNCIATION KEY

---

mixer • mock   763

¹**mo·bile** \'mō-bəl, -ˌbīl, *also* -ˌbēl\ *adj* [ME *mobyll*, fr. MF *mobile*, fr. L *mobilis*, fr. *movere* to move] (15c) **1** : capable of moving or being moved: MOVABLE <a ~ missile launcher> **2 a** : changeable in appearance, mood, or purpose <~ face> **b** : VERSATILE **3** : relating to a mobile—**mo·bil·i·ty** \mo-'bil-ət-e\ *n*

²**mo·bile** \'mō-ˌbēl\ *n* (1936) : a construction or sculpture frequently of wire and sheet metal shapes with parts that can be set in motion by air currents; *also* : a similar structure (as of paper or plastic) suspended so that it moves in a current of air

-mobile *comb form* [auto*mobile*] **1:** motorized vehicle <snow*mobile*> **2:** automotive vehicle bringing services to the public <blood*mobile*> <book*mobile*>

mobile home *n* (1949) : a dwelling structure built on a steel chassis and fitted with wheels that is intended to be hauled to a usu. permanent site—compare MOTOR HOME

mo·bi·li·za·tion \ˌmō-bə-lə-'zā-shən\ *n* (1799) **1** : the act of mobilizing **2** : the state of being mobilized

mo·bi·lize \'mō-bə-ˌlīz\ *vb* **-lized; -liz·ing** *vt* (1838) **1 a** : to put into movement or circulation <~ financial assets> **b** : to release (something stored in the organism) for bodily use **2 a** : to assemble and make ready for war duty **b** : to marshal (as resources) for action <~ support for a proposal> ~ *vi* : to undergo mobilization

Mö·bi·us strip \ˈmœ-bē-əs-, ˈmə(r), ˌmō-\ *n* [August F. *Möbius* † 1868 Ger. mathematician] (1904) : a one-sided surface that is constructed from a rectangle by holding one end fixed, rotating the opposite end through 180 degrees, and applying it to the first end

Möbius strip

mob·oc·ra·cy \mä-'bä-krə-sə\ *n* (1754) **1** : rule by the mob **2** : the mob as a ruling class— **mob·o·crat** \'mä-bə-ˌkrat\ *n* – **mob·o·crat·ic** \ˌmä-bə-'kra-tik\ *adj*

mob·ster \'mäb-stər\ *n* (1917) : a member of a criminal gang

moc·ca·sin \'mä-kə-sən\ *n* [Virginia Algonquian *mockasin*] (ca. 1612) **1 a** : a soft leather heelless shoe or boot with the sole brought up the sides of the foot and over the toes where it is joined with a puckered seam to a U-shaped piece lying on top of the foot **b** : a regular shoe having a seam on the forepart of the vamp imitating the seam of a moccasin **2 a** : WATER MOCCASIN **b** : a snake (as of the genus *Natrix*) resembling a water moccasin

moccasin flower *n* (1680) : any of several lady's slippers (genus *Cypripedium*); esp : a once common woodland orchid (*C. acaule*) of eastern No. America with pink or white moccasin-shaped flowers

mo·cha \'mō-kə\ *n* [*Mocha*, Arabia] (1773) **1 a** : a superior Arabian coffee consisting of small green or yellowish beans **b** : a coffee of superior quality **2** : a dark chocolate-brown color

¹**mock** \'mäk, 'mok\ *vb* [ME, fr. MF *mocquer*] *vt* (15c) **1** : to treat with contempt : DERIDE **2** : to disappoint the hopes of **3** : DEFY, CHALLENGE **4 a** : to imitate (as a mannerism) closely : MIMIC **b** : to mimic in sport or derision ~ *vi* : JEER, SCOFF **syn see** RIDICULE, COPY – **mock·er** *n* – **mock·ing·ly** \'mä-kiŋ-le, 'mo\ *adv*

²**mock** *n* (15c) **1** : an act of ridicule or derision : JEER **2** : one that is an object of derision or scorn **3** : MOCKERY **4 a** : an act of imitation **b** : something made as an imitation

³**mock** *adv* (ca. 1619) : in an insincere or counterfeit manner – **usu. used in combination** <*mock*-serious>

\ə\abut \ᵊ\kitten, F table \ər\further \a\ash \ā\ace \ä\cot, cart \au̇\out \ch\chin \e\bet \ē\easy \g\go \i\hit \ī\ice \j\job \ŋ\sing \ō\go \o\law \oi\boy \th\thin \th\the \ü\loot \u̇\foot \y\yet \zh\vision \à, k, ᵉ, œ, ᵫ, ᵫ̄, ᵊ\see Guide to Pronunciation

352 Thesauruses

A thesaurus is, in a sense, the opposite of a dictionary. You go to a dictionary when you know the word but need the definition. You go to a thesaurus when you know the definition but need the word. For example, you might want a word for *fear* (a certain kind of fear) to complete the following sentence:

Joan experienced a certain amount of _____ over the upcoming exam.

If you have a thesaurus in dictionary form, simply look up the word *fear* as you would in a dictionary. If, however, you have a traditional thesaurus, you must first look up your word in the alphabetical index at the back of the book. You might find this entry for *fear* in the index:

FEAR 860
Fearful painful 830
timid 862

The numbers after *fear* are guide numbers, not page numbers. (Guide numbers are similar to the topic numbers in your handbook.) For instance, if you look up number 860 in the body of the thesaurus, you will find a long list of synonyms for the word *fear*. These include *timidity, fearfulness, diffidence, apprehensiveness, solicitude, anxiety, misgiving, mistrust, suspicion,* and *qualm.* You select the word *anxiety,* and your sentence becomes

Joan experienced a certain amount of <u>anxiety</u> over the upcoming exam.

---

259   PERSONAL AFFECTIONS   859-861

860. FEAR—*N.* **fear,** timidity, diffidence, apprehensiveness, fearfulness, solicitude, anxiety, care, apprehension, misgiving, mistrust, suspicion, qualm, hesitation.

trepidation, flutter, fear and trembling, perturbation, tremor, restlessness, disquietude, funk *[colloq.].*

fright, alarm, dread, awe, terror, horror, dismay, consternation, panic, scare; stampede *[of horses].*

V. **fear,** be afraid, apprehend, dread, distrust; hesitate, falter, wince, flinch, shy, shrink, fly.

tremble, shake, shiver, shudder, flutter, quake, quaver, quiver, quail.

frighten, fright, terrify, inspire (or excite) fear, bulldoze *[colloq.],* alarm, startle, scare, dismay, astound; awe, strike terror, appall, petrify, horrify.

Adj. **afraid,** frightened, alarmed, fearful, timid, timorous, tremulous, nervous, diffident, fainthearted, shaky, afraid of one's shadow, apprehensive; aghast, awe-struck, awe-stricken, horror-stricken, panic-stricken.

861. [absence of fear] COURAGE—*N.* courage, bravery, valor, boldness, spirit, daring, gallantry, prowess, heroism, chivalry, audacity, rashness, dash, defiance, confidence, self-reliance; manhood, manliness, nerve, pluck, mettle.

353 Books and Pamphlets

You know what a book or pamphlet is. But do you know how to make the best use of one? Follow these guidelines.

1. Check out the information at the front. The original publication date can tell you whether or not the information is current. Library of Congress subject headings can tell you if the book will be useful to you or not. The preface may give you a good overview of the book's content and its overall purpose.

2. Scan the book. Examine the table of contents for the specific topics you need. Look for headings and subheadings within chapters. Read introductory paragraphs and summaries before deciding if reading in depth will prove useful.

3. Search the index for the topics you need. Determine whether there are plenty of pages on your topic or just a few.

4. Look through the appendix and glossary at the back of the book for important information—statistics, tables, graphs, definitions.

5. Check the author's notes and bibliography for other useful sources on your topic.

354 Organizational Publications

If a factory, a school system, a TV station, an emergency ward, or a modeling agency didn't have its own in-house informational publications, it would probably fall apart at the seams. Here are some kinds you may expect to come across in the work world:

Instructions and Manuals help readers complete a task—from operating a computer to putting together a swing set.

Reports contain information about an organization's day-to-day activities and long-term goals. Reports provide organized data and an analysis of the data.

Policy and Procedure Statements spell out official positions. These statements give the reader guidelines for working with an organization. They can range from a refund policy to FDA regulations on egg processing.

Sales and Public Relations Material describe a company and promote its products and services. From a simple pamphlet to a complete catalog, such documents give useful information—features, cost, after-sale support.

Company Handbooks provide important information on how a company works, its policies and procedures, its benefits and expectations, and much more.

355 Yearbooks, Almanacs, Atlases, . . .

Ready to do some number crunching? Some globe-trotting (with your fingers doing the trotting)? Some name-dropping? First practice up on reading charts, tables, and graphs; then turn to books or on-line databases like these:

Yearbooks cover major developments on specific topics during the previous year.

> *Statistical Abstract of the United States: The National Data Book,* produced by the Department of Commerce, provides statistical information about the U.S., from population figures to data on geography, social trends, politics, employment, and business.

Almanacs are regular (usually annual) publications filled with diverse facts and statistics. Originally almanacs were used as community calendars and information books. Today they're broader in scope but function the same way.

> *The World Almanac and Book of Facts* presents information on many topics: business, politics, history, religion, social programs, sports, education, and the year's major events.

Atlases are just a bunch of maps, right? Well, they include maps, but they also contain data on countries, transportation, climate, and more.

> *The Rand McNally Commercial Atlas and Marketing Guide* includes maps of the U.S. and its major cities as well as information on transportation and communication, economics, and population.

> *Street Atlas USA on CD-ROM* allows you to call up street maps for any place in the United States. Are you heading for Helena, Montana? Hannibal, Missouri? Call it up and print out a map of the city.

Directories are lists of people and groups. (Directories are now widely used on the Internet.)

> *The National Directory of Addresses and Telephone Numbers* provides nationwide coverage of companies, associations, schools, etc.

Guides and Handbooks offer guidelines and models for exploring a topic, a program, an area of knowledge, or a profession.

> *Occupational Outlook Handbook,* published by the Department of Labor, explores the job market—where jobs are and might be and how to prepare for the workplace.

Indexes are powerful information tools. Many books contain an index— an alphabetical listing of topics and their location in the book. Large indexes in book or computer form, such as the *Readers' Guide to Periodical Literature,* work on the same principle. They list items published on specific topics during specific time periods and explain where to find them. (See 372-374.)

356 Periodicals

A periodical is a story told bit by bit—the story of a trial on a newscast, a sports series in a newspaper, or a hobby in a magazine.

> A periodical is . . .
>
> a publication (*Reader's Digest, New England Journal of Medicine*) or radio/TV program (*20/20, All Things Considered*, your local news) that is produced at regular time periods and focuses on a specific topic for a specific audience.

Types of Periodicals

Newspapers and Newscasts   provide up-to-date information on current events, from politics to natural disasters (*USA Today, The Wall Street Journal, The MacNeil/Lehrer Newshour*).

Journals   provide specialized information for a special audience (*Journal of Labor Economics,* an academic journal; *Provider: For Long-Term Care Professionals,* a journal for nursing and home-care professionals).

Magazines   provide general information weekly or monthly to a less specialized audience (*Time, Consumer Reports, Popular Mechanics*).

Tips on Using Periodicals

- Understand that periodicals can take on many forms: print, television, video, microfilm, computer network, and CD-ROM.

- Recognize a periodical's goals. What is the editorial slant? Is the information complex or simple, narrow or broad? How reliable is the information? Is this periodical the best type for your topic? For example, will a 30-second news story on TV give you accurate and detailed information on a new tax law?

- Check the date of the periodical. Is the information current? On the other hand, don't assume that the most recent edition gives you the best, most accurate information.

357 CD-ROM's

Many libraries are in the process of switching from print versions to CD-ROM versions of their most popular reference tools. The reason is that users can search CD-ROM databases much more quickly than books, and that CD-ROM's are such compact sources of information. Here are some of the types of CD-ROM's commonly kept by libraries:

- national and even international telephone directories
- encyclopedias and atlases
- lists of books in print
- government statistics and health information
- various guides to magazines and newspapers

Using CD-ROM

358 Quick Guide

The great thing about CD-ROM's is that they're easy to use; but even so, they take some practice. The following may help:

1. Make sure you have the right CD-ROM. Because they do not display their contents as obviously as a book, it's easy to get the wrong one.

2. Each database has a different set of rules for searching. Be sure you understand how to conduct a search, or ask for help. Become adept at keyword searching. (See 368.) Identify the word and the synonyms that most clearly pinpoint your subject. Combine these words with AND, OR, or NOT to find the exact information you need.

3. Understand what the limits of your CD-ROM are. Its database "back files" may not go back far enough to meet your needs. If you are searching for a magazine article from three years ago and your CD-ROM's back file is one year, you won't find what you need.

4. Find out how frequently the CD-ROM has been updated. Most CD's are updated monthly, but some busy librarians may not have had a chance to load the latest version.

5. If you need to be absolutely sure that you have the latest information on a subject, don't rely on CD-ROM. You may need to find the latest print materials, or conduct an on-line computer search. (See 375-383 for more.)

Finding Information

Have you ever waited until the last minute to write a paper or finish an important project? Then, late Sunday afternoon, it's off to the library or into an encyclopedia or computer program to find some quick, ready-made information. At least that's the plan. It worked last time. But what if you can't find the information you're looking for? What if the library yields no sources, the encyclopedia article is too short, and your computer isn't able to access the files you need? Now what?

Maybe a better approach would be to take some time now—with no deadlines staring you in the face—to learn how to find the right information quickly and efficiently.

What's Ahead?

This chapter of your handbook can help you understand better how and where to find information.

Discovering Information Pathways
Places Information Is Stored
Using Libraries
Using Computers
Using Other Sources of Information

360 Discovering Information Pathways

Are you about to embark on an information quest? If you had a plan, you could journey by phone, by letter, by computer network. You could scale mountains of data or slog through streams of office correspondence. You could observe the wildlife in direct field observations. All in all, you could have a nice trip. Or, if you had no clue where to begin, you might decide to look at a map. Here, then, is a kind of map you could follow the next time you need to locate information:

Define Your Destination
Why do you need information? What do you want to do with it?
- Answer a question?
- Finish a project?
- Seize an opportunity or follow a dream?

Spell out this purpose, and then decide what info you need.

Look for Maps to Your Destination
Use general reference works to get the big picture of the topic and directions to more detailed resources.
- Talk to an information expert (librarian, computer specialist, etc.).
- Check out dictionaries, encyclopedias, handbooks.
- Search catalogs, databases, indexes, bibliographies.
- Decide whether you need to gather primary information yourself.

Locate Specific Resources
Using the directions you found in general references, find the more specific and focused resources you need. Here are some possibilities:
- Do an interview.
- Watch a specific program or presentation.
- Call up the report on a database.
- Get a book or an article from the public library.

Work with Your Resources
Work through the resources you've gathered and find the specific information you need.
- Record, understand, organize, analyze, synthesize, and evaluate the information you've uncovered. (See 324-360.)
- Make choices and decisions; share information.

361 Places Information Is Stored

libraries
public
school
special ....legal, medical
government
corporate
private

computer resources
disks ....CD-ROM
video
laser

networks...............................E-mail
Internet
on-line services

mass media
radio
television
print

learning sites
museums, zoos
science centers
special places ....parks
historical sites
plants and facilities

government
municipal
state
national

testing sites
laboratories
research centers
think tanks

conventions gatherings
sales
professional
hobby shows
fairs

workplace
corporate database
company files
bulletin boards

362 The Library

Is a library simply shelves of dusty books? A place to catch a nap, sneak a snack, or deal some cards? The territory of gray-haired librarians in horn-rimmed glasses?

If that's what you think, maybe you haven't been to a good library recently. Yes, a library is books. But it's also much more—it's an information center that not only stores books, magazines, newspapers, videos, microfilms, and CD-ROM's but also hooks you into information sources around the globe. Libraries are places where information is hap'nin'.

363 Understanding the Average Library

Because of all the new technology, libraries are changing every day. Not to worry. Underneath all that new library razzle dazzle, you'll still find the same basic components as before—human experts to ask for advice, catalogs to search, and collections of materials to explore in many forms.

librarians: Librarians are information experts who manage the library's materials, guide you to resources, and help you perform on-line, CD-ROM, and database searches.

catalogs: Catalogs are databases that guide you to the materials you need. The traditional card catalog is a cabinet with small drawers and alphabetically arranged cards. The modern on-line catalog is a computerized database. Both catalogs refer to the library's material using either the Dewey Decimal or Library of Congress numbering system.

collections: A library's collection is all the materials it contains. It varies greatly from one library to the next, but the collection usually includes the following:

- **books**—fiction and nonfiction (See 353.)

- **periodicals**—magazines, journals, newspapers (See 356.)

- **reference materials**—directories, indexes, handbooks, encyclopedias (See 347, 348, 355.)

- **audiovisual materials**—videotapes, CD's, audiotapes, microfilm

- **special materials**—government documents, local history, artwork, pamphlets

- **computer resources**—the catalog itself, CD-ROM items, on-line databases, and Internet access (See 375-383.)

364 Using the Library

Talk to a Librarian

If you're looking for information, the main branch of a public library is probably your best choice. Smaller branches may be fine for finding a good book to read, but if it's time to get serious about research, head for a large public library with a big reference department.

Librarians are your biggest resource. Don't forget to ask for help.

- 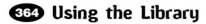 **Ask the reference librarian for help.** She or he is an expert on the reference room and can often save you hours of work.

- **Get the book you need.** If your library does not have a book you need, ask for an interlibrary loan. If a book you want has been checked out, ask them to reserve it and call you when it comes in.

- **Let your fingers do the walking.** If you are working away at home and suddenly need to know a simple fact, you can call the library and get the answer.

Check Out the Card Catalog

Libraries offer either computerized card catalogs, manual card catalogs, or both. In either case, books are generally arranged by author, title, and subject. Many card catalogs offer additional information, and some even provide brief descriptions of the book. The card catalog can be a logical starting point if you have an author, title, or subject in mind.

NOTE: Often it's enough just to get a couple of call numbers and then to go to that section of the library and browse through the books.

Browse Through an Index

An index is an alphabetical listing of topics and their location in a book. Many nonfiction books have indexes in the back that will help you identify whether the subject you are researching is covered in the book. The indexes listed below give you a quick way to find recent information.

Readers' Guide to Periodical Literature ● This index is a great place to find current articles on your subject that have appeared in general interest magazines, such as *Newsweek* and *Seventeen.* Once you've gotten familiar with the shade of green that these guides are always published in, you will spot them quite easily in the reference room.

Business Periodicals Index ● This index has information on many topics and covers business-related periodicals from *Forbes* to *Automotive News.* The information here is more technical than in magazines indexed in the *Readers' Guide,* but that may be just what you need.

New York Times Index ● The *New York Times* is a highly respected newspaper, and the beauty of this index is that it gives summaries of all the articles that have been published in the paper. Sometimes the summary will be all you need. If you want to read the article, many libraries provide microfilm that you can view on a special machine.

365 Finding Books

You can locate books in a library through two methods. First, you can browse the shelves using the classification scheme (how the books are grouped by subject) to focus your search. Second, you can use the catalog to find a book's call number, telling you its exact spot on a shelf.

366 The Card Catalog

The **card catalog** is an index (listing) of nearly all the materials in the library. The traditional catalog is a "dictionary catalog" in which subject, author, and title cards are filed alphabetically. Each book has at least three entry cards: one for the general subject, one for the author's name, and one for the title. A book may also have more cards for additional subjects. Once you've found your title, copy down the call number.

SUBJECT CARD

OCCUPATIONS--UNITED STATES — Subject heading

331.702 Farr, Michael J.
AME   America's top technical and trade jobs
/ 2nd. ed. Michael J. Farr. -- Indianapolis: — Publisher and copyright date
JIST, 1994.

1. Labor market--United States
2. Employment forecasting--United States

AUTHOR CARD

331.702 Farr, Michael J. — Call number
AME   America's top technical and trade jobs — Title and publication
/ 2nd. ed. Michael J. Farr. -- Indianapolis: information
JIST, 1994.

ISBI

1. Labor market--United States
2. Employment forecasting--United States
3. Occupations--United States

TITLE CARD

America's top technical and trade jobs — Title heading

331.702 Farr, Michael J. — Author
AME   America's top technical and trade jobs
/ 2nd. ed. Michael J. Farr. -- Indianapolis: — Subject
JIST, 1994.   headings
ISBN

1. Labor market--United States
2. Employment forecasting--United States
3. Occupations--United States
4. Vocational guidance--United States
5. Job hunting--United States

ISBN   1-563-70041-7

367 The Computerized Catalog

The computerized or on-line catalog can make finding information easier and faster. What follows is a typical start-up screen and some basic guidelines to get you started.

> Welcome to the Rapid City Public Access On-line Catalog
>
> Databases:
>
> 1. author, title, subject searching
> 2. general periodical index
> 3. information about system libraries
>
> To make a selection, type a number and then press [RETURN] >>>

Let's say you need to find a book. By simply typing in the number 1, you are ready to begin. After making a series of choices, you may come up with a screen that looks like the one shown below. Either print out the screen or write down the information you need (perhaps the title and call number).

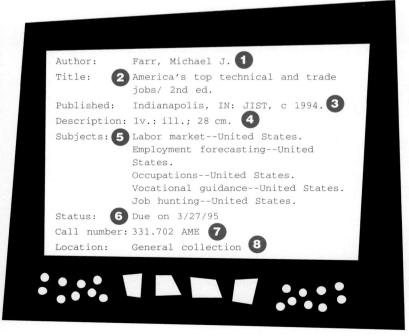

Author: Farr, Michael J. **1**
Title: **2** America's top technical and trade jobs/ 2nd ed.
Published: Indianapolis, IN: JIST, c 1994. **3**
Description: 1v.: ill.; 28 cm. **4**
Subjects: **5** Labor market--United States.
             Employment forecasting--United States.
             Occupations--United States.
             Vocational guidance--United States.
             Job hunting--United States.
Status: **6** Due on 3/27/95
Call number: 331.702 AME **7**
Location: General collection **8**

1 Author's name

2 Title heading

3 Publisher and copyright date

4 Descriptive information

5 Subject heading(s)

6 Library status

7 Call number

8 Location information

368 Keyword Searching

Because an on-line catalog is a computerized database, it offers you tremendous power to find material through a technique called keyword searching. How does it work?

◎ By following commands or choosing items from menus, you can search all of the catalog's entries to see which ones have a particular word in them—an author's name, a word in a title, or a word that describes its subject matter.

◎ In a few seconds, the computer will tell you how many entries contain that keyword. You can then look at each entry to see how useful the material might be and to get the call number. Some catalogs even tell you if the material is in the library or signed out.

For example, if you want information on the fish industry, you might type "fisheries" when the computer asks for your keyword and get a list of 15 books with that word in their titles or as their subject.

369 Broadening or Narrowing a Search

You can further control your search by combining keywords using commands such as *or*, *and,* and *not*.

Broadening a Search

To broaden a search, use "or." For example, if you want works on traditional fisheries and modern fish farming, you might type "fisheries **or** aquaculture" and get 25 entries with either keyword in them.

Narrowing a Search

Sometimes too many possibilities make your research difficult. Using "and" or "not" lets you limit your options. For example, typing "fisheries **and** oil spills" would give you only entries that contain both keywords—and far fewer entries than if you had typed "or." Similarly, if you typed "oil spills **not** *Exxon Valdez*," you would get entries on oil spills, but entries with the *Exxon Valdez* spill as their central topic would be excluded.

This question remains: How do you choose your keywords? You may refer to the on-line catalog instructions, get help from a librarian, or look at the Library of Congress subject headings inside a book on the same subject.

Terms for Broadening or Narrowing a Search

AND: find records that contain more than one term / bats and radar

OR: find records that contain either term / teen or adolescent

NOT: exclude records that contain a term / oil spills not Exxon Valdez

370 Locating Books by Call Number

You can use either the card catalog or the on-line catalog to help you identify books (and other library materials) related to your research. To find a book on the shelves, you will need to use the **call number** listed on the catalog card or on-line entry. This call number refers to the classification system used to arrange books. (The most common system used in high schools and public libraries is the Dewey Decimal classification system.) Here is a sample call number:

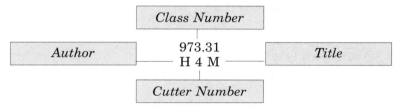

Class Number

Author   973.31   Title
          H 4 M

Cutter Number

INSIDE

info

All books are arranged by call numbers except fiction books and individual biographies. Fiction is usually kept in a separate section of the library where the books are arranged by the author's last name. Biographies are arranged on separate shelves by the last name of the person written about.

371 Searching the Shelves

When you go to the shelves to get your book, you must remember to look carefully at the call numbers. Because some call numbers contain several decimal points and are longer than others, they can easily distract you into looking in the wrong place for your book. For instance, the call number 973.2 is located on the shelf after a book with the call number 973.198. (See the illustration below.) Also, you will most likely find several books with the same number. Whenever this happens, the books are arranged alphabetically by the author's last name.

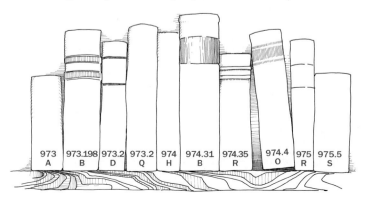

| 973 | 973.198 | 973.2 | 973.2 | 974 | 974.31 | 974.35 | 974.4 | 975 | 975.5 |
| A | B | D | Q | H | B | R | O | R | S |

372 Finding Articles in Periodicals

The best tool for locating articles in periodicals (magazines and journals) is the journal indexes that can be found in the reference or periodical section of the library. The most widely used journal index is the **Readers' Guide to Periodical Literature**. Some libraries also carry a CD-ROM version of this index. Other libraries carry a similar computer index called the **General Periodicals Index**.

373 Readers' Guide to Periodical Literature

If you are looking for information on a current topic, the *Readers' Guide* will direct you to specific magazine articles. It will also help you find magazine articles from years ago.

Locating Articles

Because there are thousands of periodicals, finding one article sounds difficult. But you can do it if you follow these steps:

1 **Discover what article you want by using an index:**
- a hard-copy version of the *Readers' Guide to Periodical Literature* or an index that lists periodicals on one specific subject (For more information on indexes, check 355.)
- an on-line catalog version of the hard-copy *Readers' Guide* or several indexes combined in one database
- a CD-ROM or on-line database that gives you either whole articles or lists of articles to look up

2 **Check the library's current list of periodicals.**

Look especially at the dates and issues the library has and what form the periodical is in (hard copy or microfilm).

3 **Locate and get the article.**

You might have to give your librarian a call slip listing the periodical's title, date, and volume so that he or she can get it for you. Or you might have to get the periodical yourself by checking in the periodical collection.

NOTE: What if you can't get the article at your library? Request it through interlibrary loan. Ask your librarian how to do this.

A Closer Look at the *Readers' Guide*

- Articles are arranged alphabetically by subject and author; the title of the article is listed under each of these two entries.
- Each subject entry is divided into subtopics whenever there are several articles on the same subject listed together.
- The *Readers' Guide* is cross-referenced, giving other subject headings where you may find additional articles on related topics.

374 Sample *Readers' Guide* Page

"SEE ALSO" REFERENCE

PAGE NUMBER(S)

VOLUME

NAME OF MAGAZINE

NAME OF AUTHOR

SUBTOPIC

DATE

"SEE" CROSS-REFERENCE

TITLE OF ARTICLE

SUBJECT ENTRY

AUTHOR ENTRY

ENVIRONMENTAL MOVEMENT
See also
Conservation of resources
Environmental associations
Industry and the environment
Minorities and the environment
Field observations [interview with W. Berry] J. Fisher-
Smith. il por *Orion* v12 p50-9 Aut '93
Pacific Northwest
Reconciling rural communities and resource conservation
[Pacific Northwest; with editorial comment by Timothy
O'Riordan] K. Johnson. bibl f il *Environment* v35
p inside cover, 16-20+ N '93
Vancouver Island (B.C.)
Brazil of the North? [battle over logging in Vancouver
Island's Clayoquot Sound area] C. A. White. il *Canada
and the World* v59 p8-9 S '93
ENVIRONMENTAL POLICY
See also
Air pollution—Laws and regulations
Genetic research—Environmental aspects
Industry and the environment
The compensation game [taking cases] F. Williams.
il por *Wilderness* v57 p28-33 Fall '93
Images of home [population and the environment] C. A.
Douglas. il *Wilderness* v57 p10-22 Fall '93
Unfunded federal environmental mandates. P. H. Abelson.
Science v262 p1191 N 19 '93
International aspects
The best environment of 1993. il *Time* v143 p74 Ja 3 '94
Public opinion
Of global concern: results of the Health of the planet sur-
vey [cover story] R. E. Dunlap and others. bibl f il
Environment v35 p6-15+ N '93
United States
See Environmental policy
ENVIRONMENTAL RACISM *See* Minorities and the
environment
ENVIRONMENTAL REGULATIONS *See* Environmental
policy
ENVIRONMENTAL SYSTEMS PRODUCTS INC.
Playing favorites [L. Weicker fires L. Goldberg over
Connecticut state contract for auto emissions testing]
C. Byron. il pors *New York* v27 p12-13 Ja 10 '94
ENVIROTEST SYSTEMS CORPORATION
Playing favorites [L. Weicker fires L. Goldberg over
Connecticut state contract for auto emissions testing]
C. Byron il pors *New York* v27 p12-13 Ja 10 '94
EPHRON, NORA
about
Sleepless in Seattle's Nora Ephron [interview] C. Krupp.
il por *Glamour* v91 p147-8 Ag '93
EPIDEMICS
See also
AIDS (Disease)

375 Computer Networks

We've already seen that computers can be a valuable source of information. Most libraries these days could hardly operate without them. If you've ever used a computerized card catalog, you were probably hooked on it immediately. The same goes for learning to use a CD-ROM to research old magazine articles or business databases.

376 Personal Networks

But libraries are no longer the only place where you can use power-ful computers to retrieve information. Personal computers are finding their way into more schools, offices, and homes than ever. And when hooked up to a modem and a telephone line, PC's open up a world of news, databases, conversation, and more. Imagine using your home computer to do the following:

◉ Access the computerized card catalog at your local library—or at a library hundreds of miles away

◉ Grab information about a product directly from the manufacturer, without waiting on hold or paying for a long-distance call

◉ Explore the libraries of hundreds of government agencies, and copy selected documents to your PC for viewing or printout

NOTE: Think of computer networking as just another program on your PC, only this one doesn't process words or crunch numbers. Instead, it calls other computers and exchanges data with them.

377 On-line Services

If you're new to computer networking, you might want to start by subscribing to an on-line service such as Prodigy, Compuserve, or America Online. On-line services offer their members numerous infor-mational sources:

◉ Reference materials, such as electronic encyclopedias, popular magazines and newspapers, and business and financial references

◉ Forums where you can discuss subjects you're interested in and receive comments and answers from other members (Most on-line services have hundreds of these forums, divided into specific subject areas and staffed by knowledgeable experts.)

◉ Electronic mail from other members on the service, or from anyone on the Internet

INSIDE

info

Be careful. Most on-line services charge by the hour, and while some offer several "free" hours each month, those can be eaten up quickly. Either watch your usage closely or sign up for a plan that has a flat monthly fee.

378 The Internet

There are millions of computer networks around the world. Computer networks are set up so that more than one user can get access to the same information. Many medium-sized and large corporations have all of their employees "wired" together in computer networks. It makes sharing possible, which can be a big help when you're trying to locate information. By learning to "surf the Net," you can turn your desktop PC into a global library.

Once you have an account with an on-line service such as Prodigy, Compuserve, or America Online, you are ready to begin using the Internet. Before you do, though, you need to understand how the system works and what tools you have available to you. The list that follows should help.

379 **Electronic Mail (E–Mail):** E-mail gives network users a channel for sending messages to electronic mailboxes. Your account should come with instructions on using the electronic mail program to communicate with other people on your local network, or over the Internet.

- An Internet e-mail address consists of the name of the person you are mailing to, followed by the @ ("at") symbol, followed by the name of the computer they're on (**Example:** president@whitehouse.gov).

- You must enter an e-mail address exactly as it is given to you, otherwise your e-mail will "bounce" (return to sender).

INSIDE info

Keep paper and pencil handy so that you can jot down e-mail addresses. Some computers have on-line "white pages" for searching out names and addresses. Usually, however, the best way to find out someone's e-mail address is to call them up and ask.

380 **File Transfer Protocol (FTP):** You can use the Internet's FTP tool to transfer whole files, such as computer programs or informational documents, anywhere in the world.

- Many files are available for anonymous FTP; that is, FTP where you log in to another computer over the Internet, using "anonymous" as your logging name and typing in your e-mail address instead of a password. Anonymous FTP was set up to allow a free exchange of available information to anyone with Internet access.

- Usually transferring files over the Internet requires two steps: FTP to bring the file from another computer to your local Internet, and then another step to download the file onto your own PC.

- A database named Archie allows you to search the entire Internet for files available for anonymous FTP. Like a computerized card catalog, it uses keywords you type in to locate the specific files you're interested in.

381 **World Wide Web (WWW):** One of the most exciting and popular uses of the Internet is to display words, pictures, and sounds by a complex technology called the World Wide Web, also known simply as "the Web."

- Millions of Web "pages" are available for browsing. They are called pages because Web technology lets pictures and text be arranged in a way that resembles pages from a book.

- The Web also uses "hypertext links" that connect WWW pages to one another. You might be reading a Web page about travel in Africa, and by selecting the word "Congo" be instantly switched to a full-color map of that African nation.

- There are special WWW pages that allow you to search the entire Internet according to keywords you type in. You can then go to any of the Web pages that come up as a result of your search.

382 **Usenet News:** All of these electronic libraries are great to have, but what if you need a librarian? That's why there's Usenet News, a collection of thousands of electronic bulletin boards on topics ranging from astronomy to motorcycles to personal finance to Zoroastrianism. Millions of people read Usenet "newsgroups," as these bulletin boards are called, every week.

- It's best to get acquainted with a newsgroup before posting any new messages to it. Look around for a frequently-asked questions file (FAQ) for the newsgroup—most have one. FAQ's are often chock-full of useful information, and if you're interested enough in the subject, they are worth downloading to your PC.

- Remember that messages on Usenet are like having a conversation with a friend—not like reading an encyclopedia. Check things you read in newsgroups against other sources to make sure the information you're getting is accurate.

Netiquette

Use the Internet wisely by observing network etiquette (called Netiquette):

1. Don't bother strangers by sending junk mail or starting unnecessary conversations.

2. Use the Internet efficiently by working with nearby networks if possible and doing lengthy operations, such as file transfers, outside of peak-use hours.

3. Be aware of laws covering copyrighted material, licensing, and software shipping, especially across national boundaries.

4. Avoid too much game playing with the Internet and activities that interfere with others' work.

383 Tips for Traveling on the Information Superhighway

Before you strike out in search of productive information, you might want to consider the following advice.

1. Cut yourself some slack.

Sometimes a search can get complicated. Computer networks often experience traffic jams, and Internet computers occasionally shut down without warning. Be patient, detour to another destination, and try again later.

2. Work intelligently.

Because finding information is intelligence work, use your smarts to do the following:

- Narrow your search to a few key questions
- Know what you need to do and then let deadlines tell you what to do next
- Judge the quality of the information you are getting
- Use the resources you find to discover more resources
- Understand how the information is organized and presented

3. Realize that the technology you use to find information is just a tool, not magic.

Like a hammer or saw, an information tool—from a book to CD-ROM—becomes useful to you with practice. Learn what each technology can and cannot do. Don't saw with a hammer.

4. Cope with frustration.

When you do find information, you may find that it is too simple or too complex for your needs. Don't despair. Use what you can and move on.

5. Get to know the right people.

Information specialists are everywhere—beside you in the workplace, in libraries, in other companies, in government. Make them your allies.

6. Arrange information around you for efficiency.

Information resources that you use often should be close at hand. What good does your phone book do in the attic?

SPEAKING

Speaking and Listening

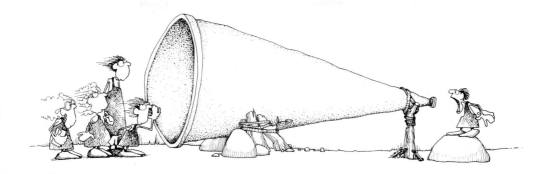

Understanding the Process

Speaking and listening well on the job means more than just flapping your lips and answering "Uh-huh" once in a while. It means knowing your situation as well as you know your coworkers. It means considering others as much as you consider yourself and listening and observing more than you speak. It means knowing the special language of your office or work site and exercising compassion, fairness, and good judgment. In short, it means following the speaker's Golden Rule:

Speak unto others as you would have them speak unto you.

What's Ahead?

This chapter provides an overview of communicating in the workplace, with special emphasis on speaking and listening. Here's what you'll find:

Elements in the Process
Speaking Effectively
The Advantages of the Spoken Message
The Listening Process in Action
Listening Effectively

385 Elements in the Speaking/Listening Process

Let's sort out the six main elements of a speaking and listening situation:

- Situation
- Sender
- Message
- Code
- Text
- Receiver

These make better sense if you weave them into a single sentence: "In a specific *situation,* a *person* (or *sender*) uses the language *code* to send a *message,* in the form of a *text,* to a specific *receiver.*"

Sounds easy. We do it almost unconsciously. However, a few definitions and cautions might be helpful:

Situation

Definition: "Situation" means the set of circumstances in the workplace (as in "Sorry, can't talk long . . . we're about to call a meeting"). Just as importantly, it may mean what's going on in the company or the world: Is the supervisor's mother ill? Is the national economy in a slump?

Difficulty: It's often hard to tell exactly what the situation is. Those who tell us what it is sometimes don't really know; those who know often don't tell.

Sender

Definition: The "sender" is the speaker or writer of a message.

Difficulty: Sometimes the sender is speaking in his or her own behalf. But sometimes the speaker represents someone else: an office, a position, a committee.

Message

Definition: The "message" is the information, idea, or attitude that the sender wants to send.

Difficulty: Sometimes the surface message doesn't agree with the "submessage," or message beneath the surface. And sometimes the submessage means more than the message itself (**Example:** "Clean out your desk before Tuesday" could mean "You're fired!").

Code

Definition: The "code" is the language that people in the workplace agree to speak.

Difficulty: This means more than "Do you speak English?" It also means: Do you speak a special jargon in this field? Do any of your terms have double meanings? Are there certain words or phrases you should avoid using?

Text

Definition: The "text" is the shape or form the message takes: spoken word, electronic transfer, body language, etc.

Difficulty: Each form or medium has its limitations and may force you to alter the message—or cause a misunderstanding. In E-mail, for example, if you type in ALL CAPITALS, the receiver will think you're "flaming" him, or showing disrespect. In spoken messages, the problem is that the "text" disappears as soon as it is spoken. Someone may have to take notes, and the new written text form may not be accurate.

Receiver

Definition: The "receiver" is the one who "gets" the message.

Difficulty: Sometimes sensitive messages fall into the wrong hands or are overheard by the wrong receiver. Sometimes messages are sent without sensitivity to the feelings, values, or responsibilities of the receiver. If the text of a message is not carefully worded, it may bring work to a halt just as surely as a broken machine does.

THE BOTTOM LINE

Now that you have a basic understanding of the elements involved in a speaking and listening situation, you should be ready to look more closely at what you can do to improve your own communication skills.

387 Speaking Effectively

Think Before You Speak

◉ Think about the subject and why you want to speak. Doing so can help you decide exactly what to say and how to say it.

◉ Think about the person you are speaking with both before and while you speak. This will help you shape your message so that what you say and the way you say it fit your listener.

Learn from Looking

◉ Pay attention to where you are and to anyone who is within hearing distance. This will help you make the message appropriate for the setting and the listeners.

◉ Look at your listener. Eye contact tells the person you care about the conversation and about him or her.

◉ Pay attention to how your listener looks and tailor your comments accordingly. Does she look puzzled? Is he nodding for you to go on? Be responsive to your listeners and help them understand your message.

Be Aware of Your Own Nonverbal Messages

◉ Be aware that you are *always* communicating, even when you're not saying a word. The expression on your face, how closely you stand to the listener, the gestures you use, and even your posture—all are forms of nonverbal communication.

◉ Be sure that your verbal and nonverbal messages match. Some researchers say that over 90 percent of communication is nonverbal. If you're talking about cooperation as you're pounding your fist on the desk, people will believe your fists more than your words.

Listen to Your Listener

◉ Pay attention to feedback from your listener. While you're talking, the listener may say things like "Oh," "Really?" "Hmmm, I wonder," or "Ah, I see." Your listener may laugh, groan, or sigh. Each word or sound is feedback—a hint that indicates whether the listener understands you.

◉ Know when to quit. If you've made your points and you're confident the listener understands, end the conversation. If your listener has additional questions, tell him you'll get back to him with the answers, and do so.

388 Advantages/Disadvantages of the Spoken Message

	Advantages	Disadvantages
Most Spoken Messages	• In addition to words, speaker is able to communicate with tone, pause, rhythm, etc. • Speaker can easily change or rephrase a message. • Speaker can get immediate feedback. • Speaker can send message quickly. • Listener can get message in little time.	• Speaker cannot take back a message. • Unless message is recorded, listener has only one chance to hear entire message, and no chance to review parts of message. • Unless message is recorded, only those who hear message receive it.
One-on-One (Person-to-Person)	• Message can be personal. • Speaker can shape message to fit an individual and a specific setting. • Form is quick, convenient. • Speaker gets immediate feedback. • Form is effective for short, simple messages. • Speaker can leave a message with an answering service.	• Speaker can be interrupted with questions and comments. • May take more time than sending a written message. • Long-distance call is more expensive than a letter. • Speaker's call may interfere with listener's activity. • Listener may be unavailable at speaker's convenience.
Voice Mail	• Form is quick, convenient. • Speaker can send message to more than one person. • Speaker can send message at his or her convenience. • Listener can retrieve message at his or her convenience. • Listener can review message. • Speaker can revise message while speaking. • Listener has a record of message.	• Form requires equipment. • Form is less personal than person-to-person conversation. • Listener cannot see facial expressions or gestures. • Message can be intercepted by someone who knows your code. • Once message is sent, speaker cannot retrieve it. • There is no way to clarify confusing messages.

389 The Listening Process in Action

"Okay, team, now listen up! We've got three seconds on the clock. Jill, you stand under the basket and pass the ball to . . . Jill . . . hey, Jill! Didn't you hear me?"

Hearing and listening are not the same on the basketball court or on the job. As Steil, Barker, and Watson explain in their book, *Effective Listening,* listening is a process. Watch how the process works in the scene below.

A Day at the Park

You're sitting in Yankee Stadium. It's the bottom of the eighth inning and the Yanks are behind the Texas Rangers 5 to 2. It's noisy. Fans are yelling, music is blasting, and a plane flies overhead. Then from way up in the top row comes, "Caaaarameled apples! I got caaaarameled apples!"

The listening process has been set in motion. Sound waves carry the vendor's gargled call from his mouth into your ear. Inside your ear are a tiny hammer and anvil. The sound waves make the hammer hit the anvil, and that sends an electronic message to your brain. The moment that the message hits your gray matter, you **hear**, or *sense,* sound.

But hearing is not the same as listening. Hearing is nothing more than the physical activity of sound waves moving from the vendor's mouth to your brain. That's it. Listening is more complex. Listening is a four-step process during which you (1) sense sound, (2) interpret it, (3) evaluate it, and (4) respond to it.

Let's go back to the ballpark. The vendor's voice reaches your brain, and you **hear or sense** something. That's step #1.

In a split second your brain **interprets** the message and decides what it means. Your brain thinks about the message, "Caaaarameled apples! I got caaaarameled apples!" Then it decides, "Hey, some dude is selling carameled apples and thinks that I may want one." That's the end of step #2.

Next, your brain **evaluates** the message—it decides whether you agree with the message. You think, "Hmmm, carameled apples, huh? Do I need a carameled apple?"

"No," you think, "I don't need one. Shoot, who needs a carameled apple?" And then you imagine that sweet, sticky caramel wrapped around a cool, juicy apple, and you think, "But do I want a carameled apple? Do I *want* one?"

"Yes, I do," you decide. "I want a carameled apple!" That's the end of step #3.

Finally, you **respond**—you do something in response to having heard, interpreted, and evaluated the message. You stand up, turn around, raise your arm, and yell, "Caaaarameled apple! I want a caaaarameled apple! Right here, right now! Caaaarameled apple!" That's the end of step #4. You just finished the process of listening.

390 Listening Effectively

Prepare to Listen

- Have a positive attitude. If you are motivated to listen well, you probably will.
- Keep an open mind about the speaker and topic. Don't decide whether you agree or disagree until after you've heard it all.
- Prepare by reading or thinking about what you may hear.
- Have a goal. Decide what you want to gain by listening: get facts, learn a process, understand an idea.

Avoid Bad Listening Habits

- Don't fake it—acting as though you're listening (nodding now and then, laughing along) while you're actually daydreaming.
- Don't listen only for the parts of the message that you can use to support your own arguments, or to focus the conversation on yourself.
- Avoid thinking about what you are going to say next. Keep your mind focused on the speaker.

Get the Message

- Concentrate on hearing all the words and sensing all the nonverbal cues: gestures, facial expressions, and vocal tone.
- Listen for major points and supporting details; think about the relationship between those points.
- Listen for signal words that tell you something about the message— words like *as a result, next, second, more important.*
- Determine the speaker's purpose: to convince, to explain, to inform.
- Listen for bias or prejudice. Is the speaker fair and objective?
- Think about how the speaker uses emotion and humor. Are they used to manipulate the audience or to help them understand?
- Take notes thoughtfully. Jot down main points, conclusions, and questions.

Digest the Message

- Review your notes and think about the message.
- Ask questions such as "How does this relate to me?" and "How can I use the information?"
- Summarize the entire message in one sentence.
- Discuss the importance of the message with others.

391

Listening Stages

	Barriers	**Breakthroughs**
Stage 1: Sensing Sounds	• other competing sounds • difficulty in hearing	• Close windows or doors. • Move away from competing noise source and closer to speaker. • Turn down radio or TV.
Stage 2: Interpreting	• halfhearted attention • being distracted by another conversation or activity	• Pay full attention to both verbal and visual cues. • If you're unable to shift your focus, tell the speaker and arrange an alternate time: "Charlie, I'd love to hear your idea, but right now I have to finish this job. Can we talk in half an hour?"
Stage 3: Evaluating	• not trying to understand the other person • thinking of your next response instead of what's being said • jumping to conclusions	• If you're unsure of any point, ask questions. • Give a short summary of what the speaker said to make sure you understand. • Decide whether you agree with the message.
Stage 4: Responding	• being too quick to respond or too fearful to respond	• Give appropriate feedback: a smile, a nod, a comment, or even another question.

THE BOTTOM LINE

The highest level of listening involves a quality called empathy. Empathy is looking at and listening to the world through the eyes and ears of the speaker. No one is born with this skill, but like any other skill, it can be learned.

Communicating
with Another Person

Alaina sometimes fails to explain to her employees exactly how to do a new task. She's like a broken record. She says, "Just get started. You'll figure it out." Well, her secretary figured out the electric pencil sharpener, but without good instruction, she goofed up the computerized filing system.

Casey feels overworked. But instead of stating his concern to his team leader in private, he spouts sarcastic comments when the leader strolls through the office.

When person-to-person communication breaks down in this way, everybody in the workplace loses. Better communication begins when coworkers learn more respectful attitudes, as well as effective techniques for sharing information and dealing with conflicts.

What's Ahead?

This chapter looks at ways to improve your ability to communicate with other people:

Communicating with Respect

Giving and Taking Instructions

Giving and Taking Criticism

Dealing with Conflict

393 Communicating with Respect

Open communication requires that two people respect both themselves and each other.

1. Respect yourself by

- ◉ believing that your own thoughts and feelings have value,
- ◉ taking responsibility for what you think and how you feel, and
- ◉ expecting others to respect what you think and feel.

2. Respect the other person by

- ◉ using an appropriate name or title (see chart, 394),
- ◉ asking only for a reasonable amount of the person's time,
- ◉ explaining things clearly at the other person's level of understanding, and
- ◉ wearing appropriate dress and using good manners.

Know Your Listener

Is your message worth the other person's time? That depends. Will your message help the listener do her or his job? Who else wants a slice of this person's time? What does the other person already know about the subject? Has the listener asked for the message? Does the listener have an attitude toward what you are about to say? Does the listener have any "pet peeves"?

In any work situation, it is politically wise to spend some energy getting to know the jobs, the sensitivities, and the personalities of others. Such knowledge will help you to be tactful. Speaking to someone you haven't bothered to learn about is like sending them junk mail.

Know Your Stuff

The best compliment you can pay to a listener is to prepare well before communicating a message. Think it through: facts, background, and implications. If you are proposing something, research your topic well, and anticipate the likeliest objections. If you are citing problems, also propose solutions. Know your subject well enough so that you can describe it from more than one angle.

Send a Clear Message

You can send a clear message by

- using words your listener will understand,
- putting the most important ideas either first or last,
- communicating not only *what* but *why* and *what next,* and
- concentrating on not being <u>mis</u>understood.

394

Addressing Another Person

Female

Ms. .... formal, appropriate when not wanting to designate a female's marital status

Mrs. (married)
Miss (unmarried) ..... formal

Madam, Ma'am .... appropriate when speaking to an adult whose name you do not know

Male

Mr. .... formal, respectful of a person's position or age

Sir .... appropriate when speaking to an adult whose name you do not know

Male or Female

Professor, President, Representative, Prime Minister,
Senator .... formal, preferred over Mr., Ms., Miss, or Mrs.

Pastor, Reverend,
Father, Rabbi .... formal

Doctor .... formal, particularly appropriate in academic
(Academic,   settings or formal introductions
Ph.D., Ed.D.)

Doctor .... formal and informal
(Medical)

Nurse ....appropriate in a clinic or hospital when you don't know the person's name

Officer ....formal, appropriate for a police officer or security guard

Boss, Chief ....informal, rarely appropriate except for a chief of police or fire chief

Person's
first name ....informal, generally inappropriate for a person in authority (teacher, supervisor) or a person older than you

395 Communicating Instructions

Supervisor:	*(Pointing to keys on the counter.)* Hal, those are keys to a white '95 Transport parked by the loading dock. Run that thing in here, balance the wheels, rotate the tires, and check the right front for a slow leak.	*Instructions include a gesture and a step-by-step process, but they do not include details like where the loading dock is or how to do each step.*
Hal:	Ninety-five white Transport, balance, rotate, and check left front for a leak?	*Question asks supervisor to confirm the steps and task.*
Supervisor:	Right front.	*Supervisor corrects detail.*
Hal:	Right front. Got it. *(Hal leaves to do the task.)*	*Feedback shows that Hal understands.*

The Process in Action

The above conversation takes place in a Pontiac garage and is an example of a kind of spoken "shorthand" that people use who know each other and their jobs well. Both characters speak clearly, get to the point quickly, and listen carefully.

While spoken shorthand is common in the workplace, giving and taking instructions is often a longer process, one that includes asking questions, showing, explaining, describing, and sometimes teaching.

Tips for Successful Instruction

● Think and speak clearly.

● Demonstrate the procedure (if possible), explaining as you go.

● Use proper terms and define them when necessary.

● Cover all steps and directions.

● Watch the listener's face carefully for signs of boredom or confusion.

396 Giving Instructions

Think about the entire task: Visualize each of the steps that make up the task. List each step, with a drawing if necessary.

Summarize the task: Help the listener see the whole task by giving him or her the big picture first. Use comparisons, or analogies, to further help the listener see what this task is like.

Organize the task: Break the task into a logical, step-by-step process and explain how to do each step. Again, use drawings or gestures to help clarify. Also include accurate distances and directions (up, down, north, south, etc.).

Repeat as necessary: Reword and repeat your explanation for any steps that are especially complicated. Speak slowly and clearly. Use short sentences—or long pauses—during the most important part of the explanation.

Ask for questions: Ask the listener if she or he has any questions. Answer each one clearly.

Review the process: Ask the person(s) you are instructing to review the process for you by performing the task or talking you through it step-by-step.

Taking Instructions

Listen to the summary: Try to understand the whole task before the instructor gets into the specific steps.

Listen to the steps: Pay attention and think about how to do each step. (Take notes if necessary.)

Ask for clarification: Ask questions or restate (in your own words) what you have been told to help you understand the whole task and each of the steps.

Follow the steps in order: Follow the instructions you've been given. Make sure you finish the task correctly and on time.

Ask for help: If you try to do the task and are not making good progress, ask for help. Don't risk a major mistake just because you're afraid to ask.

397 Communicating Criticism

> *Hey, I said, "Cut the 2" x 4" at a 35° angle!" You sleeping or what?*
>
> *You know, Terry, you're the grossest eater I've ever met.*
>
> *Are you serious? You still don't know how to log on to the Internet? Hmm . . .*

Has anyone ever criticized you like this? Then you know how insensitive criticisms can sting. Giving and taking criticism constructively is an indispensable skill for living and working. But criticism that is too broad, too harsh, or too personal often ends up hurting more than helping.

The Process in Action

Criticism is a valuable tool and a useful form of instruction, but only when it helps a speaker and listener work together to identify a problem and fix it. Here are examples of helpful instruction and helpful criticism:

◉ When you pitch a curveball, spread your fingers over the seams like this. (instruction)

◉ Not bad, but your fingers are too close together. Spread 'em out. Yeah, like that. (criticism)

◉ Then release the ball with a snap of the wrist like this. (instruction)

◉ Good try, but remember to snap it, really snap it! A twist will give you a hang ball, and you want a curve. (criticism)

Obviously the pitching instructor above knows how to both instruct and criticize. Most successful people do. People who don't learn the skills limit themselves. A person who cannot give criticism well has a limited ability to help someone else correct a problem. A person who cannot take criticism well is limited to using only his or her ideas and insights.

Tips for Giving Criticism

Because criticism is a form of instruction, follow the tips for giving instruction on the previous page. In addition, keep these guidelines in mind:

● Stay calm. Don't blow the situation out of proportion.
● Be courteous, concise, and fair.
● Avoid sarcasm, temper tantrums, or any form of rudeness.
● Listen carefully to identify any old, new, or hidden problems.
● Stick to the issue at hand.
● Keep the discussion impersonal.
● Leave the door open for further discussion or action.

398 Giving Criticism

Think about the problem: Limit criticism to a problem that the listener can understand and fix. Think about what the problem is and how the listener can solve it.

Think about your goal: What do you want to happen after you speak?

Think about the listener: Will the person benefit from the criticism? Does the listener have special needs that will make it difficult to use the criticism constructively?

Think about the setting: Is this setting the best time and place to give the criticism?

Shape the message: State the problem and solution clearly. Attack the problem, not the person. When appropriate, mention things that the person does well.

Rehearse the message: Practice by saying the criticism out loud or to yourself.

Deliver the message: Speak in an honest, positive tone. Observe closely in order to learn if the listener

- understands the problem,
- takes ownership of the problem,
- is committed to working toward a solution, and
- feels your support in achieving the solution.

Taking Criticism

Listen for the message: Listen for main points in the message by asking, "What is the problem?" Listen for the solution by asking, "What is my part in the solution, and will it fix the problem?"

Respect the speaker: Think about the person's ideas rather than how to defend yourself against those ideas, regardless of how the speaker delivers the criticism.

Value criticism: Remember, it helps you to understand that a problem exists, why it exists, and how it can be resolved.

Respect yourself: Take and use criticism daily. Respect yourself by being one who takes criticism calmly, evaluates it carefully, uses what is good, and courteously disposes of the rest.

(399) Dealing with Conflict

People in school and the workplace often disagree: It's all part of the learning and workplace process. When a disagreement helps people to identify a problem and make an improvement, it is a constructive conflict; when a disagreement hurts people or gets in the way of their work, it is a destructive conflict. Conflicts may take one of three forms: win/win, win/lose, or lose/lose.

Win/Win conflicts are constructive. In a win/win situation, both parties
- focus on solving the problem rather than defeating the other party,
- usually give up something, but gain something as well.

> A letter carrier disagrees with his supervisor about the time she allows him to deliver his route. After a few weeks of frustration, he gives her a plan for a slightly reorganized route. She reviews the plan and makes an additional change, and the two agree that both their changes are an improvement.

Win/Lose conflicts also may be constructive, at least for one of the parties. In a win/lose conflict,
- each party tries to solve a problem by defeating the other;
- one party gets what he or she wants, and the other does not.

> A short-tempered chemist in a research lab is very bright, but she regularly blames lab technicians when experiments are not successful. The technicians file a series of complaints with the manager. After the first complaint, the manager cautions the chemist; after the second, he writes a warning to the chemist; and after the third complaint, the chemist is fired. The chemist loses her job, but the working conditions of other employees improve.

Lose/Lose conflicts are nearly always destructive. Both parties usually
- try to defeat each other rather than find a mutual solution,
- lose things they care about, and are unhappy with the outcome.

> The owner of a wedding-supply store asks two employees to meet with a prospective bride to suggest flower arrangements and table decorations for the wedding reception. Rather than work together, the two employees offer different suggestions and criticize each other's ideas in front of the bride. The woman leaves the store without buying anything. The owner is not happy with either employee.

400 Resolving Conflict

Begin by listening carefully and thinking clearly. Before you can resolve any conflict, there must be (1) a clear understanding of the problem and (2) an appropriate solution. You need to listen and think to get the information you need.

Be honest, clear, and direct. If the other person feels that you're not being totally open, he or she will not trust you.

Do not use harsh or slanted language in order to win. You may lose not only the conflict and the other person's respect, but also respect for yourself.

Avoid the tension and hostility of lose/lose conflicts. Lose/lose conflicts tend to get increasingly emotional as each party abandons hope for a constructive solution and tries instead to defeat the opposition. Just as it's wise to run away from an angry swarm of hornets rather than fight, it's also wise to walk away from spiraling lose/lose conflicts.

Show goodwill even if you lose in a conflict. Remember that as time moves on, specific conflicts come and go, but you may have to work with that person for a long time.

Distinguish between a meaningful argument and a quarrel. While a meaningful argument is worth your time because it is an opportunity to identify a problem and solve it, a quarrel wastes your time and may hurt someone.

Settling Issues

Consider deferring by giving in to the other person

- when you discover you are wrong,
- when the issue is more important to the other person, or
- to let others learn by making their own mistakes.

Consider compromising by giving up something

- when there is not enough time to seek a win/win outcome,
- when the issue is not important enough to negotiate at length, or
- when the other person is not willing to seek a win/win outcome.

Consider cooperating by working to reach a common goal

- when the issue is too important for a compromise,
- when a long-term relationship is important, or
- when the other person is willing to cooperate.

Figure adapted from LOOKING OUT/LOOKING IN, Seventh Edition by Ronald B. Adler and Neil Towne, copyright © 1993 by Holt, Rinehart and Winston, Inc., reproduced by permission of the publisher.

401 Human Needs and Communication

Abraham Maslow, a famous psychologist, developed a theory to explain why people do what they do. Maslow said that all people have specific needs like the steps on a ladder. The first step represents some basic needs that must be met before a person can move on to anything else. Once those are taken care of, she or he can step up to the second rung, and so on.

Step 5	**The Need to Make the World Better** helping others meet their needs
Step 4	**The Need to Achieve, to Be "Somebody"** being good at some skill or activity getting recognition for something
Step 3	**The Need to Belong** being part of a family being part of the group
Step 2	**Basic Need for Safety** physical and emotional safety avoiding threatening situations
Step 1	**Basic Physical Needs** food, shelter, clothing

The Process in Action

Maslow's ladder can help you understand your own and others' needs in the workplace by remembering that people go up and down the ladder all the time.

Let's say you go to your after-school job as a cashier at Delightful Foods. You have a snack before you start (Step 1). You're at your assigned station feeling safe and ready to work (Step 2), and you've waved hello to the other cashiers who, all things considered, are an OK group (Step 3). As the afternoon wears on, you realize that you're good at what you do. No errors, no problems (Step 4). It's almost time to go home when your boss comes over and asks if you can stay an extra hour. Your stomach reminds you that it's time to eat (Step 1) and as much as you try, that's all you can think about for the next hour.

INSIDE info

What happened to you is what happens to everyone. Your needs must be met in a certain sequence, and when they're not, it's hard to concentrate on other things.

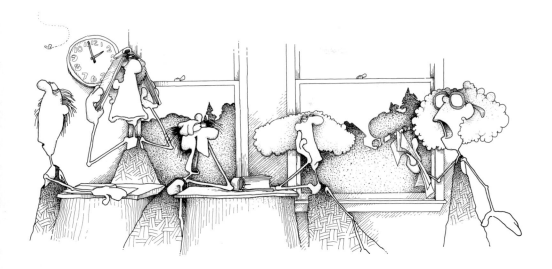

Communicating with a Group

Have you heard of a solar oven? By bouncing rays of sun off reflectors so that they all meet at one point, you can generate enough heat to broil a steak. When all members of a group are focused on the same task, something similar happens: useful work gets done.

What's the key to making your group "cook" like a solar oven? It can be stated in three words: communicate, communicate, and communicate. (Check out the group pictured above—postures, eyes, hands—do they look like they're communicating?) Following are some communication tips that should improve your group's focus.

What's Ahead?

This section of your handbook covers the following group-related topics:

What Is a Group?
Listening in a Group
Observing and Responding in a Group
Disagreeing in a Group
Working in a Group

403 What is a group?

A collection of individuals is not a group, but it may become one. For example, seven people who happen to step into an elevator at the same time are not a group. However, if that elevator gets stuck between floors, the individuals will probably form a group as they respond to their problem. They'll talk, interact, and try to find a way out of the elevator. In the process they will influence or affect each other.

> A group is
>> a small number of people
>> who get together,
>> communicate,
>> do something (like solve a problem),
>> and influence or affect each other.

Becoming a Group Is a Process

Groups don't just happen. Forming a group is a process during which people go through the following stages:

1. Groping: During this stage individuals usually aren't clear about
- the purpose of the group,
- the direction of the group, or
- the role each individual will play in the group.

2. Griping: This stage is the adjustment stage during which individuals adjust to
- the task of the group
- and the roles and personalities of others.

During this stage individuals often get frustrated and feel like griping.

3. Grasping: As people communicate and interact, they begin to understand each other as well as the purpose and direction of the group. Members begin listening, observing, and feeling more comfortable.

4. Grouping: People start working together by sharing ideas, responding to and clarifying one another's ideas, and accomplishing something together that they could not do alone. Individuals think of themselves as a team. Leaders emerge and efficient work begins.

404 Listening in a Group

Listening skills help group members understand each other and work together. The three tips below will help your group listen better.

1 Listen actively.

- ⊙ Think about the speaker's main point and supporting argument.
- ⊙ Listen with your eyes—watch gestures and facial expressions.
- ⊙ Take notes.
- ⊙ Think about how the message relates to what others have said.
- ⊙ Concentrate on what the speaker is saying rather than on how you will respond.
- ⊙ Think about how the message relates to the group's task.

2 Know when and how to interrupt.

It's rarely appropriate to interrupt a speaker, and then it's usually the group leader's responsibility to do it. But if you do interrupt, do it for the right reasons, and do it politely.

Right reasons:

- **For clarification:** "Excuse me, Samona, but how would your proposal help meet our goal to . . . ?"
- **For steering discussion:** "Pardon me, Mr. Lu, but I think you're now talking about the topic that we'll discuss this afternoon."
- **To keep someone from "hogging" discussion:** "Excuse me, Alexis, but I believe Becky made that point earlier. Would you care to add something?"
- **For scheduling purposes:** "Pardon me, Ms. Whitefeather. Our next session begins in five minutes, so would you please summarize your remaining points."

Wrong reasons:

- Because you *weren't listening carefully*
- Because you *disagree with the speaker's statement*
- Because you *are losing an argument or are angry*

3 Learn how to respond when interrupted.

If a person asks you to repeat something, do it. If the person asks again and is not paying attention, you may choose to reply, "I'll be happy to repeat that point, Andrea, but please let me finish my thought." Always respond politely—even when the person interrupting you is not polite.

405 Observing and Responding in a Group

Group members must work as a team. In order to do that, each person must observe and respond to (1) the needs of other individuals and (2) the needs of the group.

Respond to the needs of individuals . . .

◉ **Help everyone feel included.** Employees in the company you work for are meeting to evaluate your new computer software. You observe someone new in the meeting slouching in her chair and not communicating. You suspect that she may not feel welcome, so you respond by saying, "Juanita, I think you've used the software we're talking about. What do you think?"

◉ **Be sensitive to people who need more information.** You're in a hospital staff meeting and are about to report on a new patient monitoring system when you observe that two student nurses are sitting in on the session. You think that the students may need help following the report, and you respond by giving additional details about each part of the new system.

Respond to the needs of the group . . .

◉ **Encourage discussion.** A radio station manager speaking to a group of DJ's introduces new guidelines for choosing music. When he observes that the group seems frustrated by the guidelines, the manager responds by encouraging them to talk about it. "What do you think?" he asks. "Would these guidelines help us attract a broader audience?"

◉ **Snuff out confusion.** A personnel director is discussing retirement policy with a group of factory workers. When she observes that a number of people seem confused by the term "mutual funds," she responds by pointing out a definition in their handouts.

Tips for Responding

Purposeless chatter wastes time. Before you speak, ask yourself if your comment passes the tests below. If it doesn't, don't speak.

- Is my comment related to the topic being discussed?
- Is it appropriate at this point in the discussion?
- Does it add something new without simply repeating what someone else has already said?
- Does it help clarify a point or answer a question?

406 Disagreeing in a Group

An effective group listens to the ideas of all its members, evaluates the ideas, and then chooses the best one. In the process individuals must be able to disagree constructively—to communicate honestly without feeling threatened or defensive.

Disagreeing constructively may be the most difficult part of group discussion. The rules below will help you disagree in ways that help the group.

Rule 1: **Be tactful.**

Use "I" statements, not "you" statements. In other words, never blame or accuse others in the group. Instead, report your thoughts and feelings as your thoughts and feelings—nothing more, nothing less.

NOT: "You're dodging the issue!"

BUT: "I'd like to address this issue more directly."

Rule 2: **Disagree with a person's idea or work, not with the person himself or herself.**

Preserve goodwill by making sure the person understands that your disagreement has nothing to do with her worth as a human being.

> "I disagree with your proposal, Natalie, because the information on customer satisfaction includes data from only the last six months, not the entire year."

NOTE: With this approach, Natalie is likely to take your criticism well and hear what you have to say. Saying "I disagree with you," however, would be taken personally.

Rule 3: **Communicate your ideas honestly, but don't let your emotions get in the way of your ideas.**

If you're too angry to explain your ideas clearly, you probably should be quiet or take a time-out until you get control of your emotions.

If you can't speak your ideas without getting emotional, try writing them out and then reading only what you've written.

Rule 4: **Be willing to disagree when you can do it constructively.**

Communicating disagreement is sometimes necessary. In fact, when members of a group aren't able to voice their disagreement, they can become victims of "groupthink."

> *Groupthink is a condition in which all members support an idea or policy not because they agree with it, but because they're unable or unwilling to disagree.*

407 Working in a Group

When a group gets together to do its work, it usually concentrates on one or more of the following activities: *brainstorming, problem solving, informing,* and *decision making.*

408 Brainstorming

Brainstorming is a group activity that is used to come up with many ideas quickly. Groups brainstorm for many reasons:

● To generate ideas for raising money

● To list ideas for weekend activities

● To collect ideas for volunteer projects

● To list problems the group must address

Brainstorming usually includes these three steps: *generating, discarding,* and *evaluating.*

Generating: This step is like popping popcorn. Group members have one objective—to "pop" as many ideas as possible, as quickly as possible.

◉ The leader states the discussion topic or problem clearly.

◉ A secretary records the group's ideas—usually on a board or large sheet of paper where participants can see them.

◉ Participants pitch ideas as quickly as they pop into their minds.

◉ All ideas or solutions are welcome, even strange or far-out ones.

◉ The goal is quantity as well as quality—the more good ideas the better.

◉ Members listen carefully so one person's idea can trigger another's.

◉ Nothing is allowed that slows or gets in the way of new ideas:

• No person may judge another—all ideas are equally valuable regardless of who offers them.

• No one may make negative or questioning remarks like "That's not possible," "Wouldn't this cost too much?" or "But could we develop the product in time?"

Discarding: Group members look at their list of ideas and discard any duplicates.

Evaluating: Group members discuss the value of each idea and weed out the weaker ones until they find the best ones.

409 Problem Solving

No one can whistle a symphony. It takes an orchestra to play it. The same is true of some problems in school, the workplace, and society. Only groups can solve certain kinds of problems:

● Major disagreements between individuals

● Problems in the classroom or on the job

● Special needs in the community

A group will solve its problems more effectively if it has a method, one that allows it to work through its problem step by step:

1. Define the problem.

What is it?

2. Analyze the problem.

What are the causes?
Who or what is affected?
How do we know these things?

3. Set standards for choosing the best solution.

What should a solution accomplish?
How can we avoid solutions that create other problems?
What are we willing to pay for a solution (in terms of money, time, and effort)?

4. Identify possible solutions.

What solutions are available?
What solutions have been tried and how have they worked?
Which new solution would avoid past failures?

5. Select the best solution.

Which solution best meets our standards?

6. Decide how to evaluate whether the solution is working.

Before implementing a solution, decide how to test it after you have used it for a while.

7. Implement the solution.

Set guidelines for how and when the work must be done.
Assign people to put the solution into effect.
Assign people to evaluate the solution.

410 Presenting Information

Presenting information is a common activity for groups both in school and at work. Groups gather and present information for a variety of reasons:

- **To explain new policies or programs**
- **To provide training for new people**
- **To report on new products or procedures**

1. The leader introduces the topic and explains why the group needs information about it.

2. The speaker presents information on the topic—often with the help of handouts, displays, and projections.

3. The speaker or leader directs the group in a discussion about what the information means and why it is important. Individuals ask questions and give their opinions, but only if their comments help someone in the group better understand the information.

4. The discussion concludes when group members understand the information.

411 Making Decisions

Nearly all groups need to make decisions during or after the discussion process. Three methods groups can use for decision making are *authority, majority,* and *consensus.*

Authority The group will discuss the problem or topic and may make its recommendation, but one authority figure makes the final decision. Usually this person is the group leader. Occasionally an expert is invited to listen to the discussion and make the decision.

Majority The group decides by voting, and the side with the greatest number of votes wins. For example, if a 10-member group votes on two choices, a majority of votes is 6, or more than half of 10. However, if the same group votes on 3 choices, the majority will not necessarily be more than half. For example, the vote may go as follows: choice one—3 votes, choice two—3 votes, and choice three—4 votes. In this case, choice three has the majority, even though 4 is fewer than half of 10.

Consensus A group decides by consensus when *all* members agree to support a solution. Not all members will agree that it's the "best" solution, but they will all agree that it's a solution they can live with. Consensus decision making is time-consuming because it requires a lot of discussion and compromise. On the other hand, because all members feel that a decision is at least partly their own, a consensus decision will have more overall support than a majority decision.

Communicating in Meetings

If three clerks in a Fort Worth department store stop to talk about the sale on nightgowns—is that a business meeting? If four Idaho state troopers pull off the highway to have a cup of coffee and discuss how to handle slow cars in the fast lane—is that a business meeting? Yes, both are business meetings. But neither is a formal meeting. Formal meetings follow certain rules and procedures that participants should know.

What's Ahead?

This section of your handbook deals with the following meeting issues:

Formal vs. Informal Meetings

Officers and Their Responsibilities

Order of Business for a Meeting

Common Parliamentary Motions

413 Formal vs. Informal Meetings

In both schools and the workplace, most groups use a combination of formal and informal procedures. For example, the staff at the local school library may hold its weekly meetings with no prepared agenda (informal), but the head librarian will keep detailed minutes (formal). During the monthly meeting of shopping-mall personnel, store managers and security officers may discuss closing-time security measures. The mall manager leading the meeting may ask for a few minutes of open discussion (informal). However, when she thinks it's time to make a decision, she will call for a motion and a vote (formal).

Business Meeting Procedures

Knowing the difference between informal and formal procedures will help you understand which kind is being used during a meeting, and how you can participate. The table below lists characteristics of both.

Informal Procedure	Formal Procedure
• no prepared agenda	○ prepared agenda
• no minutes taken during meeting, though some participants may take notes	○ detailed minutes taken of topics discussed, key comments, all motions, people who make and second motions, and all decisions
• good for short conferences and making on-the-spot decisions	○ good for making a far-reaching decision requiring a record of both the decision and the dialogue that led to it
• usually unscheduled and held when needed	○ usually held on a regular, scheduled basis
• generally efficient for small groups	○ generally efficient for larger groups
• decisions made by authority or consensus—whichever is appropriate at the time	○ decisions made according to the rules in the group's constitution
• no elected or appointed leader	○ formally elected or appointed leader
• people speak and make decisions using rules of common courtesy	○ people speak and make decisions according to the rules of parliamentary procedure

414 Formal Meetings

In 1876 Henry M. Robert simplified a set of British rules known as parliamentary law. He wrote them in a handbook called *Robert's Rules of Order*. Today we use these rules to conduct meetings of all kinds—from the U.S. Senate to your town council to your high-school class.

Principles of Parliamentary Procedure

Parliamentary rules are a set of guidelines designed to help a group work together. The guidelines are based on the following principles:

1. **A group must work in a peaceful, orderly way.**

2. **The group makes decisions by "majority rule"** (they vote, and the side with one vote more than half the total number of votes wins).

3. **The minority must be treated fairly and respectfully.**

4. **The group chooses its own officers, who must serve the needs of the group.**

5. **All members are equal and have the opportunity to do the following:**
- attend meetings,
- be informed about what's going to happen in a meeting,
- have copies of the group's rules and policies,
- make motions,
- vote,
- nominate candidates for office,
- run for office,
- disagree with the group,
- inspect the official records of the group, and
- be treated according to the group's rules, even when being disciplined by the group.

TAKE NOTE

Each company or organization will have its own bylaws or special procedures for holding formal meetings. The principles of parliamentary procedure will be changed slightly to fit those bylaws.

415 Officers and Their Responsibilities

To help them do their work efficiently, groups usually have at least four officers: *president* (sometimes called the chairperson or chair), *vice president, secretary,* and *treasurer.* The group gives these officers the responsibility of acting on behalf of the group.

The President

As president, or main officer of your group, you have the following responsibilities:

Before the meeting . . .

- Prepare an agenda that lists what you plan to do during the meeting.
- Arrange for a meeting place that has adequate furniture and necessary audiovisual equipment.
- Send group members copies of the agenda along with the time and place of the meeting, how long the meeting will probably last, and any other necessary information.

During a meeting . . .

- Call the meeting to order, welcome members, and explain the purpose of the meeting.
- Introduce each topic clearly and keep the discussion focused.
- Encourage all members to participate; prevent any members from "hogging" the discussion.
- When the group seems unclear about where it is headed, summarize the discussion and point out the order of the agenda.
- When the group is unclear whether they agree on an issue, ask for a consensus with a question like "Do we agree that . . . ?"
- Resolve conflicts fairly.
- Don't push your own ideas or try to manipulate the discussion.
- Stay within the time scheduled for the meeting, but don't allow the group to make poor decisions because of lack of time.
- Bring the discussion to a conclusion and adjourn the meeting.

416

The Vice President

As vice president, you have the following duties:

- Chair a meeting when the president is absent.
- Take the office of the president if he or she resigns or is permanently unable to do the work.
- Represent the president when he or she asks you to.
- Do any assignments that the group's constitution requires the vice president to do.

Secretary

As secretary, you are the primary record keeper and correspondent. You do the following:

- Write minutes—the official record of what happens in each meeting. (See 222, 224.)
- Send correspondence when asked to do so.
- During meetings you
  - check attendance,
  - read minutes of the previous meeting,
  - give the secretary's report in which you tell about correspondence the group has received or correspondence you have sent, and
  - search minutes for information requested by members.

Treasurer

As treasurer, you have the following responsibilities:

- Keep the group's financial records, including a record of all money coming in and going out.
- Pay the group's bills and send bills to those who owe money to the group.
- During meetings you (1) distribute copies of the financial report and (2) present the information, including what was spent and taken in since the last meeting, and the current balance.

417 Order of Business for a Meeting

"Order of business" refers to how a meeting is organized, and includes the following activities:

1. **Call to Order:** The president or chairperson says something like "This meeting will now come to order," or "I believe everyone is here, so let's begin."

2. **Approving the Agenda:** The chair asks the group to look at the agenda and suggest necessary additions or changes.

3. **Reading the Minutes:** The chair asks the secretary to read the minutes aloud. Afterward, the chair asks, "Are there any additions or corrections?" If members have any corrections, those are made. Then the chair asks for a motion to approve the minutes. After the motion has been approved, the chair says, "The minutes are approved." (At this point the minutes become an official—and legal—record of the meeting.)

4. **Officers' Reports:** Officers may present reports. If a report includes lots of detail, an officer usually hands out printed copies.

5. **Committee Reports:** Committees who have been given a task are invited to give a report. If they have nothing to present, the committee chairperson says, "No report at this time."

6. **Old Business:** The chair asks, "Is there any old business we need to discuss?" "Old business" includes issues from previous meetings that need further discussion, as well as updates on issues discussed earlier.

7. **New Business:** The chair says, "We'll now deal with the new business." This includes items printed in or added to the agenda.

8. **Announcements:** The chair asks for announcements. Usually these include information about future meetings or issues related to the agenda.

9. **Adjournment:** The chair closes the meeting by asking for a motion to adjourn. If the motion is made and approved, the chair says, "This meeting is adjourned."

418 Making Motions

How do you get things done in a formal meeting? You make a motion. A motion is an idea for the group to think about and act on. In informal discussion, a motion sounds like a suggestion: "I think that we ought to buy the lot next door and make a playground out of it."

In a formal meeting, you say essentially the same thing, but you say it more precisely and as a recommendation rather than a suggestion: "I move that Brier Patch Child Care buy the lot north of our property, landscape it, and use it as a playground."

Being precise is important because the secretary will record exactly what you say, and the group will discuss the statement and vote on it. A carelessly worded motion leaves the group unclear about what you want them to do. As a result, everyone wastes time trying to understand or change the motion.

How to Make a Motion

1. To "address" (or get the attention of) the chair, you usually just raise your hand.

2. The chair "recognizes" you (or invites you to speak) by saying, "Yes, Meko . . ."

3. You state the motion by saying, "I move that . . ." The secretary writes down exactly what you say.

4. The chair asks for a "second" by saying, "Is there support for the motion?" If someone says "Support" or "I second that," the motion is ready for discussion.

5. The chair or the secretary reads the motion to the group.

6. The chair then asks for discussion, and members give their opinions.

7. The motion may be "amended" (changed) or "tabled" (action on it is postponed), but eventually the group will vote to accept or reject the motion.

THE BOTTOM LINE

There are different kinds of motions for various tasks, with different rules for each. For example, some motions need to be seconded and voted on while others do not. For details, see the table of "Common Parliamentary Motions" on the next page.

419 Common Parliamentary Motions

Motion	Purpose	Needs Second	Debatable	Amendable	Vote	May Interrupt Speaker	Subsidiary Motion Applied
I. MAIN MOTIONS							
1. Main Motion (general) Main Motions (specific)	To introduce business	Yes	Yes	Yes	Majority	No	Yes
a. To reconsider	To reconsider previous motion	Yes	When original motion is	No	Majority	Yes	No
b. To rescind	To nullify or wipe out previous action	Yes	Yes	Yes	Majority or two-thirds	No	No
c. To take from the table	To consider tabled motion	Yes	No	No	Majority	No	No
II. SUBSIDIARY MOTIONS							
2. To lay on the table	To defer action	Yes	No	No	Majority	No	No
3. To call for previous question	To close debate and force vote	Yes	No	No	Two-thirds	No	Yes
4. To limit or extend limits of debate	To control time of debate	Yes	No	Yes	Two-thirds	No	Yes
5. To postpone to a certain time	To defer action	Yes	Yes	Yes	Majority	No	Yes
6. To refer to a committee	To provide for special study	Yes	Yes	Yes	Majority	No	Yes
7. To amend	To modify a motion	Yes	When original motion is	Yes (once only)	Majority	No	Yes
8. To postpone indefinitely	To suppress action	Yes	Yes	No	Majority	No	Yes
III. INCIDENTAL MOTIONS							
9. To raise a point of order	To correct error in procedure	No	No	No	Decision of chair	Yes	No
10. To appeal for decision of chair	To change decision on procedure	Yes	If motion does not relate to indecorum	No	Majority or tie	Yes	No
11. To suspend rules	To alter existing rules and order of business	Yes	No	No	Two-thirds	No	No
12. To object to consideration	To suppress action	No	No	No	Two-thirds	Yes	No
13. To call for division of house	To secure a countable vote	No	No	No	Majority if chair desires	Yes	Yes
14. To close nominations	To stop nomination of officers	Yes	No	Yes	Two-thirds	No	Yes
15. To reopen nominations	To permit additional nominations	Yes	No	Yes	Majority	No	Yes
16. To withdraw a motion	To remove a motion	No	No	No	Majority	No	No
17. To divide motion	To modify motion	No	No	Yes	Majority	No	Yes
IV. PRIVILEGED MOTIONS							
18. To fix time of next meeting	To set time of next meeting	Yes	No, if made when another question is before the assembly	Yes	Majority	No	Yes
19. To adjourn	To dismiss meeting	Yes	No	Yes	Majority	No	No
20. To take a recess	To dismiss meeting for specific time	Yes	No, if made when another question is before the assembly	Yes	Majority	No	Yes
21. To raise question of privilege	To make a request concerning rights of assembly	No	No	No	Decision of chair	Yes	No
22. To call for orders of the day	To keep assembly to order of business	No	No	No	None unless objection	Yes	No
23. To make a special order	To ensure consideration at specified time	Yes	Yes	Yes	Two-thirds	No	Yes

Giving a Speech

420 Okay, so the Golden Age of Oratory died with Demosthenes. That doesn't mean you won't have to stand up publicly some day and speak well. You may have to introduce a special guest, present the results of a group project, make a sales pitch, or, if you're lucky, accept an award.

What are you going to do—stammer and shake? Why not be ready? In this section, you'll find ways to get your mind, your muscles, your material, and your mouth under control. This way, giving a speech may seem like an opportunity, not some strange form of punishment.

What's Ahead?

To help you communicate well in all situations, this section of your handbook explains the process of preparing and presenting a speech:

> Preparing to Speak
> Writing the Speech
> Rehearsing and Delivering the Speech

⬤421 Preparing to Speak

When you first get your assignment to speak, your first impulse will be to worry about yourself. Do I know enough? Can I find the right words? Fight that feeling. In fact, turn it inside out: become intensely interested in everything but yourself—your audience, the occasion, your purpose, and the topic. That will calm the jitters and at the same time prepare you to communicate.

Think about your audience by asking . . .

⊚ What are their ages, backgrounds, and interests?
⊚ What do they already know? What do they want to know?

Think about the occasion by asking . . .

⊚ Who asked me to speak and why?
⊚ Where will I speak, and is the occasion formal or informal?
⊚ What else is happening? What comes before and after my speech?
⊚ How much time do I have?

Think about your purpose by asking . . .

⊚ Am I going to inform my audience about a person, topic, or process?
⊚ Am I going to persuade them to do or believe something?
⊚ Am I going to try to entertain them?

NOTE: You may have several purposes, but you still need to decide which one is most important.

Think about your topic by asking . . .

⊚ Am I required to speak on a specific topic? A general subject area? A topic of my own choosing?
⊚ What topic do I already know something about or have an interest in? (Also see 015.)
⊚ Where can I find possible topics if no personal topics come to mind? (See 011-012.)
⊚ Where can I find additional information if I need it?

THE BOTTOM LINE

Once you've thought about your audience, the occasion, your purpose, and your topic, you should be able to put together a purpose or thesis statement. Begin the statement with a simple "My purpose is . . . " and follow with one of the three specific purposes (to inform, to persuade, to entertain). Finish your statement with your specific topic.

"My purpose is to persuade my audience that they cannot depend on the current Social Security system to provide their retirement needs."

422 Choosing the Method for Delivering the Speech

There are three basic methods for delivering a speech. The method you choose depends on your purpose and the time you have to prepare the speech.

Impromptu Use this method when you've had little or no time to prepare. Sometimes you may be able to jot down a few words to help you present your ideas in an orderly way, but basically you will speak "off the cuff," putting your speech together as you give it. Here are some basic characteristics of the impromptu speech:

- Sounds informal and "live."
- Allows speaker to shape the speech in response to audience's laughter or applause.
- Little preparation needed.
- ▼ **Drawback:** Hard to "time" and no time to gather evidence.

Outline Use this method when you have more time and want to shape the speech more carefully. Write out the main ideas you plan to talk about in outline form, not word for word. You may choose to write the outline on note cards and then use the cards when you give the speech. (See 119-120 for more on outlining.)

- Speaker can prepare speech, giving him or her more confidence than impromptu.
- As with impromptu, speaker can use eye contact and gestures freely.
- Like impromptu, allows freedom to adapt speech in response to the audience.
- Sounds conversational: more formal than impromptu, but less formal than manuscript.
- ▼ **Drawback:** Unless you fill in and smoothly connect all the parts as you speak, your speech may sound merely like an outline.

Manuscript When you want precision and formality, use this method. Write out exactly what you plan to say. Then (1) memorize and recite the speech, (2) read it to your audience, or (3) get very familiar with the manuscript so you can keep eye contact with the audience, glancing at your paper only on occasion.

- Lets speaker choose exact words of speech—nothing is changed or forgotten during delivery.
- Gives nervous or shy speaker confidence.
- Speaker can "time" speech exactly.
- When done effectively, the method can be precise and powerful.
- ▼ **Drawback:** When writing is weak, or speaker has little eye contact, formal speeches can sound stiff.

423 Writing the Speech

The way you gather information, organize your ideas, and write them down depends primarily on (1) the kind of speech you're giving and (2) your method of delivery. For example, if you're giving a 10-minute impromptu speech during a business meeting, you probably will have no time to gather information and only a few minutes to outline your thoughts.

On the other hand, if you're giving an informational speech at an industrial convention, you may have six months to search for information, to write out the speech in manuscript form, and to rehearse the delivery.

INSIDE

The first step in writing any speech is searching for information. For help on how and where to find information, look in the "Finding Information" chapter, 359-383.

After collecting your facts and details, organize them into a speech with an introduction, a body, and a conclusion using the guidelines that follow.

424 Introduction

The introduction helps you set the tone and direction of your speech and serves several important purposes:

- ◉ getting the attention of your audience,
- ◉ introducing your topic,
- ◉ stating your central idea, or purpose,
- ◉ briefly identifying the main points, and
- ◉ making your audience eager to hear what else you have to say.

Start-Up Techniques

To get the audience's attention and focus it on your topic, use one or more of the following techniques:

- ● An amazing fact or a startling statement
- ● A funny story or an attention-grabbing illustration
- ● A short demonstration or a colorful visual aid
- ● A series of questions or a short history of the topic
- ● A strong statement about why the topic is important to you and your audience

425 Body

The body of a speech carries your message. It includes your main arguments and supporting evidence. As a result, the way you organize information in the body is very important. In fact, the organization must be so effective that the audience understands the information after hearing it only once! Six popular methods for organizing the body of your speech are listed below, along with a sample topic for each method.

Order of Importance: Arrange information according to its importance: least to greatest, or greatest to least.

> Speech listing reasons for buying a new drill press for the machine shop

Chronological Order: Arrange information according to the time order in which events take place.

> Instructions for sending a message on an E-mail system

Comparison/Contrast: Give information about subjects by comparing them (showing similarities) and contrasting them (showing differences).

> Proposal for choosing one fax machine rather than another

Cause and Effect: Give information about a situation or problem by showing (1) the causes of the problem and (2) the effects of the problem.

> Report on what causes mail service to slow down during the holidays

Order of Location: Arrange information about subjects according to where things are located in relation to each other.

> A walking tour of your school for a group of senior citizens

Problem/Solution: Describe a problem and then present a solution to solve it.

> Presentation showing how an asphalt product seals cracks in concrete streets

426 Conclusion

A good conclusion helps focus the whole speech and leaves your audience with a clear picture of

- what they have heard,
- why it's important, and
- what they should do about it.

TAKE NOTE

To write a conclusion that leaves a clear picture, you may want to (1) restate your thesis statement and (2) use some of the techniques listed in 424.

⟨427⟩ Rehearsing and Delivering the Speech

Good writers understand the need to revise their writing. Similarly, good speakers understand that preparing the script, revising, and rehearsing are necessary steps in the speaking process. How you prepare the script for delivery depends on your delivery method.

Impromptu: For an impromptu speech, think about your purpose and write an abbreviated outline that includes the following:

- Your opening sentence
- Two or three phrases, each of which summarizes one main point
- Your closing sentence

> I. Opening sentence
> II. Phrase #1
>   Phrase #2
>   Phrase #3
> III. Closing sentence

Outline: For an outline speech, one that you have time to research and prepare, think carefully about your topic, purpose, and audience. Then outline your speech as follows:

- Opening statement in sentence form
- All main points in sentence form
- Supporting points written as phrases
- Quotations written in full
- All supporting numbers, technical details, and sources listed
- Closing statement in sentence form
- Notes indicating visual aids you plan to use

> I. Opening statement
>   A. Point with support
>   B. Point (purpose or thesis)
> II. Body (with 3-5 main points)
>   A. Main point with details
>   B. Main point with details
>   C. Main point with details
> III. Closing statement
>   A. Point, including restatement of thesis
>   B. Point, possibly a call to action

Manuscript: For a full manuscript speech, write the finished copy neatly, following these guidelines:

- Pages double-spaced
- Pages or cards numbered
- Abbreviations used only when you plan to say them (*FBI,* but not *w/o*)
- All sentences on same page, not running from one page to the next
- All difficult words marked for pronunciation
- Script marked for interpretation (See copy-marking symbols on next page.)

Save Now or Pay Later

Imagine that you've just finished school, gotten a good job, worked hard all week, and this $1.00 bill represents your whole paycheck. *[hold up dollar bill]* As your employer, I'm about to hand you the check when I stop, tear off about 20% like this, give it to Uncle Sam and say, "Here is my employee's income tax."

428 Rehearsing the Speech

Rehearse the speech until you're comfortable with it. Ask a family member or friend to listen and give you feedback, or use a tape recorder or video recorder so you can hear and see yourself. Practice the following techniques:

1. Stand, walk to the lectern (or front of the room), and face the audience with your head up and back straight.

2. Speak loudly and clearly.

3. Don't rush. Take your time and glance at your notes when you need them.

4. Think about what you're saying so your audience hears the feeling in your voice.

5. Talk with your hands—use gestures that help you communicate.

6. Talk with your eyes and expressions by looking at the audience as you speak.

7. Use audiovisual equipment if it is available and appropriate.

8. Conclude the speech by picking up your materials and walking carefully to your seat.

429 Marking for Interpretation

As you decide what changes you need to make in your copy, note them on your speech. Do the same for changes in delivery. Putting notes about delivery on your paper is called "marking your copy" and involves using a set of symbols to represent voice patterns. These symbols will remind you to pause in key places during your speech or to emphasize a certain word or phrase. Below is a sample list of copy-marking symbols.

Copy-Marking Symbols
Inflection *(arrows)* .... for a rise in pitch, for a drop in pitch.
Emphasis *(underlining or boldface)* .... for additional <u>drive</u> or **force**.
Color *(curved line or italic)* .... for additional feeling or *emotion*.
Pause *(dash, diagonal, ellipsis)* .... for a pause—or / break . . . in the flow.
Directions *(brackets)* .... for movement [*walk to chart*] or use of visual aids [*hold up chart*].

430 Adding Visual Aids

Once your speech is written (or outlined), think about where you might use visual aids—charts, graphs, pictures—to make it easier for your audience to follow what you are saying. The graph below goes with the "Model Speech" on the following pages.

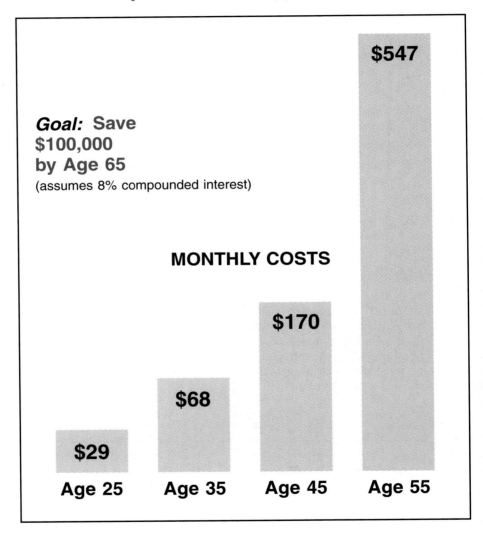

Goal: Save $100,000 by Age 65
(assumes 8% compounded interest)

MONTHLY COSTS

$547

$170

$68

$29

Age 25   Age 35   Age 45   Age 55

THE BOTTOM LINE

When it's time to deliver the speech, remember who you are. You are an important person who has thought about a topic and has something worthwhile to say. Speak loudly, clearly, and confidently.

431 Model Speech

"Save Now or Pay Later" is a persuasive speech by student writer Burnette Sawyer. Burnette's topic is the failing Social Security system. Her purpose is to show her classmates that they can't depend on Social Security to provide their retirement needs. Watch how she builds her argument by showing the audience how the problem affects each of them personally. (Also notice her use of *italics* to add vocal color and **boldface** to add emphasis.)

Save Now or Pay Later

Speaker begins with imaginary anecdote, or story.

Imagine that you've just finished school, gotten a good job, worked hard all week, and this $1.00 bill represents your whole paycheck. *[hold up dollar bill]* As your employer, I'm about to hand you the check when I stop, tear off about 20% like this, give it to Uncle Sam and say, "Here is my employee's income tax." Then I tear off another 30% like this, give that to Uncle Sam, too, and say, "And here is her Medicare and Social Security tax."

Speaker tears dollar bill to emphasize her point.

Finally, I give you this half and say, "Here, hard worker, this is your *whole paycheck.*"

Does that sound like science fiction?

A reference to a famous person is used to add believability.

Senator Alan Simpson doesn't think so. In the last issue of *Modern Maturity,* he says that unless we change the Social Security system, *our generation* will have to pay 20% of our paychecks as income tax and 30% as Social Security tax. That means we can keep just **50%** of what we earn.

Appeal to fear is used to keep audience interested.

But the news gets **worse**. Remember this 30% that we paid to Social Security? *[hold up piece of dollar bill]* Well, that won't be enough money for us to live on when we get to be 65 in the year 2043. Remember that year, 2043—we'll get back to that soon.

Speaker states problem and solution.

What's the problem? The Social Security system *can't insure* our financial security. What's the solution? We have to start our own savings plans, and the *earlier* the *better*.

Ever since it started back in 1935, the Social Security system has never been *secure*. While the system has been "fixed" a number of times, the "fixes" haven't done the job. For example, writer Keith Carlson points out that in 1983 Congress raised payroll taxes, extended the retirement age, and said that the system would be in good financial shape until 2056.

432

But then, says Carlson, *just nine years later,* a report came out saying that Congress had been *wrong.* The report said that Social Security money wouldn't even last until 2056—it would run out by 2043. Remember that year, 2043? *That's* the year we're supposed to retire—at age 65!

Do you think this news is bad? Just two months ago, the *AARP Bulletin* reported on the Bipartisan Commission on Entitlement and Tax Reform. The commission warned that entitlement programs like Social Security are growing so fast they could "bankrupt the country" by the year 2029—when we're **only 52!**

Will the U.S. government take the action necessary to secure the Social Security system? *Don't count on it.* As Senator Simpson, a member of the Bipartisan Commission, said in *Modern Maturity,* "We've been playing political chicken with the federal budget for decades."

So what should we do? Run for Congress and change the system? That's not a bad idea, except the track record for Social Security shows that one more fix-it job won't fix the system. Besides, we have to be 30 years old to be U.S. senators, and we have to start our own retirement plans long before then.

In fact, in his book, *Retirement 101,* Willard Enteman says that we should start a personal savings plan the day we get our first checks. In sociology class last week, Mr. Christians made the same point. He gave us this graph *[hold up graph]* that shows that if our goal is to save $100,000 by age 65, we better start *early* before saving gets too expensive.

You can see that if we start here, when we're 25, we can reach $100,000 by saving just $29 a month. If we wait until here, when we're 35, we'll have to save $68 a month. If we wait until here, when we're 45, we'll have to put away $170 a month. And if we wait until we're 55, we'll need $547 a month.

Look at the difference. To reach $100,000 by age 65 would cost $29 a month if we start at 25, and $547 a month if we start at 55.

What's my point? The Social Security system *can't promise us* financial security when we retire.

What's the solution? We have to start our own savings plans—and the *earlier* we start, the *easier* it will be to reach our goals.

• Irony is used to emphasize the year the system may run dry.

• The speaker uses a quotation to support her point.

• The speaker uses a graph to help make her point clear. (See 430.)

• The conclusion repeats the main point and calls the audience to action.

433 A Closer Look at Style

More than any other president of recent times, John F. Kennedy is remembered for the appealing style and tone of his speeches. By looking at sample portions of his speeches, you should get a better feel for how style and tone can help strengthen the spoken word. By using special stylistic devices (*allusion, analogy, anecdote,* etc.), you can improve the style and impact of your speech.

By using special appeals (*democratic principle, common sense, pride,* etc.), you can control the tone or feeling of what you have to say. (The type of appeal used is listed above each excerpt.)

434 **Allusion** is a reference in a speech to a familiar person, place, or thing.

Appeal to the Democratic Principle

One hundred years of delay have passed since *President Lincoln* freed the slaves, yet their heirs, their grandsons, are not fully free (Radio and Television Address, 1963).

435 **Analogy** is a comparison of an unfamiliar idea to a simple, familiar one. The comparison is usually quite lengthy, suggesting several points of similarity. An analogy is especially useful when attempting to explain a difficult or complex idea.

Appeal to Common Sense

In our opinion the German people wish to have one united country. If the Soviet Union had lost the war, the Soviet people themselves would object to a line being drawn through Moscow and the entire country defeated in war. We wouldn't like to have a line drawn down the Mississippi River . . . (Interview, November 25, 1961).

436 **Anecdote** is a short story told to illustrate a point.

Appeal to Pride, Commitment

Frank O'Connor, the Irish writer, tells in one of his books how as a boy, he and his friends would make their way across the countryside and when they came to an orchard wall that seemed too high and too doubtful to try and too difficult to permit their voyage to continue, they took off their hats and tossed them over the wall—and then they had no choice but to follow them.

This nation has tossed its cap over the wall of space, and we have no choice but to follow it. Whatever the difficulties, they will be overcome (San Antonio Address, November 21, 1963).

437 **Antithesis** is balancing or contrasting one word or idea against another, usually in the same sentence.

Appeal to Common Sense, Commitment

Mankind must put an end to war, or war will put an end to mankind (Address to the U.N., 1961).

438 **Irony** is using a word or phrase to mean the exact opposite of its literal meaning, or to show a result that is the opposite of what would be expected or appropriate; an odd coincidence.

Appeal to Common Sense

They see no harm in paying those to whom they entrust the minds of their children a smaller wage than is paid to those to whom they entrust the care of their plumbing (Vanderbilt University, 1961).

439 **Negative definition** is describing something by telling what it is *not* rather than, or in addition to, what it is.

Appeal for Commitment

. . . members of this organization are committed by the Charter to promote and respect human rights. Those rights are not respected when a Buddhist priest is driven from his pagoda, when a synagogue is shut down, when a Protestant church cannot open a mission, when a cardinal is forced into hiding, or when a crowded church service is bombed (United Nations, September 20, 1963).

440 **Parallel structuring** is the repeating of phrases or sentences that are similar (parallel) in meaning and structure; **repetition** is the repeating of the same word or phrase to create a sense of rhythm and emphasis.

Appeal for Commitment

Let every nation know, whether it wishes us well or ill, that we shall *pay any price, bear any burden, meet any hardship, support any friend, oppose any foe,* in order to assure the survival and the success of liberty (Inaugural Address, 1961).

441 **Quotations**, especially of well-known individuals, can be effective in nearly any speech.

Appeal for Emulation or Affiliation

At the inauguration, Robert Frost read a poem which began "the land was ours before we were the land's"—meaning, in part, that this new land of ours sustained us before we were a nation. And although we are now the land's—a nation of people matched to a continent—we still draw our strength and sustenance . . . from the earth (Dedication Speech, 1961).

442 **Rhetorical question** is a question posed for emphasis of a point, not for the purpose of getting an answer.

Appeal to Common Sense, Democratic Principle

"When a man's ways please the Lord," the Scriptures tell us, "he maketh even his enemies to be at peace with him." And is not peace, in the last analysis, basically a matter of human rights—the right to live out our lives without fear of devastation—the right to breathe air as nature provided it—the right of future generations to a healthy existence (Commencement Address, 1963)?

(443) Speech Terms

Acoustics: The science of sound or the way the walls, floor, ceiling, and other parts of a room react to sound. The quality of speech sounds depends in part on the acoustics of the room in which they are produced.

Ad-lib: Making up or composing the words to a speech as you deliver it.

Articulation: The uttering of speech sounds in a clear, distinct manner.

Cadence: The rhythm or flow of a speech. Your goal is to make your cadence as smooth as possible.

Climax: The high point or peak in a speech.

Color: The emotional treatment given certain key words in a speech to convey the special meaning or connotation of those words. The volume and pitch of the voice are changed to add color.

Commentary: An organized group of remarks or observations on a particular subject; an interpretation, usually of an important social issue.

Continuity: The state or quality of being continuous or unbroken. A speech with continuity will move smoothly from the introduction through the conclusion by use of effective linking or transitional devices.

Editorial: A carefully organized piece of writing in which an opinion is expressed.

Emphasis: Giving more attention to a particular word or phrase than to the others. This can be done by varying the volume, pace, pitch, or color of the voice.

Enunciation: The clearness or crispness of a person's voice. If a speaker's enunciation is good, it will be easy to understand each word he or she says.

Eye Contact: The communicating a person does with his or her eyes during a speech. It is very important that a speaker establish sincere eye contact with the audience so that full communication can take place.

Force (Drive): The amount of pressure or punch behind the speaker's voice; *loudness*.

Gesture: The motion a speaker uses to emphasize a point. Hand and body gestures are usually effective additions to a speech, although they can also be visual distractions and take away from the speaker's effectiveness. You should keep gestures as natural as possible and not overuse them.

Impromptu: A speech given with little time for preparation.

Inflection: The rising and falling in the pitch of the voice.

Interpretation: The act of figuring out or explaining the meaning of a piece of literature or writing.

Manuscript: The written copy of the speech used during a presentation.

Monotonous: A voice that is unchanging in inflection or color; *dull*.

Oratory: The art of public speaking.

Pace: The rate of movement or overall speed of a speech.

Pause: The momentary stopping in a speech to give additional emphasis to a particular word, phrase, or idea.

Pitch: The highness or lowness of a voice. By properly varying the pitch of the voice, the speaker can emphasize or color the words in the script.

Presence: The sense of closeness of the speaker to the audience. If a speaker is sincere and open with the audience, he or she is more likely to be believed.

Projection: Directing or throwing the voice so it can be heard at a distance; speaking loudly.

Rate: The speed (fastness or slowness) of the speech.

Repetition: The repeating of words or phrases to add a sense of balance and rhythm to a piece of writing, as with the Gettysburg Address: ". . . of the people, by the people, and for the people."

Resonance: The prolonging of a sound through vibration. In the speech process, the resonance is amplified by the chest, throat, and nose.

Speech: The process of communicating with the voice through a combination of breathing, resonating, and articulating.

Stage Fright: The tension or nervousness a speaker feels when he or she is preparing to deliver or is actually delivering a speech.

ISSUES

ISSUES

ISSUES

Issues in the Workplace

Preparing for the Workplace

444   A strong back, the desire to work, and a high-school diploma are all that you need to earn a good living, right?

"Wrong," say the business leaders and educators who wrote the *SCANS Report*—a government study of the kind of education needed to survive in the twenty-first century. Hard work and a high-school diploma used to be enough 20, 30, or 40 years ago, but not today. In our information age, workers need more.

It's important that you discover just what it is you need to fit into the changing workplace, and how to get it.

> ### What's Ahead?
>
> This section of your handbook provides answers to questions about your career:
>
> Changes in the Workplace
> The Workforce of the Future
> Preparing for Changes in the Workplace
> Basic Competencies
> Foundational Skills
>
> ➤

445 Changes in the Workplace

The traditional workplace was based on the "strategy" developed by people like Henry Ford. In order to build cars as cheaply as possible, he used an assembly line in which workers functioned like parts in a machine—turning, lifting, attaching, and tightening, but not thinking and acting on their own. Henry Ford wanted management to do the thinking, to give the orders, and to evaluate the end product.

The modern workplace is different. Today workers think for themselves, communicate their ideas to team members, make decisions together, and produce their product well enough so they don't need constant supervision. Why these changes? Because businesses have learned that just as a Model-T can't compete in a race with a new Saturn, the old ways can't compete with the new.

Characteristics of Traditional and Modern Workplaces

	TRADITIONAL	MODERN
Strategy	mass production	flexible production
	long production runs to cut production costs	production customized to produce the best product
	centralized control—one person or group manages	decentralized control—management shares authority
Production	fixed automation for efficiency	flexible automation for quality
	end-of-line quality control—management evaluates product	on-line quality control—workers evaluate product as they make it
	individuals work alone doing pieces of the task	multiskilled workers work in teams to do the task together
	management has authority to evaluate and decide	workers have authority and responsibility to make decisions
Hiring and Human Resources	labor-management confrontation	labor-management cooperation
	workers with minimal qualifications accepted	workers screened for basic skills and abilities
	workers treated as a cost	workers treated as an investment of the business
Job Ladders	advancement by seniority	advancement by certified skills and performance
Training	mostly for supervisors	training for everyone
	specialized for craft workers	broad skills sought and taught

446 The Workforce of the Future

While 1992 isn't far behind us, and 2005 is just around the corner, the U.S. Labor Department says that the workforce "back then" was very different from the one ahead. How will it change? The workforce in 2005 will

- **be older** (groups aged 45 and older will increase the most),
- **be located more in the South and West,**
- **have a larger percentage of women and minorities,**
- **be more concentrated in service industries,**
- **be less concentrated in manufacturing, and**
- **receive more on-the-job training.**

Changes in Job Opportunities

Changes in society cause changes in the job market. Take the population, for example. By 2005 the percentage of elderly people will have increased. Because elderly people generally require more health care than other age groups, the U.S. Department of Labor says that by 2005 health care will be one of the strongest job-producing professions we have.

The increased use of technology is probably the most forceful cause of change in the job market today. Every day, advances in technology kill off old jobs and create new ones. For example, as the auto industry increases its use of robots to build cars, many jobs that used to be done by humans are disappearing. At the same time, however, the industry is creating new jobs for workers who can design, program, operate, and fix robots.

New Workplace Skills

How do changes like these affect you? The new jobs often require additional skills like those listed later in this section under "Foundational Skills" (452). If you are currently developing these skills, you should have many opportunities to land a good job in the future. If you aren't, you should begin working on these skills immediately.

 INSIDE

 info

The U.S. government keeps track of the growth of over 2,250 occupations and publishes that information in documents you can get from your school counselor or local library. These publications list jobs in a variety of ways, including "Occupations with the Largest Job Growth" and "Occupations with the Largest Job Decline." (See the tables on the next two pages.)

447 Occupations with the Largest Job Growth: 1992–2005

Occupations with the largest job growth are those that should continue to provide jobs in the future.

Occupation (Employment Numbers in Thousands)	Employment 1992	Employment 2005	Percent Change
Home health aides	347	827	+138
Human services workers	189	445	+136
Personal and home care aides	127	293	+130
Computer engineers and scientists	211	447	+112
Systems analysts	455	956	+110
Physical and corrective therapy assistants/aides	61	118	+93
Physical therapists	90	170	+88
Paralegals	95	176	+86
Teachers, special education	358	625	+74
Medical assistants	181	308	+71
Correction officers	282	479	+70
Child care workers	684	1,135	+66
Travel agents	115	191	+66
Radiologic technologists and technicians	162	264	+63
Nursery workers	72	116	+62
Medical records technicians	76	123	+61
Teachers, preschool and kindergarten	434	669	+54
Speech-language pathologists and audiologists	73	110	+51
Flight attendants	93	140	+51
Guards	803	1,211	+51
Insurance adjusters, examiners, and investigators	147	220	+49
Respiratory therapists	74	109	+48
Psychologists	143	212	+48
Cooks, restaurant	602	879	+46
Nursing aides, orderlies, and attendants	1,308	1,903	+45
Teacher aides and educational assistants	885	1,266	+43
Food preparation workers	1,223	1,748	+43
Registered nurses	1,835	2,601	+42
Licensed practical nurses	659	920	+40
Teachers, secondary	1,263	1,724	+37
Waiters and waitresses	1,756	2,394	+36
Gardeners and groundskeepers	884	1,195	+35
Receptionists and information clerks	904	1,210	+34
Accountants and auditors	939	1,243	+32
Maintenance repairers, general utility	1,145	1,464	+28
Truck drivers, light and heavy	2,391	3,039	+27
Cashiers	2,747	3,417	+24
General office clerks	2,688	3,342	+24
Clerical supervisors and managers	1,267	1,568	+24
Salespeople, retail	3,660	4,446	+21
Teachers, elementary	1,456	1,767	+21

448 Occupations with the Largest Job Decline: 1992–2005

Occupations with the largest job decline are those that will produce fewer jobs in the future than they do now.

Occupation (Employment Numbers in Thousands)	Employment 1992	Employment 2005	Percent Change
Directory assistance operators	27	13	-51
Central office operators	48	24	-50
Telephone installers and repairers	40	20	-50
Computer operators, except peripheral equipment	266	161	-39
Central office installers and repairers	70	45	-36
Child care workers, private household	350	227	-35
Cleaners and servants, private household	483	326	-32
Billing, posting, and calculating machine operators	93	66	-29
Sewing machine operators, garment	556	393	-29
Telephone and cable TV line installers and repairers	165	125	-24
Cutting and slicing machine setters and operators	94	73	-23
Head sawyers and sawing machinery operators, setters, and setup operators	59	46	-22
Packaging and filing machine operators	319	248	-22
Farmers	1,088	857	-21
Machine forming operators, metal and plastic	155	123	-21
Switchboard operators	239	188	-21
Textile machine operators	192	157	-18
Machine tool cutting operators, metal and plastic	114	95	-17
Welding machine setters and operators	97	80	-17
Farmworkers	849	716	-16
Typists and word processors	789	664	-16
Butchers and meat cutters	222	191	-14
Electrical and electronic equipment assemblers, precision	150	129	-14
Crushing and mixing machine operators	133	117	-12
Electrical and electronic assemblers	210	187	-11
Inspectors, testers, and graders, precision	625	559	-10
Bartenders	382	350	-8
Bank tellers	525	502	-4
Industrial machinery mechanics	477	462	-3

THE BOTTOM LINE

Stay up on changes in the job market. Talk to your counselor or use *The Occupational Outlook Handbook* (published by the U.S. Department of Labor) for the latest updates on job growth and decline.

449 Preparing for Changes in the Workplace

How can you prepare for a workplace that's changing? A group of leaders in business, industry, and education recently spent three years answering this question. That group, the Secretary's Commission on Achieving Necessary Skills, wrote its answer in four publications called the *SCANS Reports*. The commission urges you to get an education in which you learn . . .

competence • using (1) resources, (2) interpersonal skills, (3) information, (4) systems, and (5) technology.

foundational skills • developing (1) basic skills, (2) thinking skills, and (3) personal qualities.

What follows below and on the next two pages are detailed lists of the competency and foundational skills needed in the workplace. Discuss the lists with your counselor and your parents or guardian; then use the information as you

- choose courses in high school,
- choose research projects in your classes,
- think about where you want to go to school after high school,
- choose part-time jobs and internships,
- read about and consider different occupations, and
- choose an occupation.

450 Basic Competencies

Competencies are abilities that all workers need to be successful. For example, the first "resource" in the list below is *time*. To be competent, a worker must use time well. (In the lists that follow, the statement after each italicized item explains what it means to use the item competently.)

Resources: A competent worker identifies, organizes, plans, and uses resources.

- ◉ *Time* • Selects goal-related activities, ranks them, and prepares and follows schedules.
- ◉ *Money* • Uses or prepares budgets, makes forecasts, keeps records, and makes adjustments as necessary.
- ◉ *Materials and Facilities* • Acquires, stores, distributes, and uses materials and space efficiently.
- ◉ *Human Resources* • Assesses skills and assigns work accordingly; evaluates performance and provides feedback.

451

2

Interpersonal Skills: A competent worker cooperates with others.

- *Participates as a Member of a Team* • Contributes to group effort.
- *Teaches Others* • Shares knowledge and skills with others.
- *Serves Clients or Customers* • Works to keep customers happy.
- *Exercises Leadership* • Communicates ideas clearly; persuades and convinces others; responsibly challenges existing procedures and policies.
- *Negotiates* • Exchanges information to help resolve conflicts or problems.
- *Works with Everyone* • Works well with women and men from all backgrounds.

3

Information: A competent worker acquires and uses information.

- *Acquires and Evaluates Information*
- *Organizes and Applies Information*
- *Interprets and Communicates Information*
- *Uses Computers to Process Information*

4

Systems: A competent worker understands complex systems and relationships.

- *Understands Systems* • Knows how social, workplace, and technical systems work.
- *Monitors and Corrects Performance* • Watches for trends and predicts their impact on the system; figures out what causes poor performance and corrects it.
- *Recommends or Designs Systems* • Suggests changes to existing systems and develops new or alternative systems to improve performance.

5

Technology: A competent worker uses a variety of technologies.

- *Selects Technology* • Chooses procedures, tools, or equipment, including computers and related technologies.
- *Applies Technology to Task* • Understands overall procedures for setup and operation of equipment.
- *Maintains and Troubleshoots Equipment* • Prevents, identifies, or solves problems with equipment, including computers and other technologies.

452 Foundational Skills

Just as you build a house on a strong foundation, you build competence on strong foundational skills. For example, the first item in the previous list is time. Efficient use of time may involve drawing up a work schedule for a group of people. However, to develop a schedule you need *foundational skills:* **math skills** to work with numbers of hours, minutes, and workers; **thinking and problem-solving skills** to decide how many people are needed for a specific task; and **personal qualities** like integrity and honesty to schedule everyone's time fairly.

Basic Skills:

- ◉ *Reading* • You will need to locate, understand, and interpret information in books, documents, manuals, and schedules.

- ◉ *Writing* • You will need to communicate thoughts and information in writing, letters, manuals, reports, directions, graphs, and flowcharts.

- ◉ *Arithmetic/Mathematics* • You will need to do simple computations and solve practical math problems.

- ◉ *Listening* • You will need to interpret and respond to verbal messages and other cues.

- ◉ *Speaking* • You will need to organize and share ideas orally.

Thinking Skills:

- ◉ *Creative Thinking* • You will need to come up with new ideas.

- ◉ *Decision Making* • You will need to make good decisions.

- ◉ *Problem Solving* • You will need to recognize problems and come up with a plan of action.

- ◉ *Knowing How to Learn* • You will need to continue learning in order to acquire and apply new knowledge and skills.

- ◉ *Reasoning* • You will need to figure out how certain objects are related and use that information to solve problems.

Personal Qualities:

- ◉ *Responsibility* • You will need to meet your employer's schedule: get to work on time, finish tasks on time, etc.

- ◉ *Self-Esteem* • You will need to be understanding, flexible, and polite in group settings.

- ◉ *Self-Management* • You will need to set personal goals, check your own progress, and exhibit self-control.

- ◉ *Integrity/Honesty* • You will need to be ethical in attitude and actions.

Workplace Ethics

453   The educators and business people who wrote the U.S. Labor Department's *SCANS Report* concluded that one of the most important issues in today's workplace is the issue of ethics, or personal values. They argue that businesses cannot thrive unless employers and employees act ethically, following professional standards of conduct. To act ethically, they suggest, everyone needs five qualities at the core of his or her character: responsibility, self-esteem, sociability, self-management, and honesty.

What's Ahead?

The qualities listed above will help you in general, both in school and on the job. This section offers you information that will help you apply these traits to specific problems in the workplace.

> Traits of a Successful Worker
>
> Information Ethics
>
> Discrimination in the Workplace

454 Traits of a Successful Worker

The five qualities needed for success in the workplace are listed below, along with a brief explanation of what each means to you and other workers. (Adapted from *Learning a Living: SCANS Report.*)

Responsible

- Work hard for excellence, even if a task is unpleasant.
- Pay attention to detail.
- Work toward high standards of attendance, punctuality, and attitude.

Confident

- Believe in your own self-worth, skills, and abilities.
- Be aware of how your emotions, behavior, and attitude can affect others, and take responsibility for your actions.

Sociable

- Be friendly, sensitive, and polite to others.
- Be interested in what others say and do.
- Be flexible so you can interact with people from different backgrounds.

Self-Managing

- Know your own abilities, skills, and knowledge.
- Set realistic personal goals and be self-motivated to achieve them.
- Use others' criticism and feedback to improve yourself.

Honest/Ethical

- Know your community's and organization's codes of ethics.
- Know how behavior that violates these codes hurts individuals and organizations.
- Be committed to ethical behavior in the workplace.

455 Information Ethics

Nearly every day we hear about new technology for gathering, processing, storing, or sending. Unfortunately, these new devices can make unethical behavior quite easy. Look at the problems that follow and think about the solutions to each.

456 Copying Information

Problem

Copying copyrighted material

Packages of information like books, songs, videos, television programs, films, and computer programs are usually copyrighted. For example, this handbook is copyrighted. On the second page you will see the following information:

> Copyright © 1996 by D.C. Heath and Company,
> a Houghton Mifflin Company. All rights reserved.

This statement tells you that Houghton Mifflin Company owns the copyright, and you may not make copies of anything in the book without their permission. While the law allows limited copying for certain purposes, nearly all copying of copyrighted material is illegal.

Solutions:

1. Check your school or company policy on copying. Most places display printed policies to help employees make ethical decisions.

2. If you're copying information to use in a research paper or report, use the rules for crediting the source. Failure to credit the source is wrong—it's called *plagiarism*.

Problem

Copying non-copyrighted material

Things like copy machines, VCR's, computers, scanners, and the Internet make copying non-copyrighted material easy. However, while copying a non-copyrighted piece may not be illegal, it can be unethical.

Solutions:

1. Don't copy a non-copyrighted piece without permission or without giving credit for it.

2. If you're working on the Internet, remember that you're responsible for working within the limits of copyright laws and rules of ethics. In general, downloading (or copying) copyrighted material without permission from the owner of the copyright is illegal; downloading non-copyrighted material without permission is unethical.

457 Misusing Information

Problem

Presenting information out of context

With devices like CD-ROM's and electronic banks of quotations, it's easy to pick up a quotation or statistic and use it out of context so that it seems to support your argument.

Solution:

Remember that when you use information that is not your own, you are ethically (and sometimes legally) responsible for how you use it. Always state quotations accurately and give the context in which they were presented.

If you quote statistics, be sure that you understand what they mean, and that you present them clearly so your reader understands.

Problem

Presenting information incorrectly

In order to do their work well, people on the job need information that is correct and clear. If the information is incorrect, or if they don't understand it, they could hurt themselves or someone else.

Solutions:

1. Take responsibility for information that you share.
2. Be sure that you understand it.
3. Check your source to make sure the information is current.
4. Check other sources to make sure the information is reliable.
5. Present the information clearly.

TAKE NOTE

Be sure that the person who receives the information understands it. Check back with her or him if there seems to be confusion or hesitation.

458 Abusing Information

Problem

Stealing business secrets

Stealing information by eavesdropping on others' conversations, recording telephone calls without permission from the participants, or secretly videotaping conversations is unethical.

Solution:

Get permission from the participants to record any conversation, and use the information only for the purposes they have agreed to.

Problem

Looking at information that is private

In nearly all business settings, you will be able to read information that is not intended for your use. For example, as a student intern in a college administrator's office, you may be able to log on to the office computer bank and nose through a friend's grade transcript.

Solution:

Unless your supervisor instructs you to look at information in a computer bank, that information is off-limits, and looking is unethical.

Problem

Sharing private information

In many businesses you will need to use private information to do your job. For example, if you work in a personnel office, you will have access to personal details about employees. Sharing that information with anyone outside the context of official business is always unethical.

Solution:

If you're uncertain whether you may share information, ask your supervisor, and above all, use your common sense.

Problem

Hoarding information

People who have information have a certain power over those who don't have it. For example, a student with a home computer hooked up to Internet has an advantage over a student who doesn't have such ready access to information.

Solution:

In school and the workplace, you must work with others, sharing information that enables you to succeed together.

459 Discrimination in the Workplace

Identifying Discrimination

Discrimination means noticing differences and making judgments on the basis of what you notice. The ability to discriminate can be good; in fact, it's necessary. For example, if you pick wild mushrooms for your dinner, you'd better be able to tell the difference between poisonous and nonpoisonous varieties. You also need to discriminate when you buy clothing, choose an occupation, or choose courses that will prepare you for that occupation.

Misusing Discrimination

We misuse our ability to discriminate when we notice differences between people and judge them or treat them unfairly on the basis of those differences. In U.S. culture today we often unfairly judge people on the basis of race, gender, religion, age, disabilities, and even occupations. This kind of discrimination is both unethical and illegal.

INSIDE

info

Title VII of the 1964 Civil Rights Act prohibits discrimination based on the following:

> **race, color, or national origin**
> **age or gender**
> **religion**
> **pregnancy**
> **disability**

Dealing with Discrimination

Many organizations and businesses have policy statements that define discrimination and outline the procedure to follow if you are a victim of discrimination. If you think that someone is discriminating against you, or if you want to avoid discriminating against someone else, do the following:

1. Check the policy statements or talk with your supervisor so you are clear about whether discrimination is taking place.

2. If possible, talk with the person involved, point out the discrimination, and tell him or her that you want this behavior to stop.

3. If the behavior does not stop, follow the steps outlined in the policy statement for dealing with the problem. (See your supervisor or the personnel manager for help to work through those steps.)

4. If these people do not help, or if they are the ones who are discriminating, see *their* supervisor.

5. If none of these steps resolves the problem, file a complaint with the Equal Employment Opportunity Commission (E.E.O.C.). A librarian can help you find an address or a phone number.

Setting Goals and Making Plans

At some point in the not-so-far-off future, you will need to begin making plans for a career. You could take the easy way out and simply flip a coin or spin a wheel—or you could do it the right way.

The first step in the planning process is to set some goals—both short- and long-term goals. Setting goals will help you think about what you want to do in life. After that, you can begin the process of achieving your goals. You can, for example, outline a specific strategy for planning your career. That strategy will include finding and organizing information on various career areas and measuring your progress along the way.

What's Ahead?

This section of your handbook will help you set goals and make career plans.

Setting Goals

Making Career Plans

Building a Career Portfolio

461 Setting Goals

If you want to achieve a major goal—your primary goal—you'll need to set smaller secondary goals to help you get there. **Secondary goals** have several benefits. They

- help you divide the project into manageable pieces,
- focus your energy on the specific steps that allow you to achieve your primary goal,
- help you manage your time,
- give you specific ways to evaluate your progress, and they
- are flexible—if one doesn't work, you can set another secondary goal without losing sight of the main one.

Below is a list that begins with one primary goal—to get a job as an X-ray technician. Notice that as you read down the list, each goal is a little narrower than the one above it. Notice also that if you start at the bottom and read up, the list seems like a stairway lifting you step-by-step toward your primary goal.

Primary goal: Get a job as an X-ray technician

Secondary goals:
- Get the tech-college training I need for the job
- Get the high-school diploma required by the tech school
- Choose a high-school program meeting the requirements of the tech school I need to attend
- Get a job (or volunteer) in the X-ray department of a local hospital
- Talk with the guidance counselor about course options, considering my interest in being an X-ray technician

462 Connecting Short-Range to Long-Range Goals

By the time you've reasoned your way back to "right now," you'll understand how your short-range goals should be linked to your long-range goals. Here's a chart you can use to help with the planning.

Lifetime Goal
Career Goal
10-Year Goal
5-Year Goal
1-Year Goal
This Month's Goal
This Week's Goal
Today's Goal
What am I doing now?

463 Planning a Career

The difference between going to school with a career plan and going to school without a career plan is like the difference between treading water and swimming. Like treading water, doing schoolwork without a plan will keep you busy, but you won't know where you're heading or whether you're making progress. A career plan helps you focus on your goals and measure your progress.

464 A Career Plan

You can get a model plan to follow by checking with your school counselor. But you can begin now by gathering the information that goes into any career plan:

1. **Statement indicating the kind of work you want to do** (health care, for example)
   - list of specific jobs (physical therapist, X-ray technician, etc.)

2. **Degrees or certification needed to obtain these jobs**
   - list of specific programs and courses leading to the certification
   - institutions where you might take these courses

3. **Work experiences needed to reach the goals**
   - list of possible places to get those experiences

4. **Records of your past accomplishments**
   - courses you've taken
   - work experiences
   - awards
   - test scores (college-entrance exams or aptitude tests)

5. **People or organizations that could help you**
   - relatives and friends with knowledge or business connections related to your occupational choice
   - school counselor and teachers
   - community leaders

6. **Plan-of-action** (including dates) for reaching your goals
   - list of courses to take
   - projects or work experiences to explore
   - college-entrance applications to complete, tests or interviews needed

465 A Career Portfolio

While a career plan is a tool that you use to prepare for a job, a career portfolio is a tool that you use to get the job. The portfolio is both an answer book and an advertisement. It answers the employer's questions about who you are, what you want to do, and why you are qualified to do it. The portfolio also helps you sell yourself by highlighting your training, skills, and potential to do good work.

Your Portfolio

Like the career plan, you must prepare the career portfolio carefully and update it regularly. Your portfolio should include the following:

1. Résumé (See "The Résumé," 206-207.)

2. Grade transcripts (or address of school office that will send them)

3. Letters of recommendation, or address of school office that will send them (See "The Request Letter," 205.)

4. List of references (people the employer could call to ask about you)

5. Diplomas and certificates

6. Awards

7. Appropriate projects and publications:

- high-school science project if you're interviewing for a science scholarship
- slides of your artwork if you're interviewing for an internship in graphic arts
- articles you've written for the school newspaper if you're interviewing for a job that involves writing
- samples of desktop-published documents, spreadsheets, or database lists you may have created using various software packages

THE BOTTOM LINE

A career plan and career portfolio are two of the most valuable tools that you will ever give yourself. While knowledgeable people like parents, teachers, and counselors can help, only you can make your plan, update it regularly, and follow it. And only you can put together and continue to update your portfolio.

466 Computer Terms

Access is to open and look into a computer file.

Applications software is a computer program designed for a specific purpose, such as word processing, desktop publishing, accounting, etc.

Backup is a duplicate copy of a program or file made to protect the original copy in case it is lost, stolen, or destroyed.

Binary is the number system commonly used by computers because the values 0 and 1 can easily be represented electronically in the computer.

Bit (binary digit) is the basic unit of computer memory; one binary digit.

Boot is to start up a computer system by loading a program into the memory.

Bug is an error in a computer program.

Bulletin board is a service that permits users to leave, store, or receive messages by computer modem.

Byte is eight bits of information acting as a single piece of data.

CD-ROM is a compact disk that can hold large amounts of information, including moving video images.

Character is a letter or number used to display information on a computer screen or printer.

Chip is a small piece of silicon containing thousands of electrical elements. Also known as an integrated circuit.

Circuit board is a flat, rigid board inside a computer used to hold and electronically connect computer chips and other electrical elements.

Clear is to erase stored or displayed data.

Command is an instruction to a computer to perform a special task like "print."

Computer is a machine that can accept data, process it according to a stored set of instructions, and then output the results.

Computer program is a piece of software containing statements and commands that tell the computer to perform a function or task.

Configuration is a computer and all devices connected to it.

Control character is a character that is entered by holding down the control key while hitting another key. The control character "controls" or changes information that is printed or displayed.

CPU (Central Processing Unit) is the hardware portion of a computer, the "brain" of the computer that controls all other devices.

Crash is to have a computer or program stop working.

CRT (Cathode Ray Tube) is the computer screen; the electronic vacuum tube found in a TV.

Cursor is a pointer on the computer screen that shows you where the next character typed from the keyboard will appear.

Data is information given to or produced by a computer.

Database is a program or collection of information that is organized in such a way that a computer can sort it quickly.

Debug is to remove errors from a computer program.

Desktop publishing is using a computer, software, and a laser printer to produce professional-looking documents.

Device is a piece of computer hardware designed to perform a certain task. A monitor, printer, and disk drive are examples of computer devices.

Directory is the table of contents for all files on a disk.

Disk is a magnetic storage device used to record computer information. Each disk appears flat and square on the outside; inside, the disk is circular and rotates so that information can be stored on its many circular tracks.

Disk drive is the device that writes and reads information onto the disk.

Documentation is writing and graphics that explain how to use and maintain a piece of hardware or software.

DOS (Disk Operating System) is a software system that allows a computer to operate by communicating with and controlling disk drives.

Download is to transfer programs or files from one computer to another.

Drag is to move the cursor across the screen by sliding the mouse.

Edit is to change an original document or program by adding, deleting, or replacing certain parts.

467

E-mail (Electronic mail) is a system that uses telecommunications to send messages from one computer to another.

Error is a programming mistake that will cause the program to run incorrectly or not run at all.

Error message is a message, displayed or printed, that tells you what error or problem is present in a program.

Execute is to run a computer program.

Exit is to leave or quit a program.

Fax (facsimile) is a device used to scan and transmit printed pages over the phone lines from one location to another.

File is a collection of computer information stored under a single name.

Floppy disk is a storage device made of a thin, magnetically coated plastic.

Font is the style or kind of type a printer uses; most printers have several fonts or typestyles to choose from.

Footprint is the space on a desk or table taken up by a computer.

Format is to prepare a blank disk for use (also initialize).

Fuzzy is approximate; not exact.

Global search is a computer search throughout an entire document for words or characters that need to be located or changed.

Graphics is information that is displayed as pictures or images.

Hacker is a skilled programmer or someone who spends a lot of time working with computers.

Hard copy is a printed copy.

Hardware is the electronic and mechanical parts of a computer system. A floppy disk is hardware; the program stored on it is software.

Header is information or graphics automatically printed at the top of each page.

Icon is a small picture or graphic used to identify computer folders or files.

Input is information placed into a computer from a disk drive, keyboard, or other device.

Instruction is machine language that commands an action to be taken by the CPU of a computer.

Interactive is a computer system in which the operator and computer frequently exchange information.

Interface is the hardware and software that are used to link one computer or computer device to another.

Internet (See 378.)

K (Kilobyte) is a term used when describing the capacity of a computer memory or storage device. For example, 16K equals 16 x 1,024 or 16,384 bits of memory.

Keyboard is an input device used to enter information into a computer by striking keys that are labeled much like those on a typewriter.

Laser printer is a high-resolution printer that prints by laser. The more dots per inch (DPI) a laser printer has, the better the printout.

Library is a collection of programs.

List is a display or printout of a computer program or file.

Load is to take information from an external storage device and place or load it into a computer's memory.

LOGO is a language that combines pictures and words in order to teach programming to children.

Loop is a series of instructions that is repeated, usually with different data on each pass.

Main memory is the memory that is built into a computer.

Memory is the chips in the computer that store information and program instructions until they are needed.

Menu is a detailed list of choices presented in a program from which a user can select.

Merge is to combine data from two or more different sources.

Microcomputer is a small computer using a microprocessor as its processing unit.

Modem (modulator demodulator) is a device that allows computers to communicate over telephone lines.

Monitor is a video screen on which information from a computer can be displayed.

Mouse is a small manual device that controls the pointer on the screen.

Multimedia is a combination of text, video, graphics, voice, music, and animation.

Multiuser is a program that allows several computers to share information from the same source.

Network is a series of computers (or other devices) connected together.

468

Output is information that a computer sends out to a monitor, printer, or modem.

Peripheral is a device connected to a computer such as a plotter, disk drive, or printer.

Printout is a copy of a computer page or program printed on paper.

Processor is the part of the computer that receives language instructions and controls all other parts of the computer.

Program is a piece of software or set of instructions that tells the computer what to do.

Programmer is a person involved in the writing, editing, and production of a computer program.

Programming language is the language used when writing a computer program.

Prompt is a question appearing on the screen that asks the user to put information into the computer.

RAM (Random Access Memory) is the part of the computer's memory where data, instructions, and results can be recorded and stored.

Resolution is the quality of the "picture" on a computer screen.

ROM (Read-Only Memory) is the part of the computer's memory containing the permanent instructions for the computer; new data cannot be recorded on this part of the computer's memory.

Save is to take a program or file from main memory and store it on disk, cassette, or hard drive for later use.

Scanner is a device used to "read," or scan, an image or a picture and send it into a computer.

Sector is a fraction of the recording surface on a disk; a sector is a fraction of a track.

Software is the program that tells a computer how to perform a certain task.

Spreadsheet is a program used to organize numbers and figures into a worksheet form so they are easier to read.

Statement is an instruction in a program that tells the computer to perform a specific task.

Storage is the main memory or external devices where information or programs can be stored.

String is a group of consecutive letters, numbers, and characters treated as one unit.

Subroutine is a group of statements that can be found and used from several different places in a main program.

Surfing is exploring the Internet with no particular goal in mind.

System is the collection of hardware and software that work together to form a working computer.

Telecommunications is sending and receiving information from one computer to another over phone lines, satellites, etc.

Terminal is a "computer" consisting of a keyboard and a monitor; it doesn't actually contain a computer (CPU) but shares a computer with other terminals.

Text is the words, letters, and numbers that can be read by an individual.

Track is a fraction of the recording surface on a disk. (A track can be compared to the space used by each song on an album.) The number of tracks on a disk varies.

User is a person using a computer.

Virus is a bug deliberately but secretly hidden in a computer system in order to wipe out stored information.

Word is a string of bits treated as a single unit by a computer.

Word processor is a program (or computer) that helps a user to write letters, memos, and other kinds of text.

World Wide Web (See 381.)

Write-enable notch is the small, rectangular cutout in the edge of a disk's jacket used to protect the contents of a disk. If the notch is closed or covered by a write-protect tab, information cannot be written on the disk.

Write-protect is to cover up the write-enable notch (or opening), making it impossible for new information to be written on the disk. The information on the disk is now protected from being overwritten.

469 Business Terms

Advertising is any paid message made through the media to sell a product.

Back order is an order accepted by a seller for future delivery, usually because the item is out of stock.

Bargaining unit is a particular group of people that a union will represent.

Bid is (1) a price a buyer is willing to pay for an item (*ex.* shares of stock); (2) a written price offer from a seller.

Bill is an itemized list of charges for goods or services.

Bill of sale is a document proving the transfer of ownership of goods.

Board of directors is a group of top managers, elected by the shareholders of a corporation, that develops broad company policy and goals and has legal responsibility to run the business.

Boycott is the refusal to do business with a company, person, or nation as a punishment or way of influencing their actions.

Brand name is a design, symbol, or term that identifies the goods or services of a specific company and distinguishes them from those of competitors.

Breakeven is a point at which the income from selling a product equals all of the costs to develop, manufacture, and market that product.

Business is (1) an organization that attempts to earn a profit by supplying goods or services that people need and want; a company; (2) a collective term referring to all businesses in general.

C.O.D. (cash on delivery) is a payment due at the time shipped goods are received.

Commission is a salesperson's earnings directly related to sales made or profits the company has earned through that person's efforts.

Commodities are goods traded in the marketplace, especially ones that can be transported.

Common carrier is a company that transports passengers or goods for a fee and whose services are available to the public (*ex.* railroad; trucking company).

Competition is a situation in which various companies provide similar goods or services. Companies may compete directly (*ex.* Coke and Pepsi) or less directly (*ex.* soft-drink and milk distributors).

Consumer is a private person who uses a product or service.

Corporation is a form of business owned by stockholders in which the business's assets and liabilities are separate from that of its owners.

Demand is the circumstance in which consumers want goods or services and have the ability to pay for them.

Direct marketing is the direct interaction between seller and buyer, except for selling in person (*ex.* catalog or letter).

Distribution channel is the means (stores, mail, etc.) by which goods and services reach the consumer.

Entrepreneur is a person who takes on the personal and financial risk of starting a business and keeping it going.

Ethics are a group of principles that outline how individuals and businesses should behave.

Exporting is the selling of goods and services to countries other than your own.

Finished goods are the completed and packaged products of a company.

Fortune 500 is a list of the 500 largest American companies, published every year in *Fortune* magazine.

Generic brand is a food or household item with a plain label containing no advertising or brand name.

Goods are products or items that can be seen and held.

Green marketing is providing packaging and products friendly to the environment and using this fact as a selling point.

Importing is purchasing goods and services from other countries.

International cartel is a group of nations or producers who band together to control the price and flow of certain goods (*ex.* OPEC's control of petroleum).

Inventory is a supply of goods on hand that has not been used up or sold.

Label is part of a product's packaging that lists the brand name or symbol, the name and address of the manufacturer or distributor, ingredients, size, and recommended use.

Labor is the physical and mental efforts that people contribute to the production of a product.

470

Lead time is the time between the discovery of a need for a material and the actual delivery date.

Management is (1) persons who supervise a store or company; (2) the process through which people seek to meet goals by efficiently using available resources such as labor and equipment.

Manufacturing is the process of coordinating material, people, equipment, and money to create finished goods; production.

Market is (1) potential buyers who have both the authority and the ability to purchase; (2) to offer for sale.

Marketing is the activities businesses use to plan, price, promote, and distribute goods and services to consumers.

Mass production is the process of manufacturing an item in large quantities, which results in lower costs per unit than small-scale production.

Media is the means of mass communication such as radio, television, or magazines.

Middleman is any person or company that is in the distribution channel.

Middle management is the second level of management, those persons who develop plans and procedures for carrying out the decisions made by top management.

Need is a person's awareness of lacking something that is useful or desirable.

Order is the instruction to buy or supply goods or services.

Organization chart is a visual description showing how a business is organized, how work is divided, and who has authority and responsibility.

Partnership is a business in which two or more people share ownership.

Perishables are goods and products likely to decay or spoil, be fragile or easily damaged.

Planning is seeking to prepare for the future by creating goals and objectives for the present; usually carried out by the management team.

Point-of-purchase advertising is the promotion of a product through a display at the buying location.

Price is (1) the value placed on goods or services being sold; (2) to set a charge for an item; (3) to seek out the cost of an item.

Private carrier is a method of transporting goods by the same company that produces the goods. Compare *common carrier*.

Product is (1) something made by human or mechanical means; (2) something formed by nature or resulting from agriculture.

Promotion is (1) activity to advertise goods or services; (2) job advancement.

Quality control is the process of measuring a manufactured part against a standard model to find poorly made parts that may cause a product to fail. The goal of quality control is to increase customer satisfaction.

Raw materials are farm products (*ex.* wheat, cotton, soybeans) or natural products (*ex.* coal, lumber, iron ore) used in producing manufactured goods.

Retailer is a business that sells goods to consumers for use rather than for resale.

Salary is the payment made to employees for regular work based on performing a specific job, rather than on an hourly rate (*ex.* many managers are paid a salary). Compare with *wage*.

Sales are (1) the exchange of goods for a price; (2) the special offering of goods at reduced prices.

Service is a useful activity that meets a need (*ex.* barber).

Shareholders are the owners of stock in a corporation.

Sole proprietor is one who owns and operates a business exclusively.

Stock is (1) the finished goods on hand or in storage and ready for sale; (2) the shares of a company sold to the public making them owners.

Subsidiary is a business owned by another company (parent company).

Supply is the amount of goods or services that are available to the marketplace.

Target market is a group of consumers at which a company directs its marketing activities.

Trade is the organized exchange of commodities usually on a large scale; commerce.

Union is an association of employees designed to help each other get satisfactory wages, benefits, and working conditions.

Wage is payment for work based on an hourly or weekly rate or by the piece. Compare with *salary*.

Wholesaler is a business selling products to others for resale or for use in making other products.

471 Insurance Terms

Accident insurance is insurance that covers injury or liability from accidents. See *health insurance*.

Adjuster is a representative of the insurance company who determines the cause of the accident, the amount of loss, and how much is to be paid on an insurance claim.

Annuity is insurance that pays regular periodic income for life or a set period of time.

Appraisal is an expert's estimate of value.

Beneficiary is the person or group who is eligible to receive insurance settlements.

Bond is a guarantee against financial loss caused by an accident or by the actions of another individual who fails to keep a promise.

Cancellation is a formal decision to discontinue an insurance policy.

Cash surrender value is the cash value of an insurance policy that builds up over time and may be borrowed by the insured person. Some types of policies do not have a cash surrender value.

Casualty insurance is an insurance contract that provides compensation for loss or injury to person or property.

Claim is a request to an insurance company for payment for loss.

Clause is a distinct section or provision in a document.

Coinsurance is a policy that covers a risk also covered by another insurance company.

Coverage is the amount of protection against loss given by an insurance policy.

Deductible is the amount of a loss that will be paid by the insured person each time a claim is submitted.

Disability insurance is insurance against the loss of income and covers expenses due to becoming unable to work.

Fraud is an attempt to cheat.

Health insurance is insurance coverage for the expenses of sickness and injury; medical insurance.

HMO (Health Maintenance Organization) is health-insurance coverage provided by an organization that hires doctors to care for prepaid subscribers.

Homeowner's insurance is a policy that covers fire, theft, liability, and damage to contents of a dwelling.

Lapsed policy is an insurance policy that has ended because the premiums were not paid.

Liability is the legal responsibility for loss or injury to others.

Life insurance is insurance that guarantees payment of a specified amount of money to a beneficiary on the death of the insured person. See *straight life* and *term life*.

Major medical is health-insurance coverage of all medical and hospital expenses resulting from illness or injury.

Maturity is the date on which an insurance policy becomes payable.

Medicaid is medical insurance subsidized by the federal government.

Medicare is medical insurance for those over 65 subsidized by the federal government.

No-fault insurance is a form of automobile liability insurance in some states that covers loss regardless of responsibility.

Policy is a written contract between the insured person and an insurance company that explains the terms and limits of the contract.

Premium is a periodic payment to cover the cost of insurance.

Redlining is discrimination when issuing property insurance based on location. (Refers to drawing a red line around an area on a map. Redlined areas often include the homes of racial minorities or the poor.)

Social Security is the federal insurance for the aged, widowed, orphans, and disabled.

Straight life (whole life) is life insurance that provides protection during the insured person's whole lifetime at a fixed premium. Compare with *term life*.

Term life is life insurance that provides coverage for a specific period of time at a set rate. After that period of time, the rate may increase. Compare with *straight life*.

Title insurance is insurance against any defects in title to real estate.

Umbrella policy is a policy that covers many types of risk (*ex.* homeowner's insurance).

Underwriting is assuming the risk of offering insurance in exchange for a premium.

472 Financial and Accounting Terms

Accounting is a system of recording financial activities.

Accounts receivable are the amounts due from customers for goods or services given.

Assets are real estate and other property of value owned by a business or person.

Audit is an examination of financial accounts.

Balance sheet is a financial report of the total assets, liabilities, and the owner's equity on a specific date.

Budget is a plan of expected income and expenses.

Capital is the assets or money used to produce goods or invest in some other way.

Controller (comptroller) is the chief financial officer of a business.

CPA (Certified Public Accountant) is a licensed accountant who meets a state's requirements to practice.

Creditors are people or businesses to whom money is owed.

Credit rating is a measure of how one has or hasn't paid loans in the past. Used to determine risk in offering new loans or giving credit.

Debt is the amount owed by a borrower.

Deficit is the condition when a company or government owes more than its income.

Depreciation is the gradual decline in value through age or use. Used in preparing tax returns for businesses.

Disbursement is the paying out of money.

Equity is the difference between the fair market value of a property and how much is still owed on it.

Expense is the cost of goods or services that reduce a business owner's equity or profits for an accounting period.

Fiscal year is the year for accounting purposes (*ex.* July 1 through June 30 or October 1 through September 30).

Fixed costs are expenses that are not affected by the amount of output in a business (*ex.* rent). Compare with *variable costs.*

General ledger is an accounting journal or computer program where all business financial transactions are recorded and the accounts are balanced.

Gross profit is the difference between total sales income and the cost of the goods sold.

Income is money received from sales, wages, profits, and investments.

Income statement is a financial report showing the results of a business's operations in terms of revenue (money taken in), expenses, and the difference between the two (net income).

Interest is (1) percentage fee charged for borrowing money or for receiving credit; (2) percentage paid by a bank or other savings institution as income on deposited money.

Liabilities are amounts owed to creditors; accounts payable.

Net is the profit (or loss) left after subtracting charges, costs, and expenses.

Output is the amount produced by a person in a given period of time.

Overhead is the total direct expense of running a business.

Overtime is payments at higher than normal rate for extra hours worked during the day or week.

Petty cash is money kept on hand for small, daily expenses.

Profit is the net amount earned after all costs are deducted.

Purchase order (PO) is an itemized list of goods being bought and their prices that is sent to a vendor.

Purchase requisition is a form used within a company to start the process for the purchase of needed items.

Revenue is the amount of money earned from the sale of goods or services or other business activities.

Secured loan is a cash loan with assets offered as security (collateral) for the loan.

Statement of cash flow is a financial report showing a business's cash income and outflow over a period of time.

Variable costs are expenses that are directly affected by the amount of output in a business (*ex.* raw materials). Compare with *fixed costs.*

Vendor is a person or business that sells supplies or materials to a company.

Venture capital is money lent to a new business in exchange for an eventual share of the profits.

Wages are payments for labor at an hourly or piecework rate.

LEARNING

Reading, Thinking, Learning

Reading Strategies

473   Over the years, you've spent a lot of time reading. In the early years, reading meant learning patterns and sounds, how words work together to form sentences, and then how sentences work together to form paragraphs and stories. Now, the word *reading* has an entirely different meaning for you. Rather than "learning to read," most of your time is spent "reading to learn." Reading now means studying, taking notes, summarizing, reviewing, and so on.

    From now on, most of the reading you do will be reading to learn, or study-reading. Your goal will be to read, remember, and use the main ideas in order to write a report, take part in a discussion, or operate a piece of equipment. Luckily, there are a number of strategies that can help you do this more efficiently, from SQ3R to mapping to acronyms. And they're not as difficult or as mysterious as they sound.

What's Ahead?

Throughout this section of your handbook, you will be introduced to strategies, guidelines, and organizers to help you improve your reading and study skills:

- Guidelines for Reading to Learn
- Strategies for Study-Reading
- Strategies for Remembering
- Using Context Clues
- Understanding Literary Terms

474 Guidelines for Reading to Learn

The guidelines below will help you put together a personal learning plan, one that may include several new study-reading strategies.

Before you read . . .

- Understand your assignment.
- Gather all the materials you need to read and to take notes (notebook, handouts, reference books, etc.).
- Decide how much time you will need to do the reading and when and where you will do it. (Find a quiet, well-lighted spot.)
- Try to avoid doing your reading when you are overly hungry or tired; take short breaks to stretch and rest your eyes.

As you read . . .

- Get to know your textbook and what it contains; use the index, glossary, and special sections.
- Use a specific approach to your study-reading—KWL, SQ3R, mapping, or graphic organizers, for example. (See 475-479.)
- Look over the whole chapter before you begin reading to get an overall picture of what the selection is about; if there are questions that go with the reading, look them over, too.
- Read the titles and headings and use them to ask yourself questions about what may be coming up next; notice words or phrases in *italics* or **boldface**.
- Look closely at maps, charts, graphs, and other illustrations to help you understand and remember important information.
- Take good notes on everything you read—summarize, outline, star, underline, or highlight important information.
- Use all of your senses when you read. Try to imagine what something looks, feels, and tastes like; draw illustrations.
- Adjust your reading speed to fit the assignment. Read difficult material slowly; reread if necessary.

After you read . . .

- Review your notes at the end of the reading session, again the next day, and as needed after that.
- Always summarize difficult material out loud (either to yourself or to someone else); make note cards or an outline to use later.
- Keep a list of things you want to check on or ask someone about.

475 Strategies for Study-Reading

Much of the reading you will be asked to do in school and later at work will involve study-reading, reading that you are expected to remember and apply. There are many strategies you can use to help. Among the most popular are KWL, mapping, graphic organizers, and SQ3R.

476 KWL

To use the KWL strategy, all you need to do is set up a chart like the one below and fill it in each time you read. You will be surprised by how helpful it can be.

K	W	L
List what you **KNOW**	List what you **WANT** to know	List what you **LEARNED**

477 Mapping

When you use this strategy, you actually draw a map of whatever you are reading. Mapping is much like clustering; but in mapping, the ideas come from the reading, not from your personal experiences. Simply place the subject of your reading in the center and "map" out the details as you read.

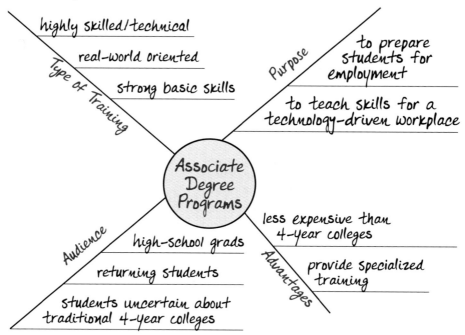

478 Graphic Organizers

A third study-reading strategy is the graphic organizer. Simply draw and fill in one of the following organizers as you read or study. (*Remember:* You can change any of these organizers to fit your needs.)

Describing: Write the subject you want to describe in the circle. List the important details on the spokes as you read.

Finding Cause and Effect: Simply fill in the causes on the first set of lines and the effects on the bottom set.

Cause
_____

_____
_____
_____

↓

Effect
_____

_____
_____
_____

Finding Sequence: If the topic you are studying has a definite sequence, list the facts and details in order beneath it.

Topic _____

1 _____

2 _____

3 _____

4 _____

Comparing and Contrasting: Write the two things you want to compare or contrast on the top lines. Then list all the ways they are similar; next list the ways they differ. (Also see "The Venn Diagram," 550-551.)

_____   _____

Similarities

_____
_____
_____

Differences
↔
_____
↔
_____
↔
_____

Identifying a Problem/Solution: List the problems on the left, the solutions on the right.

Problem   Solution
→
_____   _____

_____   _____

_____   _____

Finding Examples: List the main topic in the center and the examples that relate to it on all sides.

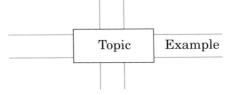

479 SQ3R

Another popular technique for reading and remembering is the SQ3R method. SQ3R stands for the five steps in the study-reading process: *Survey, Question, Read, Recite,* and *Review.*

Survey: The first step in the SQ3R study method is "survey." When you survey a reading assignment, you try to get a big picture of what the assignment is about. To survey, you must look briefly at each page, paying special attention to the headings, chapter titles, illustrations, and boldfaced type. It is also a good idea to read the first and last paragraphs. This should give you a good overall picture, or survey.

Question: As you do your survey, you should begin to ask yourself questions about the reading material. One quick way to do this is to turn the headings into questions. Asking questions will make you an "active" rather than a "passive" reader. It will keep you thinking about what may be coming up next.

Read: Read your material carefully from start to finish. Look for main ideas in each paragraph or section. Take notes as you read, or stop from time to time to write a brief summary. Read the difficult parts slowly. (Read them again if necessary.) Use context clues to help you figure out some of the most difficult passages. (See 485.) Look up unfamiliar words or ideas.

Recite: One of the most valuable parts of the SQ3R method is the reciting step. It is very important that you recite out loud (or whisper) what you have learned from your reading. It is best to stop at the end of each page, section, or chapter to answer the *who, what, when, where, why,* and *how* questions. By reciting this information out loud, you can test yourself on how well you understand what you have read. You may then go back and reread if necessary.

Review: The final step in the SQ3R study method is the review step. You should review as soon as you finish reading. If you have some questions to answer about the assignment, do them immediately. If you have no questions to answer, summarize the assignment in a short writing. You may also make an outline, note cards, illustrations, etc., to help you review and remember what you have read. (Also see 480-483.)

Strategies for Remembering

In addition to using a reading strategy, there are several specific strategies you can use to help you remember what you have read:

480 Association

The association method is a memory strategy in which each idea being studied is associated with a more memorable word, picture, or idea. For example, if you were supposed to remember the first 10 amendments to the Constitution (the Bill of Rights), you would begin by setting up an association for the four basic rights in the First Amendment. What do most people "see" when they visualize the early colonists who helped set up the Bill of Rights? Pilgrims (religion), Benjamin Franklin (printing press), Patrick Henry (speech), Boston Tea Party (protest or petition)? You, of course, may see an entirely different set of images.

481 Acronym

Another way to remember facts is to use an acronym, a "word" created by using the first letter(s) of several related words. (VISTA, for example, is an acronym for Volunteers In Service To America.) To create an acronym for the First Amendment, you would use the first letter(s) of the words *press, religion, petition,* and *speech.* One possibility is the word (acronym) **preps**, which is made up of the "re" from "religion" and the first letters from the other three. The First Amendment can easily be associated with firsts, beginnings, or preparations; the acronym *preps* can then be used to help you remember the first four basic rights, which are? Without looking!

482 Strange Sentences

A slightly different version of the acronym technique is to compose a sentence so silly or strange that you will have no trouble remembering it. Say, for example, that you needed to remember the countries of Central America and match them to their places on a map. They are (from top to bottom) Mexico, Belize, Guatemala, Honduras, El Salvador, Nicaragua, Costa Rica, and Panama. Your sentence would have to contain words beginning (in order) with M . . . b . . . g . . . h . . . e . . . n . . . c . . . p. Want to give it a try? How about "My brother George has extremely noisy car pipes"? Anything equally strange will work.

483 Rhymes, Songs, Jingles, and Raps

Anything that has rhyme and rhythm is easier to remember than a straight list of facts. Remember either of these? *"I before e, except after c . . ." "In 1492, Columbus sailed . . ."* Put your imagination (and talent) to work: Compose rhymes, songs, jingles, and raps to help you remember ideas and facts. You'll be surprised and pleased with the results.

484 Improving Reading Comprehension Skills

One of the biggest challenges for readers of all ages is handling new or difficult words, reading complicated material, or understanding technical terms. A strategy that will help you sharpen your word recognition skills and improve your overall reading comprehension is the strategy of using context clues. (The context of a word is the text, or the written words, around it.)

Below is a paragraph that contains a number of terms you may or may not be familiar with. Read the paragraph and try to determine the meanings of the boldfaced words by using context clues from the surrounding text.

Business counselors are becoming more and more popular in today's small-business market. These **counselors** serve as advisers to assist **entrepreneurs** and new business owners in setting up and running their businesses. They help both owners and managers by giving them advice on solving business-related issues such as creating marketing plans, hiring personnel, or keeping records of day-to-day **transactions**. The advice they give on daily completion of tasks and record keeping alone may be worth the cost of their services. Their help in the establishment of **personnel systems**, those all-important procedures for working successfully with employees, is also worth a great deal. In some ways, business counselors are similar to attorneys, accountants, and computer **consultants**, in that they help owners of small businesses by being there to answer questions when they arise. Everyday business dealings can quickly become unmanageable without the proper **stratagem** laid out by experts like business counselors. Since everyone wants new businesses to succeed and not fall into **insolvency** because of poor decisions or the lack of knowledge, business counselors are looked upon more and more as a good investment. Most business **agencies**, including the Better Business Bureau, often recommend business counselors to people interested in starting a new business.

485 Using Context Clues

If you just read the paragraph on the previous page about business counselors, you probably used a few context clues to figure out the meanings of some of the boldfaced words. The list below includes six types of context clues that you can use to help you further develop your reading strategies. Read the list carefully to get a feel for how each type of context clue works.

Types of Context Clues

1. Clues supplied through **synonyms:**

These **counselors** serve as *advisers* to assist **entrepreneurs** *and new business owners* in setting up and running their businesses.

2. Clues contained in **comparisons and contrasts:**

Since everyone wants new businesses to *succeed* and not fall into **insolvency** because of poor decisions or lack of knowledge, business counselors are looked upon more and more as a good investment.

3. Clues contained in a **definition or description:**

Their help in the establishment of **personnel systems,** those *all-important procedures for working successfully with employees,* is also worth a great deal.

4. Clues that appear in a **series:**

In some ways, business counselors are similar to *attorneys, accountants,* and computer **consultants**, in that they help owners of small businesses by being there to answer questions when they arise.

5. Clues provided by the **cause and effect:**

Everyday business dealings can quickly become unmanageable without the proper **stratagem** laid out by experts like business counselors.

6. Clues derived from **examples:**

Most business **agencies**, *including the Better Business Bureau,* often recommend business counselors to people interested in starting a new business.

Now that you have looked at these six types of context clues, go back into the paragraph on the previous page and use these strategies to find the meanings of all eight of the boldfaced terms. Then use these same context clues in your own reading.

INSIDE

Some context clues are not so direct as the six types listed above. There may be indirect clues found in the tone or feeling of a passage. Still, indirect clues can be very helpful. The more clues you find, the closer you can get to the specific meaning of a word and—more importantly—to the overall meaning of the passage.

486 Literary Terms

Allegory is a story in which people, things, and actions represent an idea or a generalization about life; allegories often have a strong moral or lesson.

Alliteration is the repetition of initial consonant sounds in words such as "rough and ready." Here is another example of alliteration from "Runaway Warning" by Anne-Marie Oomen: "**Our gang paces the pier like an old myth . . .**"

Allusion is a reference in literature to a familiar person, place, thing, or event.

Analogy is a comparison of two or more similar objects, suggesting that if they are alike in certain respects, they will probably be alike in other ways as well.

Antagonist is the person or thing working against the story's protagonist, or hero.

Assonance is the repetition of vowel sounds without the repetition of consonants, as in these words from "Sounds of Silence" by Paul Simon:

"My words like silent rain drops fell . . ."

Caricature is a picture or an imitation of a person's features or mannerisms exaggerated to be comic or absurd.

Climax is the high point, or turning point, in a story—usually the most intense point.

Comedy is literature that deals with life in a humorous or satiric manner. In comedy, human errors or problems appear funny. Comedies end on a happy note.

Conflict is the problem or struggle in a story that triggers the action. There are five basic types of conflict:

Person vs. Person: One character in a story has a problem with one or more of the other characters.

Person vs. Society: A character has a problem with some element of society: the school, the law, the accepted way of doing things, and so on.

Person vs. Self: A character has a problem deciding what to do in a particular situation.

Person vs. Nature: A character has a problem with some natural happening (a snowstorm, an avalanche, the bitter cold, or any other element of nature).

Person vs. Fate (God): A character has to battle what seems to be an uncontrollable problem. Whenever the problem seems to be a strange or unbelievable coincidence, fate can be considered the cause of the conflict.

Dialogue is the conversation carried on by the characters in a literary work.

Drama is the form of literature known as plays.

Exposition is the part of a play or a story that explains the background or situation in which the work is set.

Falling action is the action of a play or story that works out the decision arrived at during the climax. It ends with the resolution.

Figurative language is language used to create a special effect or feeling. It is characterized by figures of speech—language that compares, exaggerates, or means something other than what it first appears to mean. (See "Figure of speech.")

Figure of speech is a literary device used to create a special effect or feeling by making some type of interesting or creative comparison. The most common types are antithesis, hyperbole, simile, metaphor, personification, and understatement.

Antithesis is an opposition, or contrast, of ideas: "It was the best of times, it was the worst of times, it was the age of wisdom, it was the age of foolishness."
— Charles Dickens, *A Tale of Two Cities*

Hyperbole (hi-pur´-ba-li) is an overstatement, or exaggeration: "I have seen this river so wide it had only one bank."
—Mark Twain, *Life on the Mississippi*

Metaphor is a comparison of two unlike things in which no word of comparison (*as* or *like*) is used: "A green plant is a machine that runs on solar energy."
—*Scientific American*, April 1988

Personification is a literary device in which the author speaks of or describes an animal, object, or idea as if it were a person: "The rock stubbornly refused to move."

Simile is a comparison of two unlike things in which a word of comparison (*like* or *as*) is used: "She stood in front of the altar, shaking like a freshly caught trout."
—Maya Angelou, *I Know Why the Caged Bird Sings*

Understatement is stating an idea with restraint to emphasize what is being talked about. Mark Twain once described Tom Sawyer's Aunt Polly as being "prejudiced against snakes." Since she was terrified of snakes, this way of saying so is called understatement.

487

Flashback is returning to an earlier time (in a story) for the purpose of making something in the present more clear.

Foreshadowing is giving hints and clues of what is to come later in a story.

Imagery is the words or phrases a writer selects to create a certain picture in the reader's mind. Imagery is usually based on sensory details: "The sky was dark and gloomy, the air was damp and raw, the streets were wet and sloppy."

—Charles Dickens

Irony is using a word or phrase to mean the exact opposite of its literal or normal meaning. There are three kinds of irony:

> **Dramatic irony,** in which the reader or the audience sees a character's mistakes or misunderstandings, but the character himself does not.

> **Verbal irony,** in which the writer says one thing and means another. ("The best substitute for experience is being sixteen.")

> **Irony of situation,** in which there is a great difference between the purpose of a particular action and the result.

Mood is the feeling a piece of literature arouses in the reader: happiness, sadness, peacefulness, etc.

Moral is the particular value or lesson the author is trying to get across to the reader. The "moral of the story" is a common phrase in Aesop's fables.

Narration is writing that tells about an event or a series of events: a story.

Narrator is the person who is telling the story.

Onomatopoeia is the use of a word whose sound suggests its meaning, as in *clang, buzz,* and *twang.*

Oxymoron is a combination of contradictory terms, as in *jumbo shrimp.*

Parable is a short, descriptive story that illustrates a particular belief or moral.

Paradox is a statement that seems contrary to common sense yet may, in fact, be true: "The coach called this a good loss."

Parody is a form of literature intended to mock a particular literary work or its style; a comic effect is intended.

Plot is the action or sequence of events in a story. (See "Plot line.")

Plot line is the graphic display of the action or events in a story: exposition, rising action, climax, falling action, and resolution.

Point of view is the vantage point from which the story is told. In the first-person point of view, the story is told by one of the characters: "I don't know what I'm doing tonight. What about you?" In the third-person point of view, the story is told by someone outside the story: "The simple fact is he lacked confidence. He would rather do something he wasn't all that crazy about doing than risk looking foolish."

Protagonist is the main character, or hero, of the story.

Resolution, or denouement, is the portion of the play or story where the problem is solved. It comes after the climax and falling action and is intended to bring the story to a satisfactory end.

Rising action is the series of conflicts or struggles that build a story or play toward a climax.

Romance is a form of literature that presents life as we would like it to be rather than as it actually is. Usually, it has a great deal of adventure and excitement.

Satire is a literary tone used to ridicule or make fun of human vice or weakness, often with the intent of correcting or changing the subject of the satiric attack.

Setting is the time and place in which the action of a literary work occurs.

Stereotype is a pattern or form that does not change. A character is "stereotyped" if she or he has no individuality and fits the mold of that particular kind of person.

Style is how the author uses words and sentences to form his or her ideas. Style is also thought of as the qualities and characteristics that distinguish one writer's work from the work of others.

Symbol is a person, a place, a thing, or an event used to represent something else: the dove is a symbol of peace. Characters in literature are often symbols of good or evil.

Theme is the statement about life a particular work is trying to get across to the reader. In stories written for children, the theme is often spelled out clearly at the end. In more complex literature, the theme will not be so clearly spelled out.

Tone is the overall feeling, or effect, created by a writer's use of words. This feeling may be serious, mock-serious, humorous, satiric, and so on.

Tragedy is a literary work in which the hero is destroyed by some character flaw and by forces beyond his or her control.

Improving Vocabulary Skills

Increasing your vocabulary—the words you understand and use comfortably—will improve your reading, writing, and speaking skills. As your vocabulary grows, your reading rate and comprehension level will grow, too.

One of the easiest, most natural ways to improve your vocabulary is to read. That means reading whatever you *need* to read and—just as important—whatever you *want* to read. Having a dictionary and thesaurus handy can also help. Another important way to improve your vocabulary is the one this chapter will concentrate on—using word parts to break apart and understand words.

What's Ahead?

This section introduces you to a very efficient vocabulary-building strategy: using prefixes, suffixes, and roots to understand the meanings of unfamiliar words better.

Using Word Parts
Prefixes, Suffixes, and Roots

489 Using Word Parts

One of the most useful tools for building your vocabulary is the ability to chop unfamiliar words into pieces so that you can examine each part of the word, namely the *prefix, suffix,* and *root.* To do this, you need to know how each part works. Here are some examples.

Prefixes: A **prefix** is a word part that is added to the beginning of a base word:

Base Word	Prefix	New Word
typical	a	atypical

The prefix *a* means "not." Knowing this meaning will help you understand and remember that *atypical* means "not typical."

Suffixes: A **suffix** is a word part that is added to the ending of a base word:

Base Word	Suffix	New Word
assist	ant	assistant

The suffix *ant* means "the performer or agent of a task." Knowing this meaning will help you remember that *assistant* means "someone who assists."

Roots: A **root** is a base upon which a word is built:

Root Word	Meaning	Word
bibl	*"book"*	bibliography
graph	*"write"*	

Knowing that the root *bibl* means "book" and *graph* means "write" will help you to remember that *bibliography* means "a written list of books."

A Study Plan

You already know and use many common prefixes, suffixes, and roots every day. To increase your speaking and writing vocabulary, study the meanings of those prefixes, suffixes, and roots that are not familiar to you. The following pages contain nearly 500 of them! Scan down one of the pages until you come to a word part that is "new." Learn its meanings and at least one of the sample words listed.

THE BOTTOM LINE

By learning two or three new word parts a day (and a word that each is used in), you will soon become an expert. For example, by learning that *hydro* means "water," you have a good start at adding all these words to your vocabulary: *hydrogen, hydrofoil, hydroid, hydrolysis, hydrometer, hydrophobia, hydroplane,* and *hydrosphere.*

490 Prefixes

Prefixes are those word parts that come *before* the root word (pre = before). Depending upon its meaning, a prefix changes the intent, or sense, of the base word. As a skilled reader, you will want to know the meanings of the most common prefixes and then watch for them when you read.

a, an [not, without] amoral (without a sense of moral responsibility), atypical, atom (not cutable), apathy (without feeling), anesthesia (without sensation)

ab, abs, a [from, away] abnormal, abduct, absent, avert (turn away)

acro [high] acropolis (high city), acrobat, acronym, acrophobia (fear of height)

ambi, amb [both, around] ambidextrous (skilled with both hands), ambiguous, amble

amphi [both] amphibious (living on both land and water), amphitheater

ante [before] antedate, anteroom, antebellum, antecedent (happening before)

anti, ant [against] anticommunist, antidote, anticlimax, antacid

be [on, away] bedeck, belabor, bequest, bestow, beloved

bene, bon [well] benefit, benefactor, benediction, benevolent, bonanza, bonus

bi, bis, bin [both, double, twice] bicycle, biweekly, bilateral, biscuit, binoculars

by [side, close, near] bypass, bystander, by-product, bylaw, byline

cata [down, against] catalog, catastrophe, catapult, cataclysm

cerebro [brain] cerebral, cerebrum, cerebellum

circum, circ [around] circumference, circumnavigate, circumspect, circular

co, con, col, com [together, with] copilot, conspire, collect, compose

coni [dust] coniosis (disease that comes from inhaling dust)

contra, counter [against] controversy, contradict, counterpart

de [from, down] demote, depress, degrade, deject, deprive

deca [ten] decade, decathlon, decapod (ten feet)

di [two, twice] divide, ditto, dilute, dioxide, dipole, dilemma

dia [through, between] diameter, diagonal, diagram, dialogue (talk between people)

dis, dif [apart, away, reverse] dismiss, distort, distinguish, diffuse

dys [badly, ill] dyspepsia (digesting badly), dystrophy, dysentery

em, en [in, into] embrace, enslave

epi [upon] epidermis (upon the skin, outer layer of skin), epitaph, epithet

eu [well] eulogize (speak well of, praise), euphony, eugenics

ex, e, ec, ef [out] expel (drive out), ex-mayor, exorcism, eject, eccentric (out of the center position), efflux

extra, extro [beyond, outside] extracurricular, extraordinary (beyond the ordinary), extrovert

for [away or off] forswear (to renounce an oath)

fore [before in time] forecast, foretell (to tell beforehand), foreshadow

hemi, demi, semi [half] hemisphere, demitasse, semicircle (half of a circle)

hex [six] hexameter, hexagon

homo [man] Homo sapiens, homicide (killing man)

hyper [over, above] hypersensitive (overly sensitive), hyperactive

hypo [under] hypodermic (under the skin), hypothesis

il, ir, in, im [not] illegal, irregular, incorrect, immoral

in, il, im [into] inject, inside, illuminate, illustrate, impose, implant, imprison

infra [beneath] infrared

inter [between] intercollegiate, interfere, intervene, interrupt (break between)

intra [within] intramural, intravenous (within the veins)

intro [into, inward] introduce, introvert (turn inward)

macro [large, excessive] macrodent (having large teeth), macrocosm

mal [badly, poorly] maladjusted, malnutrition, malfunction, malady

meta [beyond, after, with] metaphor, metamorphosis, metaphysical

mis [incorrect, bad] misuse, misprint

miso [hate] misanthrope, misogynist

491

mono [one] monoplane, monotone, monochrome, monocle

multi [many] multiply, multiform

neo [new] neopaganism, neoclassic, neophyte, neologism

non [not] nontaxable (not taxed), nontoxic, nonexistent, nonsense

ob, of, op, oc [toward, against] obstruct, offend, oppose, occur

oct [eight] octagon, octameter, octave, octopus

paleo [ancient] paleoanthropology (pertaining to ancient man), paleontology (study of ancient life-forms)

para [beside, almost] parasite (one who eats beside or at the table of another), paraphrase, paramedic, parallel, parody

penta [five] pentagon (figure or building having five angles or sides), pentameter, pentathlon

per [throughout, completely] permanent, pervert (completely turn wrong, corrupt), perfect, perceive, persuade

peri [around] perimeter (measurement around an area), periphery, periscope, pericardium, period

poly [many] polygon (figure having many angles or sides), polygamy, polyglot, polychrome

post [after] postpone, postwar, postscript, posterity

pre [before] prewar, preview, precede, prevent, premonition

pro [forward, in favor of] project (throw forward), progress, promote, prohibition

pseudo [false] pseudonym (false or assumed name), pseudo, pseudopodia

quad [four] quadruple (four times as much), quadriplegic, quadratic, quadrant, quadruped

quint [five] quintuplet, quintuple, quintet, quintile

re [back, again] reclaim, revive, revoke, rejuvenate, retard, reject, return

retro [backward] retrospective (looking backward), retroactive, retrorocket

se [aside] seduce (lead aside), secede, secrete, segregate

self [by oneself] self-determination, self-employed, self-service, selfish

sesqui [one and a half] sesquicentennial (one and one-half centuries)

sex, sest [six] sexagenarian (sixty years old), sexennial, sextant, sextuplet, sestet

sub [under] submerge (put under), submarine, subhuman, substitute, subsoil

suf, sug, sup, sus [from under] suffer, sufficient, suggest, support, suspect, suspend

super, supr [above, over, more] supervise, superman, supernatural, supreme

syn, sym, sys, syl [with, together] synthesis, synchronize (time together), synonym, sympathy, symphony, system, syllable

trans, tra [across, beyond] transoceanic, transmit (send across), transfusion, tradition

tri [three] tricycle, triangle, tripod, trinomial, tristate

ultra [beyond, exceedingly] ultramodern, ultraviolet, ultraconservative

un [not, release] unfair, unnatural, unbutton

under [beneath] underground, underneath, underlying

uni [one] unicycle, uniform, unify, universe, unique (one of a kind)

vice [in place of] vice president, vice admiral, viceroy

492 ## Numerical Prefixes

Prefix	Symbol	Multiples and Submultiples	Equivalent	Prefix	Symbol	Multiples and Submultiples	Equivalent
tera	T	10^{12}	trillionfold	deci	d	10^{-1}	tenth part
giga	G	10^{9}	billionfold	centi	c	10^{-2}	hundredth part
mega	M	10^{6}	millionfold	milli	m	10^{-3}	thousandth part
kilo	k	10^{3}	thousandfold	micro	u	10^{-6}	millionth part
hecto	h	10^{2}	hundredfold	nano	n	10^{-9}	billionth part
deka	da	10	tenfold	pico	p	10^{-12}	trillionth part

493 Suffixes

Suffixes come at the end of a word. Very often a suffix will tell you what kind of word it is (noun, adverb, adjective, etc.). For example, words ending in -*dom* are usually nouns, -*ly* words are usually adverbs, and words ending in -*able* are usually adjectives.

able, ible [able, can do] capable, agreeable, edible, visible (can be seen)

age [act of, state of, collection of] salvage (act of saving), storage, forage

al [relating to] sensual, gradual, manual, natural (relating to nature)

an, ian [native of, relating to] African, Canadian (native of Canada)

ance, ancy [action, process, state] allowance, assistance, defiance, truancy

ant [performer, agent] assistant, servant

ary, ery, ory [relating to, quality, place where] dictionary, bravery, dormitory

ate [cause, make] liquidate, segregate (cause a group to be set aside)

cian [having a certain skill or art] musician, beautician, magician, physician

cule, ling [very small] molecule, ridicule, duckling (very small duck), sapling

cy [action, function] hesitancy, prophecy, normalcy (function in a normal way)

dom [quality, realm, office] freedom, kingdom, wisdom (quality of being wise)

ee [one who receives the action] employee, nominee (one who is nominated)

en [made of, make] silken, frozen, oaken (made of oak), wooden, lighten

ence, ency [action, state of, quality] difference, conference, urgency

er, or [one who, that which] baker, miller, teacher, racer, amplifier, doctor

escent [in the process of] adolescent (in the process of becoming an adult), obsolescent, convalescent

ese [a native of, the language of] Japanese, Vietnamese

esis, osis [action, process, condition] genesis, hypnosis, neurosis, osmosis

ess [female] actress, goddess, lioness

et, ette [a small one, group] midget, octet, baronet, majorette

fic [making, causing] scientific, specific

ful [full of] frightful, careful, helpful

fy [make] fortify, simplify, amplify

hood [order, condition, quality] manhood, womanhood, brotherhood

ic [nature of, like] metallic (of the nature of metal), heroic, poetic, acidic

ice [condition, state, quality] justice, malice, prejudice

id, ide [a thing connected with] fluid, fluoride, bromide

ile [relating to, suited for, capable of] juvenile, senile (related to being old)

ine [nature of] feminine, medicine

ion, sion, tion [act of, state of, result of] contagion, aversion, infection (state of being infected)

ish [origin, nature, resembling] foolish, Irish, clownish (resembling a clown)

ism [system, condition, characteristic] alcoholism, heroism, Communism

ist [one who, that which] artist, dentist, violinist

ite [nature of, quality of, mineral product] Israelite, dynamite, graphite

ity, ty [state of, quality] captivity, clarity

ive [causing, making] abusive (causing abuse), exhaustive

ize [make] emphasize, publicize, idolize

less [without] baseless, careless (without care), artless, fearless, helpless

ly [like, manner of] carelessly, fearlessly, hopelessly, shamelessly

ment [act of, state of, result] contentment, amendment (state of amending)

ness [state of] carelessness, restlessness

oid [resembling] asteroid, spheroid, tabloid, anthropoid

ology [study, science, theory] biology, anthropology, geology, neurology

ous [full of, having] gracious, nervous, spacious, vivacious (full of life)

ship [office, state, quality, skill] friendship, authorship, dictatorship

some [like, apt, tending to] lonesome, threesome, gruesome

tude [state of, condition of] gratitude, aptitude, multitude (condition of being many)

ure [state of, act, process, rank] culture, rupture (state of being broken)

ward [in the direction of] eastward, forward, backward

y [inclined to, tend to] cheery, crafty, faulty

494 Roots

Knowing the root of a difficult word can go a long way toward helping you figure out its meaning—even without a dictionary. Because improving your vocabulary is so important to success in all your classes (and beyond school), learning the following roots will be very valuable.

acer, acid, acri [bitter, sour, sharp] acrid, acerbic, acidity (sourness)

acu [sharp] acute, acupuncture

ag, agi, ig, act [do, move, go] agent (doer), agenda (things to do), agitate, navigate (move by sea), ambiguous (going both ways), action

ali, allo, alter [other] alias (a person's other name), alibi, alien (from another place), alloy, alter

alt(us) [high, deep] altimeter (a device for measuring heights), altitude

am, amor [love, liking] amiable, amorous, enamored

anni, annu, enni [year] anniversary, annually (yearly), centennial (occurring once in 100 years)

anthrop [man] anthropology (study of mankind), misanthrope (hater of mankind), philanthropy (love of mankind)

arch [chief, first, rule] archangel (chief angel), architect (chief worker), monarchy (rule by one person)

aster, astr [star] aster (star flower), asterisk, asteroid, astronomy (star law), astronaut (star traveler; space traveler)

aud, aus [hear, listen] audible (can be heard), auditorium, audio, audition, auditory, audience, ausculate

aug, auc [increase] augur, augment (add to; increase), auction

auto, aut [self] automobile (self-moving vehicle), autograph (self-writing), automatic (self-acting), autobiography

belli [war] rebellion, belligerent (warlike or hostile)

bibl [book] Bible, bibliography (a written list of books), bibliomania (craze for books), bibliophile (book lover)

bio [life] biology (study of life), biography, biopsy (cutting living tissue)

brev [short] abbreviate, brevity, brief

cad, cas [to fall] cadaver, cadence, caducous (falling off), cascade

calor [heat] calorie (a unit of heat), calorify (to make hot), caloric

cap, cip, cept [take] capable, capacity, capture, reciprocate, accept, except

capit, capt [head] decapitate (to remove the head from), capital, captain, caption

carn [flesh] carnivorous (flesh-eating), incarnate, reincarnation

caus, caut [burn, heat] caustic, cauldron, cauterize (to make hot; burn)

cause, cuse, cus [cause, motive] because, excuse (to attempt to remove the blame or cause), accusation

ced, ceed, cede, cess [move, yield, go, surrender] procedure, proceed (move forward), cede (yield), concede, intercede, precede, recede, secede

centri [center] concentric, centrifugal, centripetal, eccentric (out of center)

chrom [color] chrome, chromosome (color body in genetics), Kodachrome, monochrome (one color), polychrome

chron [time] chronological (in order of time), chronometer (time-measured), chronicle (record of events in time), synchronize (make time with, set time together)

cide, cise [cut down, kill] suicide (self-killer), homicide (man, human killer), pesticide (pest killer), germicide (germ killer), insecticide, decide (cut off uncertainty), precise (cut exactly right), incision, scissors

cit [to call, start] incite, citation, cite

civ [citizen] civic (relating to a citizen), civil, civilian, civilization

clam, claim [cry out] exclamation, acclaim, proclamation, clamor

clud, clus, claus [shut] include (to take in), conclude, recluse (one who shuts himself away from others), claustrophobia (abnormal fear of being shut up)

cognosc, gnosi [know] recognize (to know again), incognito (not known), prognosis (forward knowing), diagnosis

cord, cor, cardi [heart] cordial (hearty, heartfelt), concord, discord, courage, encourage (put heart into), discourage (take heart out of), coronary, cardiac

corp [body] corporation (a legal body), corpse, corpulent

cosm [universe, world] cosmos (the universe), cosmic, cosmopolitan (world citizen), cosmonaut, microcosm

495

crat, cracy [rule, strength] democratic, autocracy

crea [create] creature (anything created), recreation, creation, creator

cred [believe] creed (statement of beliefs), credo (a creed), credence (belief), credit (belief, trust), credulous (believing too readily, easily deceived), incredible

cresc, cret, crease, cru [rise, grow] crescendo (growing in loudness or intensity), concrete (grown together), increase, decrease, accrue (to grow)

crit [separate, choose] critical, criterion (guideline used in choosing)

cur, curs [run] current (running or flowing), concurrent, concur (run together, agree), incur (run into), recur, occur, courier, precursor (forerunner), cursive

cura [care] curator, curative, manicure (caring for the hands)

cycl, cyclo [wheel, circular] Cyclops (a mythical giant with one eye in the middle of his forehead), unicycle, bicycle, cyclone (a wind blowing circularly)

deca [ten] decade, decalogue, decathlon

dem [people] democracy (people-rule), demography (vital statistics of the people: deaths, births, etc.), epidemic (on or among the people)

dent, dont [tooth] dental (relating to teeth), denture, dentifrice, orthodontist

derm [skin] hypodermic (injected under the skin), dermatology (skin study), epidermis (outer layer of skin), taxidermy (arranging skin; mounting animals)

dict [say, speak] diction (how one speaks, what one says), dictionary, dictate, dictator, dictaphone, dictatorial, contradict, predict, verdict, edict, benediction

doc [teach] indoctrinate, doctrine

domin [master] dominate, dominion, predominant, domain

don [give] donate, condone

dorm [sleep] dormant, dormitory

dox [opinion, praise] doxy (belief, creed, or opinion), orthodox (having the correct, commonly accepted opinion), heterodox (differing opinion), paradox (seemingly contradictory)

drome [run, step] syndrome (run-together symptoms), hippodrome (a place where horses run)

duc, duct [lead] induce (lead into, persuade), seduce (lead aside), produce, reduce, aquaduct (water leader or channel), viaduct, conduct, conduit, subdue

dura [hard, lasting] durable, duration, endurance

dynam [power] dynamo (power producer), dynamic, dynamite, hydrodynamics

endo [within] endoral (within the mouth), endocardial (within the heart), endoskeletal

equi [equal] equinox, equilibrium

erg [work] energy, erg (unit of work), allergy, ergophobia (morbid fear of work), ergometer, ergograph

fac, fact, fic, fect [do, make] factory (place where workers make goods of various kinds), fact (a thing done), manufacture, amplification, confection

fall, fals [deceive] fallacy, falsify

fer [bear, carry] ferry (carry by water), coniferous (bearing cones, as a pine tree), fertile (bearing richly), defer, infer, refer

fid, fide, feder [faith, trust] confidante, Fido, fidelity, confident, infidelity, infidel, federal, confederacy

fila, fili [thread] filament (a threadlike conductor heated by electrical current), filter, filet, filibuster, filigree

fin [end, ended, finished] final, finite, finish, confine, fine, refine, define, finale

fix [fix] fix, fixation (the state of being attached), fixture, affix, prefix, suffix

flex, flect [bend] flex (bend), reflex (bending back), flexible, flexor (muscle for bending), inflexibility, reflect

flu, fluc, fluv [flowing] influence (to flow in), fluid, flue, flush, fluently, fluctuate (to flow in an unsteady motion)

form [form, shape] uniform, conform, deform, reform, perform, formative, formation, formal, formula

fort, forc [strong] fort, fortress (a strong point), fortify (make strong), forte (one's strong point), fortitude

fract, frag [break] fracture (a break), infraction, fragile (easy to break), fraction (result of breaking a whole into equal parts), refract (to break or bend)

gam [marriage] bigamy (two marriages), monogamy, polygamy (many spouses or marriages)

gastr(o) [stomach] gastric, gastronomic, gastritis (inflammation of the stomach)

gen [birth, race, produce] genesis (birth, beginning), genetics (study of heredity), eugenics (well-born), genealogy (lineage by race, stock), generate, genetic

geo [earth] geology, geography (earth-writing), geometry (earth measurement), geocentric (earth-centered)

496

germ [vital part] germination (to grow), germ (seed; living substance, as the germ of an idea), germane

gest [carry, bear] congest (bear together, clog), congestive, gestation

gloss, glot [tongue] glossary, polyglot (many tongues), epiglottis

glu, glo [lump, bond, glue] agglutinate (make to hold in a bond), glue, conglomerate (bond together)

grad, gress [step, go] grade (step, degree), gradual (step-by-step), graduate (make all the steps, finish a course), progress

graph, gram [write, written] graph, graphic (written; vivid), autograph (self-writing), photography (light-writing)

grat [pleasing] congratulate (express pleasure over success), gratuity (a tip for pleasing service), grateful, ingrate

grav [heavy, weighty] grave, gravitate, aggravate, gravity

greg [herd, group, crowd] gregarian (belonging to a herd), congregation (a group functioning together), segregate

helio [sun] heliograph (an instrument for using the sun's rays to send signals), heliotrope (a plant that turns to the sun)

hema, hemo [blood] hemorrhage (an outpouring or flowing of blood), hemoglobin, hemophilia

here, hes [stick] adhere, cohere, cohesion

hetero [different] heterogeneous (different in birth), heterosexual

homo [same] homogeneous (of same birth or kind), homonyn (word with same name or pronunciation as another)

hum, human [earth, ground, man] humus, exhume (to take out of the ground), humane (compassion for other humans)

hydr, hydra, hydro [water] dehydrate (take water out of), hydrant, hydraulic, hydrogen, hydrophobia (fear of water)

hypn [sleep] hypnosis, Hypnos (god of sleep), hypnotherapy (treatment of disease by hypnosis)

ject [throw] deject, inject, project (throw forward), eject, object

join, junct [join] adjoining, enjoin (to lay an order upon; to command), juncture, conjunction, injunction, conjunction

juven [young] juvenile, rejuvenate (to make young again)

lau, lav, lot, lut [wash] launder, lavatory, lotion, ablution (a washing away), dilute (to make a liquid thinner)

leg [law] legal (lawful; according to law), legislate (to enact a law), legislature, legitimize (make legal)

levi [light] alleviate (lighten a load), levitate, levity (light conversation; humor)

liber, liver [free] liberty (freedom), liberal, liberalize, deliverance

liter [letters] literary (concerned with books and writing), literature, literal, alliteration, obliterate

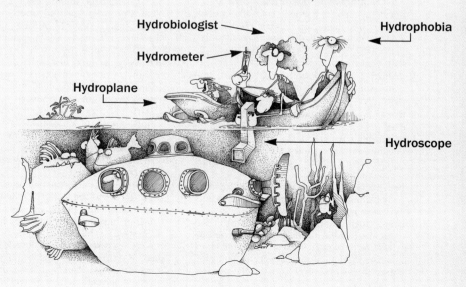

Hydrobiologist

Hydrophobia

Hydrometer

Hydroplane

Hydroscope

497

loc, loco [place] locality, locale, location, allocate (to assign; to place), relocate (to put back into place), locomotion

log, logo, ology [word, study, speech] catalog, prologue, dialogue, logogram (a symbol representing a word), zoology (animal study), psychology (mind study)

loqu, locut [talk, speak] eloquent (speaking well and forcefully), loquacious (talkative), colloquial (informal talk)

luc, lum, lus, lun [light] translucent (letting light come through), lumen (a unit of light), luminary (a heavenly body), luster (sparkle; shine)

magn [great] magnify (make great, enlarge), magnificent, magnanimous, magnate, magnitude, magnum

man [hand] manual, manage, manacle, manufacture, manicure, maneuver

mand [command] remand (order back), mandatory (commanded), mandate

mania [madness] mania (insanity; craze), monomania (mania on one idea), kleptomania, pyromania, maniac

mar, mari, mer [sea, pool] marine, marsh (wetland, swamp), maritime (relating to the sea and navigation)

matri [mother] matrimony (state of wedlock), maternal (relating to the mother), matriarchate (rulership of women)

medi [half, middle, between, halfway] mediate (come between, intervene), medieval (pertaining to the Middle Ages), mediterranean (lying between lands), mediocre, medium

mega [great] megaphone (great sound), megalopolis (great city; an extensive urban area including a number of cities), megacycle (a million cycles), megaton

mem [remember] memoir, memo (a note; a reminder), commemoration (the act of remembering by a memorial or ceremony), memento, memorable

meter [measure] meter (a metric measure), voltameter (instrument to measure volts), barometer, thermometer

micro [small] microscope, microfilm, microcard, microwave, micrometer (device for measuring small distances), omicron, micron (a millionth of a meter), microbe (small living thing)

migra [wander] migrate (to wander), emigrant (one who leaves a country), immigrate (to come into the land)

mit, miss [send] emit (send out, give off), remit (send back, as money due), submit, admit, commit, permit, transmit (send across), omit, intermittent (sending between, at intervals), mission, missile

mob, mot, mov [move] mobile (capable of moving), motionless (without motion), motor, emotional (moved strongly by feelings), motivate, promotion, demote

mon [warn, remind] admonish (warn), monument (a reminder or memorial of a person or event), monitor, premonition (forewarning)

mor, mort [mortal, death] mortal (causing death or destined for death), immortal (not subject to death), mortality (rate of death), mortician (one who prepares the dead for burial), mortuary (place for the dead, a morgue)

morph [form] amorphous (with no form, shapeless), metamorphosis (a change of form, as a caterpillar into a butterfly)

multi [many, much] multifold (folded many times), multilinguist (one who speaks many languages), multiped (an organism with many feet), multiply

nat, nasc [to be born, to spring forth] innate (inborn), natal, native, nativity, renascence (a rebirth; a revival)

neur [nerve] neuritis (inflammation of a nerve), neuropathic (having a nerve disease), neurologist (one who practices neurology), neural, neurosis, neurotic

nom [law, order] autonomy (self-law, self-government), astronomy, gastronomy (stomach law or study), economy

nomen, nomin [name] nomenclature, nominate (name someone for an office)

nov [new] novel (new; strange; not formerly known), renovate (to make like new again), novice, nova, innovate

nox, noc [night] nocturnal, equinox (equal nights), noctilucent (shining by night)

numer [number] numeral (a figure expressing a number), numeration (act of counting), enumerate (count out, one by one), innumerable

omni [all, every] omniscient (all-knowing), omnipotent (all-powerful), omnipresent, omnivorous

onym [name] anonymous (without name), pseudonym (false name), antonym (against name; word of opposite meaning), synonym

oper [work] operate (to labor; function), cooperate (work together), opus (a musical composition or work)

ortho [straight, correct] orthodox (of the correct or accepted opinion), orthodontist (tooth straightener), orthopedic

pac [peace] pacifist (one for peace only; opposed to war), pacify (make peace, quiet), Pacific Ocean (peaceful ocean)

498

pan [all] Pan-American, panacea (cure-all), pandemonium (place of all the demons; wild disorder), pantheon

pater, patr [father] paternity (fatherhood, responsibility, etc.), patriarch (head of the tribe, family), patriot

path, pathy [feeling, suffering] pathos (feeling of pity, sorrow), sympathy, antipathy (against feeling), apathy (without feeling), empathy

ped, pod [foot] pedal (lever for a foot), impede (get the feet in a trap, hinder), pedestal (foot or base of a statue), pedestrian (foot traveler), centipede, tripod

pedo [child] orthopedic, pedagogue (child leader; teacher), pediatrics (medical care of children)

pel, puls [drive, urge] compel, dispel, expel, repel, propel, pulse, impulse, pulsate, compulsory, expulsion, repulsive

pend, pens, pond [hang, weigh] pendant (a hanging object), pendulum, suspend, appendage, pensive (weighing thought)

phil [love] philosophy (love of wisdom), philanthropy, philharmonic, bibliophile, Philadelphia (city of brotherly love)

phobia [fear] claustrophobia (fear of closed spaces), acrophobia (fear of high places), aquaphobia (fear of water)

phon [sound] phonograph, phonetic (pertaining to sound), symphony (sounds with or together)

photo [light] photograph (light-writing), photoelectric, photogenic, photosynthesis

plac, plais [please] placid (calm, peaceful), placebo, placate, complacent

plu, plur, plus [more] plural (more than one), pluralist (a person who holds more than one office), plus

pneuma, pneumon [breath] pneumatic (pertaining to air, wind, or other gases), pneumonia (disease of the lungs)

poli [city] metropolis (mother city; main city), police, politics, Indianapolis, megalopolis, Acropolis (high city)

pon, pos, pound [place, put] postpone (put afterward), component, opponent (one put against), proponent, expose, impose, deposit, posture, impound

pop [people] population (the number of people in an area), popular, populous (full of people)

port [carry] porter (one who carries), portable, transport (carry across), report, export, import, support, transportation

portion [part, share] portion (a part; a share, as a portion of pie), proportion (the relation of one share to others)

prehend [seize] apprehend (seize a criminal), comprehend (seize with the mind), comprehensive (seizing much)

prim, prime [first] primacy (state of being first in rank), prima donna (the first lady of opera), primitive, primary, primeval

proto [first] prototype (the first model made), protocol, protagonist, protozoan

psych [mind, soul] psyche (soul, mind), psychiatry (healing of the mind), psychology, psychosis (serious mental disorder), psychotherapy (mind treatment), psychic

punct [point, dot] punctual (being exactly on time), punctuation, puncture, acupuncture

reg, recti [straighten] regiment, regular, rectify (make straight), correct, direct, rectangle

ri, ridi, risi [laughter] deride (mock; jeer at), ridicule (laughter at the expense of another; mockery), ridiculous, derision

rog, roga [ask] prerogative (privilege; asking before), interrogation (questioning; the act of questioning), derogatory

rupt [break] rupture (break), interrupt (break into), abrupt (broken off), disrupt (break apart), erupt (break out), incorruptible (not breakable)

sacr, sanc, secr [sacred] sacred, sacrosanct, sanction, consecrate, desecrate

salv, salu [safe, healthy] salvation (act of being saved), salvage, salutation

sat, satis [enough] saturate, satisfy (to give as much as is needed), satient (giving pleasure), satiate, saturate

sci [know] science (knowledge), conscious (knowing, aware), omniscient (knowing everything)

scope [see, watch] telescope, microscope, kaleidoscope (instrument for seeing beautiful forms), periscope, stethoscope

scrib, script [write] scribe (a writer), scribble, inscribe, describe, subscribe, prescribe, manuscript (written by hand)

sed, sess, sid [sit] sediment (that which sits or settles out of a liquid), session (a sitting), obsession (an idea that sits stubbornly in the mind), possess, preside (sit before), president, reside, subside

sen [old] senior, senator, senile (old; showing the weakness of old age)

499

sent, sens [feel] sentiment (feeling), consent, resent, dissent, sentimental (having strong feeling or emotion), sense, sensation, sensitive, sensory, dissension

sequ, secu, sue [follow] sequence (following of one thing after another), sequel, consequence, subsequent, prosecute, consecutive (following in order), second (following first), ensue, pursue

serv [save, serve] servant, service, subservient, servitude, preserve, conserve, reservation, deserve, observe

sign, signi [sign, mark, seal] signal (a gesture or sign to call attention), signature (the mark of a person written in his own handwriting), design, insignia (distinguishing marks), significant

simil, simul [like, resembling] similar (resembling in many respects), assimilate (to make similar to), simile, simulate (pretend; put on an act to make a certain impression)

sist, sta, stit [stand] assist (to stand by with help), persist (stand firmly; unyielding; continue), circumstance, stamina (power to withstand, to endure), status (standing), state, static, stable, stationary, substitute (to stand in for another)

solus [alone] solo, soliloquy, solitaire, solitude

solv, solu [loosen] solvent (a loosener, a dissolver), solve, absolve (loosen from, free from), resolve, soluble, solution, resolution, resolute, dissolute (loosened morally)

somnus [sleep] insomnia (not being able to sleep), somnambulist (a sleepwalker)

soph [wise] sophomore (wise fool), philosophy (love of wisdom), sophisticated (world wise)

spec, spect, spic [look] specimen (an example to look at, study), specific, spectator (one who looks), spectacle, aspect, speculate, inspect, respect, prospect, retrospective (looking backward), expect, introscopic, conspicuous

sphere [ball, sphere] sphere (a planet; a ball), stratosphere (the upper portion of the atmosphere), hemisphere (half of the earth), spheroid

spir [breath] spirit (breath), conspire (breathe together; plot), inspire (breathe into), aspire (breathe toward), expire (breathe out; die), perspire, respiration

string, strict [draw tight] stringent (drawn tight; rigid), strict, restrict, constrict (draw tightly together), boa constrictor

stru, struct [build] construe (build in the mind, interpret), structure, construct, instruct, obstruct, destruction, destroy

sume, sump [take, use, waste] consume (to use up), assume (to take; to use), sump pump (a pump that takes up water), presumption

tact, tang, tag, tig, ting [touch] tactile, contact (touch), intact (untouched, uninjured), intangible (not able to be touched), tangible, contagious (able to transmit disease by touching), contiguous, contingency

tele [far] telephone (far sound), telegraph (far writing), telegram, telescope (far look), television (far seeing), telephoto (far photography), telecast, telepathy (far feeling)

tempo [time] tempo (rate of speed), temporary, extemporaneously, pro tem (for the time being), contemporary (those who live at the same time)

ten, tin, tain [hold] tenacious (holding fast), tenant, tenure, untenable, detention, retentive, content, pertinent, continent, obstinate, contain, abstain, pertain, detain

tend, tent, tens [stretch, strain] tendency (a stretching; leaning), extend, intend, contend, pretend, superintend, tender, extent, tension (a stretching, strain), pretense

terra [earth] terrain, terrarium, territory, terrestrial

test [to bear witness] testament (a will; bearing witness to someone's wishes), detest, attest (bear witness to), testimony (words of a witness)

the, theo [God, a god] monotheism (belief in one god), polytheism (belief in many gods), atheism, theology

therm [heat] thermometer, therm (a unit of heat), thermal, thermos bottle, thermostat, hypothermia (subnormal temperature)

thesis, thet [place, put] antithesis (place against), hypothesis (place under), synthesis (put together)

tom [cut] atom (not cutable; smallest particle of matter), appendectomy (cutting out an appendix), tonsillectomy, dichotomy (cutting in two; a division), anatomy

500 **tort, tors** [twist] torture (twisting to inflict pain), retort (twist back, reply sharply), extort (twist out), distort (twist out of shape), contort, torsion (act of twisting, as a torsion bar)

tox [poison] toxic (poisonous), intoxicate, antitoxin

tract, tra [draw, pull] tractor, attract, subtract, tractable (can be handled), abstract (to draw away)

trib [pay, bestow] tribute (to pay honor to), contribute (to give money to a cause), attribute, retribution, tributary

turbo [disturb] turbulent, disturb, turbid, turmoil

typ [print] type, prototype (first print; model), typical, typography, typewriter, typology (study of types, symbols), typify

ultima [last] ultimate, ultimatum (the final or last offer that can be made)

uni [one] unicorn (a legendary creature with one horn), unify (make into one), university, unanimous, universal

vac [empty] vacate (to make empty), vacuum (a space entirely devoid of matter), evacuate (to remove troops or people), vacation, vacant

vale, vali, valu [strength, worth] equivalent (of equal worth), valiant, validity (truth; legal strength), evaluate (find out the value), value, valor (value; worth)

ven, vent [come] convene (come together, assemble), intervene (come between), venue, convenient, avenue, circumvent (come or go around), invent, convent, venture, event, advent, prevent

ver, veri [true] very, aver (say to be true, affirm), verdict, verity (truth), verify (show to be true), verisimilitude

vert, vers [turn] avert (turn away), divert (turn aside, amuse), invert (turn over), introvert (turn inward), convertible, reverse (turn back), controversy (a turning against; a dispute), versatile

vic, vicis [change, substitute] vicarious, vicar, vicissitude

vict, vinc [conquer] victor (conqueror, winner), evict (conquer out, expel), convict (prove guilty), convince (conquer mentally, persuade), invincible

vid, vis [see] video (television), evident, provide, providence, visible, revise, supervise (oversee), vista, visit, vision

viv, vita, vivi [alive, life] revive (make live again), survive (live beyond, outlive), vivid, vivacious (full of life), vitality, vivisection

voc [call] vocation (a calling), avocation (occupation not one's calling), convocation (a calling together), vocal

vol [will] malevolent, benevolent (one of goodwill), volunteer, volition

volcan, vulcan [fire] volcano (a mountain erupting fiery lava), vulcanize (to undergo tremendous heat), Vulcan (Roman god of fire)

volvo [turn about, roll] revolve, voluble (easily turned about or around), voluminous (winding), convolution (a twisting or coiling)

vor [eat greedily] voracious, carnivorous (flesh-eating), herbivorous (plant-eating), omnivorous (eating everything), devour (eat greedily)

zo [animal] zoo (short for zoological garden), zoology (study of animal life), zodiac (circle of animal constellations), protozoa (one-celled animals)

501 # The Human Body

arthral	joint	**gastro**	stomach	**oral**	mouth
audio	hearing	**glos**	tongue	**osteo**	bone
capit	head	**hem**	blood	**ped**	foot
card	heart	**man**	hand	**pneuma**	lungs
corp	body	**myo**	muscle	**psych**	mind
dactyl	finger	**nephro**	kidney	**rhino**	nose
dent	tooth	**neur**	nerve	**sarco**	flesh
derm	skin	**oculo**	eye	**spir**	breath

Reading Charts and Graphs

Graphs, tables, diagrams, and maps all have something in common: they're all "information pictures." They express information in pictures (visually) rather than in words (verbally). They may, in fact, contain a few words, but most of the information is expressed visually.

These information pictures, often called charts, can help us in a variety of ways. A good chart can make complex information easy to understand. It can show in one picture what it might take hundreds of words to tell. Remember the old saying, *One picture is worth a thousand words*? That's why a chart makes a big impression: It doesn't just tell—it shows.

What's Ahead?

This section will help you understand and read the most common kinds of charts:

> Graphs (line, pie, bar, stacked bar)
> Tables (schedule, distance, comparison)
> Diagrams (picture, line, graphic)
> Maps (special, weather)

503 Graphs

Graphs are popular forms of charts because they are easy to create and read. Graphs are pictures of information, not pictures of things you can see. The most common kinds are line graphs, pie graphs, and bar graphs.

504 Line Graph ● A line graph shows how things change over time. It starts with an L-shaped grid. The horizontal line of the grid stands for passing time (seconds, minutes, years, centuries, etc.). The vertical line of the grid shows the subject of the graph. The graph below is a double-line graph showing the number of deaths due to firearms compared to deaths due to motor vehicles.

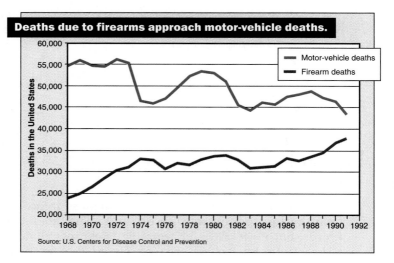

Deaths due to firearms approach motor-vehicle deaths.

Source: U.S. Centers for Disease Control and Prevention

505 Pie Graph ● A pie graph shows proportions and how each proportion, or part, relates to the other parts as well as to the whole "pie." In the sample pie graphs below, you can see at a glance how the number of people with a college background has changed from 1975 to 1990.

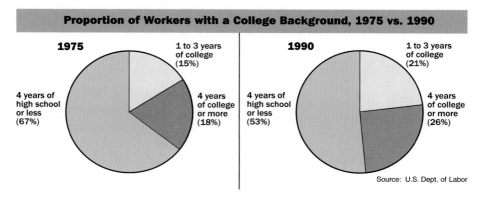

Proportion of Workers with a College Background, 1975 vs. 1990

Source: U.S. Dept. of Labor

506 **Bar Graph** ● A bar graph uses bars (sometimes called columns) to stand for the subjects of the graph. Unlike a line graph, it does not show how things change over time. Instead, a bar graph is like a snapshot that shows how things compare at one point in time.

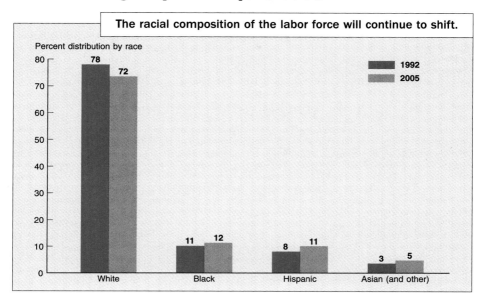

The racial composition of the labor force will continue to shift.

507 **Stacked Bar Graph** ● A stacked bar graph is a special kind of bar graph that gives more detailed information than a regular bar graph. Besides comparing the bars, it compares parts within the bars themselves.

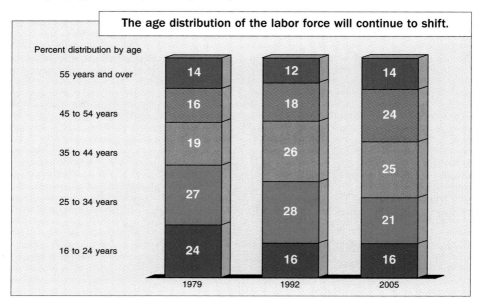

The age distribution of the labor force will continue to shift.

508 Tables

Tables organize words and numbers so that it's easy to see how they relate to one another. Most tables have rows (going across) and columns (going down). Rows contain one kind of information, while columns contain another kind of information. Examples are schedules, distance tables, comparison tables, and conversion tables. (See 790-798.)

509 Schedule ● One of the most common and useful tables is the schedule. Read schedules *very* carefully; each one is a little bit different.

MILWAUKEE TO O'HARE BUS SCHEDULE

Reading schedules: Find the time you want to arrive at O'Hare in the right-hand column. Read straight across to your left on the same line to your pickup point; that is the time you will leave from that point. (Disregard all other times.)

Lv **Marquette** University Library 1415 Wisconsin Ave.	Lv **Milwaukee** Amtrak Station 5th & St. Paul Sts.	Lv **Milwaukee** United Limo 4960 S. 13th St.	Lv **Mitchell** Field Airport	Lv **Racine Jct.** Colony Inn I-94 & Hwy. 20	Lv **Kenosha Jct.** Burger King I-94 & Hwy. 50	Ar **O'Hare** Airport Upper Level - All Airlines
4:30 AM	4:45 AM	5:00 AM	5:10 AM	5:25 AM	5:40 AM	6:40 AM
5:45 AM	6:00 AM	6:15 AM	6:25 AM	6:40 AM	6:55 AM	7:55 AM
8:30 AM	8:45 AM	9:00 AM	9:10 AM	9:25 AM	9:40 AM	10:40 AM
11:05 AM	11:20 AM	11:35 AM	11:45 AM	Noon	12:15 PM	1:15 PM
12:30 PM	12:45 PM	1:00 PM	1:10 PM	1:25 PM	1:40 PM	2:40 PM
1:45 PM	2:00 PM	2:15 PM	2:25 PM	2:40 PM	2:55 PM	3:55 PM
4:15 PM	4:30 PM	4:45 PM	4:55 PM	5:10 PM	5:25 PM	6:25 PM
7:15 PM	7:30 PM	7:45 PM	7:55 PM	8:10 PM	8:25 PM	9:25 PM

510 Distance Table ● Another common kind of table is a distance or mileage table. To read a distance table, find the place you're starting from and the place you're going to. Then find the place where the row and the column meet—that's how far it is from one place to the other.

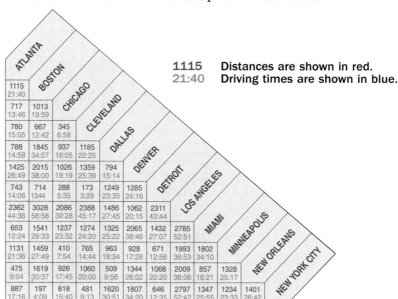

1115
21:40

Distances are shown in red.
Driving times are shown in blue.

ATLANTA											
1115 21:40	BOSTON										
717 13:46	1013 19:59	CHICAGO									
780 15:05	667 12:42	345 6:58	CLEVELAND								
788 14:58	1845 34:57	937 18:05	1185 22:25	DALLAS							
1425 26:49	2015 38:00	1026 19:19	1359 25:39	794 15:14	DENVER						
743 14:06	714 13:44	288 5:35	173 3:29	1249 23:35	1285 24:16	DETROIT					
2362 44:36	3028 56:58	2086 39:28	2388 45:17	1486 27:45	1062 20:15	2311 43:44	LOS ANGELES				
653 12:24	1541 29:33	1237 23:32	1274 24:20	1325 25:22	2065 38:46	1432 27:07	2785 52:51	MIAMI			
1131 21:36	1459 27:49	410 7:54	765 14:44	963 18:34	928 17:28	671 12:56	1993 36:53	1802 34:10	MINNEAPOLIS		
475 9:04	1619 30:37	926 17:45	1060 20:00	509 9:56	1344 26:02	1068 20:20	2009 38:06	857 16:21	1328 25:17	NEW ORLEANS	
887 17:16	197 4:09	818 15:40	481 9:13	1620 30:51	1807 34:20	646 12:35	2797 52:42	1347 25:55	1234 23:33	1401 26:42	NEW YORK CITY

511 **Comparison Table** ● A comparison table is used to show how two (or more) people, places, or things are alike (or not alike). Usually a comparison table covers a span of several months or years to show how much things have changed. The table below compares employment projections for six counties in 1994, 2004, and 2014.

Employment Projections by Industry
(by county, in thousands)

Industry	Year	Kenosha	Milwaukee	Ozaukee	Racine	Washington	Waukesha
Total employment	1994	54.79	631.48	42.01	93.17	50.55	214.64
	2004	58.10	660.76	51.36	99.49	59.56	259.64
	2014	64.28	708.30	59.18	104.82	65.23	288.10
Farming	1994	0.81	0.22	0.67	1.14	1.40	1.17
	2004	0.70	0.19	0.57	0.98	1.26	1.04
	2014	0.63	0.17	0.51	0.89	1.15	0.94
Ag. Services	1994	0.37	1.87	0.46	0.62	0.45	1.68
	2004	0.44	2.09	0.52	0.72	0.51	1.91
	2014	0.50	2.33	0.58	0.81	0.57	2.14
Construction	1994	2.79	10.23	1.75	3.64	3.43	13.19
	2004	3.17	22.12	2.16	4.10	4.71	16.14
	2014	3.51	23.48	2.39	4.31	5.57	17.21
Manufacturing	1994	9.84	105.68	9.90	26.30	13.08	45.94
	2004	8.87	98.23	10.93	27.01	15.16	54.63
	2014	8.59	96.36	11.52	27.62	16.32	59.42
Transportation	1994	1.87	30.11	0.91	3.15	1.92	9.21
	2004	2.05	30.90	1.04	3.56	2.27	11.50
	2014	2.32	32.45	1.12	3.90	2.49	12.98
Wholesale trade	1994	1.54	29.94	1.65	3.05	1.87	18.34
	2004	1.71	29.11	2.17	3.17	2.56	24.61
	2014	1.96	29.65	2.67	3.29	3.19	29.75
Retail trade	1994	12.57	104.22	7.48	16.87	8.30	35.29
	2004	14.53	109.54	9.29	18.22	9.71	41.75
	2014	17.34	118.89	10.89	19.54	10.68	45.78
Finance	1994	2.76	57.72	3.28	3.99	3.92	19.13
	2004	3.16	61.10	4.05	4.04	4.82	24.42
	2014	3.71	66.06	4.69	4.08	5.45	28.17
Services	1994	14.66	211.87	11.92	24.77	10.54	53.49
	2004	16.06	238.95	16.40	27.86	12.50	65.29
	2014	18.14	270.44	20.57	30.41	13.71	72.36
Government	1994	7.56	69.34	3.96	9.60	5.59	16.77
	2004	7.38	68.22	4.18	9.78	6.00	17.88
	2014	7.55	68.16	4.21	9.93	6.04	18.83

512 Diagrams

A diagram is a drawing designed to show how something is constructed, how its parts relate to one another, or how it works. The two most common types of diagrams are the picture diagram and the line diagram.

513 Picture Diagram ● A picture diagram is just that—a picture or drawing of the subject being discussed. Often, some parts are left out of the diagram to emphasize the parts the writer wants to show. For example, the diagram below shows the parts of the brain responsible for certain functions. Most diagrams come before or after a written explanation, as does the sample below.

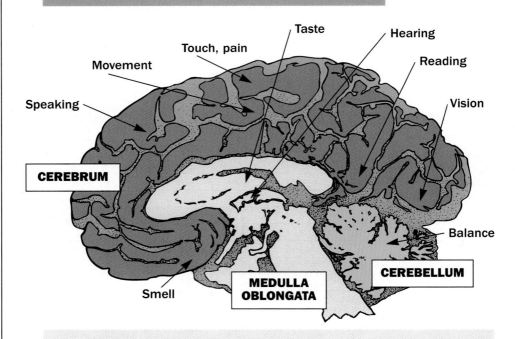

The Structure and Function of the Brain

Taste · Hearing · Touch, pain · Reading · Movement · Speaking · Vision · CEREBRUM · Balance · CEREBELLUM · Smell · MEDULLA OBLONGATA

The **cerebrum** makes up about 85 percent of the brain mass and is the seat of conscious thought processes: speaking, movement, reading, seeing, smelling, etc. The **cerebellum** automatically coordinates movement and balance with sense perceptions. The **medulla oblongata** controls automatic movements: swallowing, breathing, heartbeat, circulation, posture, etc.

514 <u>Line Diagram</u> ● Another type of diagram is a line diagram. A line diagram uses lines, symbols, drawings, and words to help you picture things that you can't actually see (or are difficult to see all at once). The diagram below helps you to see how to properly set up a complete stereo system.

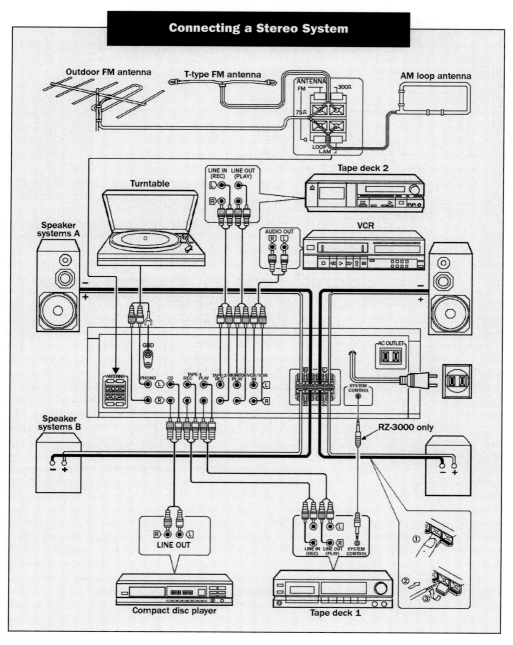

Connecting a Stereo System

515 **Graphic Diagram** ● A third type of diagram is a graphic diagram in which several graphics are combined or overlapped to emphasize the parts the writer wants to show. For example, the diagram below overlaps three graphics from a computer screen to show the process of translating DOS files so they can be used on a Macintosh computer.

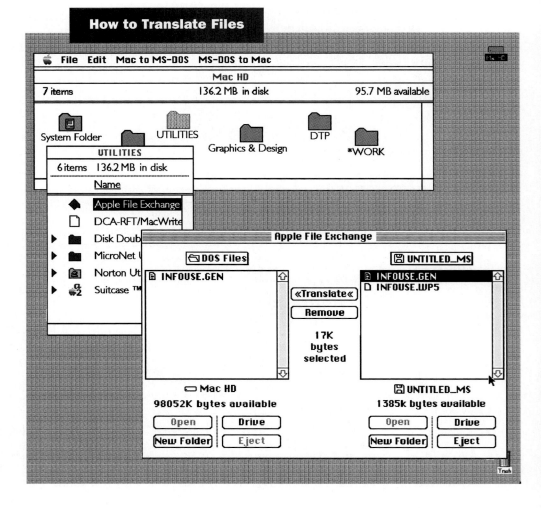

INSIDE

Most diagrams are preceded or followed by a thorough explanation of what is being shown. The diagram will help you visualize what is being discussed, but you must read the explanation completely and carefully.

516 **Maps**

Of all the information pictures we use on a regular basis, maps are probably the most useful. Road maps, special maps, political maps (see 802-818), and weather maps all play an important part in our daily lives.

517 **Special Maps** ● Some maps feature cities, states, or regions of the country for purposes of comparing one to another. In the map below, the regions of the country are compared, showing the population growth between a past 13-year span and a projected 13-year span.

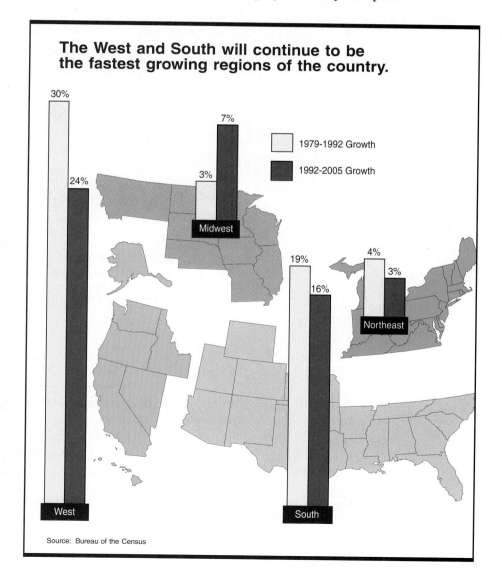

The West and South will continue to be the fastest growing regions of the country.

1979-1992 Growth

1992-2005 Growth

Source: Bureau of the Census

518 <u>**Weather Map**</u> ● Weather maps are typical of all maps—they contain an outline of a country, state, or city. But they also contain a language of words, lines, and symbols that is unique to weather maps. Study the one below, using the key as your guide.

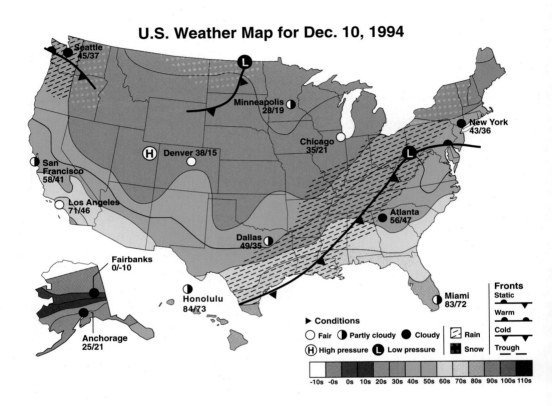

U.S. Weather Map for Dec. 10, 1994

THE BOTTOM LINE

Although no two graphs, tables, diagrams, or maps are exactly alike, there are some general guidelines you can use:

● Read the title or caption (to get the big picture).

● Read the labels or column headings (to get a better idea of what the chart is covering).

● Read the data (to get specific information).

● Read the paragraph above or below the chart (to provide background information).

● Read the key or footnotes (to clarify anything you don't understand).

Learning to Learn

519   When you face work at school or on the job, you have a choice: ride the horse, or be dragged behind it. If you don't manage your time, you'll mismanage it. If you don't take notes, you'll miss something important. If you don't write to learn, you might not learn at all.

To get the most out of your work, you have to concentrate your time, your attention, and your thoughts. You need to find out how to stuff more information and ideas into an already over-crowded brain. And you need to figure out a way to get things done on time and have time left over for sleeping and eating.

This chapter is filled with techniques—easily-learned techniques—that will help you sharpen your performance in any class, on any job.

What's Ahead?

This section of your handbook emphasizes those skills you need to be an efficient learner:

Note-Taking Skills

Writing to Learn

Completing Assignments

Managing Your Time

520 Note-Taking Skills

Memory experts tell us that within 24 hours of learning, the average person forgets at least half of what he or she learns. These same experts also tell us that the more personally involved we are in the learning process, the more likely we are to understand and remember what we have learned.

Taking notes gets you actively involved in your thinking and focuses your attention on the most important information and ideas. Just as importantly, it leaves a lasting record that will be of special value when you need to review or write.

INSIDE

info

You'll find useful tips on note taking scattered throughout the upcoming sections, 521-527.

521 Using a Note-Taking Guide

Here's a note-taking technique that should make you more active and alert in the classroom. When you read your textbook, take notes on the left two-thirds of the page. Then, when the teacher reviews the reading material with the class, follow along in your own notes, using the right one-third of the page to record any new thoughts. Write down anything that defines terms, clarifies concepts, or in some other way adds to your understanding of the material. If you are asked a question by the teacher during this process, your well-organized notes should help you answer.

NOTE: Review time is a good time to check dates, spelling of important names, and ideas that connect the facts.

March 12	Chapter 10: Apprenticeships
Outlined Reading Assignment	Class Notes
A. Renewed Interest–Medieval Europe	Learner worked for master craftsperson. The master got the benefit of free labor, and the apprentice got training and a little income. Apprenticeships lasted for seven years. After that time, apprentice free to work for wages.
1. Craft guilds set up	
a. medicine	
b. painting	
c. brewing	
2. Gender role assignments	
a. boys–all trades	
b. girls–domestic skills	
B. Changes–1700 to 1850	
1. Effects of Industrial Revolution	Fewer apprenticeships available because of changes in labor market. New machines created new trades and new demands for skilled workers but also huge demand for unskilled workers.
a. move to cities	
b. need for unskilled workers	
2. New opportunities	
a. machinists	
b. electricians	
c. tool and die makers	

522 Guidelines for Improving Note-Taking Skills

Be attentive . . .

- **Listen for any special instructions,** rules, or guidelines your instructor may have regarding notebooks and note taking.
- **Write the date and the topic** of each lecture or discussion at the top of each page of notes.
- **Write your notes in ink,** and as neatly as time will allow; leave space in the margin for working with your notes later.
- **Begin taking notes immediately.** Don't wait for something new or earthshaking before you write your first note.
- **Relate the material** you are noting to something in your life by writing a brief personal observation or reminder.

Be concise . . .

- **Summarize the main ideas,** listing only the most important details. Taking good notes does *not* mean writing down everything.
- **Write as concisely as you can.** Write your notes in phrases and thoughts rather than complete sentences.
- **Use abbreviations,** acronyms, and symbols (U.S., avg., in., ea., lb., vs., @, #, $, %, &, +, =, w/o, etc.).
- **Draw simple illustrations,** charts, or diagrams in your notes whenever they will make a point clearer.

Be organized . . .

- **Write a title or heading** for each new topic covered in your notes.
- **Listen for transitions** or signal words to help you organize your notes. Use numbers for all related ideas presented in time sequence.
- **Ask questions** when you don't understand.
- **Use a special system of marking** your notes to emphasize important information (underline, star, check, indent).
- **Label** or indicate in some way **information** that is related by cause and effect, by comparison or contrast, or by any other special way.

Be smart . . .

- **Always copy down** (or summarize) what the instructor puts on the board or an overhead projector.
- **Circle those words or ideas** that you will need to ask about or look up later.
- **Don't let your notes sit** until it is time to review for a test. Read over your notes within 24 hours and recopy, highlight, or summarize as necessary. (Use a colored marker to highlight key notes.)
- **Share your note-taking techniques,** abbreviations, or special markings with others; then learn from what they share with you.

523 Learning Logs

One of the most effective learning activities is the learning log. A learning log gets you actively involved in the learning process and gives you the opportunity to explore important ideas freely and naturally. This free flow of ideas and questions promotes true learning. (Use the guidelines for journal writing, 139, to get you started in your learning log; then refer to the list that follows for writing ideas.)

524 Guidelines for Keeping a Learning Log

1. **Write about day-to-day activities**—anything from a discussion to a demonstration. Consider what was valuable, confusing, interesting, humorous, etc.

2. **Discuss new ideas and concepts.** Consider how this new information relates to what you already know.

3. **Evaluate your progress.** Assess your strengths, your weaknesses, your relationship with other members of the group.

4. **Discuss your work with a particular audience:** a young child, a foreign exchange student, an object, an alien from another planet.

5. **Confront ideas that confuse you.** Back them into a corner until you finally understand what's so confusing.

6. **Keep a record of your thoughts and feelings.** Keeping a record can be especially helpful during an extended lab or research assignment.

7. **Start a glossary** of important and interesting vocabulary words. Use these words in your log entries.

8. **Argue for or against a topic.** The topic can be anything that comes up in a discussion, in your reading, or in a lecture.

525 Personal Note Taking

If you plan to use your learning log for reading notes, here's one method you can use. Begin by dividing a page in half. On the left side, record notes from your reading, and on the right side, record comments or questions. This written dialogue makes note taking more meaningful and provides you with material for class discussion. Here are examples of the types of comments you can make:

- A reaction to a particular point that you strongly agree or disagree with
- A question about a concept that confuses you
- A paraphrase of a difficult or complex idea
- A discussion of the importance or significance of the material
- A comment on what memory or feeling a particular idea brings to mind

526 Writing-to-Learn Activities

Writing to learn is one of the most valuable learning tools we have. The exact form your writing takes is strictly up to you. You might be perfectly satisfied with free, nonstop writing; others might find clustering or listing meaningful. Still others might enjoy a variety of writing activities similar to those that follow.

Admit slips ● Admit slips are brief pieces of writing in which you "admit" something about what is being studied. An admit slip can be a summary of last night's reading, a question about class material, a request for the instructor to review a particular point, or anything else you may have on your mind. (Admit slips are turned in at the beginning of class.)

Debates ● Try splitting your mind into two "persons." Have one side debate (disagree with) your thinking on a subject, and have the other side defend it. Keep the debate going as long as you can.

Dialogues ● In a dialogue, you create an imaginary conversation between yourself and a character (a historical figure or one from a story) or between two characters. Dialogue can bring information to life, helping you to understand a particular subject or historical period better.

Exit slips ● Write a short piece at the end of class in which you summarize, evaluate, or question something about the day's lesson. Turn in your exit slip to your instructor before you leave the classroom.

First thoughts ● You can benefit greatly from writing your immediate impressions about a topic you are preparing to study. These writings will help you focus on the task at hand and prepare you for what's ahead.

How-to writing ● Write instructions or directions for how to perform a certain task. This will help you to clarify and remember information.

Nutshelling ● Try writing down, in one sentence, the importance of something you've heard, seen, or read.

Picture outlines ● Instead of using a traditional outline, organize your thoughts into a picture outline. For example, a lecture on the basic machines underlying all technology might include a picture outline.

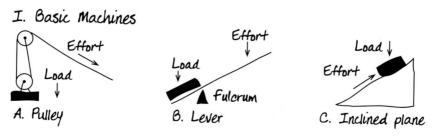

I. Basic Machines

A. Pulley   B. Lever   C. Inclined plane

527 **Pointed questions** ● Keep asking yourself *why* in your writing. Keep pressing the question until you can't push it any further.

Predicting ● Stop at a key point in a lesson and write what you think will happen next. Predicting works especially well with lessons that have a strong cause-and-effect relationship.

Role playing ● Imagine yourself in a different role (a reporter, a senior citizen, a historical or fictional character, an animal, etc.) and write about a topic from that point of view.

Stop 'n' write ● At any point in a reading assignment, stop and write. This allows you to evaluate your understanding of the topic and to reflect on what you've just read.

Summarizing ● An excellent way to learn about a subject is to summarize it in your own words, relating it to your own life whenever possible.

Textbook Summary

Cholesterol, a fatty substance found in human tissues, is primarily produced by the body. Some cholesterol enters the body as food. An important part of the membranes of every cell in the body, cholesterol is a building block in the production of bile acids (aid digestion) and hormones (chemical substances affecting many activities in the body). Though all cells can produce cholesterol, most is produced by liver cells. Special molecules called lipoproteins transport cholesterol from the liver throughout the body via the bloodstream. There are three types of lipoproteins: high-density lipoprotein (HDL), low-density lipoprotein (LDL), and very low-density lipoprotein (VLDL). Even though the body requires cholesterol, high levels of LDL- and VLDL-cholesterol (those high in saturated fats) have been linked to arteriosclerosis (hardening of the arteries) that results when fatty deposits that contain cholesterol collect on the inner walls of the blood vessels, narrowing them. This condition increases risk of stroke or heart attack.

Personal Summary

I remember hearing only bad things about cholesterol. I knew a man who had been on a low-cholesterol diet for many years. He still had high levels of "bad" cholesterol in his blood. Why does the body produce something that can cause such serious problems as heart attacks? Then I heard there's good cholesterol and that eating certain things can affect the production of the "good" cholesterol instead of the "bad." So why doesn't a diet low in LDL- and VLDL-cholesterol automatically mean only HDL, or good cholesterol, will be produced?

Unsent letters ● Write a letter to anyone on a topic related to your subject. Unsent letters allow you to personalize the subject matter and share those thoughts with another person—real or imagined.

528 Completing Assignments

In and out of school, assignments are a fact of life. They won't go away. Depending on your situation, you may find assignments more difficult these days, and time to do them more scarce. The following guidelines should help you plan and complete your work.

Planning Ahead

1. It's your responsibility to know exactly what the assignments are, when they're due, and what you must do to complete them.

2. Decide how much time you'll need to complete each assignment. Then set aside the time in your daily schedule. Each time you organize this way, you'll find that you've gotten better at estimating the time you need.

3. Decide where you'll study (library, study hall, home), and work in relative quiet. Be comfortable while you study, but don't get too comfortable.

4. Gather your materials ahead of time. Unless you really like going out at 11:00 p.m. to buy a pencil at the convenience store, keep a supply of the things you'll need. Check to make sure you have the right books and reference materials, paper, pencils, pens, etc., before you settle in to study.

INSIDE

info

If you are having trouble getting started on your assignments, try doing them at the same time and place each day. This will help you control the urge to wait until you are "in the mood" before starting. Also try to avoid doing your assignments when you are hungry or tired.

Getting It Done

◉ **Go over your directions carefully.** Look up any words you are unsure of and write down the meaning of each.

◉ **Keep track of those things you need to check with your teachers about.** All learning is an attempt to solve a problem. You must clearly understand the problem before you can solve it.

◉ **Use a study strategy.** Using the KWL or SQ3R method will help you complete the reading and studying parts of your assignments.

◉ **Make a deal with yourself.** Plan a break only after you have completed a major segment of the assignment. Hold all calls, and don't answer the door. (Families are good at running interference.)

◉ **Show pride in your work.** Complete your assignments, and turn them in on time. Welcome the suggestions your teachers may give for future improvement.

529 Managing Your Time

Managing your time is like managing your money: to spend it wisely, you have to know (1) how much you have to spend, (2) what to spend it on, and (3) how to use planning tips (like the ones below).

Planning Tips

1. **Turn big jobs into smaller ones.** Successful people will tell you that they often divide up their big jobs into smaller, more manageable steps. Spreading a project over a reasonable period of time will reduce the pressure that comes from letting everything go until the last minute. Tackle your tasks as they need to be done, and develop a process for working through the big jobs. Then follow your plan.

2. **Keep a weekly schedule.** If you haven't started a personal calendar to keep track of appointments and assignments, what are you waiting for? You'll have your day at a glance and be twice as likely to keep the appointments you write down. Design your planner to meet your needs; the more personalized you make it, the more likely it is that you'll use it.

TAKE NOTE

Planners and calendars can be purchased at a reasonable cost if that seems easier than making your own. Also, most word-processing programs have built-in notepads and calendars.

3. **Make lists.** Making a daily list of things to do may strike you as overdoing it at first, but you'll soon change your mind. You'll even sleep better at night, knowing that you've got the next day covered.

4. **Plan your study time.** Good advice, but most of us seldom take it. Good planning means having everything you need where you need it. Schedule your study time as early in the evening as you can, take short breaks, keep snacks to a minimum, interact with the page by asking questions (out loud, if no one objects), and summarize what you've learned before packing up your books.

5. **Stay flexible.** Plans do change and new things can pop up daily. Be realistic, willing to change those events that can be changed and exercising patience for those that cannot. You'll save yourself lots of wear and tear if you remain flexible and upbeat.

Taking Tests

530   Some students take to tests like monkeys to a trapeze. Others feel butterflies the size of F-16's in their stomachs. Every student can expect to feel some stress over tests since final grades often depend so heavily on them. But you need not suffer the dreaded form of paralysis called "test anxiety," with its sweaty palms and knocking knees.

    Whatever kind of test you have to take—essay, objective, or standardized—the key is being well prepared. Using this chapter, you can figure out a way to organize material, to review it (perhaps with a partner), to remember it, and, finally, to produce it on the test itself. And remember, it's usually not just facts and figures that you're expected to know, but the ideas that bind them together.

What's Ahead?

The following chapter provides a number of guidelines, tips, and models for you to follow as you begin working to improve your test-taking skills. Here are the topics covered:

531 Taking an Essay Test

One of the most common (and most challenging) tests in high school is the essay test. It's a test you'll be called on to do over and over again. And there are certain skills or strategies you should know if you hope to do well. Writing a good essay test answer is more than just writing—it's reading, thinking, planning, analyzing, judging, etc.

Too many students make the error of thinking that the best way to answer an essay question is to write down everything and anything about the topic as fast as they can. Clearly, this is not the best way to approach an essay test. Your goal is to write well, not simply to fill as many pages as possible. You have to take time to think about the essay test question and to organize an appropriate answer. If you don't, you'll probably be disappointed in the results.

The poor results many students experience on essay tests do not necessarily stem from a lack of knowledge about the subject, but rather from a lack of basic skills needed to write a good answer.

532 Understanding the Question

The first step in correctly handling an essay test question is to read the question several times until you are sure you know what the teacher is asking. As you read, you must pay special attention to the **key words** found in every essay question. Your ability to understand and respond to these key words is a basic skill necessary to handling the essay question. For example, if you are asked to *contrast* two things on a test, and you *classify* them instead, you have not given the teacher the information requested. Your score will obviously suffer.

533 Key Words

A list of key terms, along with a definition and an example of how each is used, can be found below and on the next page. Study these terms carefully. It is the first step to improving your essay test scores.

Classify: To **classify** is to place persons or things (especially animals and plants) together in a group because they are alike in one or more important ways. In science there is an order that all groups follow when it comes to classifying or categorizing: *phylum* (or *division*), *class, order, family, genus, species,* and *variety.*

Compare: To **compare** is to use examples to show how two things are similar and different, with the greater emphasis on similarities.

"Compare credit cards with debit cards."

Contrast: To **contrast** is to use examples to show how two things are different in one or more important ways.

"Contrast treasury bills with certificates of deposit."

534 **Define:** To **define** is to give a clear, concise definition or meaning for a term. To define consists of identifying the class to which a term belongs and telling how it differs from other things in that class. (See 546-547.)

> "Define what is meant by the term *computer-aided manufacturing*."

Describe: To **describe** is to give a written sketch or impression of the topic.

> "Describe the duties of a public-relations specialist."

Discuss: To **discuss** is to talk about an issue from all sides. A discussion answer must be carefully organized so that you stay on track.

> "Discuss the biological explanations for aggression."

Evaluate: To **evaluate** is to make a value judgment, to give the pluses and minuses backed up with evidence (facts, figures, instances, etc.).

> "Evaluate the contributions of the automobile to the average American's overall standard of living."

Explain: To **explain** is to make clear, to analyze, often by using a cause-effect or step-by-step explanation. (See "Cause and effect," 111.)

> "Explain how a mercury thermometer works."

Illustrate: To **illustrate** is to show by means of a picture, a diagram, or some other graphic aid. At times, however, you may use specific examples or instances to illustrate a law, rule, or principle.

> "Illustrate the food pyramid."

Justify: To **justify** is to tell why a position or point of view is good or right. A justification should be mostly positive, meaning you stress the advantages over the disadvantages.

> "Justify the use of tariffs by the United States."

Outline: To **outline** is to organize a set of facts or ideas by listing main points and subpoints. A good outline shows at a glance how topics or ideas fit together or relate to one another. (See 119-120.)

> "Outline the steps used in the scientific method."

Prove: To **prove** is to bring out the truth by giving evidence and facts to back up your point.

> "Prove that federal regulation is necessary to our banking system."

Summarize: To **summarize** is to present the main points of an issue in a shortened form. Details and examples are usually not given.

> "Summarize the various forms of flexible work schedules."

535 Planning and Writing an Essay Test Answer

In addition to a basic understanding of the key words, you must also understand the process of writing the essay answer.

1. **Read** the question several times. (Pay special attention to the key word being used in the question.)

2. **Rephrase** the question into a topic sentence (thesis statement) with a clear point. **NOTE:** It often works well to drop the question's key word from your thesis statement.

> **Question:** *Explain* the obstacles that can hinder international trade.
>
> **Thesis statement:** There are many obstacles that can hinder international trade.

3. **Outline** the main points you plan to cover in your answer. Time will probably not allow you to include all supporting details in your outline.

4. **Write** your essay (or paragraph). Begin with your thesis statement (or topic sentence). Add whatever background information may be needed, and then follow your outline, writing as clearly as possible.

536 Sample Essay Answer

One–Paragraph Answer ● If you feel that only one paragraph is needed to answer the question, use the main points of your outline as supporting details for your thesis statement. (Your thesis statement now serves as the topic sentence of your single-paragraph answer.)

> **Question:** Explain the obstacles that can hinder international trade.

Despite the fact that it is increasing every day, international trade is hindered by many obstacles. First, countries often impose trade restrictions to further their own interests. These include setting tariffs (taxes on imports) to protect native industry or to raise money, and imposing trade restrictions to further political agendas. Second, countries can impose restrictions to protect consumers, such as legal requirements for labeling or packaging. Third, national systems of measurement and infrastructure (roads, electrical current, telecommunications, etc.) are often incompatible. Fourth, the monetary exchange rates between countries can fluctuate, sometimes widely and quickly. And finally, each culture has its own values and expectations.

537 **Multi-Paragraph Answer** ● If the question is too complex to be handled in one paragraph, your opening paragraph should include only your thesis statement and any essential background information. Begin your second paragraph by rephrasing one of the main points from your outline into a suitable topic sentence. Support this topic sentence with examples, reasons, or other details. (Additional paragraphs should be handled in the same way.) If time permits, add a summary or concluding paragraph to bring all of your thoughts to a logical close.

> I. Restrictions to protect interests of country
> II. Restrictions to protect consumers
> III. Practical incompatibilities
> IV. Fluctuations of monetary exchange rates
> V. Varying customs and expectations

Despite the fact that it is increasing every day, international trade is hindered by many obstacles.

First, countries often impose restrictions to further their own interests. These include taxes on imports called tariffs, which are set up to protect native industry and/or raise money. They also include trade restrictions, which are set up to protect native industry or to further political agendas. The United States, for instance, may refuse to do business with a country because of their political differences.

Second, countries can impose complicated restrictions to protect consumers. Items sold in one country may be illegal in another, or there may be specific laws concerning product labeling, packaging, quality, or distribution.

Third, there may be practical reasons why a product from one country is unsuited to another country. For example, an American car may be too large for an Israeli road. An American blow-dryer needs a voltage adapter to be plugged into an English outlet. And many potential markets are beyond reach because they lack basic technology, including electricity.

Fourth, the monetary exchange rates between countries can fluctuate, sometimes widely and quickly. When the value of the U.S. dollar drops in relation to the Japanese yen, Japanese car manufacturers are dismayed to see the prices on their vehicles rise beyond the reach of some American consumers.

And finally, each of these cultures has its own customs and expectations—its own ways of dressing, working, traveling, and communicating. A business must understand the language and customs of its potential customers in order to make its products attractive to them.

Clearly, international trade is a complicated process requiring a good deal of knowledge about laws, systems, and cultures.

Taking an Objective Test

538 True/False

- Read the entire question before answering. Often the first half of a statement will be true or false, while the second half is just the opposite. For an answer to be true, the entire statement must be true.

- Read each word and number carefully. Pay special attention to names, dates, and numbers that are similar and could be confused.

- Be especially careful of true/false statements that contain words like *all, every, always, never*. Very often these statements will be false.

- Also watch for statements that contain more than one negative word. *Remember:* Two negatives make a positive. (Example: It is unlikely ice will not melt when the temperature rises above 32 degrees F.)

- Remember that if one part of the statement is false, the whole statement is false.

539 Matching Test

- Read through both lists quickly before you begin answering. Note any descriptions that are similar and pay particular attention to the details that make them different.

- When matching word to phrase, read the phrase first and look for the word it describes.

- Cross out each answer as you find it—unless you are told that the answer can be used more than once.

- If you get stuck when matching word to word, determine the part of speech of each word. If the word is a verb, for example, match it with another verb.

540 Multiple-Choice Test

- Read the directions very carefully to determine whether you are looking for the correct answer or the best answer. Also check to see if some questions can have two (or more) correct answers.

- Read the first part of the question very carefully, looking for negative words like *not, never, except, unless,* etc.

- Try to answer the question in your mind before looking at the choices.

- Read all the choices before selecting your answer. This is especially important on tests where you must select the best answer, or on tests where one of your choices is a combination of two or more answers. (Example: **c.** Both a and b **d.** All of the above **e.** None of the above)

- As you read through the choices, eliminate those that are obviously incorrect; then go back and reconsider the remaining choices.

541 Guidelines for Taking Tests

Organizing and Preparing Test Material

1. Ask the teacher to be as specific as possible about what will be on the test.
2. Ask how the material will be tested (true/false, multiple choice, essay).
3. Review your class notes and recopy those sections that are most important.
4. Get any notes or materials you may have missed from the teacher or another student.
5. Set up a specific time(s) to study for an exam and schedule other activities around it.
6. Look over quizzes and exams you took earlier in that class.
7. Prepare an outline of everything to be tested to get an overview of the unit.
8. Prepare a detailed study sheet for each part of your outline.
9. Attempt to predict test questions and write practice answers for them.
10. Set aside a list of questions to ask the teacher or a classmate.

Reviewing and Remembering Test Material

1. Begin reviewing early. Don't wait until the day or night before.
2. Whenever possible, relate the test material to your personal life or to other subjects you are taking.
3. Look for patterns of organization in the material you study (cause/effect, comparison, chronological, etc.).
4. Use maps, lists, diagrams, acronyms, rhymes, or any other special memory aids.
5. Use flash cards or note cards and review with them whenever you have time.
6. Recite material out loud whenever possible as you review.
7. Skim the material in your textbooks, noting key words and ideas; practice for the test by summarizing out loud.
8. Study with others only after you have studied well by yourself.
9. Test your knowledge of a subject by teaching or explaining it to someone else.
10. Review especially difficult material just before going to bed the night before the exam.

542 Taking a Standardized Test

One kind of test that will continue to come up throughout high school and beyond is the standardized test. These tests are set up to measure your skills, progress, and achievement in nearly every subject. The questions on most standardized tests follow a certain style or format. Knowing a little about these questions can help you prepare for your next standardized test. Review the guidelines below.

Standardized Tests

543 Quick Guide

1. Listen carefully to the instructions. Most standardized tests follow very strict guidelines; there is a clear procedure for you to follow and a definite time limit.

2. Skim the test. Take a quick look at the entire test to make sure you have all the pages—and that you understand what you need to do with each section.

3. Read the directions carefully. Don't assume you know what the test is asking for just by the way it looks. Most standardized tests have specific directions for each section, and no two sections are exactly alike.

4. Plan your time. Many tests are broken down into time frames, allowing you a certain amount of time for each section. If not, you will have to plan your time based on the number of questions, the difficulty level, and your own strengths and weaknesses.

5. Answer the easy questions first. Skip questions you're totally in the dark about; go back to them later.

6. Read all the choices. Don't answer a question until you've read all the choices; many choices are purposely worded alike to test your true understanding.

7. Make educated guesses. Unless you're told not to, select an answer for every question. First eliminate choices that are obviously incorrect; then use logic to guess between the remaining answers.

8. Double-check your answers. As time permits, check each of your answers to make sure you haven't made any foolish mistakes or missed any questions.

Thinking Clearly

Have you ever been asked to compare two things in an English paper or on a history test? Easier said than done, right? Or how about defining or classifying a *simple* term in science class? Not so simple? The truth is, thinking can be hard work, especially in some of your tougher classes.

That's what this chapter is about—thinking clearly in all your classes. You'll find the strategies you need not only to compare, define, and classify, but also to think creatively, solve problems, make decisions, and ask questions.

545 Thinking Operations

OBSERVE					
Watch	Listen	Taste	Feel	Smell	Perceive (sense it)

GATHER				
Collect observations	Use personal experiences	Free-write, cluster, list	Brainstorm with others	Interview others	Read, write, draw

QUESTION			
Ask: Who? What? When? Where? Why?	Ask: How? How much?	Wonder what if . . . Why not?	Look into, investigate, survey

FOCUS			
Find a main point or center of interest	Identify or define the key problem or issue	Select a way to approach the issue	Set a simple goal or purpose

ORGANIZE					
Distinguish the whole from the part	Put in meaningful order	Compare, contrast	Give reasons	Group, classify	Pro/Con (for/against)

ANALYZE			
Select best idea(s) or feature(s)	Relate it to other things	What caused it? What did it cause?	See patterns, relationships, connections

IMAGINE					
See from another point of view	Create new ideas, alternatives	Experiment, invent, design	Infer (draw conclusions)	Hypothesize (make an educated guess)	Predict, estimate

RETHINK					
Restate: "What I really mean is . . ."	Reconsider: What are the results?	Reexamine: Look for weaknesses	Rearrange: Change the order	Revise: Review rules, goals, models	Restructure: See from new perspective

EVALUATE			
Judge: Is it understandable? Is it clear? Accurate? Concise?	Criticize: Is it effective? Workable? Interesting?	Persuade: Is it worthwhile? Practical? Logical?	Argue: What are the advantages? Disadvantages?

Defining Terms

546 The Sentence Definition

The simplest way to define a term is to summarize its meaning in a single sentence, much the way a dictionary does. To build a defining sentence, you must first name the term. Then put the term into a class of objects similar to it. Finally, mention the special characteristics that make this term different from other objects in its class.

Term .... Ergonomics

Class .... is a field of technology

Characteristics .... that studies the effects of machines on people's health and safety.

NOTE: A good definition doesn't place the word you are trying to define in the definition itself. For example, do not say, "A calculator is an electronic device used to calculate numbers."

547 The Paragraph Definition

A sentence definition is bare-bones stuff. Usually we need more information (explanations and examples) to show how something looks, acts, or fits in among other things before we truly understand it. There are many kinds of details you can add to a definition sentence to expand it into a paragraph or an essay. The following paragraph definition uses several methods of expansion, all of which are included in the list below.

Ergonomics is a field of technology that studies the design of machines and objects and their effects on human health and safety. The groundwork for this science was laid during World War II when scientists needed to design military equipment that helped prevent fatigue and monotony. Today ergonomics has branched out in several directions. All workers—not just soldiers, sailors, and pilots—benefit from well-designed equipment, from cockpits to conveyor belts. All kinds of consumer products from cars to toothbrushes are designed with ergonomics in mind. Though ergonomics cannot make a boring job exciting, it can at least help prevent work from becoming a costly pain in the neck.

Definition Expanders

- Give a dictionary definition.
- Tell what people say about it.
- Describe it in detail.
- Compare it to something.
- Tell what it is *not*.
- Explain the different kinds.

548 Comparing and Contrasting

If you're like most people, you are constantly comparing and contrasting one thing to another: music groups, foods, cars, clothing—even classes. The strategies that follow will help you improve your comparing and contrasting skills and show you how to use them in all your school subjects. Here are some sample situations where you might need to use comparison and contrast:

- ◉ **History:** Review two different reports of the Great Depression.
- ◉ **English:** Write a comparison/contrast paper on two stories or poems you've read.
- ◉ **Science:** Answer an essay test question that asks you to compare a plant cell with an animal cell.
- ◉ **Math:** Compare a trapezoid to a parallelogram.

549 Choosing Two Things to Compare

If you have the freedom to choose, use this checklist to help you make a decision about which two things to compare:

✔ Choose two things **you're really interested in**.

✔ Choose two things **you know about** (or can find out about).

✔ Choose two things that **can be compared**. (See the box below.)

✔ **Have a good reason** for comparing the two.

It's important for you to know that not just *anything* can be compared. Two things can be compared only if they are two types of the same thing. They can't be compared (1) if they are two different types of things or (2) if one is an example of the other. (See the chart below and "The Venn Diagram" on the next page.)

A & B	Can Be Compared As	Can't Be Compared
Permanent & Temporary Work	Types of Work	
Permanent Work & Hobbies	Ways to Spend Time	
Permanent Work & Unemployment	Opposites	
Permanent Work & Employment		Permanent work is a type of employment

550 The Venn Diagram

Once you've chosen two things to compare, list the details about each in a Venn diagram. First list everything that fits only your first subject (permanent work) in area **A**; do the same for your second subject (temporary work) in area **B**. Then list everything A and B have in common in area **C**.

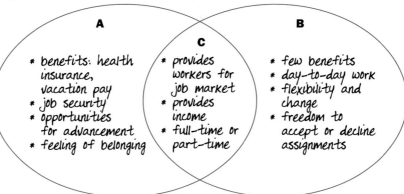

551 Organizing Your Comparison

Once you've listed all your details, you need to choose a plan for organizing your comparison. Your three choices are *whole vs. whole* (for shorter subjects), *topic by topic* (for more complicated subjects), and *similarities and differences* (for summarizing).

PLAN 1: Whole vs. Whole

- First discuss all of subject A.
- Then discuss all of subject B. As you discuss B, remind the reader of points you want to contrast with A.
- End with a conclusion that emphasizes the greatest similarity or difference.

PLAN 2: Topic by Topic

- List several topics for comparison between subject A and subject B. Arrange the topics in a meaningful order.
- Under each topic, first discuss A, then compare B.
- End by emphasizing the overall picture or the most important similarity or difference.

PLAN 3: Similarities and Differences

- First tell why you want to show similarities and differences between A and B.
- Discuss all the similarities first.
- Then discuss the differences, ending with the one you want to emphasize. (If you want to emphasize a similarity, discuss the similarities last.)

552 Classifying

Classifying may not sound like fun, but try living—or writing—without it! To think and speak clearly, you need to be able to "lump" and "split." To lump means to bunch similar things together into a single category and give the category a name. To split means to take a big lump, or class, and break it into smaller lumps, or subclasses.

For example, we can lump all those furry, barking, slobbering, floppy-eared quadrupeds together and call them "dogs." But we could split all dogs into at least two subclasses: wild and tame. For fun, we could split tame dogs into two sub-subclasses: serious (like pit bulls) and silly (like Pekingese).

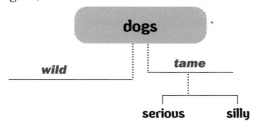

553 Writing Classification Paragraphs

When would you be asked to *lump* or *split* something? Let's say you're trying to classify the things that fall under the heading of "computer applications" for a coworker who has just learned the difference between hardware (the equipment itself) and software (the invisible stuff that's stored on disks). You might come up with something like the following:

A computer application is a software program that helps you do something practical with your computer. Computer applications can be classified according to use. Probably the most widespread application is a "word-processing" program that makes it easy to create and edit memos, reports, and other papers. Another popular application is a "spreadsheet" that lets you look like a math genius (without being in advanced calculus). To illustrate your work, you'll need a "paint" or "draw" program that can help you become an electronic artist. Put these applications together with a "page-layout" application, and you're an instant publisher.

554 Thinking Creatively

The best creative thinkers see things differently from the people around them. They see challenges rather than problems. They set aside all the rules, all the scorecards, all of what is usually expected, and begin to imagine "What would happen if . . . ?" If you sometimes find it hard to imagine, to go beyond the correct or obvious answer, maybe the suggestions below will help.

- **What if** a certain person, place, thing, or idea did not exist today? What if it suddenly appeared 100 years before its time? (What if the airplane had not yet been invented? What if it had been invented before the Civil War?)
- **What if** the world were different in some important way? (What if the sun were to shine only two hours a day? Twenty hours a day? What if it rained only twice a year? Every day?)
- **What if** two people, things, or ideas that are usually separate were brought together? (Parents and rock musicians? Ice cream and tomatoes?)
- **What if** you were to change just one important thing about an object or machine? (Change the ink in every pen to green? Cut the gas tanks on all cars to one-fourth their size?)
- **What if** a certain object could talk? (Your shoe? Your house? A newborn baby?)
- **What if** a certain object were made of another material? (Metal car tires? Grass clothes? Cardboard furniture?)
- **What if** a certain person, place, object, or idea were the opposite of what he, she, or it is now? (Homes became schools? Cars became helicopters? Forward became backward?)
- **What if** a certain object were suddenly scarce or plentiful? (What if there were suddenly very little paper? Plenty of money?)
- **What if** a certain object were a totally different size? (Two-foot pens? Twelve-foot baskets?)
- **What if** snakes could walk?

555 The Creative Mind in Action

Without creativity, you might look at an ordinary object like a pencil and think, "There's a pencil. Something to write with. It looks brand-new. It's probably worth less than a dime." But if you look at the same pencil with a creative mind—not just look at it, but look at it carefully, from every angle imaginable—you may set all sorts of mental imagery in motion. Here's proof:

The No. 2 Pencil Meets a Creative Mind

- First, notice the parts: lead point, hexagonal wooden barrel painted yellow, words "Dixon Ticonderoga 1388—2 Soft" stamped along one side in green ink on gold, triple-striped green and yellow metal collar holding a powdery pink eraser, not yet rubbed raw.

- Imagine the manufacturing process—the wood gluers, the planers, the slicers, the paint vats, the dryers, the stamps, and so on.

- Think of the tree the wood was once a part of. Where did it grow? Where on the tree was this pencil's wood located? Where are the other parts of the tree now?

- See the pencil as a bridge stretching between two places. What are they?

- Imagine the pencil as a pillar. What is it holding up?

- Who will hold this pencil before it is worn to a nub? What will be the most important thing ever written with it? What will be the funniest thing?

- How strong is it? How much weight would be needed to break it? The weight of a safe? Of a hamster? A frying pan? A six-year-old boy? A rainbow trout?

- Now it is being used as a pointer. Who is pointing it and what are they pointing at? Why?

- Imagine an occasion when this pencil might be given as a gift. What is the occasion?

- If the pencil could think, what would it be thinking as it is locked away in a drawer? As it is being used to write a letter?

- Roll the pencil around in your fingers—what does its texture bring to mind?

THE BOTTOM LINE

Get the idea? What other new ways of experiencing the pencil can you think of? Always be on the alert, thinking of new ways to look at old objects and ideas. It's an excellent way to learn—in all your classes.

556 Methods of Thinking

Different people solve problems in different ways. In the classroom, your teacher may ask you to use a specific method. If not, here are some of the possibilities you can use to make your thinking more efficient.

The Decision–Making Method

I magine the outcome or result.

D efine your goal.

E xplore (list) your options.

C hoose two or three best options.

I nvestigate the chosen options; try each one out.

D ecide on the best option.

E valuate your choice.

The Problem–Solving Method

I dentify the problem.

D escribe the problem.

E xplore possible solutions or actions.

A dopt the best plan or solution.

L ook at the effects or results.

The Scientific Method

I dentify the problem.

M ake observations.

A dvance a hypothesis, or educated guess.

G ather data and test it against your hypothesis.

I nvestigate further, observing and collecting more data.

N ote data and draw possible conclusions.

E stablish a single conclusion.

557 Asking Questions

To get the most out of your classes, you need to think—to think well, you need to ask questions. The basic questions to ask are the 5 W's and H: *Who? What? When? Where? Why?* and *How?* To go beyond the basic questions, see the chart below. It will get you started. You can then adapt the chart to fit people, places, events, and any other subject you come across.

	Description	Function	History	Value
P R O B L E M S	What is the problem? What type of problem is it? What are its parts? What are the signs of the problem?	Who or what is affected by it? What new problems may it cause in the future?	What is the current status of the problem? What or who caused it? What or who contributed to it?	What is its significance? Why? Why is it more (or less) important than other problems? What does it symbolize or illustrate?
P O L I C I E S	What type of policy is it? How broad is it? What are its most important features? What are its parts?	What is the policy designed to do? What is needed to make it work? What will be its effects?	What brought this policy about? What are the alternatives to this policy?	Is the policy workable? What are its advantages and disadvantages? Is it practical? Is it a good policy? Why or why not?
C O N C E P T S	What is the concept? What type of concept is it? What are its parts? Who or what is it related to?	Who has been influenced by this concept? Why is it important? How does it work?	When did it originate? How has it changed over the years? How may it change in the future?	What practical value does it have? Why is it superior (or inferior) to similar concepts? What is its social worth?

Thinking Logically

Thinking logically means thinking sensibly. It means going beyond your knee-jerk reaction or the first answer that pops into your head. It means looking at all sides of a question, proposing reasonable and sensible solutions, and then supporting the solutions with good reasons, interesting examples, and solid evidence. In fact, the only kind of thinking that will hold up under careful examination is logical thinking—thinking that is reasonable, reliable, and above all, believable.

So how do you go about making your thinking believable and, therefore, acceptable to your audience? Generally speaking, you must organize, support, and present your points *so well* that your audience will find it difficult to disagree with or question what you've said or written. This chapter can help you do just that.

What's Ahead?

To begin thinking more logically, you can follow the guidelines in this section.

Becoming a Logical Thinker

Making and Supporting a Point

Using Evidence and Logic

Becoming a Logical Thinker

559 Quick Guide

The steps below cover the logical thinking process from start to finish. Look each step over carefully and try to get the big picture. (Also look carefully at "Making and Supporting a Point" on the next page.) Then apply what you've learned the next time you need to use logic in an argument, a debate, or a persuasive essay.

1. **Decide on your purpose** and state it clearly on the top of your paper.

2. **Gather information** on the topic.

3. **Focus on a central point** that you feel you can support or prove. (This is called "making a claim." See 560.)

4. **Add "qualifiers"** as necessary to strengthen your claim. (See 561.)

5. **Define any terms** that may be unclear.

6. **Support your points** with evidence that is both interesting and reliable. (See 562.)

7. **Explain your evidence** and why your audience should accept it.

8. **Consider any objections** your audience could have to your explanation.

9. **Make concessions**; admit that some of your arguments may be weak. (See 563.)

10. **Point out weaknesses** in the arguments on the other side of the issue, the arguments you do not accept.

11. **Restate your point**, or central claim.

12. **Urge your audience** to accept your viewpoint.

NOTE: You will probably not use every one of these steps, or stages, each time you set out to prove a point. Each situation is different and, in addition to logic, requires some creative thinking and common sense.

Making and Supporting a Point

560 **Making Claims** ● Making a strong point, or "claim," is essential to the logical thinking process. Claims fall into three main groups: *claims of fact, claims of value,* and *claims of policy.*

Claims of fact state or claim that something is true or not true.

> Television violence causes violent behavior in children.

Claims of value state that something has or does not have worth.

> The Bigfoot Cross-Trainer is the best all-around shoe for the money.

Claims of policy assert that something ought to be done or not done.

> We need a law to prevent any more farmland from being turned into suburban housing.

561 **Using Qualifiers** ● Qualifiers are terms that make a claim more flexible. Note the difference between the two claims below:

> Teachers ignore students' excuses.

> **Some** teachers **tend to** ignore students' excuses.

The second claim is easier to defend because it makes a qualified claim, rather than an all-or-nothing claim. Here are some useful qualifiers:

almost	if . . . then . . .	maybe	probably
often	in most cases	might	usually

562 **Adding Support** ● Your central claim needs evidence for support; the more kinds of evidence you offer, and the stronger the evidence, the stronger your argument will be. Here are some types of evidence:

Observation:	"I personally observed the audience reaction to the movie."
Statistics:	"According to *Entertainment Weekly,* over 2 million people saw the movie in the first week."
Comparison:	"The movie was almost as moving as *Schindler's List.*"
Expert Testimony:	"Siskel and Ebert gave it two thumbs up."
Demonstration:	"The movie begins with a wide shot of . . ."
Analysis:	"The plot hinges on a secret that . . ."
Prediction:	"Early predictions are that it will be nominated . . ."

563 **Making Concessions** ● Concessions are "points" that you let the other side score. When your argument has some true weaknesses, it is usually best to admit it. Making a concession often adds believability to your overall claim. Here are some expressions for making concessions:

admittedly	granted	I cannot argue with
even though	I agree that	while it is true that

564 Using Evidence and Logic

An argument is a chain of reasons that a person uses to support a claim or conclusion. To use argument well, you need to know both how to draw logical conclusions from sound evidence and how to recognize and avoid false arguments, or logical fallacies.

The logical fallacies described in this section are the bits of fuzzy or dishonest thinking that crop up often in our own speaking and writing, as well as in advertisements, political appeals, editorials, and so on. You should first read through the fallacies below so that you can recognize them in the future. Then avoid them in your own writing and thinking.

Fallacies of Thinking

565 Appeal to Ignorance

One commits this logical fallacy by claiming that since no one has ever proved a claim, it must be false. Appeals to ignorance unfairly shift the burden of proof onto someone else.

> Show me one study that proves seat belts save lives.

566 Appeal to Pity

This fallacy may be heard in courts of law when an attorney begs for leniency because his client's mother is ill, his brother is out of work, his cat has a hair ball, and blah, blah, blah. The strong tug on the heart-strings can also be heard in the classroom when the student says to the teacher, "May I have an extension on this paper? I worked till my eyeballs fell out, but it's still not done."

> Imagine what it must have been like. If anyone deserves a break,
> he does.

567 Bandwagon

Another way to avoid using logic in an argument is to appeal to everyone's sense of wanting to belong or be accepted. By suggesting that everyone else is doing this or wearing that or going there, you can avoid the real question—"Is this idea or claim a good one or not?"

> Everyone on the team wears high-tops. It's the only way to go.

568 Broad Generalization

A broad generalization takes in everything and everyone at once, allowing no exceptions. For example, a broad generalization about voters might be, "All voters spend too little time reading and too much time being swayed by 30-second sound bites." It may be true that quite a few voters spend too little time reading about the candidates, but it is unfair to suggest that this is true of all voters. Here's another example:

> All teenagers spend too much time watching television.

569 **Circular Thinking**

This fallacy consists of assuming, in a definition or an argument, the very point you are trying to prove. Note how circular this sort of reasoning is:

> I hate Mr. Baldwin's class because I'm never happy in there. (But what's wrong with the class?)

570 **Either-Or Thinking**

Either-or thinking consists of reducing a solution to two possible extremes: "America: Love It or Leave It." "Put up or shut up." This fallacy of thinking eliminates every possibility in the middle.

> Either this community votes to build a new school, or the quality of education will drop dramatically.

571 **Half-Truths**

Avoid building your argument with evidence that contains part of the truth, but not the whole truth. These kinds of statements are called half-truths. They are especially misleading because they leave out "the rest of the story." They are true and dishonest at the same time.

> The new recycling law is bad because it will cost more money than it saves. (Maybe so; but it will also save the environment.)

572 **Oversimplification**

Beware of phrases like "It all boils down to . . ." or "It's a simple question of . . ." Almost no dispute is "a simple question of" anything. Anyone who feels, for example, that capital punishment "all boils down to" a matter of protecting society ought to question a doctor, an inmate on death row, the inmate's family, a sociologist, a religious leader, etc.

> Capital punishment is a simple question of protecting society.

573 **Slanted Language**

By choosing words that carry strong positive or negative feelings, a person can distract the audience, leading them away from the valid arguments being made. A philosopher once illustrated the bias involved in slanted language when he compared three synonyms for the word *stubborn:* "I am *firm.* You are *obstinate.* He is *pigheaded.*"

> No one in his right mind would ever do anything that dumb.

574 **Testimonial**

You can take Dr. Carl Sagan's word on the composition of Saturn's rings, but the moment he starts pushing exercise machines, watch out! If the testimonial or statement comes from a recognized authority in the field, great. If it comes from a person famous in another field, beware.

> Sports hero: "I've tried every cold medicine on the market, and—believe me—nothing works like Comptrol."

GUIDE

Proofreader's Guide

"It's not wise to violate the rules until you know how to observe them."

—T. S. Eliot

Marking Punctuation

Period

575 A **period** is used to end a sentence that makes a statement or that gives a command that is not an exclamation.

> **(Statement)** There is more credit and satisfaction in being a first-rate truck driver than a tenth-rate executive.
> —B. C. Forbes

> **(Mild command)** To say the right thing at the right time, keep still most of the time.
> —John W. Roper

> **(Request)** Please check the gas and fill up the oil.

NOTE: It is not necessary to place a period after a statement that has parentheses around it and is part of another sentence.

> Choosing a career in politics (career may be the wrong word to use) requires a great deal of faith in oneself.

576 A period should be placed after an initial or abbreviation.

> Mr.   Sen.   D.D.S.   Ph.D.   M.D.   Jr.   B.C.   p.m.   U.S.
> Edna St. V. Millay   Booker T. Washington   F. Scott Fitzgerald

NOTE: When an abbreviation is the last word in a sentence, use only one period at the end of the sentence.

> Grace picked up her clothes, fed her boxer, put away her CD's, did her homework, etc.

577 A period is used as a decimal point.

> The Sierra pickup had been designed from the wheels up at a cost of $2.8 billion.
> —Tim Cahill, *Road Fever*

Using the Ellipsis

578 Quick Guide

1 An **ellipsis** (three periods) is used to show that one or more words have been omitted in a quotation. (When typing, leave one space before and after each period.)

(Original)

We the people of the United States, in order to form a more per-fect Union, establish justice, insure domestic tranquility, provide for the common defense, promote the general welfare, and secure the blessings of liberty to ourselves and our posterity, do ordain and establish this Constitution for the United States of America.

–Preamble, U.S. Constitution

(Quotation)

"We the people . . . in order to form a more perfect Union . . . establish this Constitution for the United States of America."

2 If words from a quotation are omitted at the end of a sentence, the ellipsis is placed after the period or other end punctuation.

"Five score years ago, a great American, in whose symbolic shadow we stand, signed the Emancipation Proclamation. . . . But one hundred years later, we must face the tragic fact that the Negro is still not free."

—Martin Luther King, Jr., "I Have a Dream"

NOTE: If the quoted material is a complete sentence (even if it was not in the original), use a period, then an ellipsis.

(Original)

I am tired; my heart is sick and sad. From where the sun now stands I will fight no more forever.

–Chief Joseph of the Nez Percé

(Quotations)

"I am tired. . . . From where the sun now stands I will fight no more forever."

or

"I am tired. . . . I will fight no more forever."

3 An ellipsis may be used to indicate a pause.

I brought my trembling hand to my focusing eyes. It was oozing, it was red, it was . . . it was . . . a tomato!

—Laura Baginski, student writer

Comma

579 A **comma** may be used between two independent clauses that are joined by coordinating conjunctions such as these: *but, or, nor, for, yet, and, so.*

> Having good skills is important, but having a good attitude is even more important.

> I'm a great believer in luck, and I find the harder I work the more I have of it.
>
> —Thomas Jefferson

NOTE: Do not confuse a sentence with a compound verb with a compound sentence.

> She turned on the computer and booted up her program.

> Then she worked through the morning and took a lunch break at 12:30.

580 Commas are used to separate individual words, phrases, or clauses in a series. (A series contains at least three items.)

> Computers can store information, organize data, and access other information systems.

> Do what you can, with what you have, where you are.
>
> —Stephen Leacock

NOTE: Do not use commas when the items in a series are connected with *or, nor,* or *and.*

> New adjustable keyboards reduce user stress and help prevent carpal tunnel syndrome and improve speed—all at the same time.

581 Commas are used to separate adjectives that *equally* modify the same noun. (Notice in the examples below that no comma separates the last adjective from the noun.)

> He asked a very tricky, technical question.

> I gave him a long, hard look before I answered.

---

system check

To determine whether the adjectives in a sentence modify *equally* (and should be separated by commas), use these two tests:

1 Shift the order of the adjectives; if the sentence is clear, the adjectives modify equally. (If *tricky* and *technical* were shifted in the example above, the sentence would still be clear; therefore, use a comma.)

2 Insert *and* between the adjectives; if the sentence reads well, use a comma. (If *and* were inserted in the sentences above, they would still read well.)

582 Commas are used to enclose an explanatory word or phrase.

> Networking, to be effective, requires an open line of communication.
> —**Benjamin Baker**

583 A specific kind of explanatory word or phrase called an **appositive** identifies or renames a preceding noun or pronoun. (Do not use commas with *restrictive appositives*. A restrictive appositive is essential to the basic meaning of the sentence. See the second example below and 586.)

> John Matthews, an author of several career books, recognizes the importance of networking.

> Author John Matthews recognizes the importance of networking.

584 Commas are used to separate contrasted elements within a sentence.

> We work to become, not to acquire.
> —**Eugene Delacroix**

> Leadership is action, not position.
> —**Donald H. McGannon**

585 A comma should separate an adverb clause or a long modifying phrase from the independent clause that follows it.

> If you don't take care of yourself today, you may regret it tomorrow.

NOTE: A comma is usually omitted if the phrase or adverb clause follows the independent clause.

You may regret it tomorrow if you don't take care of yourself today.

586 Commas are used to enclose **nonrestrictive phrases** and clauses. Nonrestrictive phrases or clauses are those that are not essential or necessary to the basic meaning of the sentence. **Restrictive phrases** or clauses—phrases or clauses that are needed in the sentence because they restrict or limit the meaning of the sentence—are not set off with commas.

> Roy, *who had wanted to be a mechanic,* lost his right arm in an accident. **(nonrestrictive)**

> Fatigue, *which can be caused by extreme exertion,* is a major cause of accidents. **(nonrestrictive)**

NOTE: The two italicized clauses in the examples above are merely additional information; they are nonrestrictive (not required). If the clauses were left out of the sentences, the meaning of the sentences would remain clear. Clauses are restrictive if they are necessary to the sense of the sentence.

> People *who have a knack for accentuating the positive* send out good vibrations. **(restrictive)**

> Companies *that offer merit pay* usually have happier, more efficient workers. **(restrictive)**

---

system check

Remember: restrictive phrases are *required* in a sentence; nonrestrictive phrases are *not required.* Compare the following restrictive and nonrestrictive phrases:

The songwriter *Elton John* was born in England. (*Elton John* is required; do not use commas.)

Elton John, *the songwriter,* was born in England. (*The songwriter* is not required; use commas.)

---

587 Commas are used to set off items in an address and items in a date.

> Send for your personal copy of *School to Work* before June 1, 1998, from Great Source Education Group, 2700 North Richardt Avenue, Indianapolis, Indiana 46219.

NOTE: No comma is placed between the state and ZIP code. Also, no comma is needed if only the month and year are given: January 1996.

588 Commas are used to set off the exact words of the speaker from the rest of the sentence.

> "I hired Kelly because of her positive attitude," said Ms. Kane.

589 Commas are used to separate a **vocative** from the rest of the sentence. (A vocative is the noun that names the person or persons spoken to.)

> Jamie, would you please stop whistling while I'm working?

590 A comma is used to separate an interjection or a weak exclamation from the rest of the sentence.

> OK, so now what do I do?

591 Commas are used to set off a word, phrase, or clause that interrupts the movement of a sentence. Such expressions usually can be identified through the following tests: (1) They may be omitted without changing the meaning of a sentence. (2) They may be placed nearly anywhere in the sentence without changing the meaning of the sentence.

> For me, well, it was just a good job gone!
>> —Langston Hughes, "A Good Job Gone"
>
> As a general rule, the best way to double your money is to fold it and put it in your pocket.

592 Commas are used to separate a series of numbers in order to distinguish hundreds, thousands, millions, etc.

> Do you know how to write the amount $2,025 on a check?
>
> 25,000   18,620,197

593 Commas are used to enclose a title or initials and names that follow a surname.

> Until Martin, Sr., was fifteen, he never had more than three months of schooling in any one year.
>> —Ed Clayton, *Martin Luther King: The Peaceful Warrior*
>
> Hickok, J. B., and Cody, William F., are two popular Western heroes.

594 A comma may be used for clarity or for emphasis. There will be times when none of the traditional comma rules call for a comma, but one will be needed to prevent confusion or to emphasize an important idea. Use a comma in either case.

> What she does, does matter to us.
>
> It may be those who do most, dream most.   —Stephen Leacock

---

system check **Do not use a comma** that could cause confusion. There should be no comma between the subject and its verb or the verb and its object. Also, use no comma before an indirect quotation. (The commas circled below should not be used.)

My friend Greta said, that computers had always terrified her.
(misuse of a comma before an indirect quotation)

I told her to read, *Making Friends with Your Computer*.
(misuse of a comma between a verb and its object)

Semicolon

595 A semicolon is used to join two or more independent clauses that are not connected with a coordinating conjunction. (In other words, each of the clauses could stand alone as a separate sentence.)

> It used to be that people needed products to survive; now products need people to survive.
> —Nicholas Johnson

NOTE: The exception to this rule occurs when the two clauses are closely related, short, or conversational in tone. Then a comma may be used.

> Getting married is easy, staying married is hard.

596 A semicolon is used before a conjunctive adverb when the word connects two independent clauses in a compound sentence. A comma should follow the adverb in this case. (Common conjunctive adverbs are these: *also, besides, for example, however, in addition, instead, meanwhile, then,* and *therefore.*)

> John arrived about five minutes early for his interview; however, he was dressed completely wrong for the occasion.

597 A semicolon is used to separate independent clauses that are long or contain commas.

> Taking messages on the phone is easy; but when it comes to taking *clear* messages, that's a different story.

Taking messages on the phone is easy; but when it comes to taking clear messages, that's a different story.

598 A semicolon is used to separate groups of words that already contain commas.

> My favorite foods are liver and onions; peanut butter and banana sandwiches; pizza with cheese, pepperoni, onions, and mushrooms; and diet ginger ale. Does that make me weird?

Colon

599 A **colon** may be used after the salutation of a business letter.

> Dear Mr. Spielberg: Dear Attorney General Reno:

600 A colon is used between the parts of a number indicating time.

> 8:30 p.m.   9:45 a.m.   10:10 p.m.

601 A colon may be used to emphasize a word, phrase, clause, or sentence that explains or adds impact to the main clause.

> I have one goal for myself: to become the CEO of a Fortune 500 company.

> Don't ever slam a door: you might want to go back.   —Don Herold

602 A colon is used to introduce a list.

> Besides basic skills, a good employee needs two more things: a willingness to learn and a positive attitude.

---

system check → A colon should not separate a verb from its object or complement, and it should not separate a preposition from its object.

Incorrect: Dave likes: comfortable space and time to think.

Correct: Dave likes two things: comfortable space and time to think.

Incorrect: There was a show on the radio this morning about: stress and laughter.

Correct: This morning there was a show on the radio about an interesting subject: stress and laughter.

---

603 The colon is used to distinguish between title and subtitle, volume and page, and chapter and verse in literature.

> *Writers INC: School to Work*

> *Encyclopedia Americana* IV: 211

> Psalm 23:1-6

604 A colon may be used to formally introduce a sentence, a question, or a quotation.

> John Locke is credited with this prescription for a good life: "A sound mind in a sound body."

> Lou Gottlieb, however, offered this version: "A sound mind or a sound body—take your pick."

Hyphen

605 The **hyphen** is used to make a compound word.

> great-great-grandfather   mother-in-law   three-year-old
>
> And they pried pieces of baked-too-fast sunshine cake from the roofs of their mouths and looked once more into the boy's eyes.
>
> **—Toni Morrison, *Song of Solomon***

NOTE: Don't use a single hyphen when a dash (two hyphens) is required.

606 A hyphen is used to join a capital letter to a noun or participle.

> T-shirt   U-turn   V-shaped

607 The hyphen is used to join the words in compound numbers from twenty-one to ninety-nine when it is necessary to write them out. (See 678.)

> On this day in 1955, a forty-two-year-old woman was on her way home from work.
>
> **—Robert Fulghum, *It Was On Fire When I Lay Down On It***

608 A hyphen is used between the elements of a fraction, but not between the numerator and denominator when one or both of them are already hyphenated.

> four-tenths   five-sixteenths   (7/32) seven thirty-seconds

609 Use hyphens when two or more words have a common element that is omitted in all but the last term.

> We have cedar posts in four-, six-, and eight-inch widths.

610 A hyphen is usually used to form new words beginning with the prefixes *self, ex, all, great,* and *half.* It is also used to join any prefix to a proper noun, a proper adjective, or the official name of an office. A hyphen is used with the suffix *elect.*

> half-eaten   great-grandson   ex-mayor
> post-Depression   governor-elect   mid-May
>
> Self-trust is the essence of heroism.
>
> **—Ralph Waldo Emerson**

NOTE: Use a hyphen with other prefixes or suffixes to avoid confusion or awkward spelling.

> re-cover (not recover) the sofa   shell-like (not shelllike) shape

611 The hyphen is used to join numbers indicating the life span of a person and the score in a contest or vote.

> In 1954 Attorney Thurgood Marshall (1908-1993) argued the winning side of the 9-0 Supreme Court decision that school segregation is unconstitutional.

612 The hyphen is used to separate a word at the end of a line of print. A word may be divided only between syllables, and the hyphen is always placed after the syllable at the end of the line—never before a syllable at the beginning of the following line.

Guidelines for Word Division

1. Always leave enough of the word at the end of the line so that the word can be identified.

2. Never divide a one-syllable word: *rained, skills, through.*

3. Avoid dividing a word of five letters or less: *paper, study, July.*

4. Never divide a one-letter syllable from the rest of the word: *omit-ted,* not *o-mitted.*

5. Always divide a compound word between its basic units: *sister-in-law,* not *sis-ter-in-law.*

6. Never divide abbreviations or contractions: *shouldn't,* not *should-n't.*

7. When a vowel is a syllable by itself, divide the word after the vowel: *epi-sode,* not *ep-isode.*

8. Avoid dividing a number written as a figure: *1,000,000;* not *1,000,-000.* (If a figure must be broken, divide it after one of the commas.)

9. Avoid dividing the last word in a paragraph.

10. Never divide the last word in more than two lines in a row.

613 Use the hyphen to join two or more words that serve as a single adjective (a single-thought adjective) before a noun.

> In real life I am a large, big-boned woman with rough, man-working hands.
> —Alice Walker, "Everyday Use"

NOTE: When words forming the adjective come after the noun, do not hyphenate them.

> In real life, I am large and big boned.

ALSO NOTE: When the first of these words is an adverb ending in *ly,* do not use a hyphen; also, do not use a hyphen when a number or letter is the final element in a one-thought adjective.

> *freshly painted* barn (adverb ending in *-ly*)
>
> *grade A* milk (letter is the final element)

Dash

614 The **dash** is used to indicate a sudden break or change in the sentence.

> The average worker works 135 days—from January 1 to May 15—to pay all federal, state, and local taxes each year.

NOTE: A dash is indicated by two hyphens--without spacing before or after--in all handwritten material.

615 A dash is used to set off an introductory series from the clause that explains the series.

> Health, friends, family—where would we be without them?

616 A dash may also be used to show that words or letters are missing.

> Mr. — won't let us marry.
> —Alice Walker, *The Color Purple*

617 A dash may be used to emphasize a word, series, phrase, or clause.

> I have seen the future, and it is very much like the present—only longer.
> —Kehlog Albran

618 A dash is used to show interrupted or faltering speech in dialogue.

> "Well, Dad, I—ah—ran out of gas, had two flat tires, and—there was a terrible snowstorm on the other side of town."

"Well, Dad, I—ah—ran out of gas, had two flat tires, and—there was a terrible snowstorm on the other side of town."

Question Mark

619 A **question mark** is used at the end of a direct question.

> What can I know? What ought I to do? What may I hope?
> —Immanuel Kant

> Since when do you have to agree with people to defend them from injustice?
> —Lillian Hellman

620 No question mark is used after an indirect question.

> I asked him if he had ever had any formal training on a Macintosh computer.

621 When two clauses within a sentence both ask questions, one question mark is used.

> Do you often ask yourself, "What should I be?"

622 The question mark is placed within parentheses to show uncertainty.

> This August will be the 25th anniversary (?) of the first moon walk.

623 A short question within parentheses—or a question set off by dashes—is punctuated with a question mark.

> You must consult your handbook (what choice do you have?) when you need to know a punctuation rule.

> Maybe somewhere in the pasts of these humbled people, there were cases of bad mothering or absent fathering or emotional neglect—what family surviving the '50s was exempt?—but I couldn't believe these human errors brought the physical changes in Frank.
> —Mary Kay Blakely, *Wake Me When It's Over*

Exclamation Point

624 The **exclamation point** is used to express strong feeling. It may be placed after a word, a phrase, or a sentence. (The exclamation point should be used sparingly.)

> "That's not the point," said Wangero. "These are all pieces of dresses Grandma used to wear. She did all this stitching by hand. Imagine!"
> —Alice Walker, "Everyday Use"

> Su-su-something's crawling up the back of my neck!
> —Mark Twain, *Roughing It*

> She was on tiptoe, stretching for an orange, when they heard, "HEY YOU!"
> —Beverly Naidoo, *Journey to Jo'burg*

Quotation Marks

625 **Quotation marks** are used to punctuate titles of songs, poems, short stories, lectures, courses, episodes of radio or television programs, chapters of books, unpublished works, and articles found in magazines, newspapers, or encyclopedias. (For punctuation of other titles, see 632.)

"Taking Care of Business" (**song**)

"A Song for Emily" (**short story**)

"Technical Writing" (**course title**)

"When Words Are the Best Weapon" (**magazine article**)

"When Your Parachute Doesn't Open" (**chapter in a book**)

"Force of Nature" (**television episode from** *Star Trek*)

NOTE: In titles, capitalize the first word, the last word, and every word in between except articles, short prepositions, and short conjunctions.

626 Quotation marks also may be used (1) to distinguish a word that is being discussed, (2) to indicate that a word is slang, or (3) to point out that a word is being used in a special way.

(**1**) A commentary on the times is that the word "honesty" is now preceded by "old-fashioned." —**Larry Wolters**

(**2**) I drank a Dixie and ate bar peanuts and asked the bartender where I could hear "chanky-chank," as Cajuns call their music.
—**William Least Heat Moon,** *Blue Highways*

(**3**) In order to be popular, he works very hard at being "cute."

NOTE: Italics (underlining) may be used in place of quotation marks for each of these three functions.

627 Periods and commas are always placed inside quotation marks.

"Dr. Slaughter wants you to have liquids, Will," Mama said anxiously. "He said not to give you any solid food tonight."
—**Olive Ann Burns,** *Cold Sassy Tree*

628 An exclamation point or a question mark is placed inside quotation marks when it punctuates the quotation; it is placed outside when it punctuates the main sentence.

I almost croaked when he asked, "That won't be a problem, will it?"

Did he really say, "Finish this by tomorrow"?

629 Semicolons or colons are always placed outside quotation marks.

I just read "Computers and Creativity"; I now have some different ideas about the role of computers in the arts.

Marking Quoted Material
630 ## Quick Guide

1 **Quotation marks** are placed before and after direct quotations. Only the exact words quoted are placed within the quotation marks.

> Recently at Hardees' drive-thru I tested the worker's listening. She said, "A dollar fifty-six. Please drive around." And I said, "How long?" She didn't get it.

2 Quotation marks are placed before and after a quoted passage. Any word or punctuation mark that is not part of the original quotation must be placed inside brackets.

> **(Original)** First of all, it must accept responsibility for providing shelter for the homeless.

> **(Quotation)** "First of all, it [the federal government] must accept responsibility for providing shelter for the homeless."
> —Amy Douma, "Helping the Homeless"

NOTE: If you quote only part of the original passage, be sure to construct a sentence that is both accurate and grammatically correct.

> The report goes on to say that the federal government "must accept responsibility for providing shelter for the homeless."

3 If more than one paragraph is quoted, quotation marks are placed before each paragraph and at the end of the last paragraph (Example A). Quotations that are more than four lines on a page are usually set off from the text by indenting 10 spaces from the left margin ("block form"). Quotation marks are placed neither before nor after the quoted material unless they appear in the original (Example B).

Example A

Example B

4 Single quotation marks are used to punctuate a quotation within a quotation.

> Jason said, "I never read 'Casey at the Bat'!"

Italics (Underlining)

631 **Italics** is a printer's term for a style of type that is slightly slanted. In this sentence the word *happiness* is printed in italics. In material that is handwritten or typed on a machine that cannot print in italics, each word or letter that should be in italics is underlined.

> In The Road to Memphis, racism is a contagious disease. **(typed)**
>
> Mildred Taylor's *The Road to Memphis* exposes racism. **(printed)**

632 Italics are used to indicate the titles of magazines, newspapers, books, pamphlets, plays, films, radio and television programs, book-length poems, ballets, operas, lengthy musical compositions, record albums, CD's, legal cases, and the names of ships and aircraft. (Also see 625.)

> Consumer Reports **(magazine)**   Finding the Hat That Fits **(book)**
>
> Wall Street **(film)**   Home Improvement **(television program)**
>
> Death of a Salesman **(play)**   Motorist's Handbook **(pamphlet)**
>
> New York Times or New York Times **(newspaper)**

633 When one title appears within another title, punctuate as follows:

> "The Fresh Prince of Bel-Air Rings True" **(title of TV program in an article)**

634 Italics are used to indicate a foreign word that has not been adopted into the English language; they also denote scientific names.

> Most dinosaurs, including *Tyrannosaurus rex*, had large bodies but small brains.

Most dinosaurs, including Tyrannosaurus rex, had large bodies but small brains.

Parentheses

635 **Parentheses** are used to enclose explanatory or supplementary material that interrupts the normal sentence structure.

> The EPA (Environmental Protection Agency) defines waste as hazardous if it poses a danger to human health or the environment.

636 Punctuation is placed within parentheses when it is intended to mark the material within the parenthetical. Also note that words enclosed by parentheses do not have to begin with a capital letter or end with a period—even though these words may express a complete thought.

> But Mom doesn't say boo to Dad; she's always sweet to him. (Actually she's sort of sweet to everybody.)
> —**Norma Fox Mazer,** *Up on Fong Mountain*

> And, since your friend won't have the assignment (he was just thinking about calling you), you'll have to make a couple more calls to actually get it.
> —**Ken Taylor, "The Art and Practice of Avoiding Homework"**

NOTE: For unavoidable parentheses within parentheses (. . . [. . .] . . .), use brackets. Avoid overuse of parentheses by using commas instead.

Brackets

637 **Brackets** are used before and after material that a writer adds when quoting another writer.

> "Sometimes I think it [my writing] sounds like I walked out of the room and left the typewriter running." —**Gene Fowler**

NOTE: The brackets indicate that the words *my writing* are not part of the quotation but were added for clarification.

638 Place brackets around material that has been added by someone other than the author or speaker.

> "Congratulations to the astronomy club's softball team, which put in, shall we say, a 'stellar' performance." [groans]

639 Place brackets around an editorial correction.

> "Brooklyn alone has eight percent of lead poisoning [victims] nationwide," said Marjorie Moore. —**Donna Actie, student writer**

640 Brackets should be placed around the letters *sic* (Latin for "as such"); the letters indicate that an error appearing in the quoted material was made by the original speaker or writer.

> "No parent can dessert [sic] his child without damaging a human life."

Apostrophe

641 An **apostrophe** is used to show that one or more letters have been left out of a word to form a contraction.

> don't - **o** is left out   she'd - **woul** is left out   it's - **i** is left out

NOTE: An apostrophe is also used to show that one or more letters or numbers have been left out of numerals or words that are spelled as they are actually spoken.

> class of '85 - **19** is left out   good mornin' - **g** is left out

642 An apostrophe and *s* are used to form the plural of a letter, a number, a sign, or a word discussed as a word.

> A - A's   C - C's   8 - 8's
>
> You use too many *and*'s in your writing.

NOTE: When two apostrophes are called for in the same word, simply omit the second one.

> Follow closely the do's and don'ts (not don't's) on the checklist.

643 The possessive form of singular nouns is usually made by adding an apostrophe and *s*.

> Spock's ears   my computer's memory

NOTE: When a singular noun ends with an *s* or a *z* sound, the possessive may be formed by adding just an apostrophe. When the singular noun is a one-syllable word, however, the possessive is usually formed by adding both an apostrophe and *s*.

> Dallas' sports teams **(or)** Dallas's sports teams
>
> Kiss's last concert   my boss's generosity **(one-syllable word)**

644 The possessive form of plural nouns ending in *s* is usually made by adding just an apostrophe.

> Joneses' great-grandfather   bosses' office

---

system check   It will help you punctuate correctly if you remember that the word immediately before the apostrophe is the owner.

> girl's guitar **(girl is the owner)**   boss's office **(boss is the owner)**
>
> girls' guitar **(girls are the owners)**   bosses' office **(bosses are the owners)**

---

645 When possession is shared by more than one noun, use the possessive form for the last noun in the series.

> Jason, Kamil, and Elana's sound system **(All own one system.)**
>
> Jason's, Kamil's, and Elana's sound systems **(Each owns a system.)**

646 The possessive of a compound noun is formed by placing the possessive ending after the last word.

> his mother-in-law's (**singular**) career
> the secretary of state's (**singular**) spouse
>
> their mothers-in-law's (**plural**) careers
> the secretaries of state's (**plural**) spouses

647 The possessive of an indefinite pronoun is formed by placing an apostrophe and *s* on the last word. (See 719.)

> everyone's   anyone's   somebody else's

648 An apostrophe is used with an adjective that is part of an expression indicating time or amount.

> yesterday's news   a day's wage   a month's pay

Diagonal

649 A **diagonal** (also called a slash) is used to form a fraction. Also place a diagonal between *and/or* to indicate that either is acceptable (avoid this use of the diagonal in formal writing).

> My shoe size is 5 1/2 unless I'm wearing running shoes; then it's 6 1/2.
>
> A large radio/tape player is a boombox or a stereo or a box or a large metallic ham sandwich with speakers. It is not a "ghetto blaster."
> —Amoja Three Rivers, "Cultural Etiquette: A Guide"

650 When quoting more than one line of poetry, use a diagonal to show where each line of poetry ends.

> A dryness is upon the house / My father loved and tended. / Beyond his firm and sculptured door / His light and lease have ended.
> —Gwendolyn Brooks, "In Honor of David Anderson Brooks, My Father"

651

Punctuation Marks

´	Accent, acute	,	Comma	( )	Parentheses
`	Accent, grave	†	Dagger	.	Period
'	Apostrophe	—	Dash	?	Question mark
*	Asterisk	/	Diagonal/Slash	" "	Quotation marks
{ or }	Brace	¨ (ü)	Dieresis	§	Section
[ ]	Brackets	. . .	Ellipsis	;	Semicolon
^	Caret	!	Exclamation point	~	Tilde
˛ (ç)	Cedilla	-	Hyphen	_____	Underscore
ˆ	Circumflex	...	Leaders		
:	Colon	¶	Paragraph		

"Write freely and as rapidly as possible and throw the whole thing on paper. Never correct or rewrite until the whole thing is down."

—John Steinbeck

Checking Mechanics

Capitalization

652 **Capitalize** all proper nouns and all proper adjectives (adjectives derived from proper nouns). The chart below provides a quick overview of capitalization rules. The pages following explain specific or special uses of capitalization.

Capitalization at a Glance

Days of the week	**Sunday, Monday, Tuesday**
Months	**June, July, August**
Holidays, holy days	**Thanksgiving, Easter, Hanukkah**
Periods, events in history	**Middle Ages, the Renaissance**
Special events	**the Battle of Bunker Hill**
Political parties	**Republican Party, Socialist Party**
Official documents	**Declaration of Independence**
Trade names	**Oscar Mayer hot dogs, Pontiac Sunbird**
Formal epithets	**Alexander the Great**
Official titles	**Mayor John Spitzer, Senator Feinstein**
Official state nicknames	**the Badger State, the Aloha State**
Geographical names	
Planets, heavenly bodies	**Earth, Jupiter, the Milky Way**
Continents	**Australia, South America**
Countries	**Ireland, Grenada, Sri Lanka**
States, provinces	**Ohio, Utah, Nova Scotia**
Cities, towns, villages	**El Paso, Burlington, Wonewoc**
Streets, roads, highways	**Park Avenue, Route 66, Interstate 90**
Sections of the world	**the Southwest, the Far East**
Landforms	**the Rocky Mountains, the Sahara Desert**
Bodies of water	**Nile River, Lake Superior, Pumpkin Creek**
Public areas	**Yosemite, Yellowstone National Park**

653 Capitalize the first word in every sentence and the first word in a full-sentence direct quotation.

> **Some** farmers use laptop computers on their tractors out in the field.
>
> Ralph yelled to his father, "**Dad**, we need the computer in the house."

654 Capitalize the first word in each sentence that is enclosed in parentheses if that sentence comes before or after another complete sentence.

> Dad can drive the tractor while typing on his laptop computer.
> (**Is** that weird or what?)

NOTE: Do *not* capitalize a sentence that is enclosed in parentheses and is located in the middle of another sentence.

> Just about everything (**that** includes crop-rotation history, fertilization estimates, and cow biographies) is on my dad's computer.

655 Capitalize a complete sentence that follows a colon only if that sentence is a formal statement or a quotation. You may also capitalize the sentence following a colon if you want to emphasize that sentence.

> It was Sydney Harris who said this about computers: "**The** real danger is not that computers will begin to think like people, but that people will begin to think like computers."

656 Words that indicate sections of the country are proper nouns and should be capitalized; words that simply indicate direction are not proper nouns.

> Many businesses are moving to the sunny **South**. **(section of the country)**
>
> They move **south** to cut fuel costs and other expenses. **(direction)**

657 Capitalize races, nationalities, languages, and religions.

> African-American   Navajo   French   Latino   Spanish   Muslim

658 Capitalize the first word of a title, the last word, and every word in between except articles (*a, an, the*), short prepositions, and short conjunctions. Follow this rule for titles of books, newspapers, magazines, poems, plays, songs, articles, films, works of art, pictures, and stories.

> *Going to Meet the Man*   *Chicago Tribune*   "Nothing Gold Can Stay"
>
> *A Midsummer Night's Dream*   "Job Hunting in the '90s"

659 Capitalize the name of an organization, or a team and its members.

> Tampa Bay Buccaneers   American Indian Movement
>
> Tucson High School Drama Club   Republican Party

660 Capitalize abbreviations of titles and organizations. (Some other abbreviations are also capitalized. See 679-681.)

> U.S.A.   NAACP   M.D.   Ph.D.   A.D.   B.C.   R.R.   No.

661 Capitalize the letters used to indicate form or shape.

> U-turn   I-beam   S-curve   A-bomb   T-shirt

662 Capitalize words like *father, mother, uncle,* and *senator* when they are parts of titles that include a personal name, or when they are substituted for proper nouns (especially in direct address).

> Hi, **Uncle** Charley! (*Uncle* **is part of the name.**)
> My **uncle** is an optician.
> Who was the first African-American **senator**?
> It was **Senator** Hiram Revels, elected in 1870 in Mississippi.

NOTE: To test whether a word is being substituted for a proper noun, simply read the sentence with a proper noun in place of the word. If the proper noun fits in the sentence, the word being tested should be capitalized. (*Further note:* Usually the word is not capitalized if it follows a possessive— *my, his, our,* etc.)

> Did **Mom (Sue)** say we could go? (*Sue* **works in this sentence.**)
> Did your **mom (Sue)** say you could go? (*Sue* **does not work here; the word** *mom* **also follows the possessive** *your.***)**

663 Words such as *technology, history,* and *science* are proper nouns when they are the titles of specific courses, but are common nouns when they name a field of study.

> "Who teaches **History 202**?" **(title of a specific course)**
> "The same guy who teaches that **technology** course." **(a field of study)**

664 Nouns that refer to the Supreme Being are capitalized. So are the word *Bible,* the books of the Bible, and the names of other holy books.

> **God**   **Jehovah**   the **Lord**   the **Savior**   **Allah**
> **Bible**   **Book of Psalms**   **Ecclesiastes**   the **Koran**

665 Do *not* capitalize any of the following: (1) a prefix attached to a proper noun, (2) seasons of the year, (3) words used to indicate direction or position, or (4) common nouns that appear to be part of a proper noun.

Capitalize	Do Not Capitalize
American	un-American
January, February	winter, spring
The South is quite conservative.	Turn south at the stop sign.
Duluth Central High School	a Duluth high school
Governor Douglas Wilder	Douglas Wilder, our governor

Plurals

666 The **plurals** of most nouns are formed by adding *s* to the singular.

mechanic – mechanics   computer – computers

667 The plurals of nouns ending in *sh, ch, x, s,* and *z* are made by adding *es* to the singular.

lunch – lunches   wish – wishes   mess – messes   fax – faxes

NOTE: Some nouns remain unchanged when used as plurals: *deer, sheep, salmon,* etc.

668 The plurals of common nouns that end in *y*—preceded by a consonant—are formed by changing the *y* to *i* and adding *es*.

fly – flies   jalopy – jalopies   monopoly – monopolies

669 The plurals of nouns that end in *y*—preceded by a vowel—are formed by adding only *s*.

attorney – attorneys   money – moneys

NOTE: The plurals of proper nouns ending in *y* are formed by adding *s*.

670 The plurals of words ending in *o* (preceded by a vowel) are formed by adding *s*.

radio – radios   cameo – cameos   studio – studios

671 Most nouns ending in *o* (preceded by a consonant) are formed by adding *es*.

echo – echoes   hero – heroes   tomato – tomatoes

Exception: Musical terms always form plurals by adding *s*; consult your dictionary for other words of this type.

alto – altos   banjo – banjos   solo – solos   piano – pianos

672 The plurals of nouns that end in *f* or *fe* are formed in one of two ways: If the final *f* sound is still heard in the plural form of the word, simply add *s*; if the final sound is a *v* sound, change the *f* to *ve* and add *s*.

Plural ends with f sound: roof – roofs; chief – chiefs
Plural ends with v sound: wife – wives; loaf – loaves
Plural ends with either sound: hoof – hoofs, hooves

673 Many foreign words (as well as some of English origin) form a plural by taking on an irregular spelling; others are now acceptable with the commonly used *s* or *es* ending.

Foreign Words		English Words	
crisis	crises	child	children
criterion	criteria	goose	geese
radius	radii	die	dice

674 The plurals of symbols, letters, figures, and words discussed as words are formed by adding an apostrophe and an *s*.

> I groaned when I opened my grade report and saw two C's and three B's.

> But Dad just yelled a lot of *wow*'s, *yippee*'s, and *way-to-go*'s.

NOTE: Some writers omit the apostrophe when the omission does not cause confusion.

> 1990's *or* 1990s   YMCA's *or* YMCAs   CD's or CDs

675 The plurals of nouns that end with *ful* are formed by adding an *s* at the end of the word.

> three pailfuls   two tankfuls

NOTE: Do not confuse these examples with three *pails full* (when you are referring to three separate pails full of something) or two *tanks full*.

676 The plurals of compound nouns are usually formed by adding *s* or *es* to the important word in the compound.

> brothers-in-law   maids of honor   secretaries of state

677 Pronouns referring to a collective noun may be singular or plural. A pronoun is singular when the group (noun) is considered a unit. A pronoun is plural when the group (noun) is considered in terms of its individual components.

> The team prepared for its opening game. (group as a unit)

> The team prepared for their physical exams. (group as individuals)

The team prepared for their physical exams.

Numbers

678 Quick Guide

1 **Numbers** from one to nine are usually written as words; all numbers 10 and over are usually written as numerals.

two   seven   nine   10   25   106   1,079

Exception: If numbers are used infrequently in a piece of writing, you may spell out those that can be written in no more than two words.

ten   twenty-five   two hundred   fifty thousand

NOTE: Numbers being compared or contrasted should be kept in the same style.

8 to 11 years old *or* eight to eleven years old

2 Use numerals to express numbers in the following forms: money, decimal, percentage, chapter, page, address, telephone, ZIP code, time, dates, identification numbers, and statistics.

$2.39	26.2	8 percent
chapter 7	pages 287-89	July 6, 1945
44 B.C.	A.D. 79	4:30 p.m.
Highway 36	a vote of 23 to 4	24 mph

Exception: If numbers are used infrequently in a piece of writing, you may spell out amounts of money and percentages when you can do so in two or three words.

nine cents   one hundred dollars   eight percent   thirty-five percent

NOTE: Always use numerals with abbreviations and symbols.

5'4"   8%   10 in.   3 tbsp.   6 lbs. 8 oz.   90° F

3 Use words to express numbers that begin a sentence.

Fourteen students "forgot" their assignments.

NOTE: Change the sentence structure if this rule creates a clumsy construction.

Clumsy: *Six hundred thirty-nine* teachers were victims of the layoff this year.

Better: This year, 639 teachers were victims of the layoff.

4 Use words for numbers that precede a compound modifier that includes another number.

She sold twenty 35-millimeter cameras in one day.

NOTE: You may use a combination of words and numerals for very large numbers.

1.5 million   3 billion to 3.2 billion   6 billion

Abbreviations

679 An **abbreviation** is the shortened form of a word or phrase. The following abbreviations are always acceptable in both formal and informal writing:

> Mr.   Mrs.   Miss   Ms.   Dr.   a.m. (A.M)   p.m. (P.M.)

In formal writing, **do not abbreviate** the names of states, countries, months, days, units of measure, or courses of study. Do not abbreviate the words *Street, Road, Avenue, Company,* and similar words when they are part of a proper name. Also do not use signs or symbols (%, &, #, @) in place of words. The dollar sign is, however, appropriate when numerals are used to express an amount of money ($325).

680 Address Abbreviations

State Abbreviations

	Standard	Postal
Alabama	Ala.	AL
Alaska	Alaska	AK
Arizona	Ariz.	AZ
Arkansas	Ark.	AR
California	Calif.	CA
Colorado	Colo.	CO
Connecticut	Conn.	CT
Delaware	Del.	DE
District of Columbia	D.C.	DC
Florida	Fla.	FL
Georgia	Ga.	GA
Guam	Guam	GU
Hawaii	Hawaii	HI
Idaho	Idaho	ID
Illinois	Ill.	IL
Indiana	Ind.	IN
Iowa	Iowa	IA
Kansas	Kan.	KS
Kentucky	Ky.	KY
Louisiana	La.	LA
Maine	Maine	ME
Maryland	Md.	MD
Massachusetts	Mass.	MA
Michigan	Mich.	MI
Minnesota	Minn.	MN
Mississippi	Miss.	MS
Missouri	Mo.	MO
Montana	Mont.	MT
Nebraska	Neb.	NE
Nevada	Nev.	NV
New Hampshire	N.H.	NH
New Jersey	N.J.	NJ
New Mexico	N.M.	NM
New York	N.Y.	NY
North Carolina	N.C.	NC
North Dakota	N.D.	ND
Ohio	Ohio	OH
Oklahoma	Okla.	OK
Oregon	Ore.	OR
Pennsylvania	Pa.	PA
Puerto Rico	P.R.	PR
Rhode Island	R.I.	RI
South Carolina	S.C.	SC
South Dakota	S.D.	SD
Tennessee	Tenn.	TN
Texas	Texas	TX
Utah	Utah	UT
Vermont	Vt.	VT
Virginia	Va.	VA
Virgin Islands	V.I.	VI
Washington	Wash.	WA
West Virginia	W.Va.	WV
Wisconsin	Wis.	WI
Wyoming	Wyo.	WY

Canadian Provinces

	Standard	Postal
Alberta	Alta.	AB
British Columbia	B.C.	BC
Labrador	Lab.	LB
Manitoba	Man.	MB
New Brunswick	N.B.	NB
Newfoundland	N.F.	NF
Northwest Territories	N.W.T.	NT
Nova Scotia	N.S.	NS
Ontario	Ont.	ON
Prince Edward Island	P.E.I.	PE
Quebec	Que.	PQ
Saskatchewan	Sask.	SK
Yukon Territory	Y.T.	YT

Address Abbreviations

	Standard	Postal
Apartment	Apt.	APT
Avenue	Ave.	AVE
Boulevard	Blvd.	BLVD
Circle	Cir.	CIR
Court	Ct.	CT
Drive	Dr.	DR
East	E.	E
Expressway	Expy.	EXPY
Freeway	Fwy.	FWY
Heights	Hts.	HTS
Highway	Hwy.	HWY
Hospital	Hosp.	HOSP
Junction	Junc.	JCT
Lake	L.	LK
Lakes	Ls.	LKS
Lane	Ln.	LN
Meadows	Mdws.	MDWS
North	N.	N
Palms	Palms	PLMS
Park	Pk.	PK
Parkway	Pky.	PKY
Place	Pl.	PL
Plaza	Plaza	PLZ
Post Office Box	P.O. Box	PO BOX
Ridge	Rdg.	RDG
River	R.	RV
Road	Rd.	RD
Room	Rm.	RM
Rural	R.	R
Rural Route	R.R.	RR
Shore	Sh.	SH
South	S.	S
Square	Sq.	SQ
Station	Sta.	STA
Street	St.	ST
Suite	Ste.	STE
Terrace	Ter.	TER
Turnpike	Tpke.	TPKE
Union	Un.	UN
View	View	VW
Village	Vil.	VLG
West	W.	W

681 Common Abbreviations

abr. abridge; abridgment

AC, ac alternating current

ack. acknowledge; acknowledgement

acv actual cash value

A.D. in the year of the Lord (Latin *anno Domini*)

AM amplitude modulation

A.M., a.m. before noon (Latin *ante meridiem*)

ASAP as soon as possible

avg., av. average

BBB Better Business Bureau

B.C. 1. before Christ 2. British Columbia

bibliog. bibliographer; bibliography

biog. biographer; biographical; biography

C 1. Celsius 2. centigrade 3. coulomb

c. 1. circa (about) 2. cup

cc carbon copies; copies

cc. chapters

CDT, C.D.T. Central Daylight Time

cm centimeter

c.o., c/o care of

COD, C.O.D 1. cash on delivery 2. collect on delivery

co-op cooperative

CST, C.S.T. Central Standard Time

cu 1. cubic 2. cumulative

D.A. district attorney

d.b.a. doing business as

DC, dc direct current

dec. deceased

dept. department

disc. discount

DST, D.S.T. Daylight Saving Time

dup. duplicate

ea. each

ed. edition; editor

EDT, E.D.T. Eastern Daylight Time

e.g. for example (Latin *exempli gratia*)

EST, E.S.T. Eastern Standard Time

etc. and so forth (Latin *et cetera*)

ex. example

F Fahrenheit

FM frequency modulation

F.O.B., f.o.b. free on board

ft. foot

g 1. gravity 2. gram

gal. gallon

gds. goods

gloss. glossary

GNP gross national product

hdqrs. headquarters

HIV human immunodeficiency virus

Hon. Honorable (title)

hp horsepower

Hz hertz

id. the same (Latin *idem*)

i.e. that is (Latin *id est*)

illus. illustration

inc. incorporated

IQ, I.Q. intelligence quotient

IRS Internal Revenue Service

ISBN International Standard Book Number

JP, J.P. justice of the peace

Jr., jr. junior

K 1. kelvin (temperature unit) 2. Kelvin (temperature scale)

kc kilocycle

kg kilogram

km kilometer

kn knot

kw kilowatt

l liter

lat. latitude

lb. pound (Latin *libra*)

l.c. lowercase

lit. literary; literature

log logarithm

long. longitude

Ltd., ltd. limited

m meter

M.A. Master of Arts (Latin *Magister Artium*)

man. manual

Mc, mc megacycle

M.C., m.c. master of ceremonies

M.D. Doctor of Medicine (Latin *Medicinae Doctor*)

mdse. merchandise

mfg. manufacture; manufactured

mg milligram

mi. 1. mile 2. mill (monetary unit)

misc. miscellaneous

ml milliliter

mm millimeter

mpg, m.p.g. miles per gallon

mph, m.p.h. miles per hour

MS 1. manuscript 2. Mississippi 3. multiple sclerosis

Ms. Title of courtesy for a woman

MST, M.S.T. Mountain Standard Time

NE northeast

neg. negative

N.S.F., n.s.f. not sufficient funds

NW northwest

oz, oz. ounce

PA public-address system

pct. percent

pd. paid

PDT, P.D.T. Pacific Daylight Time

Pfc, Pfc. private first class

pg., p. page

P.M., p.m. after noon (Latin *post meridiem*)

P.O. 1. Personnel Officer 2. purchase order 3. postal order; post office 4. also **p.o.** petty officer

pop. population

POW, P.O.W. prisoner of war

pp. pages

ppd. 1. postpaid 2. prepaid

PR, P.R. 1. public relations 2. Puerto Rico

psi, p.s.i. pounds per square inch

PST, P.S.T. Pacific Standard Time

PTA, P.T.A. Parent-Teacher Association

qt. quart

RD rural delivery

RF radio frequency

R.P.M., rpm revolutions per minute

R.S.V.P., r.s.v.p. please reply (French *répondez s'il vous plaît*)

SE southeast

SOS 1. international distress signal 2. any call for help

Sr. 1. senior (after surname) 2. sister (religious)

SRO, S.R.O. standing room only

ST standard time

St. 1. saint 2. strait 3. street

std. standard

SW southwest

syn. synonymous; synonym

tbs., tbsp. tablespoon

TM trademark

UHF, uhf ultra high frequency

V 1. *Physics:* velocity 2. *Electricity:* volt 3. volume

VA, V.A. Veterans Administration 2. Virginia

VHF, vhf very high frequency

VIP *Informal:* very important person

vol. 1. volume 2. volunteer

vs. versus

W 1. *Electricity:* watt 2. *Physics:* (also **w**) work 3. west

whse., whs. warehouse

whsle. wholesale

wkly. weekly

w/o without

wt. weight

yd. yard (measurement)

Acronyms and Initialisms

682 An **acronym** is a word formed from the first (or first few) letters of words in a set phrase. Even though acronyms are a form of abbreviation, they are not followed by a period(s).

radar – radio detecting and ranging

CARE – Cooperative for American Relief Everywhere

NASA – National Aeronautics and Space Administration

VISTA – Volunteers in Service to America

UNICEF – United Nations International Children's Emergency Fund

683 An **initialism** is similar to an acronym except that the initials used to form this abbreviation cannot be pronounced as a word.

CIA – Central Intelligence Agency

FBI – Federal Bureau of Investigation

FHA – Federal Housing Administration

684 Common Acronyms and Initialisms

AIDS	acquired immunodeficiency syndrome	**ORV**	off-road vehicle
CETA	Comprehensive Employment and Training Act	**OSHA**	Occupational Safety and Health Administration
CIA	Central Intelligence Agency	**PAC**	political action committee
FAA	Federal Aviation Administration	**PIN**	personal identification number
FBI	Federal Bureau of Investigation	**PSA**	public service announcement
FCC	Federal Communications Commission	**REA**	Rural Electrification Administration
FDA	Food and Drug Administration	**RICO**	Racketeer Influenced and Corrupt Organizations (Act)
FDIC	Federal Deposit Insurance Corporation	**ROTC**	Reserve Officers' Training Corps
FHA	Federal Housing Administration	**SADD**	Students Against Drunk Driving
FmHA	Farmers Home Administration	**SSA**	Social Security Administration
FTC	Federal Trade Commission	**SWAT**	Special Weapons and Tactics
IRS	Internal Revenue Service	**TDD**	telecommunications device for the deaf
MADD	Mothers Against Drunk Driving	**TMJ**	temporomandibular joint
NASA	National Aeronautics and Space Administration	**TVA**	Tennessee Valley Authority
		VA	Veterans Administration
NATO	North Atlantic Treaty Organization	**VISTA**	Volunteers in Service to America
NYC	Neighborhood Youth Corps	**WAC**	Women's Army Corps
OEO	Office of Economic Opportunity	**WAVES**	Women Accepted for Volunteer Emergency Service
OEP	Office of Emergency Preparedness		

Spelling Rules

685 Quick Guide

Rule 1: Write *i* before *e* except after *c*, or when sounded like *a* as in neighbor and weigh.

Examples: receive   perceive   relief

Exceptions: This sentence contains eight exceptions: **Neither sheik dared leisurely seize either weird species of financiers.**

When the *ie/ei* combination is not pronounced *ee*, it is usually spelled *ei*.

Examples: reign   foreign   weigh   neighbor

Exceptions: fiery   friend   mischief   view

Rule 2: When a one-syllable word (*bat*) ends in a consonant (*t*) preceded by one vowel (*a*), double the final consonant before adding a suffix that begins with a vowel (*batting*).

sum—summary   god—goddess

When a multi-syllable word (*control*) ends in a consonant (*l*) preceded by one vowel (*o*), the accent is on the last syllable (*con trol´*), and the suffix begins with a vowel (*ing*)—the same rule holds true: double the final consonant (*controlling*).

prefer—preferred   begin—beginning

forget—forgettable   admit—admittance

Rule 3: If a word ends with a silent *e*, drop the *e* before adding a suffix that begins with a vowel.

state—stating—statement   like—liking—likeness

use—using—useful   nine—ninety—nineteen

NOTE: You do not drop the *e* when the suffix begins with a consonant. Exceptions include *judgment, truly, argument,* and *ninth*.

Rule 4: When *y* is the last letter in a word and the *y* is preceded by a consonant, change the *y* to *i* before adding any suffix except those beginning with *i*.

fry—fries   hurry—hurried   lady—ladies

ply—pliable   happy—happiness   beauty—beautiful

When forming the plural of a word that ends with a *y* that is preceded by a vowel, add *s*.

toy—toys   play—plays   monkey—monkeys

686 Commonly Misspelled Words

A

ab-bre-vi-ate
a-brupt
ab-scess
ab-sence
ab-so-lute (-ly)
ab-sorb-ent
ab-surd
a-bun-dance
ac-cede
ac-cel-er-ate
ac-cept (-ance)
ac-ces-si-ble
ac-ces-so-ry
ac-ci-den-tal-ly
ac-com-mo-date
ac-com-pa-ny
ac-com-plice
ac-com-plish
ac-cor-dance
ac-cord-ing
ac-count
ac-crued
ac-cu-mu-late
ac-cu-rate
ac-cus-tom (ed)
ache
a-chieve (-ment)
ac-knowl-edge
ac-quaint-ance
ac-qui-esce
ac-quired
ac-tu-al
a-dapt
ad-di-tion (-al)
ad-dress
ad-e-quate
ad-journed
ad-just-ment
ad-mi-ra-ble
ad-mis-si-ble
ad-mit-tance
ad-van-ta-geous
ad-ver-tise-ment
ad-ver-tis-ing
ad-vice (n.)
ad-vis-able

ad-vise (v.)
ae-ri-al
af-fect
af-fi-da-vit
a-gain
a-gainst
ag-gra-vate
ag-gres-sion
a-gree-able
a-gree-ment
aisle
al-co-hol
a-lign-ment
al-ley
al-lot-ted
al-low-ance
all right
al-most
al-ready
al-though
al-to-geth-er
a-lu-mi-num
al-ways
am-a-teur
a-mend-ment
a-mong
a-mount
a-nal-y-sis
an-a-lyze
an-cient
an-ec-dote
an-es-thet-ic
an-gle
an-ni-hi-late
an-ni-ver-sa-ry
an-nounce
an-noy-ance
an-nu-al
a-noint
a-non-y-mous
an-swer
ant-arc-tic
an-tic-i-pate
anx-i-ety
anx-ious
any-thing
a-part-ment
a-pol-o-gize
ap-pa-ra-tus

ap-par-ent (-ly)
ap-peal
ap-pear-ance
ap-pe-tite
ap-pli-ance
ap-pli-ca-ble
ap-pli-ca-tion
ap-point-ment
ap-prais-al
ap-pre-ci-ate
ap-proach
ap-pro-pri-ate
ap-prov-al
ap-prox-i-mate-ly
ar-chi-tect
arc-tic
ar-gu-ment
a-rith-me-tic
a-rouse
ar-range-ment
ar-riv-al
ar-ti-cle
ar-ti-fi-cial
as-cend
as-cer-tain
as-i-nine
as-sas-sin
as-sess (-ment)
as-sign-ment
as-sist-ance
as-so-ci-ate
as-so-ci-a-tion
as-sume
as-sur-ance
as-ter-isk
ath-lete
ath-let-ic
at-tach
at-tack (ed)
at-tempt
at-tend-ance
at-ten-tion
at-ti-tude
at-tor-ney
at-trac-tive
au-di-ble
au-di-ence
au-thor-i-ty
au-to-mo-bile

au-tumn
aux-il-ia-ry
a-vail-a-ble
av-er-age
aw-ful
aw-ful-ly
awk-ward

B

bach-e-lor
bag-gage
bal-ance
bal-loon
bal-lot
ba-nan-a
ban-dage
bank-rupt
bar-gain
bar-rel
base-ment
ba-sis
bat-tery
beau-ti-ful
beau-ty
be-come
be-com-ing
be-fore
beg-gar
be-gin-ning
be-hav-ior
be-ing
be-lief
be-lieve
ben-e-fi-cial
ben-e-fit (-ed)
be-tween
bi-cy-cle
bis-cuit
bliz-zard
book-keep-er
bough
bought
bouil-lon
bound-a-ry
break-fast
breath (n.)
breathe (v.)

brief
bril-liant
Brit-ain
bro-chure
brought
bruise
budg-et
bul-le-tin
buoy-ant
bu-reau
bur-glar
bury
busi-ness
busy

C

caf-e-te-ria
caf-feine
cal-en-dar
cam-paign
can-celed
can-di-date
can-is-ter
ca-noe
can't
ca-pac-i-ty
cap-i-tal
cap-i-tol
cap-tain
car-bu-ret-or
ca-reer
car-i-ca-ture
car-riage
cash-ier
cas-se-role
cas-u-al-ty
cat-a-log
ca-tas-tro-phe
caught
cav-al-ry
cel-e-bra-tion
cem-e-ter-y
cen-sus
cen-tu-ry
cer-tain
cer-tif-i-cate
ces-sa-tion

chal-lenge
change-a-ble
char-ac-ter (-is-tic)
chauf-feur
chief
chim-ney
choc-o-late
choice
choose
Chris-tian
cir-cuit
cir-cu-lar
cir-cum-stance
civ-i-li-za-tion
cli-en-tele
cli-mate
climb
clothes
coach
co-coa
co-er-cion
col-lar
col-lat-er-al
col-lege
col-lo-qui-al
colo-nel
col-or
co-los-sal
col-umn
com-e-dy
com-ing
com-mence
com-mer-cial
com-mis-sion
com-mit
com-mit-ment
com-mit-ted
com-mit-tee
com-mu-ni-cate
com-mu-ni-ty
com-par-a-tive
com-par-i-son
com-pel
com-pe-tent
com-pe-ti-tion
com-pet-i-tive-ly
com-plain
com-ple-ment
com-plete-ly
com-plex-ion
com-pli-ment

com-pro-mise
con-cede
con-ceive
con-cern-ing
con-cert
con-ces-sion
con-clude
con-crete
con-curred
con-cur-rence
con-demn
con-de-scend
con-di-tion
con-fer-ence
con-ferred
con-fi-dence
con-fi-den-tial
con-grat-u-late
con-science
con-sci-en-tious
con-scious
con-sen-sus
con-se-quence
con-ser-va-tive
con-sid-er-ably
con-sign-ment
con-sis-tent
con-sti-tu-tion
con-tempt-ible
con-tin-u-al-ly
con-tin-ue
con-tin-u-ous
con-trol
con-tro-ver-sy
con-ven-ience
con-vince
cool-ly
co-op-er-ate
cor-dial
cor-po-ra-tion
cor-re-late
cor-re-spond
cor-re-spond-
 ence
cor-rob-o-rate
cough
couldn't
coun-cil
coun-sel
coun-ter-feit
coun-try

cour-age
cou-ra-geous
cour-te-ous
cour-te-sy
cous-in
cov-er-age
cred-i-tor
cri-sis
crit-i-cism
crit-i-cize
cru-el
cu-ri-os-i-ty
cu-ri-ous
cur-rent
cur-ric-u-lum
cus-tom
cus-tom-ary
cus-tom-er
cyl-in-der

D

dai-ly
dair-y
dealt
debt-or
de-ceased
de-ceit-ful
de-ceive
de-cid-ed
de-ci-sion
dec-la-ra-tion
dec-o-rate
de-duct-i-ble
de-fend-ant
de-fense
de-ferred
def-i-cit
def-i-nite (-ly)
def-i-ni-tion
del-e-gate
de-li-cious
de-pend-ent
de-pos-i-tor
de-pot
de-scend
de-scribe
de-scrip-tion
de-sert
de-serve
de-sign

de-sir-able
de-sir-ous
de-spair
des-per-ate
de-spise
des-sert
de-te-ri-o-rate
de-ter-mine
de-vel-op
de-vel-op-ment
de-vice
de-vise
di-a-mond
di-a-phragm
di-ar-rhe-a
di-a-ry
dic-tio-nary
dif-fer-ence
dif-fer-ent
dif-fi-cul-ty
di-lap-i-dat-ed
di-lem-ma
din-ing
di-plo-ma
di-rec-tor
dis-agree-able
dis-ap-pear
dis-ap-point
dis-ap-prove
dis-as-trous
dis-ci-pline
dis-cov-er
dis-crep-an-cy
dis-cuss
dis-cus-sion
dis-ease
dis-sat-is-fied
dis-si-pate
dis-tin-guish
dis-trib-ute
di-vide
di-vine
di-vis-i-ble
di-vi-sion
doc-tor
doesn't
dom-i-nant
dor-mi-to-ry
doubt
drudg-ery
du-al

du-pli-cate
dye-ing
dy-ing

E

ea-ger-ly
ear-nest
eco-nom-i-cal
econ-o-my
ec-sta-sy
e-di-tion
ef-fer-ves-cent
ef-fi-ca-cy
ef-fi-cien-cy
eighth
ei-ther
e-lab-o-rate
e-lec-tric-i-ty
el-e-phant
el-i-gi-ble
e-lim-i-nate
el-lipse
em-bar-rass
e-mer-gen-cy
em-i-nent
em-pha-size
em-ploy-ee
em-ploy-ment
e-mul-sion
en-close
en-cour-age
en-deav-or
en-dorse-ment
en-gi-neer
En-glish
e-nor-mous
e-nough
en-ter-prise
en-ter-tain
en-thu-si-as-tic
en-tire-ly
en-trance
en-vel-op (v.)
en-ve-lope (n.)
en-vi-ron-ment
equip-ment
equipped
e-quiv-a-lent
es-pe-cial-ly
es-sen-tial

688

es-tab-lish
es-teemed
et-i-quette
ev-i-dence
ex-ag-ger-ate
ex-ceed
ex-cel-lent
ex-cept
ex-cep-tion-al-ly
ex-ces-sive
ex-cite
ex-ec-u-tive
ex-er-cise
ex-haust (-ed)
ex-hi-bi-tion
ex-hil-a-ra-tion
ex-is-tence
ex-or-bi-tant
ex-pect
ex-pe-di-tion
ex-pend-i-ture
ex-pen-sive
ex-pe-ri-ence
ex-plain
ex-pla-na-tion
ex-pres-sion
ex-qui-site
ex-ten-sion
ex-tinct
ex-traor-di-nar-y
ex-treme-ly

F

fa-cil-i-ties
fal-la-cy
fa-mil-iar
fa-mous
fas-ci-nate
fash-ion
fa-tigue (d)
fau-cet
fa-vor-ite
fea-si-ble
fea-ture
Feb-ru-ar-y
fed-er-al
fem-i-nine
fer-tile
fic-ti-tious
field

fierce
fi-ery
fi-nal-ly
fi-nan-cial-ly
fo-li-age
for-ci-ble
for-eign
for-feit
for-go
for-mal-ly
for-mer-ly
for-tu-nate
for-ty
for-ward
foun-tain
fourth
frag-ile
fran-ti-cal-ly
freight
friend
ful-fill
fun-da-men-tal
fur-ther-more
fu-tile

G

gad-get
gan-grene
ga-rage
gas-o-line
gauge
ge-ne-al-o-gy
gen-er-al-ly
gen-er-ous
ge-nius
gen-u-ine
ge-og-ra-phy
ghet-to
ghost
glo-ri-ous
gnaw
gov-ern-ment
gov-er-nor
gra-cious
grad-u-a-tion
gram-mar
grate-ful
grat-i-tude
grease
grief

griev-ous
gro-cery
grudge
grue-some
guar-an-tee
guard
guard-i-an
guer-ril-la
guess
guid-ance
guide
guilty
gym-na-si-um
gyp-sy
gy-ro-scope

H

hab-i-tat
ham-mer
hand-ker-chief
han-dle (d)
hand-some
hap-haz-ard
hap-pen
hap-pi-ness
ha-rass
har-bor
hast-i-ly
hav-ing
haz-ard-ous
height
hem-or-rhage
hes-i-tate
hin-drance
his-to-ry
hoarse
hol-i-day
hon-or
hop-ing
hop-ping
horde
hor-ri-ble
hos-pi-tal
hu-mor-ous
hur-ried-ly
hy-drau-lic
hy-giene
hymn
hy-poc-ri-sy

I

i-am-bic
i-ci-cle
i-den-ti-cal
id-io-syn-cra-sy
il-leg-i-ble
il-lit-er-ate
il-lus-trate
im-ag-i-nary
im-ag-i-na-tive
im-ag-ine
im-i-ta-tion
im-me-di-ate-ly
im-mense
im-mi-grant
im-mor-tal
im-pa-tient
im-per-a-tive
im-por-tance
im-pos-si-ble
im-promp-tu
im-prove-ment
in-al-ien-able
in-ci-den-tal-ly
in-con-ve-nience
in-cred-i-ble
in-curred
in-def-i-nite-ly
in-del-ible
in-de-pend-ence
in-de-pend-ent
in-dict-ment
in-dis-pens-able
in-di-vid-u-al
in-duce-ment
in-dus-tri-al
in-dus-tri-ous
in-ev-i-ta-ble
in-fe-ri-or
in-ferred
in-fi-nite
in-flam-ma-ble
in-flu-en-tial
in-ge-nious
in-gen-u-ous
in-im-i-ta-ble
in-i-tial
ini-ti-a-tion
in-no-cence
in-no-cent

in-oc-u-la-tion
in-quir-y
in-stal-la-tion
in-stance
in-stead
in-sti-tute
in-sur-ance
in-tel-lec-tu-al
in-tel-li-gence
in-ten-tion
in-ter-cede
in-ter-est-ing
in-ter-fere
in-ter-mit-tent
in-ter-pret (-ed)
in-ter-rupt
in-ter-view
in-ti-mate
in-va-lid
in-ves-ti-gate
in-ves-tor
in-vi-ta-tion
ir-i-des-cent
ir-rel-e-vant
ir-re-sis-ti-ble
ir-rev-er-ent
ir-ri-gate
is-land
is-sue
i-tem-ized
i-tin-er-ar-y
it's (it is)

J

jan-i-tor
jeal-ous (-y)
jeop-ard-ize
jew-el-ry
jour-nal
jour-ney
judg-ment
jus-tice
jus-ti-fi-able

K

kitch-en
knowl-edge
knuck-le

689

L

la-bel
lab-o-ra-to-ry
lac-quer
lan-guage
laugh
laun-dry
law-yer
league
lec-ture
le-gal
leg-i-ble
leg-is-la-ture
le-git-i-mate
lei-sure
length
let-ter-head
li-a-bil-i-ty
li-a-ble
li-ai-son
li-brar-y
li-cense
lieu-ten-ant
light-ning
lik-able
like-ly
lin-eage
liq-ue-fy
liq-uid
lis-ten
lit-er-ary
lit-er-a-ture
live-li-hood
liv-ing
log-a-rithm
lone-li-ness
loose
lose
los-ing
lov-able
love-ly
lun-cheon
lux-u-ry

M

ma-chine
mag-a-zine
mag-nif-i-cent
main-tain
main-te-nance
ma-jor-i-ty
mak-ing
man-age-ment
ma-neu-ver
man-u-al
man-u-fac-ture
man-u-script
mar-riage
mar-shal
ma-te-ri-al
math-e-mat-ics
max-i-mum
may-or
mean-ness
meant
mea-sure
med-i-cine
me-di-eval
me-di-o-cre
me-di-um
mem-o-ran-dum
men-us
mer-chan-dise
mer-it
mes-sage
mile-age
mil-lion-aire
min-i-a-ture
min-i-mum
min-ute
mir-ror
mis-cel-la-neous
mis-chief
mis-chie-vous
mis-er-a-ble
mis-ery
mis-sile
mis-sion-ary
mis-spell
mois-ture
mol-e-cule
mo-men-tous
mo-not-o-nous
mon-u-ment
mort-gage
mu-nic-i-pal
mus-cle
mu-si-cian
mus-tache
mys-te-ri-ous

N

na-ive
nat-u-ral-ly
nec-es-sary
ne-ces-si-ty
neg-li-gi-ble
ne-go-ti-ate
neigh-bor-hood
nev-er-the-less
nick-el
niece
nine-teenth
nine-ty
no-tice-able
no-to-ri-ety
nu-cle-ar
nui-sance

O

o-be-di-ence
o-bey
o-blige
ob-sta-cle
oc-ca-sion
oc-ca-sion-al-ly
oc-cu-pant
oc-cur
oc-curred
oc-cur-rence
of-fense
of-fi-cial
of-ten
o-mis-sion
o-mit-ted
o-pin-ion
op-er-ate
op-po-nent
op-por-tu-ni-ty
op-po-site
op-ti-mism
or-di-nance
or-di-nar-i-ly
orig-i-nal
out-ra-geous

P

pag-eant
paid
pam-phlet
par-a-dise
para-graph
par-al-lel
par-a-lyze
pa-ren-the-ses
pa-ren-the-sis
par-lia-ment
par-tial
par-tic-i-pant
par-tic-i-pate
par-tic-u-lar-ly
pas-time
pa-tience
pa-tron-age
pe-cu-liar
per-ceive
per-haps
per-il
per-ma-nent
per-mis-si-ble
per-pen-dic-u-
    lar
per-se-ver-ance
per-sis-tent
per-son-al (-ly)
per-son-nel
per-spi-ra-tion
per-suade
phase
phe-nom-e-non
phi-los-o-phy
phy-si-cian
piece
planned
pla-teau
plau-si-ble
play-wright
pleas-ant
pleas-ure
pneu-mo-nia
pol-i-ti-cian
pos-sess
pos-ses-sion
pos-si-ble
prac-ti-cal-ly
prai-rie
pre-cede
pre-ce-dence
pre-ced-ing

pre-cious
pre-cise-ly
pre-ci-sion
pre-de-ces-sor
pref-er-a-ble
pref-er-ence
pre-ferred
prej-u-dice
pre-lim-i-nar-y
pre-mi-um
prep-a-ra-tion
pres-ence
prev-a-lent
pre-vi-ous
prim-i-tive
prin-ci-pal
prin-ci-ple
pri-or-i-ty
pris-on-er
priv-i-lege
prob-a-bly
pro-ce-dure
pro-ceed
pro-fes-sor
prom-i-nent
pro-nounce
pro-nun-ci-a-
    tion
pro-pa-gan-da
pros-e-cute
pro-tein
psy-chol-o-gy
pub-lic-ly
pump-kin
pur-chase
pur-sue
pur-su-ing
pur-suit

Q

qual-i-fied
qual-i-ty
quan-ti-ty
quar-ter
ques-tion-naire
qui-et
quite
quo-tient

690

R

raise
rap-port
re-al-ize
re-al-ly
re-cede
re-ceipt
re-ceive
re-ceived
rec-i-pe
re-cip-i-ent
rec-og-ni-tion
rec-og-nize
rec-om-mend
re-cur-rence
ref-er-ence
re-ferred
re-hearse
reign
re-im-burse
rel-e-vant
re-lieve
re-li-gious
re-mem-ber
re-mem-brance
rem-i-nisce
ren-dez-vous
re-new-al
rep-e-ti-tion
rep-re-sen-ta-tive
req-ui-si-tion
res-er-voir
re-sis-tance
re-spect-a-bly
re-spect-ful-ly
re-spec-tive-ly
re-spon-si-bil-i-ty
res-tau-rant
rheu-ma-tism
rhyme
rhythm
ri-dic-u-lous
route

S

sac-ri-le-gious
safe-ty
sal-a-ry
sand-wich

sat-is-fac-to-ry
Sat-ur-day
scarce-ly
scene
scen-er-y
sched-ule
sci-ence
scis-sors
sec-re-tary
seize
sen-si-ble
sen-tence
sen-ti-nel
sep-a-rate
ser-geant
sev-er-al
se-vere-ly
shep-herd
sher-iff
shin-ing
siege
sig-nif-i-cance
sim-i-lar
si-mul-ta-ne-ous
since
sin-cere-ly
ski-ing
sol-dier
sol-emn
so-phis-ti-cat-ed
soph-o-more
so-ror-i-ty
source
sou-ve-nir
spa-ghet-ti
spe-cif-ic
spec-i-men
speech
sphere
spon-sor
spon-ta-ne-ous
sta-tion-ary
sta-tion-ery
sta-tis-tic
stat-ue
stat-ure
stat-ute
stom-ach
stopped
straight
strat-e-gy

strength
stretched
study-ing
sub-si-dize
sub-stan-tial
sub-sti-tute
sub-tle
suc-ceed
suc-cess
suf-fi-cient
sum-ma-rize
su-per-fi-cial
su-per-in-tend-ent
su-pe-ri-or-i-ty
su-per-sede
sup-ple-ment
sup-pose
sure-ly
sur-prise
sur-veil-lance
sur-vey
sus-cep-ti-ble
sus-pi-cious
sus-te-nance
syl-la-ble
sym-met-ri-cal
sym-pa-thy
sym-pho-ny
symp-tom
syn-chro-nous

T

tar-iff
tech-nique
tele-gram
tem-per-a-ment
tem-per-a-ture
tem-po-rary
ten-den-cy
ten-ta-tive
ter-res-tri-al
ter-ri-ble
ter-ri-to-ry
the-ater
their
there-fore
thief
thor-ough (-ly)
though
through-out

tired
to-bac-co
to-geth-er
to-mor-row
tongue
to-night
touch
tour-na-ment
tour-ni-quet
to-ward
trag-e-dy
trai-tor
tran-quil-iz-er
trans-ferred
trea-sur-er
tried
tru-ly
Tues-day
tu-i-tion
typ-i-cal
typ-ing

U

unan-i-mous
un-con-scious
un-doubt-ed-ly
un-for-tu-nate-ly
unique
u-ni-son
uni-ver-si-ty
un-nec-es-sary
un-prec-e-dent-ed
un-til
up-per
ur-gent
us-able
use-ful
using
usu-al-ly
u-ten-sil
u-til-ize

V

va-can-cies
va-ca-tion
vac-u-um
vague
valu-able
va-ri-ety

var-i-ous
veg-e-ta-ble
ve-hi-cle
veil
ve-loc-i-ty
ven-geance
vi-cin-i-ty
view
vig-i-lance
vil-lain
vi-o-lence
vis-i-bil-i-ty
vis-i-ble
vis-i-tor
voice
vol-ume
vol-un-tary
vol-un-teer

W

wan-der
war-rant
weath-er
Wednes-day
weird
wel-come
wel-fare
where
wheth-er
which
whole
whol-ly
whose
width
wom-en
worth-while
wor-thy
wreck-age
wres-tler
writ-ing
writ-ten
wrought

Y

yel-low
yes-ter-day
yield

Steps to Becoming a
Better Speller

1 **Be patient.** Learning to become a good speller takes time.

2 **Check the correct pronunciation of each word** you are attempting to spell. Knowing the correct pronunciation of each word is important to remembering its spelling.

3 **Note the meaning and history of each word** as you are checking the dictionary for pronunciation. Knowing the meaning and history of a word can provide you with a better notion of how and when the word will probably be used. This fuller understanding will help you remember the spelling of that particular word.

4 **Before you close the dictionary, practice spelling** the word. You can do this by looking away from the page and trying to "see" the word in your "mind's eye." Write the word on a piece of paper. Check the spelling in the dictionary and repeat the process until you are able to spell the word correctly.

5 **Learn some spelling rules.** The four rules in this handbook (685) are four of the most useful, although there are others.

6 **Make a list of the words that you misspell.** Select the first 10 and practice spelling them.

STEP A: Read each word carefully; then write it on a piece of paper. Look at the written word to see that it's spelled correctly. Repeat the process for those words that you misspelled.

STEP B: When you have finished your first 10 words, ask someone to read the words to you so you can write them again. Again, check for misspellings. If you find none, congratulations! Repeat both steps with your next 10 words.

7 **Write often.** As noted educator Frank Smith said,
"There is little point in learning to spell if you have little intention of writing." ←

"The difference between the right word and the nearly right word is the same as that between lightning and the lightning bug."

—Mark Twain

Using the Right Word

692 **a, an** ● *A* is used before words that begin with a consonant sound; *an* is used before words that begin with a vowel sound.

a heap   a uniform   an idol
an urban area   an honor   a historian

accept, except ● The verb *accept* means "to receive or believe"; the preposition *except* means "other than."

The foreman accepted the man's story about being late, but she asked why no one except him forgot to reset his clock for daylight savings time.

adapt, adopt ● *Adapt* means "to adjust or change to fit"; *adopt* means "to choose and treat as your own" (a child, an idea).

After much careful study, we adopted Peachtree's accounting system. We then adapted our computer software to work with the new program.

advice, advise ● *Advice* is a noun meaning "information or recommendation"; *advise* is a verb meaning "to recommend."

Successful people will give you great advice, so I advise you to listen.

affect, effect ● *Affect* means "to influence"; the noun *effect* means "the result."

The employment growth in a field will affect your chances of getting a job. The effect may be a new career choice.

aid, aide ● As a verb, *aid* means "to help"; as a noun, *aid* means "the help given." *Aide* is a person who acts as an assistant.

allusion, illusion ● *Allusion* is an indirect reference to something; *illusion* is a false picture or idea.

The person who makes many allusions to his abilities is usually trying to reinforce the illusion that he's exceptionally talented.

*"A lot" should be written as two words, not one.
Luckily, Buzz saw through the problem.*

693   **alot** ● *Alot* should not be one word; *a lot* (two words) is a vague descriptive phrase that should probably not be used too often, especially in formal writing.

already, all ready ● *Already* is an adverb meaning "before this time" or "by this time." *All ready* is an adjective meaning "fully prepared."

> My younger sister found a job already. She is all ready to start tomorrow.

alright ● *Alright* is the incorrect form of *all right*. (Please note, the following are spelled correctly: *always, altogether, already, almost*.)

altogether, all together ● *Altogether* means "entirely." The phrase *all together* means "in a group" or "all at once."

> All together there are 35,000 job titles to choose from. That's altogether too many to even think about.

among, between ● *Among* is used when speaking of more than two persons or things. *Between* is used when speaking of only two.

> Child-care programs are among the most important workplace benefits. They will soon be a bargaining issue between employers and workers.

amount, number ● *Amount* is used for bulk measurement. *Number* is used to count separate units. (See also **fewer, less**.)

> The number of new teachers hired next year will depend upon the amount of revenue raised by the new sales tax.

annual, biannual, semiannual, biennial, perennial ● An *annual* event happens once every year. A *biannual* event happens twice a year (*semiannual* is the same as *biannual*). A *biennial* event happens every two years. A *perennial* event is active throughout the year and continues to happen every year.

anyways ● *Anyways* is the incorrect form of *anyway*. (Also watch out for *nowheres*.)

694 **base, bass** ● *Base* is the foundation or the lower part of something. *Bass* is a deep sound or tone. *Bass* (when pronounced like *class*) is a fish.

beside, besides ● *Beside* means "by the side of." *Besides* means "in addition to."

> Other women besides Sandra Day O'Connor and Ruth Bader Ginsberg will someday sit beside the men on the United States Supreme Court.

blew, blue ● *Blew* is the verb. *Blue* is the color.

board, bored ● *Board* is a piece of wood. *Board* is also an administrative group or council.

> The school board approved the purchase of fifty 1- by 6-inch pine boards.

Bored may mean "to make a hole by drilling" or "to become weary out of dullness."

> Watching television bored Joe, so he took his drill and bored a hole in the wall where he could hang his new clock.

brake, break ● *Brake* is a device used to stop a vehicle. *Break* means "to separate or to destroy."

> I hope the brakes on my car never break.

bring, take ● *Bring* suggests the action is directed toward the speaker; *take* suggests the action is directed away from the speaker.

> Mom says that she brings home the bacon, so I have to take out the garbage.

by, bye, buy ● *By* is a preposition or an adverb. *Bye-bye* means "farewell." *Buy* means "to purchase."

> The following message was posted in front of a small corner store: "Smart people buy; the others walk by!"

can, may ● *Can* suggests ability while *may* suggests permission.

> "Can I go to the library?" literally means "Am I physically able to go to the library?" "May I go to the library?" asks permission to go.

capital, capitol ● The noun *capital* refers to a city or to money. The adjective *capital* means "major or important." *Capitol* refers to a building.

> The capitol building is in the capital city for a capital reason. The city government contributed capital for the building expense.

cent, sent, scent ● *Cent* is a coin; *sent* is the past tense of the verb "send"; *scent* is an odor or a smell.

> For 32 cents, I sent my girlfriend a mushy love poem in a perfumed envelope. She adored the scent but hated the poem.

chord, cord ● *Chord* may mean "an emotion or feeling," but it also may mean "the combination of two or more tones sounded at the same time," as with a guitar chord. A *cord* is a string or rope.

chose, choose ● *Chose* (choz) is the past tense of the verb *choose* (chooz).

> For generations, people chose their careers based on their parents' careers; in the future, people will choose their careers based on the job market.

695 **coarse, course** ● *Coarse* means "rough or crude"; *course* means "a direction or path taken." *Course* also means "a class or series of studies."

> The instructor who taught the course "Workplace Etiquette" said that all coarse workers should sign up for extra credit.

compare with, compare to ● Things of the same class are *compared with* each other; things of different classes are *compared to* each other.

complement, compliment ● *Complement* means "to complete or go well with." *Compliment* is an expression of admiration or praise.

> Employees should be complimented for work that complements the company's goals.

continual, continuous ● *Continual* refers to something that happens again and again; *continuous* refers to something that doesn't stop happening.

> Sunlight hits Peoria, Iowa, on a continual basis; but sunlight hits the earth continuously.

counsel, council ● When used as a noun, *counsel* means "advice"; when used as a verb, *counsel* means "to advise." *Council* refers to a group that advises.

> The city council was asked to counsel our student council on running an efficient meeting. Their counsel was very helpful.

dear, deer ● *Dear* means "loved or valued"; *deer* are animals. (Please note, people will think you're strange if you write that you kissed your *deer* in the moonlight.)

desert, dessert ● *Desert* is barren wilderness. *Dessert* is food served at the end of a meal. The verb *desert* means "to abandon."

die, dye ● *Die* (dying) means "to stop living." *Dye* (dyeing) is used to change the color of something.

different from, different than ● Use *different from* in formal writing; use either form in informal or colloquial settings.

faint, feint ● *Faint* means "without strength" or "to lose consciousness"; *feint* is a noun that means "a move or activity that is pretended or false."

farther, further ● *Farther* refers to a physical distance; *further* refers to additional time, quantity, or degree.

> Further research showed that walking farther would improve his health.

fewer, less ● *Fewer* refers to the number of separate units; *less* refers to bulk quantity.

> Because of spell checkers, workers can produce reports containing fewer errors in less time.

fiscal, physical ● *Fiscal* means "related to financial matters"; *physical* means "related to material things."

> The company's fiscal work is handled by its accounting staff. The physical work is handled by its maintenance staff.

for, fore, four ● *For* is a preposition meaning "because of" or "directed to"; *fore* means "earlier" or "the front"; *four* is the number 4.

696 **good, well** ● *Good* is an adjective; *well* is nearly always an adverb. (When used to indicate state of health, *well* is an adjective.)

> A good job offers opportunities for advancement, especially for those who do their jobs well.

heal, heel ● *Heal* means "to mend or restore to health." A *heel* is the back part of a human foot.

> Achilles was a young Greek soldier who died because a poison arrow pierced his heel and the wound would not heal.

healthful, healthy ● *Healthful* means "causing or improving health"; *healthy* means "possessing health."

> Healthful foods and regular exercise build healthy bodies.

hear, here ● You *hear* with your ears. *Here* means "the area close by."

heard, herd ● *Heard* is the past tense of the verb "hear"; *herd* is a large group of animals.

> Have you ever heard a herd of buffalo stampeding?

hole, whole ● A *hole* is a cavity or hollow place. *Whole* means "complete or entire."

immigrate, emigrate ● *Immigrate* means "to come into a new country or environment." *Emigrate* means "to go out of one country to live in another."

> Immigrating to a new country is a challenging experience.
> People emigrating from their homelands need to consider this.

imply, infer ● *Imply* means "to suggest or express indirectly"; *infer* means "to draw a conclusion from facts." (A writer or speaker *implies;* a reader or listener *infers.*)

> My boss implied I should drive more carefully, and I inferred he was concerned for both me and the company van.

interstate, intrastate ● *Interstate* means "existing between two or more states"; *intrastate* means "existing within a state."

it's, its ● *It's* is the contraction of "it is." *Its* is the possessive form of "it."

> It's important to know a company's policies. For instance, this company requires reading, writing, and math competency tests for its job applicants.

knew, new ● *Knew* is the past tense of the verb "know." *New* means "recent or novel."

> You probably already knew that nearly 25 percent of new job applicants are turned away for exhibiting poor verbal skills.

know, no ● *Know* means "to understand or to realize." *No* means "the opposite of yes."

> Did you know that job applicants with little or no experience have only one chance in ten of getting the job?

later, latter ● *Later* means "after a period of time." *Latter* refers to the second of two things mentioned.

697 **lay, lie** ● *Lay* means "to place." *Lay* is a transitive verb. (See 731.)

> If you lay another book on my table, I won't have room for anything else. Yesterday, you laid two books on the table. Over the last few days, you must have laid at least 20 books there.

Lie means "to recline." *Lie* is an intransitive verb. (See 734.)

> The fat cat lies down anywhere.
> It lay down yesterday on my homework.
> It has lain down many times on the kitchen table.

lead, led ● *Lead* is the present tense of the verb meaning "to guide." The past tense of the verb is *led*. When the words are pronounced the same, *lead* is the metal.

lean, lien ● The verb *lean* means "to incline or bend." The adjective *lean* means "having little or no fat." A *lien* is "a legal charge or hold on property."

learn, teach ● *Learn* means "to acquire information"; *teach* means "to give information."

> Sometimes it's easier to teach someone else a lesson than it is to learn one yourself.

leave, let ● *Leave* means "to allow something to remain behind." *Let* means "to permit."

> If you let people work at their own pace, you may leave the door open for missed deadlines.

lend, borrow ● *Lend* means "to give for temporary use"; *borrow* means "to receive for temporary use."

> I told Mom I needed to borrow $15 for a CD, but she said her lending service was for school supplies only.

liable, likely ● *Liable* means "responsible according to the law" or "exposed to an adverse action"; *likely* means "in all probability."

> The "flat tire on the freeway in rush-hour traffic" seems a likely story; but I still think you're liable to be in deep trouble for missing your final exam.

like, as ● *Like* is a preposition meaning "similar to"; *as* is a conjunction with several meanings. *Like* usually introduces a phrase; *as* usually introduces a clause.

> Like the other people in my group, I do my work as any professional would—carefully and thoroughly.

loose, lose, loss ● *Loose* (loos) means "free, untied, unrestricted"; *lose* (looz) means "to misplace or fail to find or control"; *loss* (los) means "something that is misplaced and cannot be found."

mail, male ● *Mail* refers to letters or packages handled by the postal service (also voice mail and E-mail). *Male* refers to the masculine sex.

meat, meet ● *Meat* is food or flesh; *meet* means "to come upon."

medal, metal ● *Medal* is an award. *Metal* is an element like iron or gold.

> Are the Olympic gold medals made out of solid gold metal?

*The use of minors as miners
is no minor problem.*

698   **miner, minor** ● A *miner* digs in the ground for ore. A *minor* is a person who is not legally an adult. A *minor* problem is one of no great importance.

> The use of minors as miners is no minor problem.

past, passed ● *Passed* is a verb. *Past* can be used as a noun, as an adjective, or as a preposition.

> That Escort passed my 'Vette. **(verb)**
> Many senior citizens hold dearly to the past. **(noun)**
> I'm sorry, but my past life is not your business. **(adjective)**
> Old Rosebud walked past us and never smelled the apples. **(preposition)**

peace, piece ● *Peace* means "tranquility or freedom from war." *Piece* is a part or fragment.

> Someone once observed that peace is not a condition, but a process—a process of building goodwill one piece, or one step, at a time.

people, persons ● Use *people* to refer to population, races, large groups; use *persons* to refer to individuals or human beings.

> What the American people need is a good insect repellent. The forest ranger recommends that we check our persons for wood ticks when we leave the woods.

personal, personnel ● *Personal* means "private." *Personnel* are people working at a particular job.

plain, plane ● *Plain* means "an area of land that is flat or level"; it also means "clearly seen or clearly understood."

> It's plain to see why the early settlers had trouble getting to the Great Plains.

Plane means "flat, level, and even"; it is also a tool used to smooth the surface of wood.

> I used a plane to make the board plane and smooth.

pore, pour, poor ● A *pore* is an opening in the skin. *Pour* means "a constant flow or stream." *Poor* means "needy or pitiable."

> Tough exams on late spring days make my poor pores pour.

699 **principal, principle** ● As an adjective, *principal* means "primary." As a noun, it can mean "a school administrator" or "a sum of money." *Principle* means "idea or doctrine."

> His principal gripe is lack of freedom. **(adjective)**
> The principal expressed his concern about open campus. **(noun)**
> After 20 years, the amount of interest was higher than the principal. **(noun)**
> The principle of *caveat emptor* is "Let the buyer beware."

quiet, quit, quite ● *Quiet* is the opposite of noisy. *Quit* means "to stop." *Quite* means "completely or to a considerable extent."

> The library remained quite quiet until she quit watching us.

quote, quotation ● *Quote* is a verb; *quotation* is a noun.

> "The quotation I used was from Woody Allen. You may quote me on that."

real, very, really ● Do not use *real* in place of the adverbs *very* or *really*.

> My mother's cake is usually very (not real) moist. But this cake is really stale—I mean, it's just about fossilized.

right, write, wright, rite ● *Right* means "correct or proper"; it also refers to that which a person has a legal claim to, as in *copyright*. *Write* means "to inscribe or record." A *wright* is a person who makes or builds something. *Rite* is a ritual or ceremonial act.

> Did you write that it is the right of the shipwright to perform the rite of christening—breaking a bottle of champagne on the stern of the ship?

scene, seen ● *Scene* refers to the location where something happens; it also may mean "sight or spectacle." *Seen* is part of the verb "see."

> An exhibitionist likes to be seen making a scene.

seam, seem ● *Seam* is a line formed by connecting two pieces. *Seem* means "to appear to exist."

> The ragged seams in his old coat seem to match the creases in his face.

set, sit ● *Sit* means "to put the body in a seated position." *Set* means "to place." *Set* is transitive; *sit* is intransitive.

> "How can you just sit there and watch as I set all these chairs in place?"

"How can you just sit there and watch as I set all these chairs in place?"

700 **sight, cite, site** ● *Sight* means "the act of seeing" or "something that is seen." *Cite* means "to quote" or "to summon." *Site* means "location or position."

> The building inspector cited the electrical contractor for breaking two city codes at a downtown job site.
> It was not a pretty sight when the two men started arguing.

sole, soul ● *Sole* means "single, only one"; *sole* also refers to the bottom surface of the foot. *Soul* refers to the spiritual part of a person.

> To be successful, a sole proprietor needs to put her heart and soul into her business.

some, sum ● *Some* refers to an unknown thing, number, or part. *Sum* means "the whole amount."

> Some accountant told me to deduct our expenses from the sum total of our daily receipts.

stationary, stationery ● *Stationary* means "not movable"; *stationery* refers to the paper and envelopes used to write letters.

steal, steel ● *Steal* means "to take something without permission"; *steel* is a metal.

than, then ● *Than* is used in a comparison; *then* tells when.

> Humor is more important in the workplace than most people realize. Then again, so is hard work.

their, there, they're ● *Their* is the possessive personal pronoun. *There* is an adverb used to point out location. *They're* is the contraction for "they are."

> If there is a comfortable place for workers to relax during their breaks, they're more likely to do a good job.

threw, through ● *Threw* is the past tense of "throw." *Through* means "passing from one side of something to the other."

to, too, two ● *To* is a preposition that can mean "in the direction of." *To* also is used to form an infinitive. *Too* means "also" or "very." *Two* is the number 2.

> Two common causes of visual problems in the workplace are lights that fail to illuminate properly and computer screens that glare too much.

vain, vane, vein ● *Vain* means "valueless or fruitless"; it may also mean "holding a high regard for one's self." *Vane* is a flat piece of material set up to show which way the wind blows. *Vein* refers to a blood vessel or a mineral deposit.

> The weather vane indicates the direction of the wind; the blood vein determines the direction of flowing blood; the vain mind moves in no particular direction and is content to think only about itself.

vary, very ● *Vary* means "to change"; *very* means "to a high degree."

> To provide the very best working relations, the workloads should not vary greatly from worker to worker.

701 **waist, waste** ● *Waist* is the part of the body just above the hips. The verb *waste* means "to lose through inaction" or "to wear away, decay"; the noun *waste* refers to material that is unused or useless.

Her waist is small because she wastes no opportunity to exercise.

wait, weight ● *Wait* means "to stay somewhere expecting something." *Weight* refers to a degree or unit of heaviness.

ware, wear, where ● *Ware* refers to a product that is sold; *wear* means "to have on or to carry on one's body"; *where* asks the question "In what place?" or "In what situation?"

The designer boasted, "Anybody can wear my ware anywhere."

way, weigh ● *Way* means "path or route." *Weigh* means "to measure weight."

Since our dog weighs too much, we take him on walks all the way around the park.

weather, whether ● *Weather* refers to the condition of the atmosphere. *Whether* refers to a possibility.

Weather conditions affect nearly all of us, whether we are farmers, pilots, or plumbers.

who, which, that ● *Who* refers to people. *Which* refers to nonliving objects or to animals. (*Which* should never refer to people.) *That* may refer to animals, people, or nonliving objects.

who, whom ● *Who* is used as the subject of a verb; *whom* is used as the object of a preposition or as a direct object. (*Who* is used in place of *whom* for most everyday communication.)

who's, whose ● *Who's* is the contraction for "who is." *Whose* is the possessive pronoun.

"Whose car are we using, and who's going to cover our expenses?"

wood, would ● *Wood* is the stuff that trees are made of; *would* is part of the verb "will."

A carpenter who refinishes old wood would be well-advised to protect his or her eyes, nose, and mouth.

your, you're ● *Your* is a possessive pronoun. *You're* is the contraction for "you are."

If you're like most Americans, you'll hold eight jobs by your 40th birthday.

"If you scoff at language study . . . how will you scoff?"

—Mario Pei

Understanding Our Language

702 Parts of Speech

Parts of speech are the eight different ways words are used in our language—as *nouns, pronouns, verbs, adjectives, adverbs, prepositions, conjunctions,* or *interjections.*

703 Noun

A **noun** is a word that names something: a person, place, thing, or idea.

Nelson Mandela/president   Oregon/state   *The Lion King*/film
Richmond Memorial Hospital/hospital   Buddhism/religion

704 Classes of Nouns

The classes of nouns are *proper, common, concrete, abstract,* and *collective.*

A **proper noun** names a particular person, place, thing, or idea. Proper nouns are always capitalized.

Lee Iacocca   Marian Edelman **(people)** Tokyo   Wall Street **(places)**
Brooklyn Dodgers   World Series **(things)** Christianity   Judaism **(ideas)**

A **common noun** is any noun that does not name a particular person, place, thing, or idea. Common nouns are not capitalized.

electrician   woman   business   memo   government   city

A **concrete noun** names a thing that is tangible (can be seen, touched, heard, smelled, or tasted). Concrete nouns are either proper or common.

Grand Canyon   jeans   Pearl Jam   aroma   pizza

An **abstract noun** names an idea, a condition, or a feeling—in other words, something that cannot be touched, tasted, seen, or heard.

New Deal   greed   poverty   progress   freedom   hope

A **collective noun** names a group or unit.

United States   Chicago Bulls   team   crowd   community

705 Forms of Nouns

Nouns are grouped according to their *number, gender,* and *case.*

706 Number of a Noun

Number indicates whether a noun is singular or plural.

> A **singular noun** refers to one person, place, thing, or idea.
>
> employee   shop   Canadian   bully   truth   child

> A **plural noun** refers to more than one person, place, thing, or idea.
>
> employees   shops   Canadians   bullies   truths   children

707 Gender of a Noun

Gender indicates whether a noun is masculine, feminine, neuter, or indefinite.

> **Masculine:** uncle   brother   host   men   bull   rooster   stallion
>
> **Feminine:** mother   queen   hostess   women   cow   hen   filly
>
> **Neuter:** tree   cobweb   fishing rod   stapler (without sex)
>
> **Indefinite:** president   plumber   parent (masculine or feminine)

708 Case of a Noun

Case tells how nouns are related to other words used with them. There are three cases: *nominative, possessive,* and *objective.*

> **Nominative case** describes a noun used as the subject of a clause.
>
> In 1951, **Betty Nesmith Graham**, a Texas secretary, invented a liquid for painting out typing and printing errors.

A noun is also in the nominative case when it is used as a *predicate noun* (or predicate nominative). A predicate noun follows a form of the *be* verb *(is, are, was, were, been)* and repeats or renames the subject.

> Graham was also an **artist**, though her idea for a better eraser was born in her kitchen and not in her studio.

Possessive case describes a noun that shows possession or ownership.

> **Graham's** invention was eventually patented and marketed by the Liquid Paper Corporation.

Objective case describes a noun used as a direct object, an indirect object, or an object of the preposition.

> Correction fluid is great, but it can't promise **writers** perfect **papers**.
> (*Papers* is the direct object of *can promise; writers* is the indirect object.)

> For **perfection** in **correction**, you need a **computer**. (*Perfection* is the object of the preposition *for; correction* is the object of the preposition *in. Computer* is the direct object of *need.*)

Pronoun

709 A **pronoun** is a word used in place of a noun.

> I, you, she, it, which, that, themselves, whoever, me, he, they, whatever, my, mine, ours

710 All pronouns have **antecedents**. An antecedent is the noun that the pronoun refers to or replaces.

> The **judge** coughed and reached for the glass of water. The water touched *his* lips before *he* noticed the **fly** *that* lay bathing in the cool liquid. (*Judge* is the antecedent of *his* and *he*; *fly* is the antecedent of *that*.)

NOTE: Each pronoun must agree with its antecedent in number, person, and gender. (See 772-774.)

711 **Pronouns** are distinguished according to their *type, class, number, gender, person,* and *case*. There are three **types**.

> **Simple**   I, you, he, she, it, we, they, who, what
>
> **Compound** myself, yourself, himself, herself, ourselves, itself
>
> **Phrasal**   one another, each other

NOTE: There are five **classes** of pronouns: *personal, relative, indefinite, interrogative,* and *demonstrative.*

712 Forms of Personal Pronouns

The **form** of a personal pronoun indicates its number (singular or plural), its person (first, second, or third), its case (nominative, possessive, or objective), and its gender (masculine, feminine, or neuter).

713 Number of a Pronoun

The **number** of a pronoun can be either singular or plural. Singular personal pronouns include *I, you, he, she, it.* Plural personal pronouns include *we, you, they.* Notice that the pronoun *you* can be singular or plural.

> Are you (singular) going to eat that all by yourself?

> I will if you (plural) don't help me.

714 **Person of a Pronoun**

The **person** of a pronoun indicates whether that pronoun is speaking, is spoken to, or is spoken about.

First person is used in place of the name of the speaker.

"**I** am always right!"   —*Joe Bighead,* **founder and president of the National Organization of Bigheads**

"**We** won't listen to anyone else!"   —**motto of the three-member N.O.B.**

Second person is used to name the person or thing spoken to.

"Joe, **you** [singular] are wrong."—*Isabelle M. Right,* **N.O.B. vice president**

"Isabelle and Joe, **you** [plural] are both wrong."
—*Uriah R. Wrong, N.O.B.* **secretary/treasurer**

Third person is used to name the person or thing spoken about.

I. M. Right elected **herself** vice president because **she** knew that **she** was the smartest Bighead.

U. R. Wrong elected **himself** because **he** knew that **he** was the smartest.

Neither I. M. Right nor U. R. Wrong voted for Joe because **they** knew that **he** was always wrong.

715 **Case of a Pronoun**

The **case** of each pronoun tells how it is related to the other words used with it. There are three cases: *nominative, possessive,* and *objective.*

Nominative case describes a pronoun used as the *subject* of a clause. The following are nominative forms: *I, you, he, she, it, we, they.*

I like myself when things go well.
You must live life in order to love life.

A pronoun is also in the *nominative case* when it is used as a *predicate nominative.* A predicate nominative follows a form of the *be* verb (*am, is, are, was, were, been*), and it repeats the subject.

We have met the enemy, and they are **we**. Then who is **she**?

Possessive case describes a pronoun that shows possession or ownership. An apostrophe, however, is not used with a personal pronoun to show possession.

my   mine   our   ours   his   her   hers   their   theirs   its   your   yours

Objective case describes a pronoun used as the direct object, indirect object, or object of a preposition.

Mr. Clausen hired **me**. (*Me* **is the direct object of the verb** *hired*.)

He showed **me** the mailroom. (*Me* **is the indirect object of the verb** *showed*.)

He introduced me to two other clerks and said I'd be training with **them**. (*Them* **is the object of the preposition** *with*.)

716

Number, Person, and Case of Personal Pronouns

	Nominative Case	Possessive Case	Objective Case
First Person Singular	I	my, mine	me
Second Person Singular	you	your, yours	you
Third Person Singular	he	his	him
	she	her, hers	her
	it	its	it

	Nominative Case	Possessive Case	Objective Case
First Person Plural	we	our, ours	us
Second Person Plural	you	your, yours	you
Third Person Plural	they	their, theirs	them

717 ## Special Personal Pronouns

A **reflexive pronoun** is formed by adding -self or -selves to a personal pronoun. A reflexive pronoun can act as a direct object or an indirect object of the verb, the object of a preposition, or a predicate nominative.

> He loves **himself**. (direct object of *loves*)
>
> He gives **himself** pats on the back. (indirect object of *gives*)
>
> He smiles at **himself** in the mirror. (object of preposition *at*)
>
> He is truly **himself** only when he sleeps. (predicate nominative)

NOTE: A reflexive pronoun is called an **intensive pronoun** when it intensifies, or emphasizes, the noun or pronoun it refers to.

> Leo **himself** taught his children to invest their lives in others.
>
> The lesson was sometimes painful—but they learned it **themselves**.

718 ## Other Kinds of Pronouns

A **relative pronoun** relates one part of a sentence to a word in another part of the sentence. Specifically, a relative pronoun relates an adjective clause to the noun or pronoun it modifies. (The noun is underlined in each example below; the relative pronoun is in boldface.)

> The <u>man</u> **who** invented the game of Monopoly did so during the Great Depression when he was out of work.
>
> <u>Monopoly</u>, **which** he invented in the 1930's, became America's most popular game.

719 An **indefinite pronoun** refers to unnamed or unknown people or things.

> At first, **whoever** wanted a game of Monopoly would ask Darrow to make a game board and cards by hand. (**The antecedent of** *whoever* **is unknown.**)

720 An **interrogative pronoun** asks a question.

> **Who** would have thought Monopoly would become so popular? **What** is its appeal?

721 A **demonstrative pronoun** points out specific people, places, or things.

> **Those** little cards of make-believe real estate cheered up people who had lost their homes, farms, and businesses. Sixty years later, **that** board game has not lost its magic.

722

Classes of Pronouns

Personal

I, me, my, mine / we, us, our, ours
you, your, yours / they, them, their, theirs
he, him, his, she, her, hers, it, its
myself, himself, herself, itself, yourself, themselves, ourselves

Relative

who, whose, whom, which, what, that

Indefinite

all	both	everything	nobody	several
another	each	few	none	some
any	each one	many	no one	somebody
anybody	either	most	nothing	someone
anyone	everybody	much	one	something
anything	everyone	neither	other	such

Interrogative

who, whose, whom, which, what

Demonstrative

this, that, these, those

Verb
723 Forms of Verbs

A **verb** is a word that expresses action or state of being. A verb has different forms depending on its number (singular, plural); person (first, second, third); voice (active, passive); tense (present, past, future, present perfect, past perfect, future perfect); and mood (indicative, imperative, subjunctive).

724 Number of a Verb

Number indicates whether a verb is singular or plural. The verb and its subject both must be singular, or they both must be plural.

> One large **island floats** off Italy's "toe." (singular)

> Five small **islands float** inside Michigan's "thumb." (plural)

725 Person of a Verb

Person indicates whether the subject of the verb is **first**, **second**, or **third person** and whether the subject is **singular** or **plural**. Verbs usually have a different form only in third person singular of the present tense.

	Singular	Plural
First Person	I think	we think
Second Person	you think	you think
Third Person	he/she/it thinks	they think

726 Voice of a Verb

Voice indicates whether the subject is acting or being acted upon.

Active voice indicates that the subject of the verb is acting—doing something.

> As Verne **sat** helplessly by, Clyde **rolled** the winning total.

Passive voice indicates that the subject of the verb is being acted upon. A passive verb is a combination of a *be* verb and a past participle.

> The winning total **was rolled** by Clyde as Verne sat helplessly by.

727 **Tense of a Verb**

Tense indicates time. Each verb has three principal parts: the *present, past,* and *past participle.* All six of the tenses are formed from these principal parts. The past and past participle of regular verbs are formed by adding *ed* to the present form. The past and past participle of irregular verbs are usually different words. (See 736 for examples.)

Present tense expresses action that is happening at the present time, or action that happens continually, regularly.

Today, over 75 percent of all U.S. workers **work** in service industries.

Past tense expresses action that was completed at a time in the past.

A hundred years ago, more than 75 percent **worked** in agriculture.

Future tense expresses action that will take place in the future.

By the year 2000, service jobs **will make up** 80 percent of all jobs.

Present perfect tense expresses action that began in the past but continues in the present or is completed at the present.

Our economy **has seen** great changes over the years.

Past perfect tense expresses action that began in the past and was completed in the past.

We **had expected** our lives to be different from our parents'.

Future perfect tense expresses action that will begin in the future and be completed by a specific time in the future.

During our lifetimes, we **will have seen** more changes than any other generation in history.

728

| Tense | Active Voice | | Passive Voice | |
	Singular	Plural	Singular	Plural
PRESENT	I see	we see	I am seen	we are seen
	you see	you see	you are seen	you are seen
	he/she/it sees	they see	he/she/it is seen	they are seen
PAST	I saw	we saw	I was seen	we were seen
	you saw	you saw	you were seen	you were seen
	he saw	they saw	he was seen	they were seen
FUTURE	I will see	we will see	I will be seen	we will be seen
	you will see	you will see	you will be seen	you will be seen
	he will see	they will see	he will be seen	they will be seen
PRESENT PERFECT	I have seen	we have seen	I have been seen	we have been seen
	you have seen	you have seen	you have been seen	you have been seen
	he has seen	they have seen	he has been seen	they have been seen
PAST PERFECT	I had seen	we had seen	I had been seen	we had been seen
	you had seen	you had seen	you had been seen	you had been seen
	he had seen	they had seen	he had been seen	they had been seen
FUTURE PERFECT	I will have seen	we will have seen	I will have been seen	we will have been seen
	you will have seen	you will have seen	you will have been seen	you will have been seen
	he will have seen	they will have seen	he will have been seen	they will have been seen

729 ## Mood of a Verb

The **mood** of the verb indicates the tone or attitude with which a statement is made.

> **Indicative mood** is used to state a fact or to ask a question.
>
> > Can any theme capture the essence of the complex 1960's U.S. culture? President John F. Kennedy's directives (stated below) represent one ideal popular during that decade.

> **Imperative mood** is used to give a command.
>
> > "Ask not what your country can do for you. Ask what you can do for your country."

> **Subjunctive mood** is no longer commonly used; however, it continues to be used by careful writers to express the exact manner in which their statements are meant.

> **1** Use the subjunctive *were* to express a condition that is contrary to fact.
>
> > If each of your brain cells **were** one person, there would be enough people to populate 25 planets.

> **2** Use the subjunctive *were* after *as though* or *as if* to express doubt or uncertainty in the past.
>
> > Experts have sometimes talked as though the human brain **were** nothing more than a complex computer.

> **3** Use the subjunctive *be* in "that clauses" to express necessity, parliamentary motions, or legal decisions.
>
> > I propose that the following truth **be embraced**: "grayware" (brain power) is more powerful than software (computer power).

Classes of Verbs

730 ## Auxiliary Verbs

Auxiliary verbs, or helping verbs, help to form some of the **tenses** (727), the **mood** (729), and the **voice** (726) of the main verb. In the following examples, the auxiliary verbs are in boldface, and the main verbs are in italics.

> I *believe,* I **have** always *believed,* and I **will** always *believe* in private enterprise as the backbone of economic well-being in America.
> —Franklin D. Roosevelt

Common Auxiliary Verbs								
is	are	was	were	am	been	shall	will	would
did	must	can	may	have	had	has	do	should

731 **Transitive Verbs**

A **transitive** verb communicates action and is always followed by an object that receives the action and completes the meaning of the verb.

> Communicating in business often **requires** public-speaking *skills*.

Active voice • A transitive verb in the active voice directs the action from the subject to the object.

> Many adults **fear** public *speaking* more than they **fear** *snakes* or the *IRS*.

Passive voice • If a transitive verb is in the passive voice, the subject of the sentence receives the action. (In the example below, the subject *speaking* receives the action of the verb *is feared*.)

> Public speaking **is feared** by many people.

732 A **direct object** receives the action of a transitive verb directly from the subject.

> A good speaker radiates **energy**. (*Energy* is the direct object.)

733 An **indirect object** receives the action of a transitive verb, but indirectly. An indirect object names the person (*or thing*) to whom (*or to what*) or for whom (*or for what*) something is done.

> Dynamic speakers give their **audiences** wit and wisdom along with information. (*Audiences* is the indirect object.)

NOTE: When the word naming the indirect receiver of the action is contained in a prepositional phrase, it is no longer considered an indirect object.

> Our boss gave words of encouragement to **us**. (*Us* is the object of the preposition *to*.)

734 **Intransitive Verbs**

An **intransitive verb** refers to an action that is complete in itself. It does not need an object to receive the action.

> The best public speakers **energize** and **motivate**.

NOTE: Some verbs can be either *transitive* or *intransitive*.

> Her voice **projects** *authority* and *confidence*. (transitive)
> Her voice **projects** well. (intransitive)

735 A **linking verb** is a special type of intransitive verb that links the subject to a noun or an adjective in the predicate.

> A poor *speaker* **is** a *cure* for insomnia.

Common Linking Verbs

is	are	was	were	be	been	am	smell	look
seem	grow	become	appear	sound	taste	feel	remain	stand

Common Irregular Verbs and Their Principal Parts

Present Tense	Past Tense	Past Participle	Present Tense	Past Tense	Past Participle	Present Tense	Past Tense	Past Participle
am, be	was, were	been	freeze	froze	frozen	show	showed	shown
begin	began	begun	give	gave	given	shrink	shrank	shrunk
bite	bit	bitten	go	went	gone	sing	sang	sung
blow	blew	blown	grow	grew	grown	sink	sank, sunk	sunk
break	broke	broken	hang (execute)	hanged	hanged	sit	sat	sat
bring	brought	brought	hang (suspend)	hung	hung	speak	spoke	spoken
burst	burst	burst	hide	hid	hidden	spring	sprang, sprung	sprung
catch	caught	caught	know	knew	known			
choose	chose	chosen	lay	laid	laid	steal	stole	stolen
come	came	come	lead	led	led	strive	strove	striven
dive	dived	dived	lie (recline)	lay	lain	swear	swore	sworn
do	did	done	lie (deceive)	lied	lied	swim	swam	swum
drag	dragged	dragged	raise	raised	raised	swing	swung	swung
draw	drew	drawn	ride	rode	ridden	take	took	taken
drink	drank	drunk	ring	rang	rung	tear	tore	torn
drive	drove	driven	rise	rose	risen	throw	threw	thrown
eat	ate	eaten	run	ran	run	wake	woke, waked	waked
fall	fell	fallen	see	saw	seen	wear	wore	worn
fight	fought	fought	set	set	set	weave	wove	woven
flee	fled	fled	shake	shook	shaken	wring	wrung	wrung
flow	flowed	flowed	shine (light)	shone	shone	write	wrote	written
fly	flew	flown	shine (polish)	shined	shined			

737 Special Verb Forms

A **verbal** is a word that is derived from a verb, has the power of a verb, but acts as another part of speech. Like a verb, a verbal may take an object, a modifier (adjective, adverb), and sometimes a subject; but unlike a verb, a verbal functions as a noun, an adjective, or an adverb. Three types of verbals are *gerunds, infinitives,* and *participles.*

A **gerund** is a verb form that ends in *ing* and is used as a noun.

> **Getting up** each morning is the first challenge. **(subject)**
>
> I start **moving** at about seven o'clock. **(direct object)**
>
> I work at **jump-starting** my weary system. **(object of the preposition)**
>
> "Eighty percent of life is **showing up**." **(predicate noun)**

An **infinitive** is a verb form that is usually introduced by *to*; the infinitive may be used as a noun, as an adjective, or as an adverb.

> **To succeed** is not easy. **(noun subject)**
>
> That is the most important rule **to learn**. **(adjective)**
>
> Employees are wise **to work** hard. **(adverb)**

A **participle** is a verb form usually ending in *ing* or *ed*. A participle functions as a verb because it can take an object; a participle functions as an adjective because it can modify a noun or pronoun.

> The worker **stamping** orders is **tired**. The stack of **stamped** papers grows taller by the minute. (*Stamping* functions as an adjective because it modifies *worker*. It also acts as a verb with an object, *orders*. Both *tired* and *stamped* act as adjectives, modifying *worker* and *papers*.)

Adjective

738 An **adjective** describes or modifies a noun or pronoun. Articles *a, an,* and *the* are adjectives.

> Advertising is **a big** and **powerful** industry.
> (**A**, *big*, and *powerful* modify *industry*.)

Adjectives can be common or proper. **Proper adjectives** are created from proper nouns and are capitalized.

> **English** (proper noun) has been greatly influenced by advertising slogans.

> The **English** (proper adjective) language has been greatly influenced by advertising slogans.

NOTE: Some words can be either adjectives or pronouns *(that, these, many, some,* etc.). These words are adjectives if they come before a noun and modify that noun; they are pronouns if they stand alone.

> **Some** advertisements are less than truthful. (**Some** modifies *advertisements*; it is an adjective.)

> **Many** cause us to chuckle at their outrageous claims. (**Many** stands alone; it is a pronoun.)

739 A **predicate adjective** follows a form of the *be* verb (or other linking verb) and describes the subject.

> At its best, advertising is **useful**; at its worst, **deceptive**.
> (*Useful* and *deceptive* modify *advertising*.)

740 ## The Forms of Adjectives

Adjectives have three forms: *positive, comparative,* and *superlative*.

> The **positive form** describes a noun or pronoun without comparing it to anyone or anything else.
>
> > Roach-Busters is **strong** and **effective**.

> The **comparative form** (*-er* or *more*) compares two persons, places, things, or ideas.
>
> > The secret ingredient in Bug-Off is **stronger** and **more effective** than anything you'll find in Roach-Busters.

> The **superlative form** (*-est* or *most*) compares three or more persons, places, things, or ideas.
>
> > But Fatal Attraction is the **strongest, most effective** roach killer of all!

Adverb

741 An **adverb** modifies a verb, an adjective, or another adverb. An adverb tells *how, when, where, why, how often,* or *how much.*

> Sales fell **sharply**. (*Sharply* modifies the verb *fell*.)
>
> Sales were **quite** low. (*Quite* modifies the adjective *low*.)
>
> Sales dropped **very** quickly. (*Very* modifies the adverb *quickly*.)

Adverbs can be grouped in four ways: *time, place, manner,* and *degree.*

Time (These adverbs tell *when, how often,* and *how long.*)

> today, yesterday   daily, weekly   briefly, eternally

Place (These adverbs tell *where, to where,* and *from where.*)

> here, there   nearby, yonder   backward, forward

Manner (These adverbs often end in *ly* and tell *how* something is done.)

> precisely   regularly   regally   smoothly   well

Degree (These adverbs tell *how much* or *how little.*)

> substantially   greatly   entirely   partly   too

NOTE: Some adverbs can be written with or without the *ly* ending. When in doubt, use the *ly* form.

> slow, slowly   loud, loudly   fair, fairly   tight, tightly   quick, quickly

742 **The Forms of Adverbs**

Adverbs have three forms: *positive, comparative,* and *superlative.*

The **positive form** describes a verb, an adjective, or another adverb without comparing it to anyone or anything else.

> Roach-Busters works **fast**. Roach-Busters works **effectively**.

The **comparative form** (*-er* or *more*) compares two persons, places, things, or ideas.

> Bug-Off works **faster** than Roach-Busters.
>
> Bug-Off works **more effectively** than Roach-Busters.

The **superlative form** (*-est* or *most*) compares three or more persons, places, things, or ideas.

> Fatal Attraction works **fastest** of all.
>
> Fatal Attraction works **most effectively** of all!

Positive	Comparative	Superlative
well	better	best
badly	worse	worst
fast	faster	fastest
effectively	more effectively	most effectively

Preposition

743 A **preposition** is a word (or group of words) that introduces a phrase, which in turn modifies some other word in the sentence. The first noun or pronoun following the preposition is its object.

> Have you heard the one **about the boss** who hated procrastination? He put up a sign that said, "Do It Now." **Within 24 hours** his sales force quit, and his secretary went **on vacation**. (In these sentences, *boss, hours,* and *vacation* are objects of their preceding prepositions *about, within,* and *on.*)

NOTE: There are three kinds of prepositions: *simple* (at, in, of, on, with), *compound* (within, outside, underneath), and *phrasal* (on account of, on top of).

A **prepositional phrase** includes the preposition, the object of the preposition, and the modifiers of the object. A prepositional phrase may function as an adverb or as an adjective.

> Humor **on the job** can help create a positive and healthy atmosphere. (The phrase *on the job* functions as an adjective modifying the noun *humor.*)
>
> Lighthearted but hardworking employees are valued **in most places**. (The phrase functions as an adverb modifying the verb *are valued.*)

744

LIST OF PREPOSITIONS

aboard	because of	excepting	notwithstanding	round about
about	before	for	of	save
above	behind	from	off	since
according to	below	from among	on	subsequent to
across	beneath	from between	on account of	together with
across from	beside	from under	on behalf of	through
after	besides	in	onto	throughout
against	between	in addition to	on top of	till
along	beyond	in behalf of	opposite	to
alongside	but	in front of	out	toward
alongside of	by	in place of	out of	under
along with	by means of	in regard to	outside	underneath
amid	concerning	inside	outside of	until
among	considering	inside of	over	unto
apart from	despite	in spite of	over to	up
around	down	instead of	owing to	up to
aside from	down from	into	past	upon
at	during	like	prior to	with
away from	except	near	regarding	within
back of	except for	near to	round	without

Conjunction

745 A **conjunction** connects individual words or groups of words.

> When we came back to Paris, it was clear **and** cold **and** lovely.
> (The conjunction *and* connects equal adjectives.)
> —Ernest Hemingway

Coordinating conjunctions connect a word to a word, a phrase to a phrase, or a clause to a clause. The words, phrases, or clauses joined by a coordinating conjunction must be *equal* or of the *same type*.

> Civilization is a race between education **and** catastrophe.
> (The conjunction *and* joins the two objects of the preposition *between*.)
> —H. G. Wells

Correlative conjunctions are conjunctions used in pairs (*either, or; neither, nor; not only, but also; both, and; whether, or; just, as; just, so*).

> There are two ways to keep from thinking: **either** believe everything **or** doubt everything.

Subordinating conjunctions are words that connect, and show the relationship between, two clauses that are *not* equally important. A subordinating conjunction connects a dependent clause to an independent clause in order to complete the meaning of the dependent clause.

> Experience is the worst teacher; it gives the test **before** it presents the lesson. (The clause *before it presents the lesson* is dependent. It depends on the rest of the sentence to complete its meaning.)

Kinds of Conjunctions

Coordinating: and, but, or, nor, for, yet, so

Correlative: either, or; neither, nor; not only, but also; both, and; whether, or; just, as; just, so; as, so

Subordinating: after, although, as, as if, as long as, as though, because, before, if, in order that, provided that, since, so, so that, that, though, till, unless, until, when, where, whereas, while

---

NOTE: Relative pronouns (718) and conjunctive adverbs (596) can also connect clauses.

Interjection

746 An **interjection** is included in a sentence in order to communicate strong emotion or surprise. Punctuation (often a comma or an exclamation point) is used to set an interjection off from the rest of the sentence.

> **Help! Ouch! I'm stuck! Well, I guess no one hears me.**

Parts of Speech

747 **Quick Guide**

1. A **noun** is a word that names something: a person, a place, a thing, or an idea.

   Nelson Mandela/president   Oregon/state
   The Lion King/film   Buddhism/religion
   Richmond Memorial Hospital/building

2. A **pronoun** is a word used in place of a noun.

   I, you, she, it, which, that, themselves, whoever,
   me, he, they, whatever, my, mine, ours

3. A **verb** is a word that expresses action or state of being.

   is, are, was, were, bite, break, catch, drag, eat, fly,
   give, ride, run, see, sit, tear, throw

4. An **adjective** describes or modifies a noun or pronoun. (The articles *a, an,* and *the* are adjectives.)

   Advertising is **a big** and **powerful** industry.
   (*A, big,* and *powerful* modify *industry*.)

5. An **adverb** modifies a verb, an adjective, or another adverb. An adverb tells *how, when, where, why, how often,* or *how much.*

   today, yesterday, here, there, precisely, regularly,
   greatly, partly, slow, slowly, quick, quickly

6. A **preposition** is a word (or group of words) that introduces a phrase, which in turn modifies some other word in the sentence. The first noun or pronoun following the preposition is its object.

   above, across, after, by, for, from, in, of, off, on, out,
   over, through, to, until, up, with

7. A **conjunction** connects individual words or groups of words.

   and, but, or, nor, for, yet, so, because

8. An **interjection** is included in a sentence in order to communicate strong emotion or surprise. Punctuation (often a comma or an exclamation point) is used to set an interjection off from the rest of the sentence.

   Help!   Ouch!   Good grief, I'm stuck again.

"The limits of my language stand for the limits of my world."

—Ludwig Wittgenstein

Using the Language

Constructing Sentences

748 A **sentence** is made up of one or more words that express a complete thought. (NOTE: A sentence begins with a capital letter; it ends with a period, a question mark, or an exclamation point.)

> Computers deliver the universe in a box.

749 A sentence must have a **subject** and a **predicate** that express a complete thought. The subject is the element of the sentence about which something is said. The predicate is the element of the sentence that says something about the subject. (The primary part of a predicate is the word or words that function as a verb.)

> Technology fascinates many people.

NOTE: In the sentence above, *technology* is the subject—the sentence talks about technology. *Fascinates*, a verb, is the primary part of the predicate—it says something about the subject.

750 Either the subject or the predicate or both may be "missing" from a sentence, but both must be clearly **understood**.

> "What's the big deal?" (*What* is the subject; the predicate is expressed by the contraction: *'s* for *is*.)

> "Information." (*Information* is the subject; the predicate *is* is understood.)

> "Get on-line." (The subject *you* is understood; *get* is the predicate.)

751 ## The Subject

The **subject** is always a noun, or a word or phrase that functions as a noun, such as a pronoun, an infinitive, a gerund, or a noun clause.

> **Technology** makes it impossible for a business to work without some kind of gizmo. (noun)
>
> In most businesses **you** will find a computer and a fax. (pronoun)
>
> **To survive without technology** is difficult. (infinitive phrase)
>
> **Downloading information from a computer** is easy. (gerund phrase)
>
> **That the information age would arrive** was inevitable. (noun clause)

A **simple subject** is the subject without the words that modify it.

> Thirty years ago, reasonably well-trained **mechanics** could fix any car on the road.

A **complete subject** is the simple subject and all the words that modify it.

> Thirty years ago, **reasonably well-trained mechanics** could fix any car on the road.

A **compound subject** is composed of two or more simple subjects.

> Today, **mechanics** and **technicians** would need to master a half million manual pages to fix every car on the road.

752 ## The Predicate (Verb)

A **predicate** is the sentence part that says something about the subject.

> All workers **need technical skills as well as basic academic skills**.

A **simple predicate** is the predicate without the words that describe or modify it.

> Today's workplace **requires** employees to have a broad range of skills.

A **complete predicate** is the simple predicate and all the words that modify or explain it.

> Today's workplace **requires employees to have a broad range of skills**.

A **compound predicate** is composed of two or more simple predicates.

> Workers **analyze**, **reason**, **calculate**, and **troubleshoot**.

A **compound subject** and a **compound predicate** sometimes appear in the same sentence.

> Both high-school **students** and their college **counterparts need** strong interpersonal skills and **want** jobs with a future.

A **direct object** receives the action of the predicate. (See 732.)

> In the past, vocational education emphasized **hands** instead of heads.

The **direct object** may be **compound**.

> Today, educators see the **value** and **interdependence** of brainpower and hands-on skill.

Using Phrases

753 A **phrase** is a group of related words that lacks either a subject or a predicate or both.

> amazing triumphs of technology (The subject lacks a predicate.)
>
> can be found (The predicate lacks a subject.)
>
> in ancient civilizations (The phrase lacks a subject and a predicate.)
>
> Amazing triumphs of technology can be found in ancient civilizations.
> (Together, these three phrases present a complete thought.)

Types of Phrases

Phrases appear in several types: *noun, verb, prepositional, appositive, absolute,* and *verbal.*

A **noun phrase** consists of a noun and its modifiers; the whole phrase functions as a simple noun would.

> **The Great Pyramid of Khufu** was one of the Seven Wonders of the Ancient World. (subject)
>
> Modern day engineers marvel at **its incredible size and architectural perfection.** (object of preposition)

A **verb phrase** consists of a verb and its modifiers.

> Experts **have been discussing pyramid construction for many years.**

A **prepositional phrase** consists of a preposition, its object, and modifiers.

> The pyramids were built **without powerful machinery.**
> (adverb modifying the verb *were built*)
>
> What is the secret **behind the mystery?** (adjective modifying *secret*)

754

An **appositive phrase**, which stands beside another noun and renames it, consists of a noun and its modifiers. An appositive adds new information about the noun it follows.

> Khufu, **the Egyptian king who directed the construction of the Great Pyramid**, was born about 2680 B.C. (The appositive phrase renames *Khufu*.)

An **absolute phrase** consists of a noun and a participle (plus the object of the participle and any modifiers). Because it has a subject and a verbal, an absolute phrase resembles a clause; however, the verbal does not have the tense and number found in the main verb of a clause.

> **His whip cracking repeatedly**, the overseer kept everyone on task. (*Whip* is the noun; *cracking* is a present participle modifying *whip*.)

A **verbal phrase** is a phrase based on one of the three types of verbals: *gerund, infinitive,* or *participle*. (See 737.)

1 A **gerund phrase** is based on a gerund and functions as a noun.

> **Building the pyramids** took highly developed construction techniques. (subject)

> Workers succeeded in **overcoming all odds**. (object of preposition)

2 An **infinitive phrase** is based on an infinitive and functions as a noun, an adjective, or an adverb.

> **To dream** is the first step in any project. (*To dream* is the subject.)

> During his reign, Khufu mobilized almost all of Egypt's males **to work on his pyramid**. (adverb modifying the verb *mobilized*)

> Did he create a slave-labor army **to build his pyramid**? (adjective modifying the noun *army*)

3 A **participial phrase** consists of a past or present participle and its modifiers; the whole phrase functions as an adjective.

> **Transporting the blocks of limestone**, workers poured a liquid on the road to lubricate the path. (adjective modifying the noun *workers*)

> These men, **exhausted by their labor**, could not quit and find an easier line of work. (adjective modifying the noun *men*)

---

system check ➡ Phrases can add valuable information to sentences. In writing for business, however, beware of phrases that add nothing but "fat" to your sentences. For a list of phrases to abbreviate or delete, see 185.

Using Clauses

755 A **clause** is a group of related words that has both a subject and a predicate. (A phrase never has both.)

An **independent clause** presents a complete thought and can stand alone as a sentence.

> Airplanes are twentieth-century inventions, but people throughout the ages have dreamed of flying.

NOTE: The above sentence has two independent clauses joined by the conjunction *but*. Each independent clause can also be written as a sentence.

> Airplanes are twentieth-century inventions.
> People throughout the ages have dreamed of flying.

A **dependent clause** (sometimes called a **subordinate clause**) cannot stand alone as a sentence. It can, however, add important detail to a sentence.

> Because the U.S. Weather Bureau had recommended it (**dependent clause**), Wilbur and Orville Wright selected a deserted beach in Kitty Hawk, South Carolina, to test their new flying machine.

756 **Types of Clauses**

There are three basic types of dependent or subordinate clauses: *adverb, adjective,* and *noun.*

An **adverb clause** is used like an adverb to modify or place some condition upon a verb.

> **Although the Wright brothers suffered many failures**, they were finally successful. (modifies *were*)

NOTE: All adverb clauses begin with a subordinating conjunction. (See 745.)

An **adjective clause** is used like an adjective to modify a noun or pronoun. Like an adjective, an adjective clause answers the questions *what kind?* or *which one?*

> The men **who invented the first airplane** were brothers, Orville and Wilbur Wright. (Which men?)
> Orville and Wilbur Wright first performed 700 successful glider flights, **which were not powered by an engine**. (What kind?)

A **noun clause** is used in place of a noun. Noun clauses can appear as subjects, direct or indirect objects, predicate nominatives, or objects of prepositions.

> **What made later aviation possible** was the determination of people who believed humans would one day soar through the heavens like birds. (subject)

Using Sentence Variety

757 A **sentence** may be classified according to the type of statement it makes, the way it is constructed, and the arrangement of words within the sentence.

758 ## Kinds of Sentences

Sentences make different kinds of statements according to the mood of their main verbs: *declarative, interrogative, imperative, exclamatory,* or *conditional.*

Declarative sentences make statements. They tell us something about a person, a place, a thing, or an idea.

> In the mid-1800's, an Englishman named Charles Babbage invented a hand-cranked machine that could calculate logarithms.

Interrogative sentences ask questions.

> Who was Ada Lovelace?

Imperative sentences give commands. They often contain an understood subject (you).

> Check out computer history, and you'll discover that she was Babbage's sweetheart and the world's first computer programmer.

Exclamatory sentences communicate strong emotion or surprise.

> Incredible as it seems, these two mathematical geniuses went bankrupt by gambling on horse races!

Conditional sentences express wishes ("if . . . then" statements) or conditions contrary to fact.

> If their gambling system had worked, and they hadn't gone deeply in debt, the first computer might have been built a hundred years before it was.

759 ## Structure of a Sentence

A sentence may be *simple, compound, complex,* or *compound-complex* in structure, depending on the relationship between independent and dependent clauses in it.

A **simple sentence** may have a single subject or a compound subject. It may have a single predicate or a compound predicate. But a simple sentence has only one independent clause, and it has no dependent clauses. A simple sentence may, however, contain one or more phrases.

> My **back aches**. (single subject; single predicate)
>
> My **teeth** and my **eyes hurt**. (compound subject; single predicate)
>
> My **memory** and my **logic come** and **go**. (compound subject; compound predicate)
>
> **I must be getting over the hill**. (single subject: *I*; single predicate: *must be getting*; phrase: *over the hill*)

A **compound sentence** consists of two independent clauses. The clauses must be joined by a coordinating conjunction, by punctuation, or by both.

> Energy is part of youth, **so** why am I so exhausted?
> It couldn't be my fault; I take good care of myself.

A **complex sentence** contains one independent clause (in boldface) and one or more dependent clauses (in italics).

> *When I can,* **I get eight hours of sleep**. (dependent clause; independent clause)

> *When I get up on time,* and *if my brother hasn't used up all the milk,* **I eat breakfast.** (two dependent clauses; independent clause)

A **compound-complex sentence** contains two or more independent clauses (in boldface) and one or more dependent clauses (in italics).

> *If I'm not in a hurry,* **I take long, leisurely walks,** and **I stop to smell the roses.** (dependent clause; two independent clauses)

760 Arrangement of a Sentence

Depending on the arrangement of the words and the placement of emphasis, a sentence may also be classified as *loose, balanced, periodic,* or *cumulative.*

A **loose sentence** expresses the main thought near the beginning and adds explanatory material as needed.

> **A prime mover is what makes a machine run**, though there are a great number of things that fit into the category of prime mover.

A **balanced sentence** is constructed so that it emphasizes a similarity or contrast between two or more of its parts (words, phrases, or clauses).

> Everything from **dogsleds** to **windmills** to **jackhammers** requires a prime mover. (All three boldfaced nouns have a similar function in the sentence.)

A **periodic sentence** is one that postpones the crucial or most surprising idea until the end.

> Though gasoline and diesel engines are the prime movers for many kinds of machines, **the simplest prime mover is human muscle power.**

A **cumulative sentence** places the general idea in the main clause and gives it greater precision with modifying words, phrases, or clauses placed before it, after it, or in the middle of it.

> Straining forward with all their might, **the team of workhorses slowly pulled their heavy load forward** as the owner shouted words of encouragement from the sidelines.

Getting Sentence Parts to Agree

761 ## Agreement of Subject and Verb

The subject and verb of any clause must agree in both **person** and **number**. There are **three persons: first person** *(I)*, **second person** *(you)*, and **third person** *(he, she, it)*. Checking sentences for agreement in **person** is simply a matter of reading carefully. (See 725.) Checking sentences for agreement in **number** (singular or plural) requires a much closer look. Read the following guidelines.

762 ### Agreement in Number

A verb must agree in number (singular or plural) with its subject.

> The **student was** proud of her quarter grades. (Both the subject *student* and the verb *was* are singular; they are said to agree in number.)

NOTE: Do not be confused by other words that come between the subject and verb.

> The **pilot**, as well as the flight attendants, **is** required to display courtesy. (*Pilot*, not *flight attendants*, is the subject.)

763 **Delayed subjects** occur when the verb comes *before* the subject in a sentence. In these inverted sentences, the true *(delayed)* subject must be made to agree with the verb.

> There **are** many hardworking **students** in our schools.
> There **is** present among many students today a **will** to succeed.
> (*Students* and *will* are the true subjects of these sentences, not *there.*)

764 **Compound subjects** connected with *and* usually require a plural verb.

> **Strength** and **balance are** necessary for good posture.

765 **Singular subjects** joined by *or* or *nor* take a singular verb.

> Neither **Bev** nor **Connie is going** to the job fair.

NOTE: When one of the subjects joined by *or* or *nor* is singular and one is plural, the verb is made to agree with the subject nearer the verb.

> Neither **Mr. Kemper** nor his **students are able** to find the résumés. (The plural subject *students* is nearer the verb; therefore, the plural verb *are* is used to agree with *students.*)

766 The **indefinite pronouns** *each, either, neither, one, everybody, another, anybody, everyone, nobody, everything, somebody,* and *someone* are singular; they require a singular verb.

> **Everybody is** invited to the cafeteria for the group interview.

NOTE: Do not be confused by words or phrases that come between the indefinite pronoun and the verb.

> **Each** of the candidates **is** (not **are**) required to bring a list of references to the interview.

767 The **indefinite pronouns** *all, any, half, most, none,* and *some* may be either singular or plural when they are used as subjects. These pronouns are singular if the number of the noun in the prepositional phrase is singular; they are plural if the noun is plural.

> **Half** of the bottles **were** missing.
> (*Bottles,* the noun in the prepositional phrase, is plural; therefore, the pronoun *half* is considered plural, and the plural verb *were* is used to agree with it.)
>
> **Half** of the lecture **was** over by the time we arrived.
> (Because *lecture* is singular, *half* is also singular, requiring the singular verb *was.*)

768 **Collective nouns** (*faculty, committee, team, congress, species, crowd, army, pair, assembly, squad,* etc.) take a singular verb when they refer to a group as a unit; collective nouns take a plural verb when they refer to the individuals within the group.

> The **faculty is** united in its effort to make this school a better place to be.
> (*Faculty* refers to a group as a unit; it requires a singular verb: *is.*)
>
> The **faculty are** required to turn in their grades before leaving for vacation.
> (In this example, *faculty* refers to the individuals within the group. If the word *individuals* were substituted for *faculty,* it would become clear that the plural verb *are* is needed in this sentence.)

769 Some nouns that are **plural in form but singular in meaning** take a singular verb: *mumps, measles, news, mathematics, economics,* etc.

> **Economics is** sometimes called "the dismal science."

Exceptions: *scissors, trousers, tidings, robotics.*

> The **scissors are** missing again.

NOTE: Mathematical phrases usually take a singular verb.

> **Three and three is** six. **Five times six is** thirty.

770 When a **relative pronoun** (*who, which, that*) is used as the subject of a clause, the number of the verb is determined by the antecedent of the pronoun. (The antecedent is the word to which the pronoun refers.)

> This is one of the **books that are** required for English class.
> (The relative pronoun *that* requires the plural verb *are* because its antecedent *books* is plural. To test this type of sentence for agreement, read the *of* phrase first: *Of the books that are . . .*)

771 When a sentence contains a form of the *be* verb—and a noun comes before and after that verb—the verb must agree with the subject, even if the *predicate noun* (the noun coming after the verb) is different in number.

> The **cause** of his problem **was** his bad **brakes**. His bad **brakes were** the **cause** of his problem.

Agreement of a Pronoun and Its Antecedent

772 A pronoun must agree in number, person, and gender (sex) with its *antecedent*. (The *antecedent* is the word to which the pronoun refers.)

> **Bill** brought **his** laptop computer to school.
>
> (The antecedent in this sentence is *Bill*; it is to *Bill* that the pronoun *his* refers. Both the pronoun and its antecedent are singular, third person, and masculine; therefore, the pronoun is said to agree with its antecedent.)

773 Use a singular pronoun to refer to such antecedents as *each, either, neither, one, anyone, everyone, everybody, somebody, another, nobody,* and *a person*.

> **One** of the files is missing **its** (not **their**) label.

NOTE: When *a person* or *everyone* is used to refer to both sexes or either sex, you will have to choose whether to offer optional pronouns or rewrite the sentence.

> A **person** must learn to wait **his** or **her** turn. (optional pronouns)
>
> **People** must learn to wait **their** turn. (rewritten in plural form)

774 Two or more antecedents joined by *and* are considered plural; two or more singular antecedents joined by *or* or *nor* are referred to by a singular pronoun.

> **Tom** and **Bob** are finishing **their** assignments.
>
> Either **Connie** or **Sue** left **her** headset in the library.

NOTE: If one of the antecedents is masculine and one feminine, the pronouns should likewise be masculine and feminine.

> Is either **Dave** or **Phyllis** bringing **his** or **her** Frisbee?

NOTE: If one of the antecedents joined by *or* or *nor* is singular and one is plural, the pronoun is made to agree with the nearer antecedent.

> Neither the lead **singer** nor his backup **musicians** were prepared for **their** reception.

775 Treating the Sexes Fairly

When you box people in or put them down because of their sex, that is called "sexism." When you identify all human virtues with only one sex, or when you identify one sex with the whole human race, that, too, is sexism. And when you bring in sexual distinctions where they don't belong, that, too, is sexism. Sexism is unfair. And it hurts. Ask anyone who has been a victim of it.

To change our centuries-old habit of sexist thinking, we must try to change our language, for our traditional ways of speaking and writing have sexist patterns deeply imprinted in them. The assumptions built into our language teach even little children who they are and how they relate to others. For their sakes and our own, we must seek a language that implies equal value, equal potential, and equal opportunity for people of both sexes.

Portraying the Sexes in Writing

776 **Don't** typecast all men as leaders, professionals, breadwinners, etc.; don't typecast all women as subordinates, homebodies, helpers, and dependents.

Do show both women and men as doctors and nurses, principals and teachers, breadwinners and housekeepers, bosses and secretaries, pilots, plumbers, TV repairers, social workers, etc.

777 **Don't** associate courage, strength, brilliance, creativity, independence, persistence, and seriousness with only men and boys; don't associate emotionalism, passivity, and fearfulness with only women and girls.

Do portray people of both sexes along the whole range of potential human strengths and weaknesses.

778 **Don't** refer to women according to their physical appearance and to men according to their mental abilities or professional status:

> The admirable Dr. William Hicks and his wife Mary, an attractive former model, both showed up at the party.

Do refer to both on the same plane:

> Bill and Mary Hicks showed up at the party.

779 **Don't** use demeaning or sexually loaded labels when referring to women:

> girl (for secretary)   chick, fox, bombshell, knockout
>
> the weaker sex   better half, little woman

Do use respectful terms rather than labels; consider what the woman herself might wish to be called:

> secretary, Helen, Ms. Jones   professional woman, career person
>
> wife, spouse   woman, mother

780 **Don't** take special notice when a woman does a "man's job" or vice versa:

    lady doctor   male nurse   coed

Do treat men's or women's involvement in a profession as normal, not exceptional:

    doctor   nurse   student

781 **Don't** portray women as the possessions of men:

    Fred took his wife on a vacation.

Do portray women and men, husbands and wives, as equal partners:

    Fred and Wilma took a vacation.

Referring to Men and Women Together

782 **Don't** give special treatment to one of the sexes:

    The men and the ladies came through in the clutch.
    Hank and Miss Jenkins
    Mr. Bubba Gumm, Mrs. Bubba Gumm

Do use equal language for both sexes:

    The men and the women came through in the clutch.
    Hank and Mimi
    Mr. Bubba Gumm, Mrs. Lotta Gumm

Referring to People in General

783 **Don't** use "man words" to refer to all people or a person in general:

    mankind   man-hours
    man-made   the best man for the job

Do use nonsexist alternatives to man words:

    humanity   synthetic   employee hours   the best person for the job

784 **Don't** use only masculine pronouns *(he, his, him)* when you want to refer to a human being in general:

    A politician can kiss privacy good-bye when he runs for office.

Do use one of the several ways to avoid sexism:

    Reword the sentence: Running for office robs a politician of privacy.

    Express in the plural: Politicians can kiss privacy good-bye when they run for office.

    Offer optional pronouns: A politician can kiss privacy good-bye when he or she runs for office.

Addressing Your Reader

785 **Don't** assume that your reader is male:

> You and your wife will be shocked at these prices.
> After the morning shave, one feels a bit clearer in the head.

Do assume that your reader is either male or female:

> You and your spouse (or loved one) will be shocked at these prices.
> After the morning shower, one feels a bit clearer in the head.

786 **Don't** use a male word in the salutation of a business letter to someone you do not know:

> Dear Sir: Dear Gentlemen:

Do address a position when you don't know the person's name:

> Dear Personnel Officer:
> Dear Members of the Big Bird Fan Club:

Using Occupational Titles

787 **Don't** use "man words" for titles, even if the person in question is a male.

Do use neutral titles whenever possible. Do use equal language for both sexes.

What NOT to Do	What to Do
foreman	supervisor
chairman	chair; presiding officer; moderator
salesman	sales representative; salesperson
mailman	mail carrier; postal worker; letter carrier
insurance man	insurance agent
fireman	firefighter
businessman	executive; manager; businessperson
congressman	member of Congress; representative; senator

788 **Don't** use special titles to distinguish female workers from males.

Do use neutral terms for both men and women.

What NOT to Do	What to Do
steward, stewardess	flight attendant
policeman, policewoman	police officer
author, authoress	author

ALMANAC

Tables, Maps, and Time Line

Tables and Lists

World Maps

Historical Time Line

"I find that a great part of the information I have was acquired by looking up something and finding something else on the way."

—Franklin P. Adams

Tables and Lists

789 Holidays

Legal Federal Holidays

New Year's Day: January 1
Martin Luther King Day: Third Monday in January
Presidents' Day: Third Monday in February
Memorial Day: Last Monday in May
Independence Day: July 4
Labor Day: First Monday in September
Columbus Day: Second Monday in October
Veterans Day: November 11
Thanksgiving Day: Fourth Thursday in November
Christmas Day: December 25

Special Days

Valentine's Day: February 14
St. Patrick's Day: March 17
May Day: May 1
Cinco de Mayo: May 5

Mother's Day: Second Sunday in May
Father's Day: Third Sunday in June
Halloween: October 31
Kwanza: December 26

NOTE: Religious holidays such as Easter, Hanukkah, First Day of Ramadan, and Yom Kippur fall on different calendar dates each year.

790 Weights and Measures

Linear Measure

1 inch	=	2.54 centimeters
1 foot	=	12 inches
		0.3048 meter
1 yard	=	3 feet
		0.9144 meter
1 rod (or pole or perch)	=	5 1/2 yards or 16 1/2 feet
		5.029 meters
1 furlong.	=	40 rods
		201.17 meters
1 (statute) mile	=	8 furlongs
		1,760 yards
		5,280 feet
		1,609.3 meters
1 (land) league	=	3 miles
		4.83 kilometers

Square Measure

1 square inch	=	6.452 sq. centimeters
1 square foot	=	144 square inches
		929 square centimeters
1 square yard	=	9 square feet
		0.8361 square meter
1 square rod	=	30 1/4 square yards
		25.29 square meters
1 acre	=	160 square rods
		4,840 square yards
		43,560 square feet
		0.4047 hectare
1 square mile.	=	640 acres
		259 hectares
		2.59 square kilometers

Cubic Measure

1 cubic inch	=	16.387 cubic centimeters
1 cubic foot.	=	1,728 cubic inches
		0.0283 cubic meter
1 cubic yard	=	27 cubic feet
		0.7646 cubic meter
1 cord foot	=	16 cubic feet
1 cord	=	8 cord feet
		3.625 cubic meters

Chain Measure
(Gunter's or surveyor's chain)

1 link	=	7.92 inches
		20.12 centimeters
1 chain	=	100 links or 66 feet
		20.12 meters
1 furlong.	=	10 chains
		201.17 meters
1 mile.	=	80 chains
		1,609.3 meters

(Engineer's chain)

1 link	=	1 foot
		0.3048 meter
1 chain	=	100 feet
		30.48 meters
1 mile	=	52.8 chains
		1,609.3 meters

Surveyor's (Square) Measure

1 square pole	=	625 square links
		25.29 square meters
1 square chain	=	16 square poles
		404.7 square meters
1 acre	=	10 square chains
		0.4047 hectare
1 square mile or 1 section.	=	640 acres
		259 hectares
		2.59 square kilometers
1 township	=	36 square miles
		9,324 hectares
		93.24 square kilometers

Nautical Measure

1 fathom.	=	6 feet
		1.829 meters
1 cable's length (ordinary).	=	100 fathoms

(In the U.S. Navy 120 fathoms or 720 feet = 1 cable's length; in the British Navy 608 feet = 1 cable's length.)

1 nautical mile	=	6,076.10333 feet; by *international agreement in 1954*
		10 cables' length
		1.852 kilometers
		1.1508 statute miles; *length of a minute of longitude at the equator*
1 marine league	=	3.45 statute miles
		3 nautical miles
		5.56 kilometers
1 degree of a great circle of the earth.	=	60 nautical miles

Dry Measure

1 pint	=	33.60 cubic inches
		0.5505 liter
1 quart	=	2 pints
		67.20 cubic inches
		1.1012 liters
1 peck	=	8 quarts
		537.61 cubic inches
		8.8096 liters
1 bushel	=	4 pecks
		2,150.42 cubic inches
		35.2383 liters

Liquid Measure

4 fluid ounces . . . . (see next table)	=	1 gill
		7.219 cubic inches
		0.1183 liter
1 pint	=	4 gills
		28.875 cubic inches
		0.4732 liter
1 quart	=	2 pints
		57.75 cubic inches
		0.9463 liter
1 gallon	=	4 quarts
		231 cubic inches
		3.7853 liters

791 **Apothecaries' Fluid Measure**

1 minim	=	0.0038 cubic inch
		0.0616 milliliter
1 fluid dram	=	60 minims
		0.2256 cubic inch
		3.6966 milliliters
1 fluid ounce	=	8 fluid drams
		1.8047 cubic inches
		0.0296 liter
1 pint	=	16 fluid ounces
		28.875 cubic inches
		0.4732 liter

Circular (or Angular) Measure

1 minute (')	=	60 seconds (")
1 degree (°)	=	60 minutes
1 quadrant or 1 right angle . .	=	90 degrees
1 circle	=	4 quadrants
		360 degrees

Avoirdupois Weight
(The grain, equal to 0.0648 gram,
is the same in all three tables of weight.)

1 dram or 27.34 grains	=	1.772 grams
1 ounce	=	16 drams
		437.5 grains
		28.3495 grams
1 pound	=	16 ounces
		7,000 grains
		453.59 grams
1 hundredweight	=	100 pounds
		45.36 kilograms
1 ton	=	2,000 pounds
		907.18 kilograms

Troy Weight
(The grain, equal to 0.0648 gram,
is the same in all three tables of weight.)

1 carat	=	3.086 grains
		200 milligrams
1 pennyweight	=	24 grains
		1.5552 grams
1 ounce	=	20 pennyweights
		480 grains
		31.1035 grams
1 pound	=	12 ounces
		5,760 grains
		373.24 grams

Apothecaries' Weight
(The grain, equal to 0.0648 gram,
is the same in all three tables of weight.)

1 scruple	=	20 grains
		1.296 grams
1 dram	=	3 scruples
		3.888 grams
1 ounce	=	8 drams
		480 grains
		31.1035 grams
1 pound	=	12 ounces
		5,760 grains
		373.24 grams

Miscellaneous

1 palm	=	3 inches
1 hand	=	4 inches
1 span	=	6 inches
1 cubit	=	18 inches
1 Bible cubit	=	21.8 inches
1 military pace	=	$2\,^1/_2$ feet

792

Additional Units of Measure

Astronomical Unit (A.U.): 93,000,000 miles, the average distance of the earth from the sun. Used in astronomy.

Board Foot (bd. ft.): 144 cubic inches (12 in. x 12 in. x 1 in.). Used for lumber.

Bolt: 40 yards. Used for measuring cloth.

Btu: British thermal unit. Amount of heat needed to increase the temperature of one pound of water by one degree Fahrenheit.

Gross: 12 dozen or 144.

Knot: Not a distance, but a speed of one nautical mile per hour.

Light, Speed of: 186,281.7 miles per second.

Light-Year: 5,880,000,000,000 miles, the distance light travels in a year at the rate of 186,281.7 miles per second.

Pi (π): 3.14159265+. The ratio of the circumference of a circle to its diameter. For all practical purposes: 3.1416.

Roentgen: Dosage unit of radiation exposure produced by X rays.

Sound, Speed of: 1,088 ft. per second at 32° F at sea level.

793 The Metric System

In 1975, the United States signed the Metric Conversion Act, declaring a national policy of encouraging voluntary use of the metric system. Today, the metric system exists side by side with the U.S. customary system. The debate on whether the United States should adopt the metric system has been going on for nearly 200 years, leaving the United States the only country in the world not totally committed to adopting the system.

The metric system is considered a simpler form of measurement. It is based on the decimal system (units of 10) and eliminates the need to deal with fractions as we currently use them.

Linear Measure

1 centimeter	=	10 millimeters
		0.3937 inch
1 decimeter	=	10 centimeters
		3.937 inches
1 meter	=	10 decimeters
		39.37 inches
		3.28 feet
1 decameter	=	10 meters
		393.7 inches
1 hectometer	=	10 decameters
		328 feet 1 inch
1 kilometer	=	10 hectometers
		0.621 mile
1 myriameter	=	10 kilometers
		6.21 miles

Volume Measure

1 cubic centimeter	=	1,000 cubic millimeters
		.06102 cubic inch
1 cubic decimeter	=	1,000 cubic centimeters
		61.02 cubic inches
1 cubic meter	=	1,000 cubic decimeters
		35.314 cubic feet

Capacity Measure

1 centiliter	=	10 milliliters
		.338 fluid ounce
1 deciliter	=	10 centiliters
		3.38 fluid ounces
1 liter	=	10 deciliters
		1.0567 liquid quarts
		0.9081 dry quart
1 decaliter	=	10 liters
		2.64 gallons
		0.284 bushel
1 hectoliter	=	10 decaliters
		26.418 gallons
		2.838 bushels
1 kiloliter	=	10 hectoliters
		264.18 gallons
		35.315 cubic feet

Square Measure

1 square centimeter	=	100 square millimeters
		0.15499 square inch
1 square decimeter	=	100 square centimeters
		15.499 square inches
1 square meter	=	100 square decimeters
		1,549.9 square inches
		1.196 square yards
1 square decameter	=	100 square meters
		119.6 square yards
1 square hectometer	=	100 square decameters
		2.471 acres
1 square kilometer	=	100 square hectometers
		0.386 square mile

Land Measure

1 centare	=	1 square meter
		1,549.9 square inches
1 are	=	100 centares
		119.6 square yards
1 hectare	=	100 ares
		2.471 acres
1 square kilometer	=	100 hectares
		0.386 square mile

Weights

1 centigram	=	10 milligrams
		0.1543 grain
1 decigram	=	10 centigrams
		1.5432 grains
1 gram	=	10 decigrams
		15.432 grains
1 decagram	=	10 grams
		0.3527 ounce
1 hectogram	=	10 decagrams
		3.5274 ounces
1 kilogram	=	10 hectograms
		2.2046 pounds
1 myriagram	=	10 kilograms
		22.046 pounds
1 quintal	=	10 myriagrams
		220.46 pounds
1 metric ton	=	10 quintals
		2,204.6 pounds

794

HANDY CONVERSION FACTORS

TO CHANGE	TO	MULTIPLY BY
acres	hectares	.4047
acres	square feet	43,560
acres	square miles	.001562
Celsius	Fahrenheit	*1.8
		*(then add 32)
centimeters	inches	.3937
centimeters	feet	.03281
cubic meters	cubic feet	35.3145
cubic meters	cubic yards	1.3079
cubic yards	cubic meters	.7646
degrees	radians	.01745
Fahrenheit	Celsius	*.556
		* (after subtracting 32)
feet	meters	.3048
feet	miles (nautical)	.0001645
feet	miles (statute)	.0001894
feet/sec.	miles/hr.	.6818
furlongs	feet	660.0
furlongs	miles	.125
gallons (U.S.)	liters	3.7853
grains	grams	.0648
grams	grains	15.4324
grams	ounces avdp.	.0353
grams	pounds	.002205
hectares	acres	2.4710
horsepower	watts	745.7
hours	days	.04167
inches	millimeters	25.4000
inches	centimeters	2.5400
kilograms	pounds avdp.	2.2046
kilometers	miles	.6214
kilowatts	horsepower	1.341
knots	nautical miles/hr.	1.0
knots	statute miles/hr.	1.151
liters	gallons (U.S.)	.2642
liters	pecks	.1135
liters	pints (dry)	1.8162
liters	pints (liquid)	2.1134
liters	quarts (dry)	.9081

TO CHANGE	TO	MULTIPLY BY
liters	quarts (liquid)	1.0567
meters	feet	3.2808
meters	miles	.0006214
meters	yards	1.0936
metric tons	tons (long)	.9842
metric tons	tons (short)	1.1023
miles	kilometers	1.6093
miles	feet	5,280
miles (nautical)	miles (statute)	1.1516
miles (statute)	miles (nautical)	.8684
miles/hr.	feet/min.	88
millimeters	inches	.0394
ounces avdp.	grams	28.3495
ounces	pounds	.0625
ounces (troy)	ounces (avdp.)	1.09714
pecks	liters	8.8096
pints (dry)	liters	.5506
pints (liquid)	liters	1.4732
pounds ap. or t.	kilograms	.3732
pounds avdp.	kilograms	.4536
pounds	ounces	16
quarts (dry)	liters	1.1012
quarts (liquid)	liters	.9463
rods	meters	5.029
rods	feet	16.5
square feet	square meters	.0929
square kilometers	square miles	.3861
square meters	square feet	10.7639
square meters	square yards	1.1960
square miles	square kilometers	2.5900
square yards	square meters	.8361
tons (long)	metric tons	1.1060
tons (short)	metric tons	.9072
tons (long)	pounds	2,240
tons (short)	pounds	2,000
watts	Btu/hr.	3.4129
watts	horsepower	.001341
yards	meters	.9144
yards	miles	.0005682

795

ten ways to
measure *when you don't have a ruler*

1. Many floor tiles are 12-inch by 12-inch squares.
2. U.S. paper currency is 6-1/8 inches long by 2-5/8 inches wide.
3. A quarter is approximately 1 inch wide.
4. A penny is approximately 3/4 of an inch wide.
5. A standard sheet of paper is 8-1/2 inches by 11 inches.

Each of the following items can be used as a measuring device by multiplying its length by the number of times it is used to measure an area in question.

6. A shoelace   7. A tie   8. A belt
9. Your feet—placing one in front of the other to measure an area
10. Your outstretched arms from fingertip to fingertip

796 Multiplication and Division Table

A number at the top (11) multiplied by a number in the extreme left-hand column (12) produces the number where the top line and side line meet (132).

A number in the table (208) divided by the number at the top of the same column (13) results in the number (16) in the extreme left-hand column. A number in the table (208) divided by the number at the extreme left (16) results in the number (13) at the top of the column.

1	2	3	4	5	6	7	8	9	10	11	12	13	14	15	16	17	18	19	20	21	22	23	24	25
2	4	6	8	10	12	14	16	18	20	22	24	26	28	30	32	34	36	38	40	42	44	46	48	50
3	6	9	12	15	18	21	24	27	30	33	36	39	42	45	48	51	54	57	60	63	66	69	72	75
4	8	12	16	20	24	28	32	36	40	44	48	52	56	60	64	68	72	76	80	84	88	92	96	100
5	10	15	20	25	30	35	40	45	50	55	60	65	70	75	80	85	90	95	100	105	110	115	120	125
6	12	18	24	30	36	42	48	54	60	66	72	78	84	90	96	102	108	114	120	126	132	138	144	150
7	14	21	28	35	42	49	56	63	70	77	84	91	98	105	112	119	126	133	140	147	154	161	168	175
8	16	24	32	40	48	56	64	72	80	88	96	104	112	120	128	136	144	152	160	168	176	184	192	200
9	18	27	36	45	54	63	72	81	90	99	108	117	126	135	144	153	162	171	180	189	198	207	216	225
10	20	30	40	50	60	70	80	90	100	110	120	130	140	150	160	170	180	190	200	210	220	230	240	250
11	22	33	44	55	66	77	88	99	110	121	132	143	154	165	176	187	198	209	220	231	242	253	264	275
12	24	36	48	60	72	84	96	108	120	132	144	156	168	180	192	204	216	228	240	252	264	276	288	300
13	26	39	52	65	78	91	104	117	130	143	156	169	182	195	208	221	234	247	260	273	286	299	312	325
14	28	42	56	70	84	98	112	126	140	154	168	182	196	210	224	238	252	266	280	294	308	322	336	350
15	30	45	60	75	90	105	120	135	150	160	180	195	210	225	240	255	270	285	300	315	330	345	360	375
16	32	48	64	80	96	112	128	144	160	176	192	208	224	240	256	272	288	304	320	336	352	368	384	400
17	34	51	68	85	102	119	136	153	170	187	204	221	238	255	272	289	306	323	340	357	374	391	408	425
18	36	54	72	90	108	126	143	162	180	198	216	234	252	270	288	306	323	340	360	378	396	414	432	450
19	38	57	76	95	114	133	152	171	190	209	228	247	266	285	304	323	342	361	380	399	418	437	456	475
20	40	60	80	100	120	140	160	180	200	220	240	260	285	300	320	340	360	380	400	420	440	460	480	500
21	42	63	84	105	126	147	168	189	210	231	252	273	294	315	336	357	378	399	420	441	462	483	504	525
22	44	66	88	110	132	154	176	198	220	242	264	286	308	330	352	374	396	418	440	462	484	506	528	550
23	46	69	92	115	138	161	184	207	230	253	276	299	322	345	368	391	414	437	460	483	506	529	552	575
24	48	72	96	120	144	168	192	216	240	264	288	312	336	360	384	408	432	456	480	504	528	552	576	600
25	50	75	100	125	150	175	200	225	250	275	300	325	350	375	400	425	450	475	500	525	550	575	600	625

797 Decimal Equivalents of Common Fractions

Fraction	Decimal	Fraction	Decimal	Fraction	Decimal	Fraction	Decimal	Fraction	Decimal
1/2	.5000	1/12	.0833	3/5	.6000	5/6	.8333	7/9	.7778
1/3	.3333	1/16	.0625	3/7	.4286	5/7	.7143	7/10	.7000
1/4	.2500	1/32	.0313	3/8	.3750	5/8	.6250	7/11	.6364
1/5	.2000	1/64	.0156	3/10	.3000	5/9	.5556	7/12	.5833
1/6	.1667	2/3	.6667	3/11	.2727	5/11	.4545	8/9	.8889
1/7	.1429	2/5	.4000	3/16	.1875	5/12	.4167	8/11	.7273
1/8	.1250	2/7	.2857	4/5	.8000	5/16	.3125	9/10	.9000
1/9	.1111	2/9	.2222	4/7	.5714	6/7	.8571	9/11	.8182
1/10	.1000	2/11	.1818	4/9	.4444	6/11	.5455	10/11	.9091
1/11	.0909	3/4	.7500	4/11	.3636	7/8	.8750	11/12	.9167

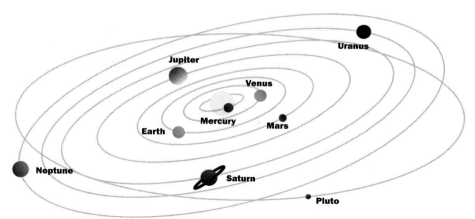

798 Planet Profusion

Our solar system is located in the Milky Way Galaxy. Even though this galaxy contains approximately 100 billion stars, our solar system contains only one star—the sun. The sun, which is the center of our solar system, has nine planets and a countless number of asteroids, meteors, and comets orbiting it. (See the illustration.) The planets are divided into two categories: the terrestrial planets—Mercury, Venus, Earth, Mars, and Pluto—which resemble Earth in size, chemical composition, and density; and the Jovian planets—Jupiter, Saturn, Uranus, and Neptune—which are much larger in size and have thick, gaseous atmospheres and low densities. (See the table below.)

	Sun	Moon	Mercury	Venus	Earth	Mars	Jupiter	Saturn	Uranus	Neptune	Pluto
Orbital Speed (in mi. per second)		.6	29.8	21.8	18.5	15.0	8.1	6.0	4.1	3.4	2.9
Rotation on Axis	24 days 16 hrs. 48 min.	27 days 7 hrs. 38 min.	59 days	243 days	23 hrs. 56 min.	1 day 37 min.	9 hrs. 55 min.	10 hrs. 39 min.	16 to 28 hours	16 hrs.	6 days
Mean Surface Gravity (Earth=1)		0.16	0.38	0.9	1.00	0.38	2.87	1.32	0.93	1.23	0.03
Density (times that of water)	100 (core)	3.3	5.4	5.3	5.5	3.9	1.3	0.7	1.2	1.6	1.0
Mass (times that of Earth)	333,000	0.012	0.055	0.82	6×10^{21} metric tons	0.11	318	95	14.6	17.2	0.0026
Approx. Weight of a Human (in lbs.)		24	57	135	150	57	431	198	140	185	4.5
No. of Satellites	9 planets	0	0	0	1	2	16	23	15	8	1
Mean Distance to Sun (in millions of miles)		93.0	36.0	67.23	92.96	141.7	483.7	886.2	1,781	2,793	3,660
Revolution Around Sun		365.25 days	88.0 days	224.7 days	365.25 days	686.99 days	11.86 years	29.46 years	84.0 years	164.8 years	247.6 years
Approximate Surface Temp. (degrees Fahrenheit)	10,000° (surface) 27,000,000° (center)	lighted side 200° dark side -230°	-315°	850°	-126.9° to 136°	-191° to -24°	-236°	-285°	-357°	-400°	-342° to -369°
Diameter (in miles)	867,000	2,155	3,031	7,520	7,926	4,200	88,700	74,600	31,570	30,800	1,420

799

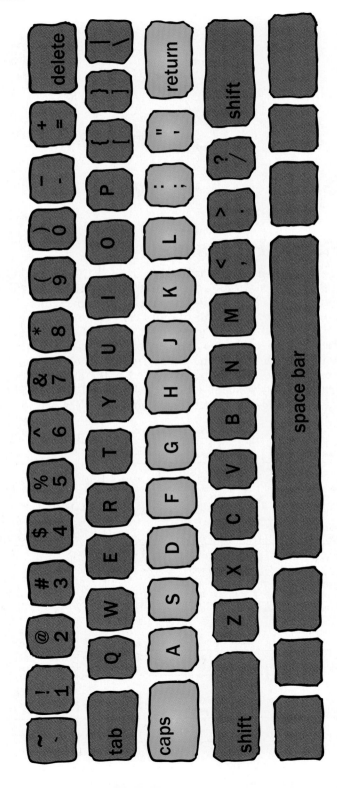

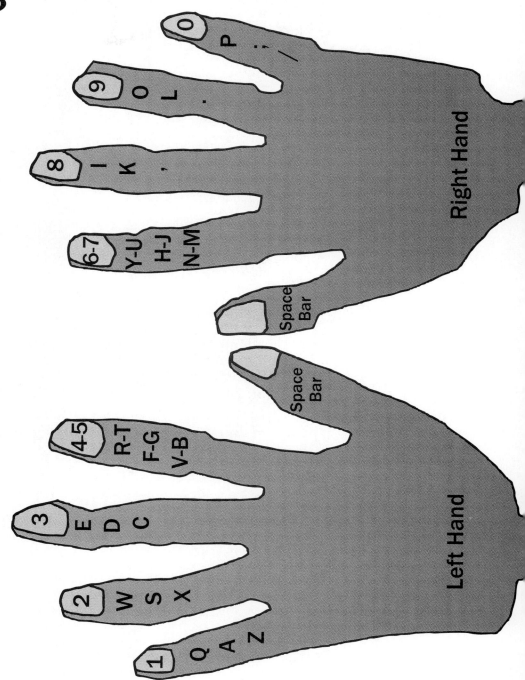

Periodic Table of the Elements

Atomic Number ——— 1

Symbol ——— **H**
Hydrogen
1.00797

Atomic Weight
(or Mass Number of most stable
isotope if in parentheses)

Legend:
- Alkali metals
- Alkaline earth metals
- Transition metals
- Lanthanide series
- Actinide series
- Other metals
- Nonmetals
- Noble gases

(Names of elements 104-109 subject to approval by
International Union of Pure & Applied Chemistry.)

1a	2a	3b	4b	5b	6b	7b	8	8	8	1b	2b	3a	4a	5a	6a	7a	0
1 **H** Hydrogen 1.00797																	2 **He** Helium 4.00260
3 **Li** Lithium 6.941	4 **Be** Beryllium 9.0128											5 **B** Boron 10.811	6 **C** Carbon 12.01115	7 **N** Nitrogen 14.0067	8 **O** Oxygen 15.9994	9 **F** Fluorine 18.9984	10 **Ne** Neon 20.179
11 **Na** Sodium 22.9898	12 **Mg** Magnesium 24.305											13 **Al** Aluminum 26.9815	14 **Si** Silicon 28.0855	15 **P** Phosphorus 30.9738	16 **S** Sulfur 32.064	17 **Cl** Chlorine 35.453	18 **Ar** Argon 39.948
19 **K** Potassium 39.0983	20 **Ca** Calcium 40.08	21 **Sc** Scandium 44.9559	22 **Ti** Titanium 47.88	23 **V** Vanadium 50.94	24 **Cr** Chromium 51.996	25 **Mn** Manganese 54.9380	26 **Fe** Iron 55.847	27 **Co** Cobalt 58.9332	28 **Ni** Nickel 58.69	29 **Cu** Copper 63.546	30 **Zn** Zinc 65.39	31 **Ga** Gallium 69.72	32 **Ge** Germanium 72.59	33 **As** Arsenic 74.9216	34 **Se** Selenium 78.96	35 **Br** Bromine 79.904	36 **Kr** Krypton 83.80
37 **Rb** Rubidium 85.4678	38 **Sr** Strontium 87.62	39 **Y** Yttrium 88.905	40 **Zr** Zirconium 91.224	41 **Nb** Niobium 92.906	42 **Mo** Molybdenum 95.94	43 **Tc** Technetium (98)	44 **Ru** Ruthenium 101.07	45 **Rh** Rhodium 102.906	46 **Pd** Palladium 106.42	47 **Ag** Silver 107.868	48 **Cd** Cadmium 112.41	49 **In** Indium 114.82	50 **Sn** Tin 118.71	51 **Sb** Antimony 121.75	52 **Te** Tellurium 127.60	53 **I** Iodine 126.905	54 **Xe** Xenon 131.29
55 **Cs** Cesium 132.905	56 **Ba** Barium 137.33	57-71* Lanthanides	72 **Hf** Hafnium 178.49	73 **Ta** Tantalum 180.948	74 **W** Tungsten 183.85	75 **Re** Rhenium 186.207	76 **Os** Osmium 190.2	77 **Ir** Iridium 192.22	78 **Pt** Platinum 195.08	79 **Au** Gold 196.967	80 **Hg** Mercury 200.59	81 **Tl** Thallium 204.383	82 **Pb** Lead 207.19	83 **Bi** Bismuth 208.980	84 **Po** Polonium (209)	85 **At** Astatine (210)	86 **Rn** Radon (222)
87 **Fr** Francium (223)	88 **Ra** Radium 226.025	89-103** Actinides (227)	104 **Db** Dubnium (261)	105 **Jl** Joliotium (262)	106 **Rf** Rutherfordium (263)	107 **Bh** Bohrium (262)	108 **Hn** Hahnium (265)	109 **Mt** Meitnerium (266)	110 (269)	111 (272)							

*Lanthanides

57 **La** Lanthanum 138.906	58 **Ce** Cerium 140.12	59 **Pr** Praseodymium 140.908	60 **Nd** Neodymium 144.24	61 **Pm** Promethium (145)	62 **Sm** Samarium 150.36	63 **Eu** Europium 151.96	64 **Gd** Gadolinium 157.25	65 **Tb** Terbium 158.925	66 **Dy** Dysprosium 162.50	67 **Ho** Holmium 164.930	68 **Er** Erbium 167.26	69 **Tm** Thulium 168.934	70 **Yb** Ytterbium 173.04	71 **Lu** Lutetium 174.967

**Actinides

89 **Ac** Actinium 227.028	90 **Th** Thorium 232.038	91 **Pa** Protactinium 231.036	92 **U** Uranium 238.029	93 **Np** Neptunium 237.048	94 **Pu** Plutonium (244)	95 **Am** Americium (243)	96 **Cm** Curium (247)	97 **Bk** Berkelium (247)	98 **Cf** Californium (251)	99 **Es** Einsteinium (252)	100 **Fm** Fermium (257)	101 **Md** Mendelevium (258)	102 **No** Nobelium (259)	103 **Lr** Lawrencium (260)

"We are citizens of the world, and the tragedy of our times is that we do not know this."

—Woodrow Wilson

World Maps

802   As you know, the world has changed dramatically in the past several years. As global citizens it is up to each of us to stay on top of those changes. Just as we once tried to understand something about each of the 50 states, we must now work to understand each of the more than 190 countries in the world. The section that follows will give you the map skills you need to begin your work.

803 Finding Direction

Mapmakers use special marks and symbols to show where things are or to give other useful information. Among other things, these marks and symbols show direction (north, south, east, and west). On most maps, north is at the top. But you should always check the **compass rose,** or directional finder, to make sure you know where north is. If there is no symbol, you can assume that north is at the top.

804 Finding Information

Other important marks and symbols are explained in a box printed on each map. This box is called the **legend**, or **key**. It is included to make it easier for you to understand and use the map. Below is a United States map legend. This legend includes symbols for state capitals and state boundaries, as well as other useful information.

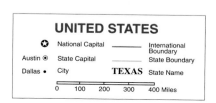

805 Measuring Distances

To measure distances on a map, use the **map scale**. (See the sample below.) Line up an index card or a piece of paper under the map scale and put a dot on your paper at "0." Now put other dots to mark off 100, 200, 300, and so on. Your paper can now be used to measure the approximate distance between points on the map.

```
├───┼───┼───┼───┤
0   100  200  300  400 Miles
```

806 Locating Countries

Latitude and **longitude lines** are another helpful feature of most maps. Latitude and longitude refer to imaginary lines that mapmakers use. When used together, these lines can be used to locate any point on the earth.

Latitude

The imaginary lines that go from east to west around the earth are called lines of latitude. The line of latitude that goes around the earth exactly halfway between the North Pole and the South Pole is called the *equator*. Latitude is measured in degrees, with the equator being 0 degrees (0°). Above the equator, the lines are called *north latitude* and measure from 0° to 90° north (the North Pole). Below the equator, the lines are called *south latitude* and measure from 0° to 90° south (the South Pole). On a map, latitude numbers are printed along the left- and right-hand sides.

Longitude

The imaginary lines that run from the North Pole to the South Pole are lines of longitude. The *prime meridian,* which passes through Greenwich, England, is 0° longitude. Lines east of the prime meridian are called *east longitude;* lines west of the prime meridian are called *west longitude.* On a map, longitude numbers are printed at the top and bottom.

THE BOTTOM LINE

The latitude and longitude numbers of a location are called its **coordinates**. In each set of coordinates, latitude is given first, then longitude. To locate a certain place on a map using its coordinates, find the point where the two lines cross. Take, for example, Australia, which has coordinates 25° S, 135° E. After finding the equator (0°), locate the line 25° south of that. Next, find the prime meridian (0°), and then the line 135° to its east. You will find Australia at the point where these two imaginary lines intersect.

807 Index to World Maps

Country	Latitude	Longitude	Country	Latitude	Longitude
Afghanistan	33° N	65° E	Georgia	43° N	45° E
Albania	41° N	20° E	Germany	51° N	10° E
Algeria	28° N	3° E	Ghana	8° N	2° W
Andorra	42° N	1° E	Greece	39° N	22° E
Angola	12° S	18° E	Greenland	70° N	40° W
Antigua and Barbuda	17° N	61° W	Grenada	12° N	61° W
Argentina	34° S	64° W	Guatemala	15° N	90° W
Armenia	41° N	45° E	Guinea	11° N	10° W
Australia	25° S	135° E	Guinea-Bissau	12° N	15° W
Austria	47° N	13° E	Guyana	5° N	59° W
Azerbaijan	41° N	47° E	Haiti	19° N	72° W
Bahamas	24° N	76° W	Honduras	15° N	86° W
Bahrain	26° N	50° E	Hungary	47° N	20° E
Bangladesh	24° N	90° E	Iceland	65° N	18° W
Barbados	13° N	59° W	India	20° N	77° E
Belarus	54° N	25° E	Indonesia	5° S	120° E
Belgium	50° N	4° E	Iran	32° N	53° E
Belize	17° N	88° W	Iraq	33° N	44° E
Benin	9° N	2° E	Ireland	53° N	8° W
Bhutan	27° N	90° E	Israel	31° N	35° E
Bolivia	17° S	65° W	Italy	42° N	12° E
Bosnia-Herzegovina	44° N	18° E	Ivory Coast	8° N	5° W
Botswana	22° S	24° E	Jamaica	18° N	77° W
Brazil	10° S	55° W	Japan	36° N	138° E
Brunei	4° N	114° E	Jordan	31° N	36° E
Bulgaria	43° N	25° E	Kazakhstan	45° N	70° E
Burkina Faso	13° N	2° W	Kenya	1° N	38° E
Burundi	3° S	30° E	Kiribati	0° N	175° E
Cambodia	13° N	105° E	North Korea	40° N	127° E
Cameroon	6° N	12° E	South Korea	36° N	128° E
Canada	60° N	95° W	Kuwait	29° N	47° E
Cape Verde	16° N	24° W	Kyrgyzstan	42° N	75° E
Central African Republic	7° N	21° E	Laos	18° N	105° E
Chad	15° N	19° E	Latvia	57° N	25° E
Chile	30° S	71° W	Lebanon	34° N	36° E
China	35° N	105° E	Lesotho	29° S	28° E
Colombia	4° N	72° W	Liberia	6° N	10° W
Comoros	12° S	44° E	Libya	27° N	17° E
Congo	1° S	15° E	Liechtenstein	47° N	9° E
Costa Rica	10° N	84° W	Lithuania	56° N	24° E
Croatia	45° N	16° E	Luxembourg	49° N	6° E
Cuba	21° N	80° W	Macedonia	43° N	22° E
Cyprus	35° N	33° E	Madagascar	19° S	46° E
Czech Republic	50° N	15° E	Malawi	13° S	34° E
Denmark	56° N	10° E	Malaysia	2° N	112° E
Djibouti	11° N	43° E	Maldives	2° N	70° E
Dominica	15° N	61° W	Mali	17° N	4° W
Dominican Republic	19° N	70° W	Malta	36° N	14° E
Ecuador	2° S	77° W	Mauritania	20° N	12° W
Egypt	27° N	30° E	Mauritius	20° S	57° E
El Salvador	14° N	89° W	Mexico	23° N	102° W
Equatorial Guinea	2° N	9° E	Moldova	47° N	28° E
Eritrea	17° N	38° E	Monaco	43° N	7° E
Estonia	59° N	26° E	Mongolia	46° N	105° E
Ethiopia	8° N	38° E	Montenegro	43° N	19° E
Fiji	19° S	174° E	Morocco	32° N	5° W
Finland	64° N	26° E	Mozambique	18° S	35° E
France	46° N	2° E	Myanmar	25° N	95° E
Gabon	1° S	11° E	Namibia	22° S	17° E
The Gambia	13° N	16° W	Nauru	1° S	166° E

Country	Latitude	Longitude
Nepal	28° N	84° E
Netherlands	52° N	5° E
New Zealand	41° S	174° E
Nicaragua	13° N	85° W
Niger	16° N	8° E
Nigeria	10° N	8° E
Northern Ireland	55° N	7° W
Norway	62° N	10° E
Oman	22° N	58° E
Pakistan	30° N	70° E
Panama	9° N	80° W
Papua New Guinea	6° S	147° E
Paraguay	23° S	58° W
Peru	10° S	76° W
Philippines	13° N	122° E
Poland	52° N	19° E
Portugal	39° N	8° W
Qatar	25° N	51° E
Romania	46° N	25° E
Russia	60° N	80° E
Rwanda	2° S	30° E
St. Kitts & Nevis	17° N	62° W
Saint Lucia	14° N	61° W
Saint Vincent and the Grenadines	13° N	61° W
San Marino	44° N	12° E
Sao Tome and Principe	1° N	7° E
Saudi Arabia	25° N	45° E
Scotland	57° N	5° W
Senegal	14° N	14° W
Serbia	45° N	21° E
Seychelles	5° S	55° E
Sierra Leone	8° N	11° W
Singapore	1° N	103° E
Slovakia	49° N	19° E
Slovenia	46° N	15° E
Solomon Islands	8° S	159° E
Somalia	10° N	49° E
South Africa	30° S	26° E
Spain	40° N	4° W
Sri Lanka	7° N	81° E
Sudan	15° N	30° E
Suriname	4° N	56° W
Swaziland	26° S	31° E
Sweden	62° N	15° E
Switzerland	47° N	8° E
Syria	35° N	38° E
Taiwan	23° N	121° E
Tajikistan	39° N	71° E
Tanzania	6° S	35° E
Thailand	15° N	100° E
Togo	8° N	1° E
Tonga	20° S	173° W
Trinidad/Tobago	11° N	61° W
Tunisia	34° N	9° E
Turkey	39° N	35° E
Turkmenistan	40° N	55° E
Tuvalu	8° S	179° E
Uganda	1° N	32° E
Ukraine	50° N	30° E
United Arab Emirates	24° N	54° E

Country	Latitude	Longitude
United Kingdom	54° N	2° W
United States	38° N	97° W
Uruguay	33° S	56° W
Uzbekistan	40° N	68° E
Vanuatu	17° S	170° E
Venezuela	8° N	66° W
Vietnam	17° N	106° E
Wales	53° N	3° W
Western Samoa	10° S	173° W
Yemen	15° N	44° E
Yugoslavia	44° N	19° E
Zaire	4° S	25° E
Zambia	15° S	30° E
Zimbabwe	20° S	30° E

Topographic Tally Table

THE CONTINENTS

	Area (Sq Km)	Percent of Earth's Land
Asia	44,026,000	29.7
Africa	30,271,000	20.4
North America	24,258,000	16.3
South America	17,823,000	12.0
Antarctica	13,209,000	8.9
Europe	10,404,000	7.0
Australia	7,682,000	5.2

LONGEST RIVERS

	Length (Km)
Nile, *Africa*	6,671
Amazon, *South America*	6,437
Chang Jiang (Yangtze), *Asia*	6,380
Mississippi-Missouri, *North America*	5,971
Ob-Irtysk, *Asia*	5,410
Huang (Yellow), *Asia*	4,672
Congo, *Africa*	4,667
Amur, *Asia*	4,416
Lena, *Asia*	4,400

MAJOR ISLANDS

	Area (Sq Km)
Greenland	2,175,600
New Guinea	792,500
Borneo	725,500
Madagascar	587,000
Baffin	507,500
Sumatra	427,300
Honshu	227,400
Great Britain	218,100
Victoria	217,300
Ellesmere	196,200
Celebes	178,700
South (New Zealand)	151,000
Java	126,700

THE OCEANS

	Area (Sq Km)	Percent of Earth's Water Area
Pacific	166,241,000	46.0
Atlantic	86,557,000	23.9
Indian	73,427,000	20.3
Arctic	9,485,000	2.6

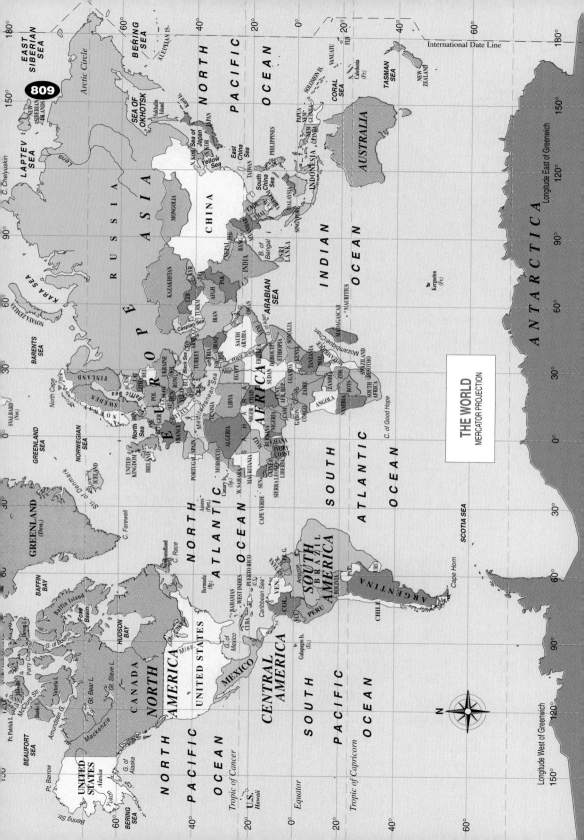

THE WORLD
MERCATOR PROJECTION

NORTH AMERICA

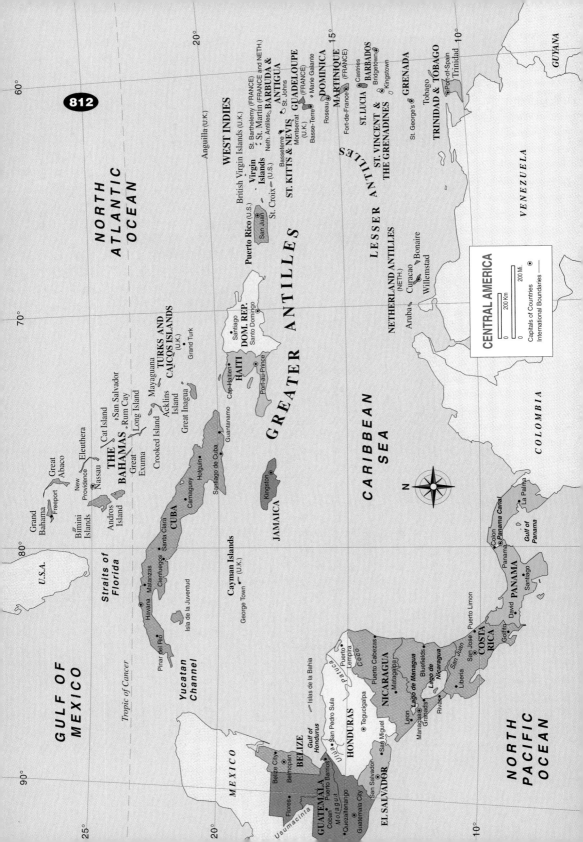

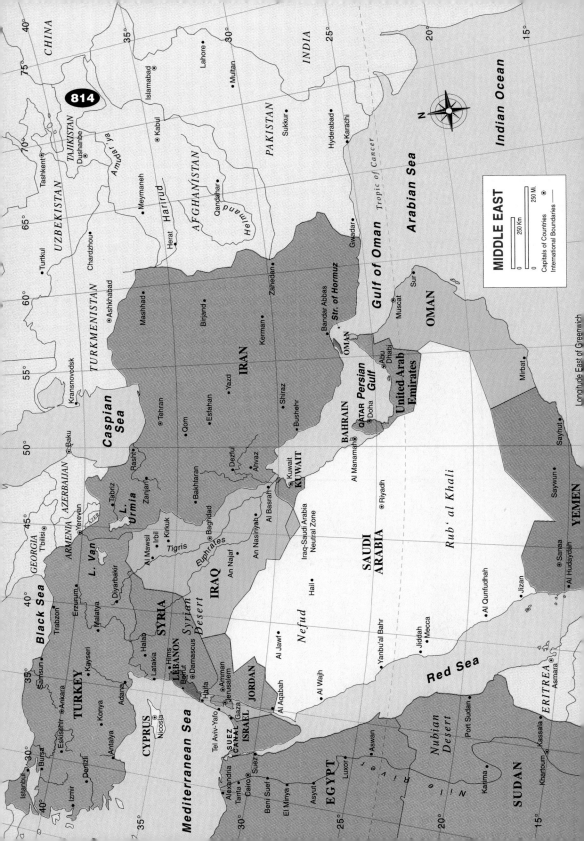

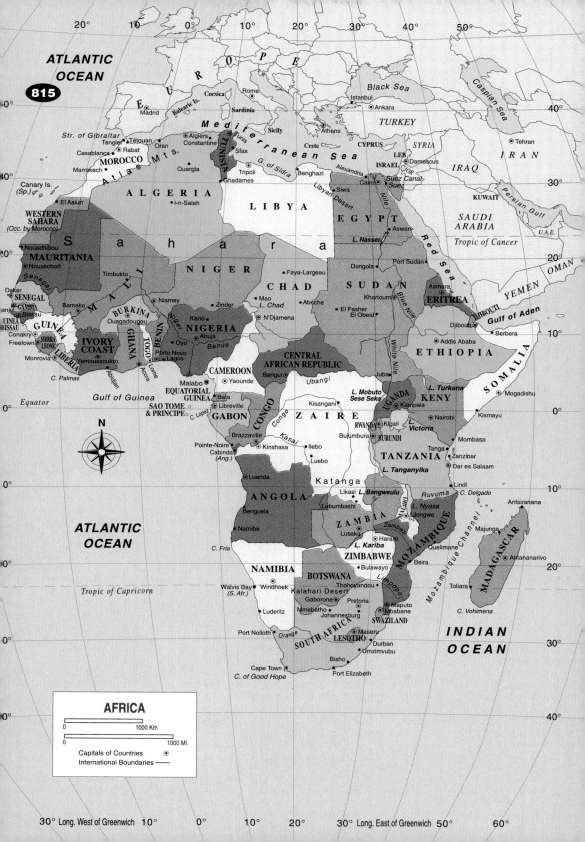

AFRICA

ATLANTIC OCEAN

815

20° 10° 0° 10° 20° 30° 40° 50°

E U R O P E

ATLANTIC
OCEAN

Str. of Gibraltar
Madrid
Balearic Is.
Corsica
Rome
Sardinia

Mediterranean Sea

Black Sea
Istanbul
Ankara
TURKEY

Caspian Sea

Tangier
Tétouan
Casablanca
Rabat
Marrakech
Oran
Algiers
Constantine
TUNISIA
Tunis
Sfax
Tripoli
Ghadames

Crete
Athens
CYPRUS
SYRIA
LEB.
Damascus

Tehran
IRAN

Canary Is.
(Sp.)
El Aaiún

MOROCCO
Atlas Mts.
Ouargla
I-n-Salah

ALGERIA

LIBYA
Libyan Desert

G. of Sidra
Benghazi
Alexandria
Cairo
Suez Canal
Suez
ISRAEL
JOR.

IRAQ
KUWAIT

Persian Gulf

**WESTERN
SAHARA**
(Occ. by Morocco)

S a h a r a

EGYPT
Siwa
L. Nasser
Aswan
Nile

**SAUDI
ARABIA**

Tropic of Cancer
U.A.E.

Nouadhibou
Nouakchott
MAURITANIA
Senegal

Timbuktu

NIGER
Mao
L. Chad

Faya-Largeau

Dongola
Port Sudan

Red Sea
OMAN

Dakar
SENEGAL
Banjul
GAMBIA
Bissau
GUINEA BISSAU
Conakry
Freetown
SIERRA LEONE
Monrovia
LIBERIA
C. Palmas

Bamako
M A L I
Niamey
Zinder
BURKINA
Ouagadougou
GHANA
Kano
NIGERIA
Abuja
Oyo
Benue
Porto Novo
Lagos
Accra
Lome
TOGO
BENIN
**IVORY
COAST**
Yamoussoukro
Abidjan

CHAD
Abéché
N'Djamena
El Fasher
El Obeid

SUDAN
Khartoum
Blue Nile
Asmara
ERITREA
DJIBOUTI
Djibouti
Berbera

Gulf of Aden

CAMEROON
Malabo
**EQUATORIAL
GUINEA**
Bata
Yaounde
Bangui
Ubangi

**CENTRAL
AFRICAN REPUBLIC**

Addis Ababa
ETHIOPIA

White Nile
Juba

L. Turkana

SOMALIA
Mogadishu

**SAO TOME
& PRINCIPE**
Libreville
C. Lopez
GABON
CONGO
Brazzaville
Pointe-Noire
Cabinda
(Ang.)
Kinshasa

Congo
Kasai
Ilebo
Luebo
Kisangani
ZAIRE

L. Mobuto
Sese Seko
UGANDA
Kampala
RWANDA
Kigali
BURUNDI
Bujumbura
L. Victoria

KENYA
Nairobi
Kismayu
Mombasa

Equator

TANZANIA
Tanga
Zanzibar
Dar es Salaam
L. Tanganyika

ANGOLA
Luanda
Benguela
Namibe
C. Fria

Katanga
Likasi
Lubumbashi
L. Bangweulu

Lindi
Ruvuma
C. Delgado

Antsiranana
MADAGASCAR
Majunga
Antananarivo

ZAMBIA
Lusaka
L. Kariba
Harare
ZIMBABWE
Bulawayo

L. Nyasa
Quionga
Zambezi
MOZAMBIQUE
Quelimane
Beira

Mozambique Channel

ATLANTIC
OCEAN

NAMIBIA
Walvis Bay
(S. Afr.)
Windhoek
Luderitz

BOTSWANA
Kalahari Desert
Gaborone
Mmabatho
Pretoria
Johannesburg

Thohoyandou
Limpopo
Maputo
Mbabane
SWAZILAND

Tropic of Capricorn

**INDIAN
OCEAN**

Port Nolloth
Orange
Cape Town
C. of Good Hope

SOUTH AFRICA
Maseru
LESOTHO
Bisho
Umzimvubu
Durban
Port Elizabeth

AFRICA

0   1000 Km
0   1000 Mi.

Capitals of Countries
International Boundaries

30° Long. West of Greenwich 10°   0°   10°   20°   30° Long. East of Greenwich 50°   60°

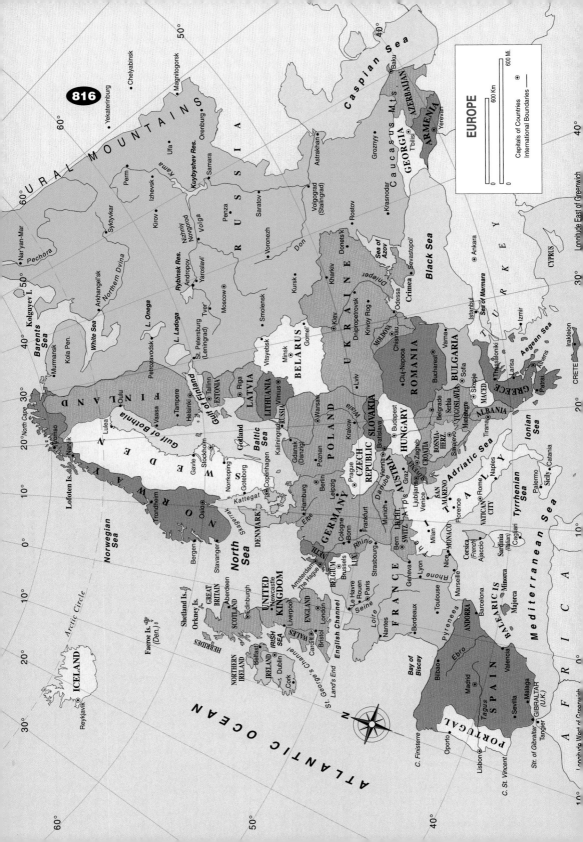

EUROPE

Capitals of Countries ⊙
International Boundaries —

600 Km
600 Mi.

816

ATLANTIC OCEAN

ICELAND
Reykjavik

Arctic Circle

Faeroe Is. (Den.)

Shetland Is.
Orkney Is.
HEBRIDES
Aberdeen
SCOTLAND
Edinburgh
GREAT BRITAIN
Newcastle
NORTHERN IRELAND
Belfast
IRELAND
Dublin
IRISH SEA
Liverpool
Cork
St. George's Channel
Land's End
WALES
Cardiff
Bristol
London
ENGLAND
UNITED KINGDOM
English Channel

URAL MOUNTAINS

Chelyabinsk
Yekaterinburg
Magnitogorsk
Orenburg
Ufa
Perm
Kama
Izhevsk
Samara
Kuybyshev Res.
Nar'yan-Mar
Pechora
Syktyvkar
Kirov
Penza
Saratov
Northern Dvina
Arkhangel'sk
Kotlas
RUSSIA
Nizhniy Novgorod
Volga
Voronezh
Murmansk
Kola Pen.
White Sea
L. Onega
L. Ladoga
Petrozavodsk
Yaroslavl'
Andropov
Rybinsk Res.
Tver
Moscow
Smolensk
Kursk
Don
Rostov
Volgograd (Stalingrad)
Astrakhan
Krasnodar
Caspian Sea
Baku
AZERBAIJAN
ARMENIA
Yerevan
GEORGIA
Tbilisi
Caucasus Mts.
Grozny
Sea of Azov
Donetsk
Sevastopol'
Crimea
Black Sea
Odessa
Krivoy Rog
Dnipropetrovsk
Dnieper
UKRAINE
Kharkiv
Kiev
Gomel
Chişinău
MOLDOVA
ROMANIA
Bucharest
Cluj-Napoca
BULGARIA
Sofia
Varna
Skopje
MACED.
Thessaloniki
Larisa
Aegean Sea
Izmir
TURKEY
Ankara
Sea of Marmara
Istanbul
Iraklion
CRETE
GREECE
Athens
Patrai
Ionian Sea
ALBANIA
Tirana
Montenegro
Serbia
YUGOSLAVIA
BOSNIA-HERZ.
Sarajevo
Belgrade
Adriatic Sea
CROATIA
Zagreb

North Cape
Tromsø
Narvik
Lofoten Is.
NORWAY
SWEDEN
Luleå
Oulu
FINLAND
Vaasa
Tampere
Helsinki
Gulf of Bothnia
Gulf of Finland
Tallinn
ESTONIA
Riga
LATVIA
Vilnius
LITHUANIA
Kaliningrad
RUSSIA
Gotland
Stockholm
Gävle
Göteborg
Norrköping
Baltic Sea
Kaliningrad
BELARUS
Minsk
Vitsyebsk
Lviv
Warsaw
POLAND
Gdansk (Danzig)
Poznań
Kraków
Wisła
Bergen
Oslo
Trondheim
Stavanger
Skagerrak
Kattegat
DENMARK
Copenhagen
North Sea
Norwegian Sea

Bodø
Hamburg
Berlin
Leipzig
Elbe
Cologne
Bonn
Frankfurt
GERMANY
Prague
CZECH REPUBLIC
Munich
Danube
Vienna
Bratislava
SLOVAKIA
Budapest
HUNGARY
AUSTRIA
Graz
SLOVENIA
Venice
Milan
ITALY
Florence
Rome
VATICAN CITY
Naples
Tyrrhenian Sea
Palermo
Sicily
Catania
San Marino
MONACO
Corsica (French)
Ajaccio
Sardinia (Italian)
Cagliari
SWITZ.
Bern
Geneva
LIECHT.
Rhine
Strasbourg
Amsterdam
The Hague
NETH.
BELGIUM
Brussels
Lille
Le Havre
Rouen
Seine
Paris
FRANCE
Nantes
Loire
Bordeaux
Toulouse
Lyon
Rhône
Nice
Marseille
Pyrenees
Bay of Biscay
ANDORRA
Barcelona
Minorca
Majorca
BALEARIC IS.
Valencia
SPAIN
Madrid
Bilbao
Ebro
C. Finisterre
Oporto
PORTUGAL
Lisbon
Tagus
C. St. Vincent
Sevilla
Malaga
GIBRALTAR (U.K.)
Str. of Gibraltar
Tangier
AFRICA
Mediterranean Sea

Longitude East of Greenwich
Longitude West of Greenwich

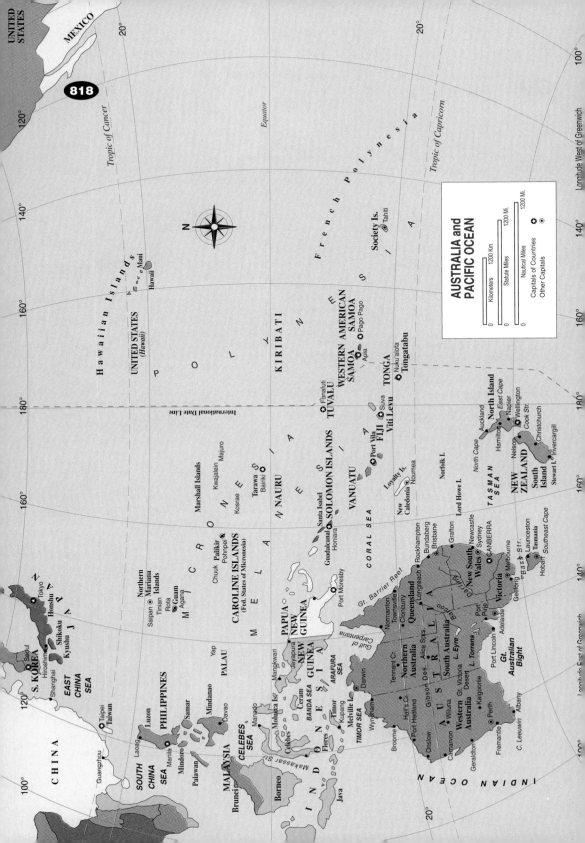

AUSTRALIA and
PACIFIC OCEAN

Kilometers   1200 Km
0
Statute Miles   1200 Mi.
0
Nautical Miles   1200 Mi.
0

⊛ Capitals of Countries
⊙ Other Capitals

818

"When I want to understand what is happening today or try to decide what will happen tomorrow, I look back."

—Oliver Wendell Holmes, Jr.

Historical Time Line

819   The historical time line covers the next 10 pages in your handbook and over 500 years of history—from 1492 when Columbus discovered the West Indies, to 1969 when the first astronauts walked on the moon, to the present time.

Along the way you'll find out some very interesting facts. Do you know when

- the first watch was invented?
- the first newspaper was printed in the U.S.?
- Washington, D.C., became the capital?
- the first photograph was taken?
- Eli Whitney invented mass production?
- women were given the right to vote?
- CD's were first developed?

Well, you'll find the answers to these and many other questions as you look through the historical time line. You should also notice that the time line is divided into three parts: **United States History, Science & Technology,** and **Daily Living**. As a result, you will be able to imagine what was going on in the White House in Washington as well as in the houses of your own hometown.

1500	1520	1540	1560	1580

UNITED STATES HISTORY

1492
Columbus reaches the West Indies.

1513
Ponce de León explores Florida; Balboa reaches Pacific.

1519
Magellan begins three-year voyage around the world.

1521
Cortez defeats Aztecs and claims Mexico for Spain.

1542
Cabrillo explores California.

1559
Spanish colony of Pensacola, Florida, lasts two years.

1565
Spain settles St. Augustine, Florida, first permanent European colony.

1570
League of the Iroquois Nations formed.

1588
England defeats the Spanish Armada and rules the seas.

1597
British Parliament sends criminals to colonies.

SCIENCE & TECHNOLOGY

1507
Book on surgery is developed.

1509
Watches are invented in Germany.

1530
Bottle corks are invented.

1531
Halley's Comet appears.

1545
French printer Garamond sets first type.

1543
Copernicus' theory proclaims a sun-centered universe.

1558
Magnetic compass is invented by John Dee.

1585
Decimals introduced by Dutch mathematicians.

1590
First paper mill is used in England.

1596
Thermometer is invented.

DAILY LIVING

1500
Game of bingo developed.

1503
Raw sugar is refined.

1507
Glass mirrors are greatly improved.

1513
Machiavelli's *The Prince* is published.

1517
Reformation begins in Europe.

1536
First songbook used in Spain.

1538
Mercator draws map with America on it.

1541
Michelangelo completes largest painting, *The Last Judgment*.

1564
First horse-drawn coach used in England.

1580
First water closet designed in Bath, England.

1582
Pope Gregory XIII introduces the modern calendar.

1589
Iron-making process patented in England.

1599
Copper coins made.

U.S. POPULATION: (NATIVE AMERICAN)   SPANISH

approximately 1,100,000   **1,021**

1600   1620   1640   1660   1680   1700

1607
England establishes Jamestown, Virginia.

1609
Henry Hudson explores the Hudson River and Great Lakes.

1619
House of Burgesses is established in Virginia.

1620
Pilgrims found Plymouth Colony.

1634
Colony of Maryland is founded.

1629
Massachusetts Bay Colony is established.

1646
First spinning school is established in Jamestown, Virginia.

1654
First Jewish colonists settle in New Amsterdam.

1664
The Dutch colony of New Netherlands becomes the English colony of New York.

1673
Marquette and Joliet explore Mississippi River for France.

1682
William Penn founds Pennsylvania.

1608
Telescope is invented.

1609
Galileo makes first observations with telescope.

1643
Galileo invents the barometer.

1650
First pendulum clocks developed by Huygens.

1629
Human temperature measured by a physician in Italy.

1668
Reflecting telescope invented by Sir Isaac Newton.

1671
First calculation machine invented.

1682
Halley's Comet is studied by Edmund Halley and named for him.

1687
Newton describes gravity and publishes *Principia Mathematica*.

1600
Shakespeare's plays are performed at Globe Theatre in London.

1605
European diseases are killing Native Americans (measles, TB, and smallpox).

1622
January 1 accepted as beginning of the year (instead of March 25).

1636
Harvard is the first college in the colonies.

1638
Stephen Daye installs first printing press in America.

1640
First book printed in the colonies.

1653
First postage stamps used in Paris.

1658
First colonial police force created in New Amsterdam.

1685
First drinking fountain used in England.

1698
First steam-powered machine, designed by Thomas Savery, pumps water.

(ENGLISH)

| 350 | 2,302 | 26,634 | 75,058 | 151,507 |

1700   1710   1720   1730   1740

UNITED STATES HISTORY

1700
France builds forts at Mackinac and Detroit to control fur trade.

1705
Virginia Act establishes public education.

1707
England (English) and Scotland (Scots) unite and become Great Britain (British).

1711
Tuscarora War fought in Carolina.

1718
France founds New Orleans.

Scotland

England

1733
Molasses Act places taxes on sugar and molasses.

1733
James Oglethorpe founds Georgia.

1735
Freedom of the press established during trial of John Peter Zenger.

1747
Ohio Company formed to settle Ohio River Valley.

1747
Trade workers organize in New York.

SCIENCE & TECHNOLOGY

1701
Seed drill that plants seeds in a row is invented by Jethro Tull.

1709
The pianoforte (first piano) is invented by Christofori Bartolommeo.

1712
Thomas Newcomen develops first practical steam engine.

1719
J. Le Blon patents four-color printing system.

1728
First dental drill is used by Pierre Fauchard.

1732
Sedatives for operations discovered by Thomas Dover.

1735
Rubber found in South America.

1738
First cuckoo clocks invented in Germany.

1742
Benjamin Franklin invents efficient Franklin stove.

1747
First civil engineering school established in France.

DAILY LIVING

1700
The Selling of Joseph by Samuel Sewall is first protest of slavery.

1701
Yale University is founded.

1704
First successful newspaper in colonies, *Boston News-Letter*, is published.

1716
First hot-water home heating system developed.

1719
Robinson Crusoe is written by Daniel Defoe.

1726
Gulliver's Travels written by Jonathan Swift.

1731
Ben Franklin begins first subscription library.

1732
Poor Richard's Almanac printed.

1736
First successful appendectomy performed.

1739
William Geld invents stereotype printing.

1742
Handel composes the *Messiah*.

1749
Pereire invents sign language for deaf.

U.S. POPULATION: (ENGLISH COLONIES)

| 250,888 | 331,711 | 466,185 | 629,445 | 905,563 |

1750	1760	1770	1780	1790	1800

1750
The French and Indian War begins.

1765
Stamp Act tax imposed on colonies.

1776
Declaration of Independence signed at Second Continental Congress on July 4.

1787
U.S. Constitution is signed.

1789
George Washington elected president.

1750
Flatbed boats and Conestoga wagons begin moving settlers west.

1770
Boston Massacre occurs.

1781
British surrender at Yorktown October 19.

1789
French Revolution begins.

1763
French and Indian War ends.

1773
Boston Tea Party occurs.

1781
United colonies adopt Articles of Confederation as first government.

1775
Revolutionary War begins.

1752
Benjamin Franklin discovers lightning is a form of electricity.

1770
First steam carriage is invented by French engineer Nicholas Cugnot.

1777
Johann Beckmann's *Guide to Technology* defines technological procedures.

1790
First U.S. patent law passed.

1758
Sextant for navigation is invented by John Bird.

1781
Uranus, first planet not known to ancient world, is discovered.

1793
Eli Whitney invents cotton gin that takes seeds out of cotton.

1764
"Spinning Jenny" for cotton is invented by James Hargreaves.

1776
Adam Smith's *Wealth of Nations* explains mechanization and division of labor.

1798
Eli Whitney invents mass production.

1752
First general hospital is established in Philadelphia.

1764
Mozart writes first symphony.

1776
Thomas Paine prints *Common Sense*.

1786
First ice-cream company in America begins production.

1760
Pencils are produced by Faber Company.

1769
Venetian blinds are first used.

1783
Bleaching fabrics with chlorine begins.

1790
Official U.S. census begins.

1757
Streetlights are installed in Philadelphia.

1783
Bell invents cylinder printing for fabrics.

1795
Food canning is introduced.

1,170,760	1,593,625	2,148,076	2,780,369	3,929,157

1800 1810 1820 1830 1840

UNITED STATES HISTORY

1800
Washington, D.C., becomes U.S. capital.

1803
Louisiana Purchase from France doubles U.S. size.

1804
Lewis & Clark explore Louisiana Territory and northwestern United States.

1812–1814
War of 1812 is fought between U.S. and Britain.

1819
U.S. acquires Florida from Spain.

1820
Missouri Compromise signed.

1825
Erie Canal opens from Albany to Buffalo, N.Y.

1830
Indian Removal Act forces Native Americans west of Mississippi River.

1836
Texans defend the Alamo.

1838
Cherokee Nation forced west on "Trail of Tears."

1846
Mexican War begins.

1848
The Associated Press (AP) formed by New York City newspapers.

1848
Gold found in California.

SCIENCE & TECHNOLOGY

1800
The battery is invented by Count Volta.

1802
Steamboat is built by Robert Fulton.

1808
Chemical symbols are developed by Jöns Berzelius.

1816
Stethoscope invented by Reneé Laënnec.

1819
Hans Christian Oestad discovers electromagnetism.

1822
William Beaumont studies digestion via exposed stomach of a wounded man.

1833
Michael Faraday produces aluminum.

1836
Samuel Morse invents telegraph.

1839
Bicycle is invented by Kirkpatrick Macmillan.

1845
The hypodermic syringe is developed.

1846
Elias Howe invents sewing machine.

DAILY LIVING

1800
Library of Congress is established.

1805
Thomas Plucknett invents the lawnmower.

1806
Gas lighting used in homes.

1815
John McAdam invents paved roads using crushed rock.

1816
Niepce takes first photograph.

1816
Fire extinguisher invented by Captain George Manby.

1812
Army meat inspector, "Uncle Sam" Wilson, becomes U.S. symbol.

1828
Webster's Dictionary is published.

1830
Mormon Church is founded.

1834
Louis Braille perfects a letter system for the blind.

1835
Samuel Colt patents a handgun with a rotating breech.

1841
Stapler is patented.

1844
Safety matches produced.

1849
Safety pin is invented.

U.S. POPULATION:

5,308,080	7,240,102	9,638,453	12,860,702	17,063,353

1850 **1860** **1870** **1880** **1890** **1900**

1853
National Council of Colored People is founded.

1860
Abraham Lincoln elected president.

1869
Florence Nightingale founds the first school of nursing.

1889
Jane Addams founds Hull House in Chicago to help immigrants.

1861
Civil War begins at Fort Sumter.

1869
Coast-to-coast railroad is finished in Utah.

1881
Samuel Gompers organizes American Federation of Labor.

1862
Lincoln proclaims abolition of slavery.

1876
Custer is defeated at Little Big Horn.

1886
Chicago labor gathering erupts into Haymarket Riot.

1865
Civil War ends.

1865
Lincoln is assassinated.

1898
U.S. defeats Spain in Spanish-American War.

1851
Isaac Singer produces sewing machine.

1860
Jean Lenoir builds internal combustion engine.

1874
Barbed wire introduced by Joseph Glidden.

1887
Radio waves produced by Hertz.

1893
First successful U.S. gasoline automobile is built.

1852
Elisha Otis invents elevator.

1861
Massachusetts Institute of Technology (MIT) founded.

1876
Alexander Graham Bell invents telephone.

1857
Atlantic cable is completed.

1865
Joseph Lister introduces antiseptic practices.

1896
Marconi invents wireless radio.

1879
Edison makes incandescent light bulb.

1898
Curies discover radium.

1851
First World's Fair is held in London, England.

1864
Red Cross is established.

1876
National Baseball League established.

1883
Four U.S. time zones are created.

1890
Workers' wages fixed at $1.50 a day.

1852
Uncle Tom's Cabin by Harriet Beecher Stowe strengthens anti-slavery movement.

1866
Hires introduces root beer.

1877
Thomas Edison invents phonograph.

1888
Pneumatic bicycle tires invented by John Dunlop.

1889
Roll film produced by George Eastman.

1855
Alexander Parks produces first synthetic plastic.

1873
Zipper invented by Whitcomb Judson.

1894
Pullman workers strike against railroad.

23,191,876   31,443,321   38,558,371   50,189,209   62,979,766

1900   1905   1910   1915   1920

UNITED STATES HISTORY

1900
First Olympics involving women held in Paris.

1906
Pure Food and Drug Act passed by Congress.

1903
Wrights' first successful airplane flight.

1909
National Association for the Advancement of Colored People (NAACP) is founded.

1913
Income tax established.

1914
Federal Trade Act promotes fair labor practices.

1914
Panama Canal opens.

1914
World War I begins.

1917
United States enters World War I.

1917
Bolshevik Revolution starts in Russia.

1918
World War I ends.

1919
League of Nations founded.

1920
Prohibition begins.

1920
Women gain vote.

SCIENCE & TECHNOLOGY

1900
Count Zeppelin launches his first zeppelin airship.

1901
Walter Reed discovers yellow fever is carried by mosquitos.

1904
New York City opens its subway system.

1905
Albert Einstein announces theory of relativity (E=mc²) of time and space.

$$E = mc^2$$

1911
First escalators are used.

1913
Henry Ford manufactures automobiles by assembly line.

1915
Coast-to-coast telephone system established.

1917
The first commercial plastic product produced.

1921
Vaccine for tuberculosis is discovered.

1922
Insulin treatment for diabetes discovered.

1922
Farnsworth develops electron scanner for television.

DAILY LIVING

1900
Motor-driven bicycles are introduced.

1901
Vacuum cleaner invented by bridge-builder Hubert Booth.

1903
First national wildlife refuge established.

1903
First World Series played.

1905
First nickelodeon movie theater established in Pittsburgh.

1905
Upton Sinclair's book *The Jungle* describes problems in meatpacking industry.

1910
Electric washing machines are introduced.

1913
Arthur Wynne invents the crossword puzzle.

1914
Red and green traffic lights introduced in Cleveland.

1916
Adamson Act sets 8-hour workday.

KDKA

1920
Johnson & Johnson introduces the Band-Aid.

1920
First radio station, KDKA, founded in Pittsburgh.

1921
John Larson invents the lie detector.

1924
The spiral-bound notebook is introduced.

U.S. POPULATION:

76,212,168   92,228,496   106,021,537

1925   **1930**   **1935**   **1940**   **1945**   **1950**

1925
John Scopes found guilty of teaching evolution.

1927
Charles Lindbergh flies solo across the Atlantic Ocean.

1929
Wall Street stock market crashes.

1931
The 102-story Empire State Building completed as tallest in the world.

1933
President Franklin Roosevelt inaugurates New Deal to end Great Depression.

1933
Prohibition is repealed.

1935
National Labor Relations Board secures right to join union.

1939
Germany invades Poland to begin World War II.

1941
U.S. enters World War II after bombing of Pearl Harbor.

1945
World War II ends.

1945
United States joins the United Nations.

1947
Taft-Hartley Act outlaws the closed union shop.

1948
Israel becomes a nation.

1926
John Baird demonstrates his television system.

1926
Alexander Fleming develops penicillin.

1930
First analog computer invented by Vannevar Bush.

1929
Clarence Birdseye introduces frozen foods.

1935
Radar is invented.

1938
Modern ballpoint pens developed.

1938
First photocopy machine produced.

1939
First jet aircraft flown.

1940
Enrico Fermi develops nuclear reactor.

1947
Edwin Land invents Polaroid camera.

1947
Bell Lab scientists invent transistor.

1949
First fax machine manufactured.

1925
Potato chips are produced in New York City.

1927
Wings wins first Academy Award for motion pictures.

1927
First "talking movie," *The Jazz Singer,* made.

1931
"Star-Spangled Banner" becomes U.S. national anthem.

1936
Mitchell's *Gone with the Wind* is published.

1937
First full-length animated film, *Snow White,* is made.

1938
"G.I. Bill of Rights" offers subsidized education.

1938
Fair Labor Standards Act sets $16, 40-hour workweek.

1939
Steinbeck's *Grapes of Wrath* is published.

1947
Jackie Robinson becomes the first black major league baseball player.

1948
First McDonald's opened.

123,202,624   132,164,569

1950 1955 1960 1965 1970

UNITED STATES HISTORY

1950
United States enters Korean War.

1953
Korean War ends.

1955
Rosa Parks refuses to follow segregation rules on Montgomery bus.

1955
Martin Luther King, Jr., begins organizing protests against black discrimination.

1959
Alaska & Hawaii become states.

1959
Labor Reform Act restricts unions.

1961
Alan Shepard becomes first U.S. astronaut in space.

1963
President John F. Kennedy assassinated in Dallas, Texas.

1965
U.S. combat troops sent to Vietnam.

1965
Civil Rights Freedom March from Selma to Montgomery, Alabama.

1968
Martin Luther King, Jr., is assassinated.

1969
Neil Armstrong and Buzz Aldrin are first men to walk on moon.

1971
Eighteen-year-olds are given right to vote.

1974
President Richard Nixon resigns.

SCIENCE & TECHNOLOGY

1951
Fluoridated water discovered to prevent tooth decay.

1951
UNIVAC 1 (first electronic computer) sold to U.S. Census Bureau.

1953
Watson and Crick map the DNA molecule.

1954
Jonas Salk discovers polio vaccine.

1957
Russia's *Sputnik I* satellite is launched.

1958
Stereo long-playing records are produced.

1960
First laser invented by Theodor Maiman.

1962
Telstar, the first communication satellite, is launched.

1965
Computer mouse invented.

1968
First U.S. heart transplant is done by Norman Shumway.

1970
The floppy disk is introduced for storing computer data.

1971
Space probe *Mariner* maps surface of Mars.

1972
DDT banned.

1974
Sears Tower (110 stories) built in Chicago.

DAILY LIVING

1950
Peanuts comic strip produced by Charles Schulz.

1951
Fifteen million American homes have television.

1953
Arthur Miller's *The Crucible* is published.

1954
Supreme Court rules school segregation is unconstitutional.

1957
Elvis Presley is the most popular rock 'n' roll musician in U.S.

1961
Peace Corps is established.

1963
Cassette music tapes developed.

1964
The Beatles appear on *The Ed Sullivan Show*.

1970
First Earth Day is observed.

1970
Dee Brown's *Bury My Heart At Wounded Knee* is published.

1970
Sesame Street television show begins.

1971
Texas Instruments introduces first pocket calculator.

U.S. POPULATION:

151,325,798   179,323,175   203,302,031

1975   1980   1985   1990   1995   2000

1975
Vietnam War ends.

1979
Iran seizes
U.S. hostages.

1976
Supreme
Court rules
death
penalty is
constitutional.

1981
U.S. hostages returned
from Iran after 444 days.

1981
Sandra Day
O'Connor
becomes first
woman on
Supreme Court.

1983
Sally Ride becomes first
U.S. woman in space.

1986
Challenger
spacecraft
explodes, killing
entire crew.

1989
Berlin Wall is
torn down.

1991
Persian Gulf War begins.

1991
Restructuring of Soviet Union occurs.

1994
Earthquake rocks Los
Angeles, killing more
than 50 people.

1975
First laser
printer
introduced.

1977
Apple
Computers
produces
first
personal
computer.

1979
Three-Mile
Island nuclear
accident occurs.

1980
Post-it notes
discovered
by accident.

1981
Scientists
identify
AIDS.

1984
Compact
discs (CD's)
developed.

1985
First interface
software, Windows,
launched by
Microsoft.

1985
PageMaker
software advances
desktop publishing.

1993
Apple's Newton Writing-Pad
computer introduced.

1994
110th and 111th
elements discovered.

1995
Federal Building
in Oklahoma City
is bombed.

1976
Alex Haley's *Roots*
is published.

1976
U.S. Bicentennial celebrated.

1977
Star Wars becomes
largest moneymaking
movie of all time.

1979
Yellow ribbons symbolize
support for return of U.S.
hostages in Iran.

1984
Geraldine
Ferraro is
first woman
nominee for
vice president.

1986
Martin Luther King
Day proclaimed
national holiday.

1988
Thirty million U.S. schoolchildren
have access to computers.

1989
Pocket
telephone
is
introduced.

1993
Connie Chung is
named first
woman to co-
anchor national
evening news team.

CBS

1993
Jurassic Park features
new computer film-
making techniques.

226,542,203   248,709,873